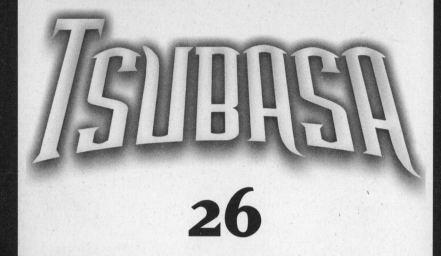

TSUBASA

26

CLAMP

TRANSLATED AND ADAPTED BY
William Flanagan

LETTERED BY
Dana Hayward

DEL REY
BALLANTINE BOOKS • NEW YORK

A Del Rey Manga/Kodansha Trade Paperback Original

Tsubasa, volume 26 copyright © 2009 CLAMP
English translation copyright © 2010 CLAMP

Published in the United States by Del Rey Books, an imprint of The Random House Publishing Group, a division of Random House, Inc., New York.

DEL REY is a registered trademark and the Del Rey colophon is a trademark of Random House, Inc.

Publication rights arranged through Kodansha Ltd.

First published in Japan in 2009 by Kodansha Ltd., Tokyo

ISBN 978-0-345-52070-8

Printed in the United States of America

www.delreymanga.com

9 8 7 6 5 4 3 2 1

Translator/Adapter—William Flanagan
Lettering—Dana Hayward

Contents

Tsubasa crosses over with *xxxHOLiC*. Although it isn't necessary to read *xxxHOLiC* to understand the events in *Tsubasa*, you'll get to see the same events from different perspectives if you read both series!

Honorifics Explained

Throughout the Del Rey Manga books, you will find Japanese honorifics left intact in the translations. For those not familiar with how the Japanese use honorifics and, more important, how they differ from American honorifics, we present this brief overview.

Politeness has always been a critical facet of Japanese culture. Ever since the feudal era, when Japan was a highly stratified society, use of honorifics—which can be defined as polite speech that indicates relationship or status—has played an essential role in the Japanese language. When you address someone in Japanese, an honorific usually takes the form of a suffix attached to one's name (example: "Asuna-san"), is used as a title at the end of one's name, or appears in place of the name itself (example: "Negi-sensei," or simply "Sensei!").

Honorifics can be expressions of respect or endearment. In the context of manga and anime, honorifics give insight into the nature of the relationship between characters. Many English translations leave out these important honorifics and therefore distort the feel of the original Japanese. Because Japanese honorifics contain nuances that English honorifics lack, it is our policy at Del Rey not to translate them. Here, instead, is a guide to some of the honorifics you may encounter in Del Rey Manga.

-san: This is the most common honorific and is equivalent to Mr., Miss, Ms., or Mrs. It is the all-purpose honorific and can be used in any situation where politeness is required.

-sama: This is one level higher than "-san" and is used to confer great respect.

-dono: This comes from the word "tono," which means "lord." It is an even higher level than "-sama" and confers utmost respect.

-kun: This suffix is used at the end of boys' names to express familiarity or endearment. It is also sometimes used by men among friends, or when addressing someone younger or of a lower station.

-chan: This is used to express endearment, mostly toward girls. It is also used for little boys, pets, and even among lovers. It gives a sense of childish cuteness.

Bozu: This is an informal way to refer to a boy, similar to the English terms "kid" and "squirt."

Sempai/Senpai: This title suggests that the addressee is one's senior in a group or organization. It is most often used in a school setting, where underclassmen refer to their upperclassmen as "sempai." It can also be used in the workplace, such as when a newer employee addresses an employee who has seniority in the company.

Kohai: This is the opposite of "sempai" and is used toward underclassmen in school or newcomers in the workplace. It connotes that the addressee is of a lower station.

Sensei: Literally meaning "one who has come before," this title is used for teachers, doctors, or masters of any profession or art.

-[blank]: This is usually forgotten in these lists, but it is perhaps the most significant difference between Japanese and English. The lack of honorific means that the speaker has permission to address the person in a very intimate way. Usually, only family, spouses, or very close friends have this kind of permission. Known as *yobisute*, it can be gratifying when someone who has earned the intimacy starts to call one by one's name without an honorific. But when that intimacy hasn't been earned, it can be very insulting.

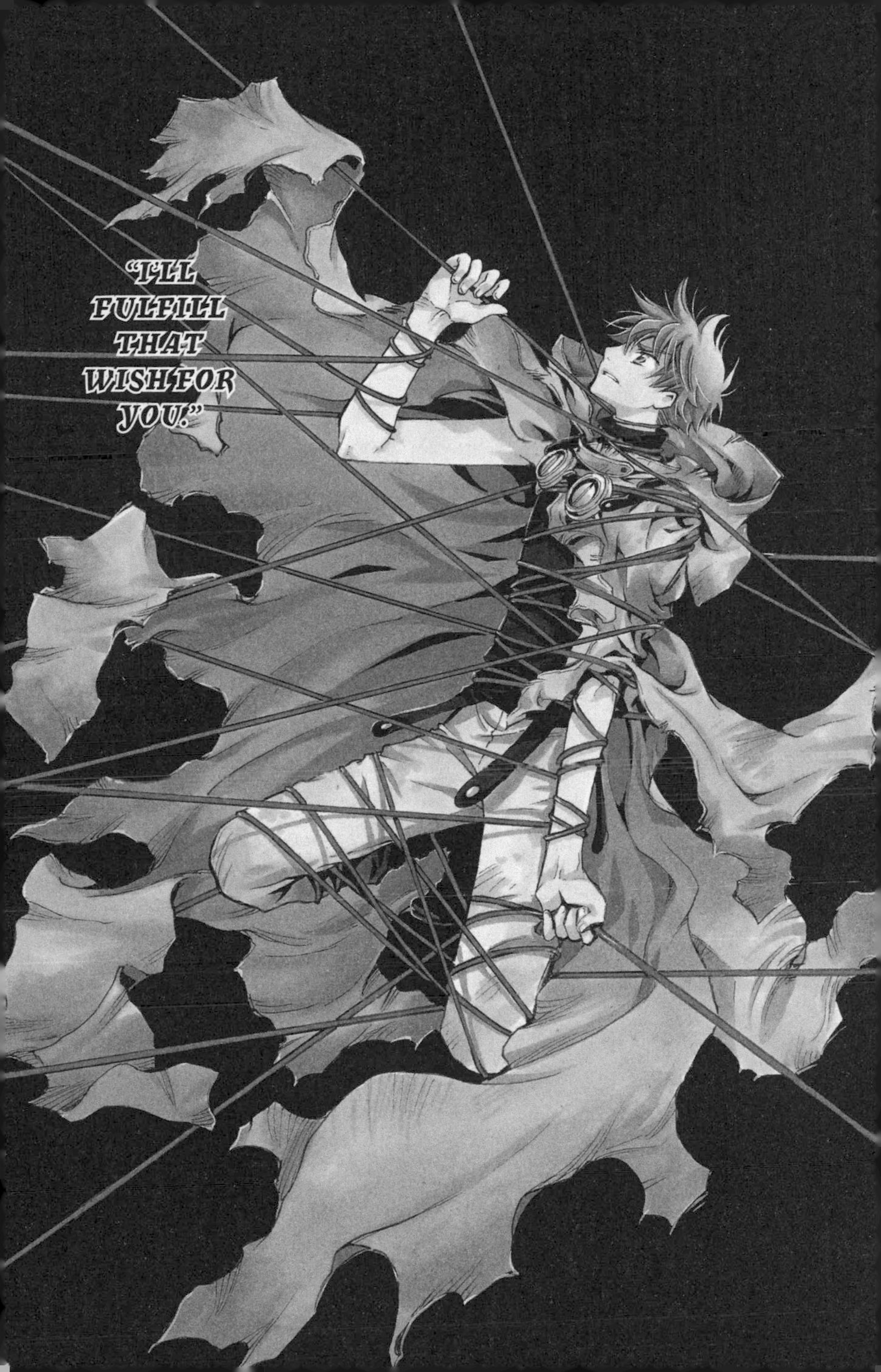
"I'LL FULFILL THAT WISH FOR YOU."

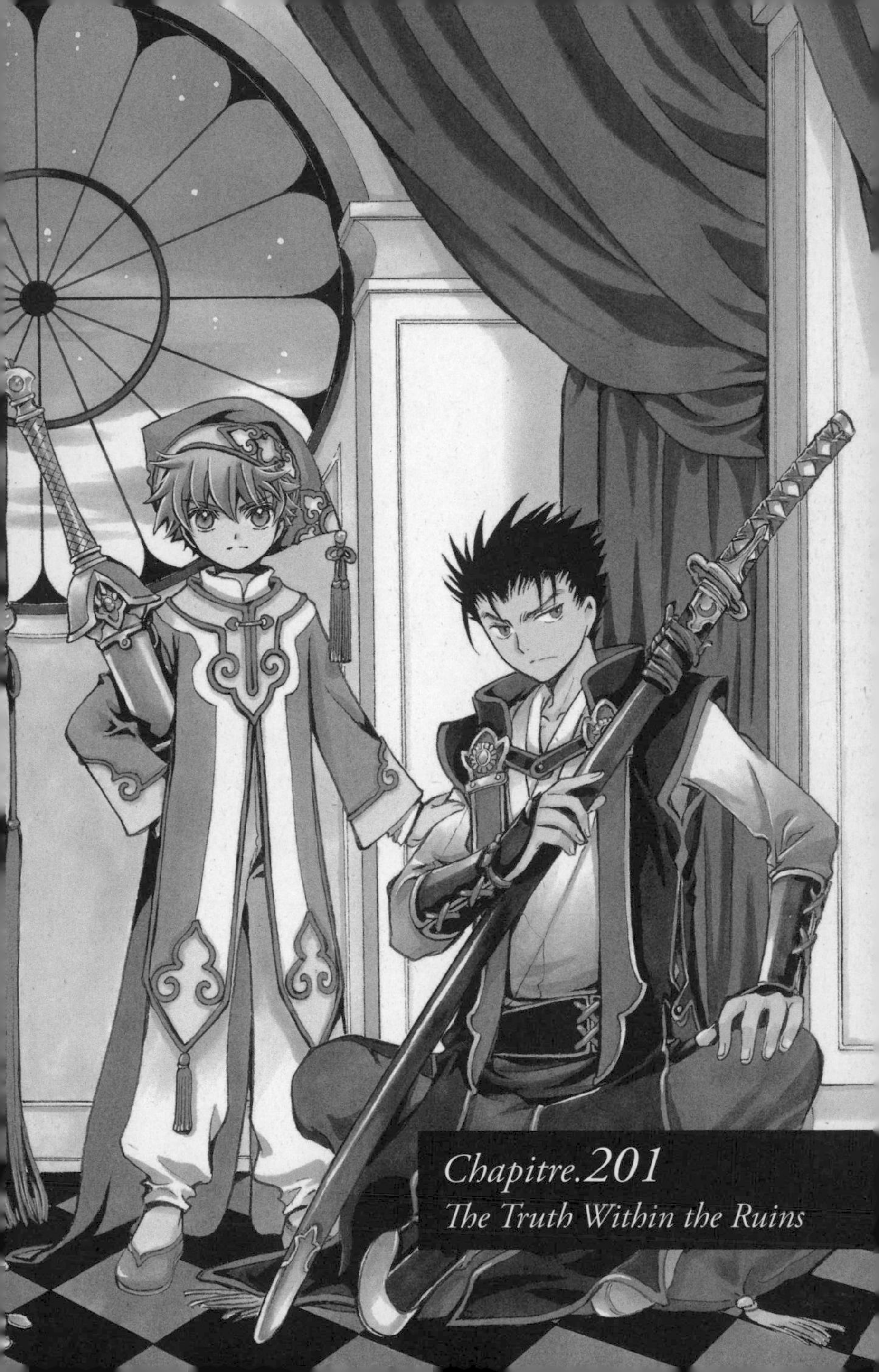
Chapitre.201
The Truth Within the Ruins

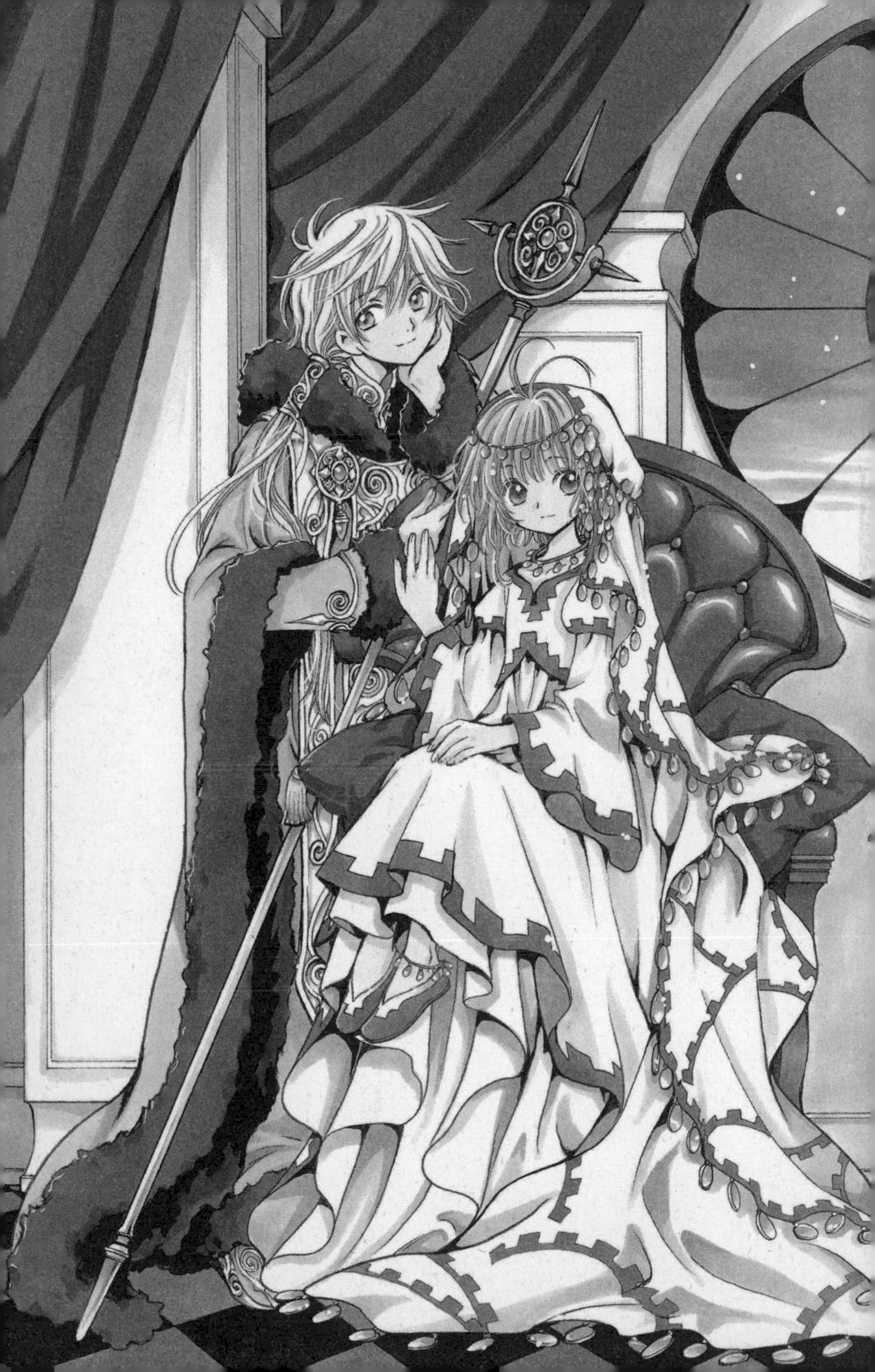

ツバサ
RESERVoir CHRoNiCLE

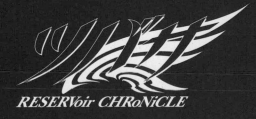

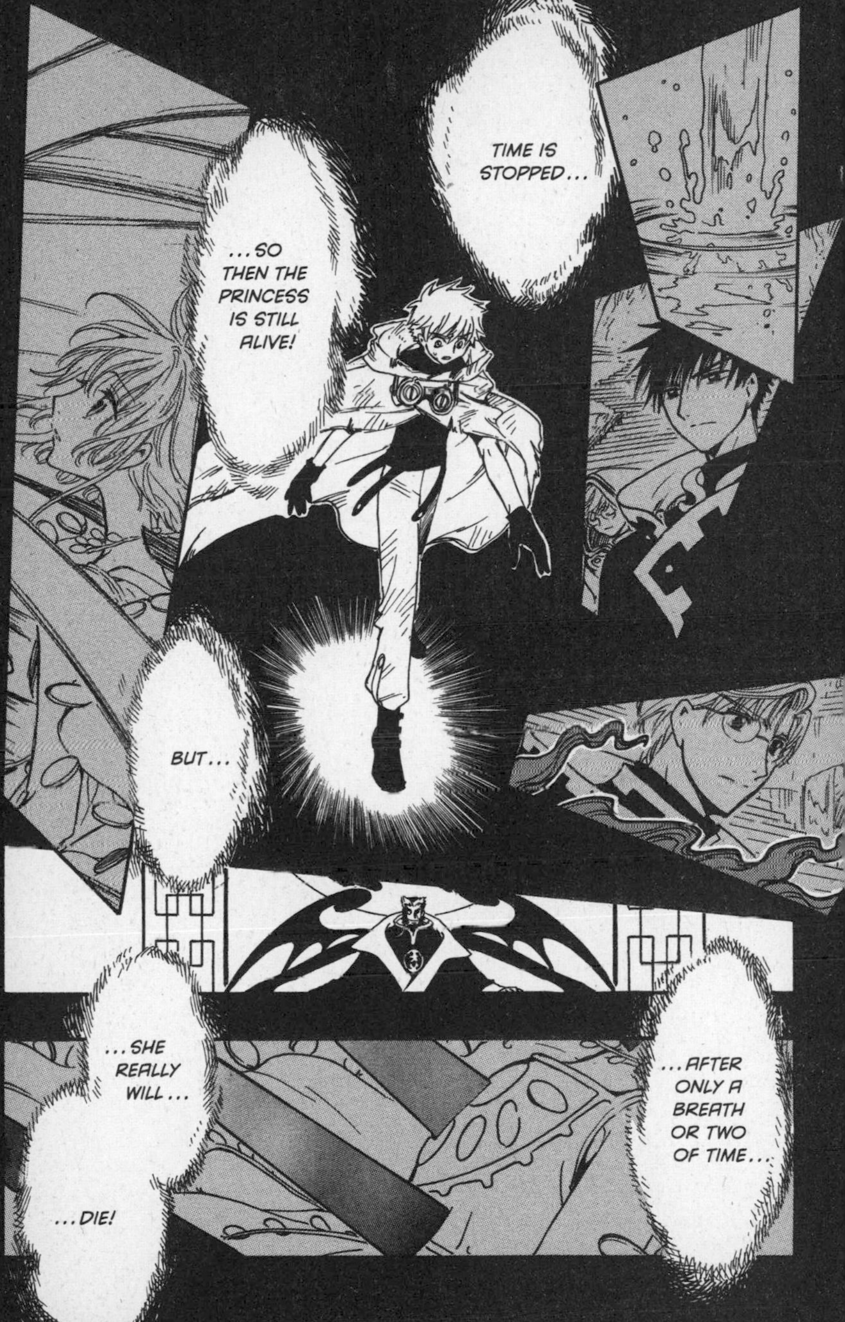
TIME IS STOPPED...
...SO THEN THE PRINCESS IS STILL ALIVE!
BUT...
...AFTER ONLY A BREATH OR TWO OF TIME...
...SHE REALLY WILL...
...DIE!

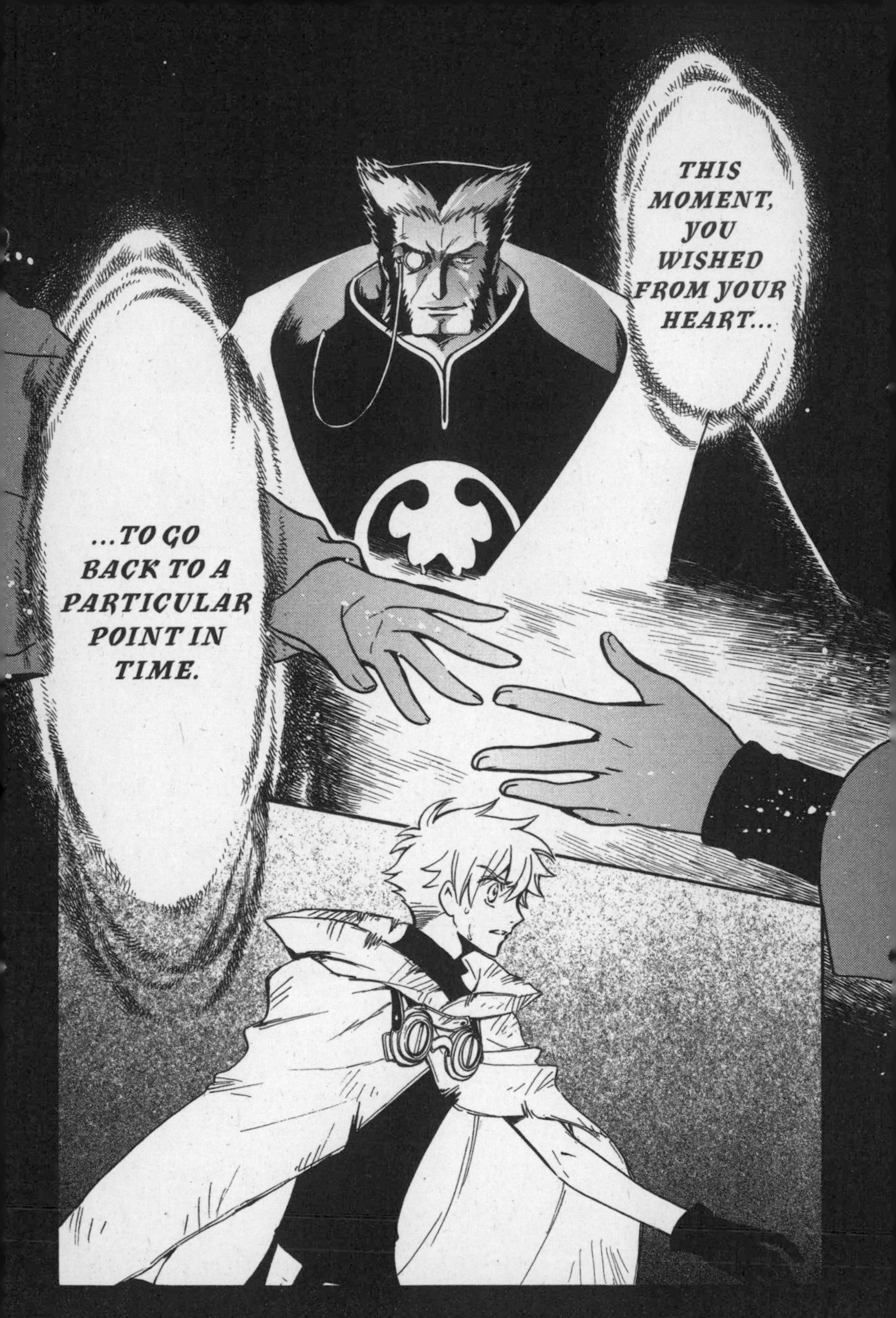
THIS MOMENT, YOU WISHED FROM YOUR HEART...
...TO GO BACK TO A PARTICULAR POINT IN TIME.

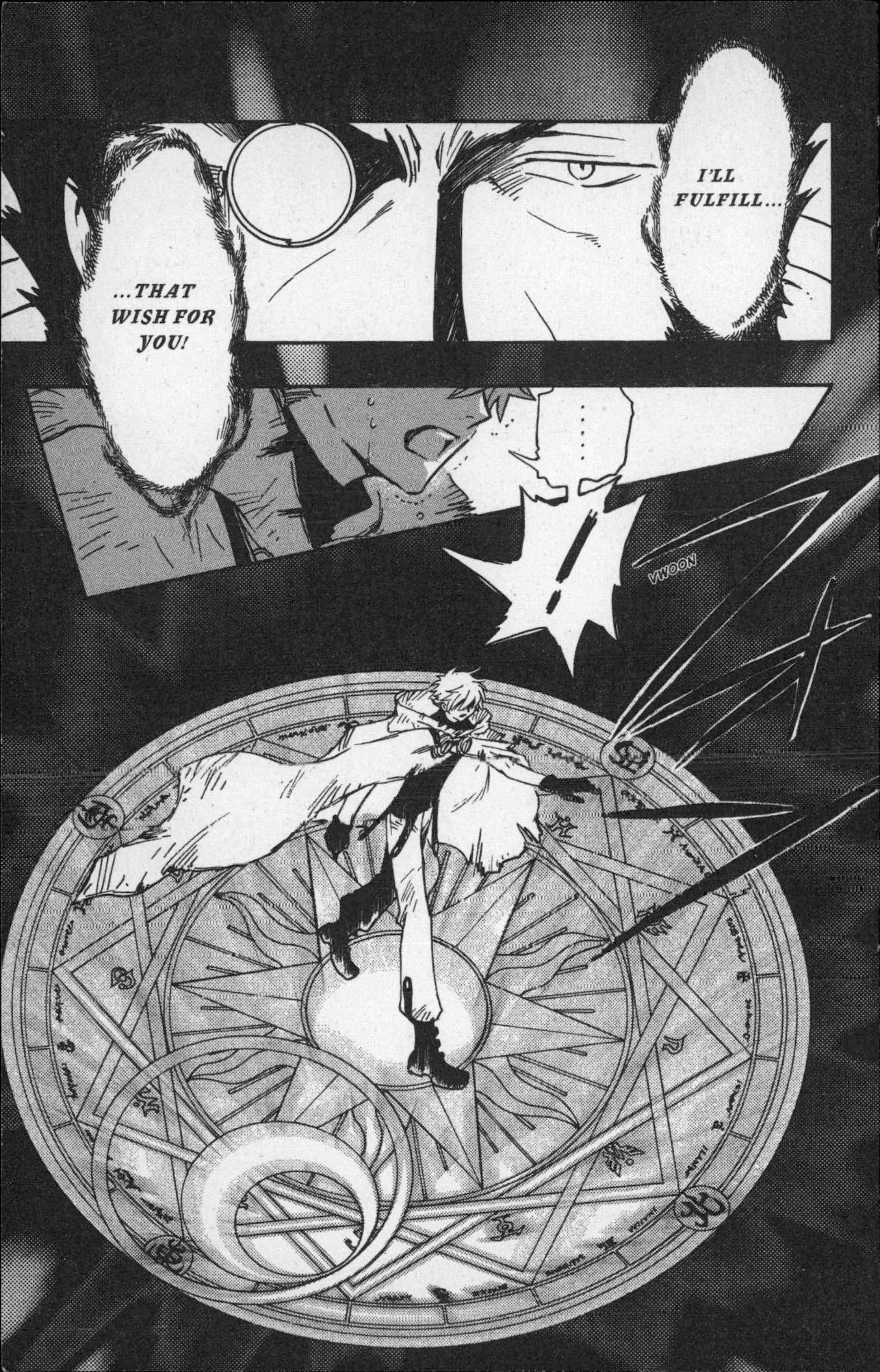
I'LL FULFILL...
...THAT WISH FOR YOU!
VWOON

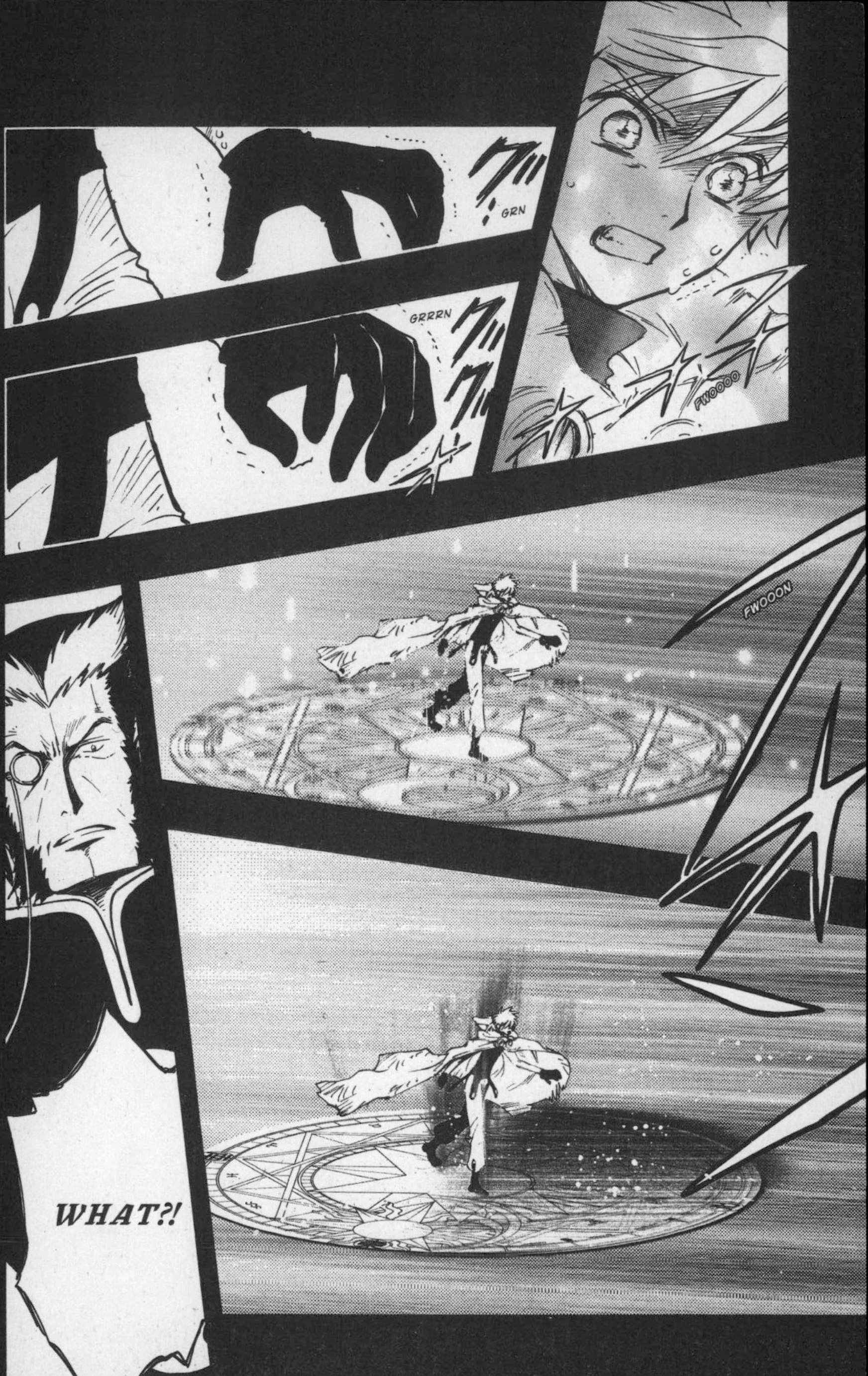
FWOOOO
GRN
GRRRN
FWOOON
WHAT?!

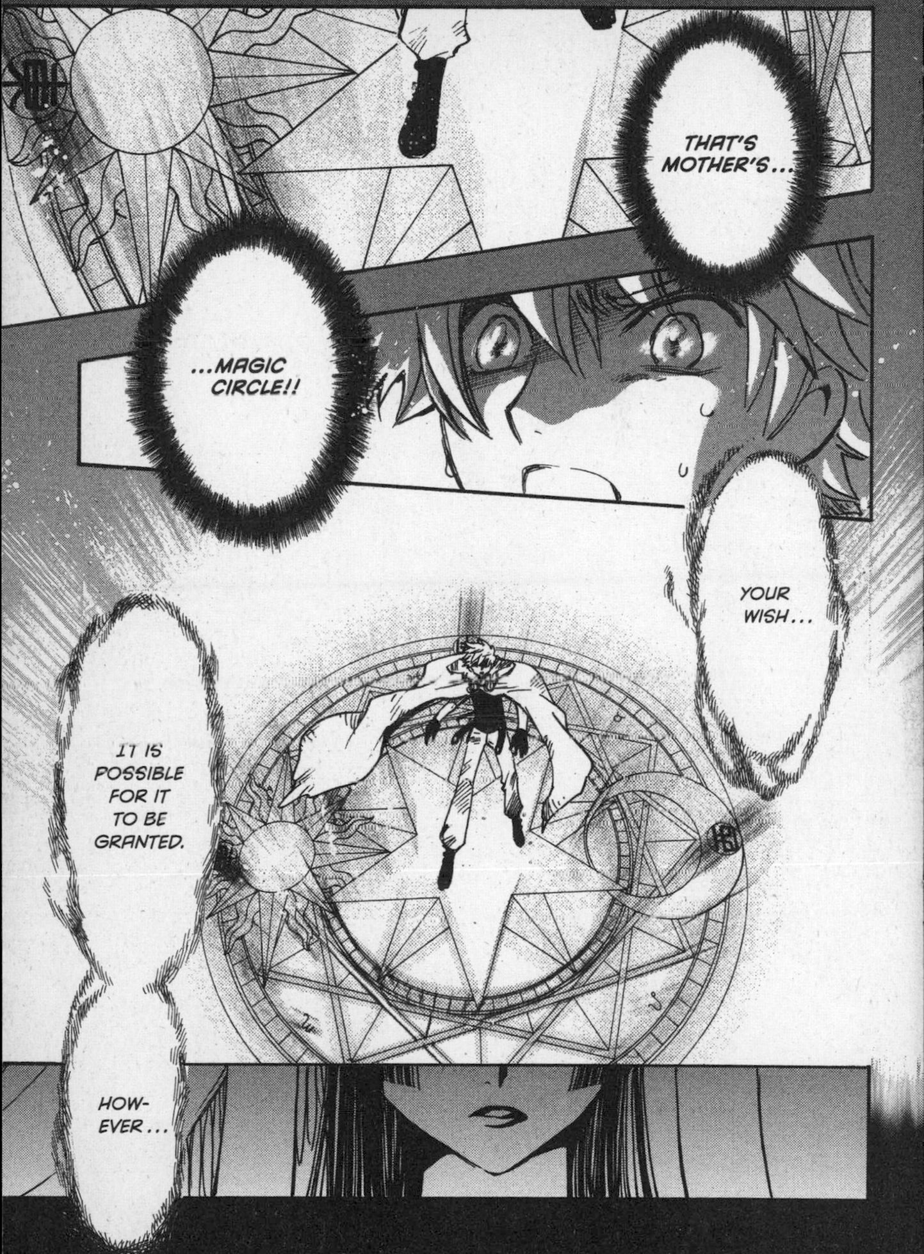
THAT'S MOTHER'S...
...MAGIC CIRCLE!!
YOUR WISH...
IT IS POSSIBLE FOR IT TO BE GRANTED.
HOW-EVER...

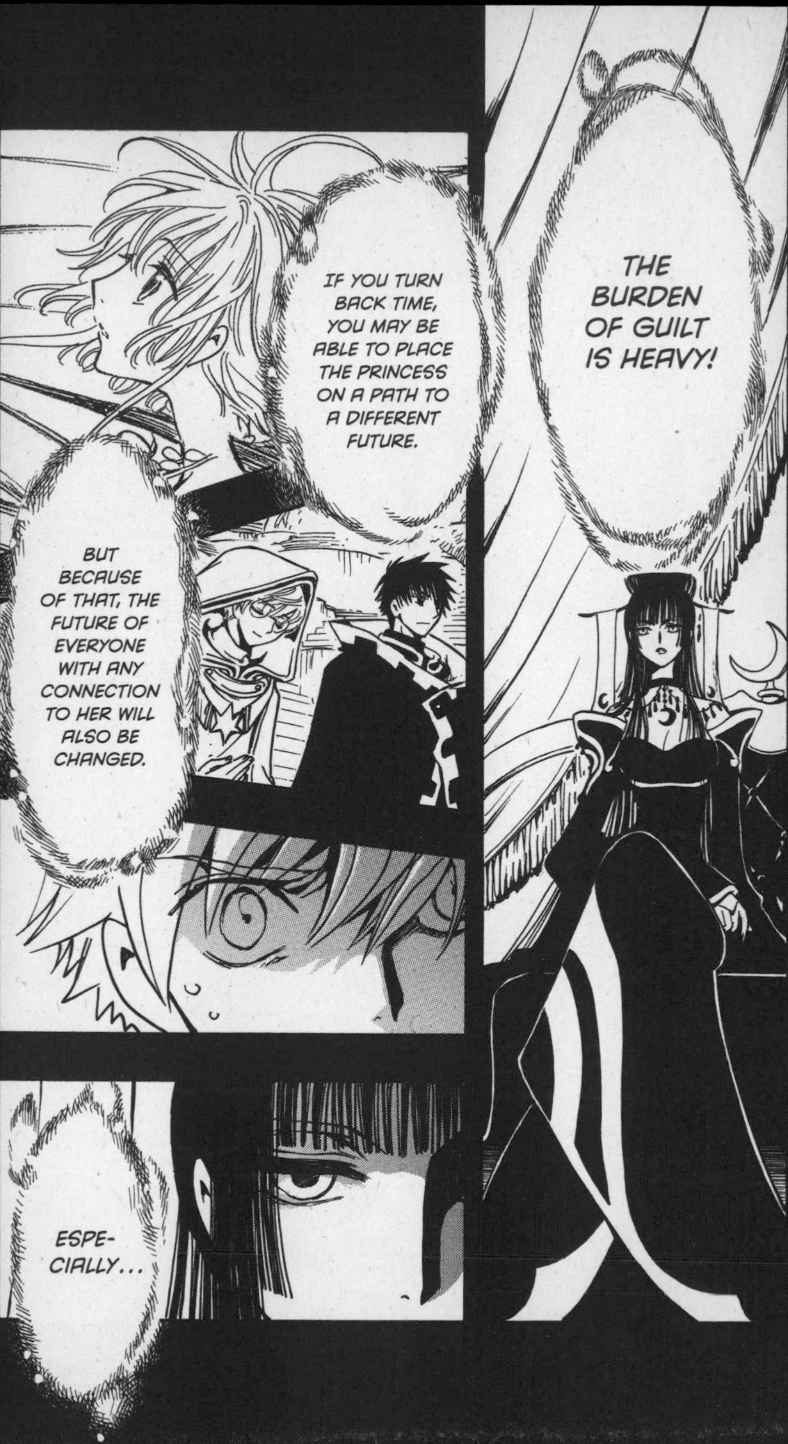
THE BURDEN OF GUILT IS HEAVY!
IF YOU TURN BACK TIME, YOU MAY BE ABLE TO PLACE THE PRINCESS ON A PATH TO A DIFFERENT FUTURE.
BUT BECAUSE OF THAT, THE FUTURE OF EVERYONE WITH ANY CONNECTION TO HER WILL ALSO BE CHANGED.
ESPE-CIALLY...

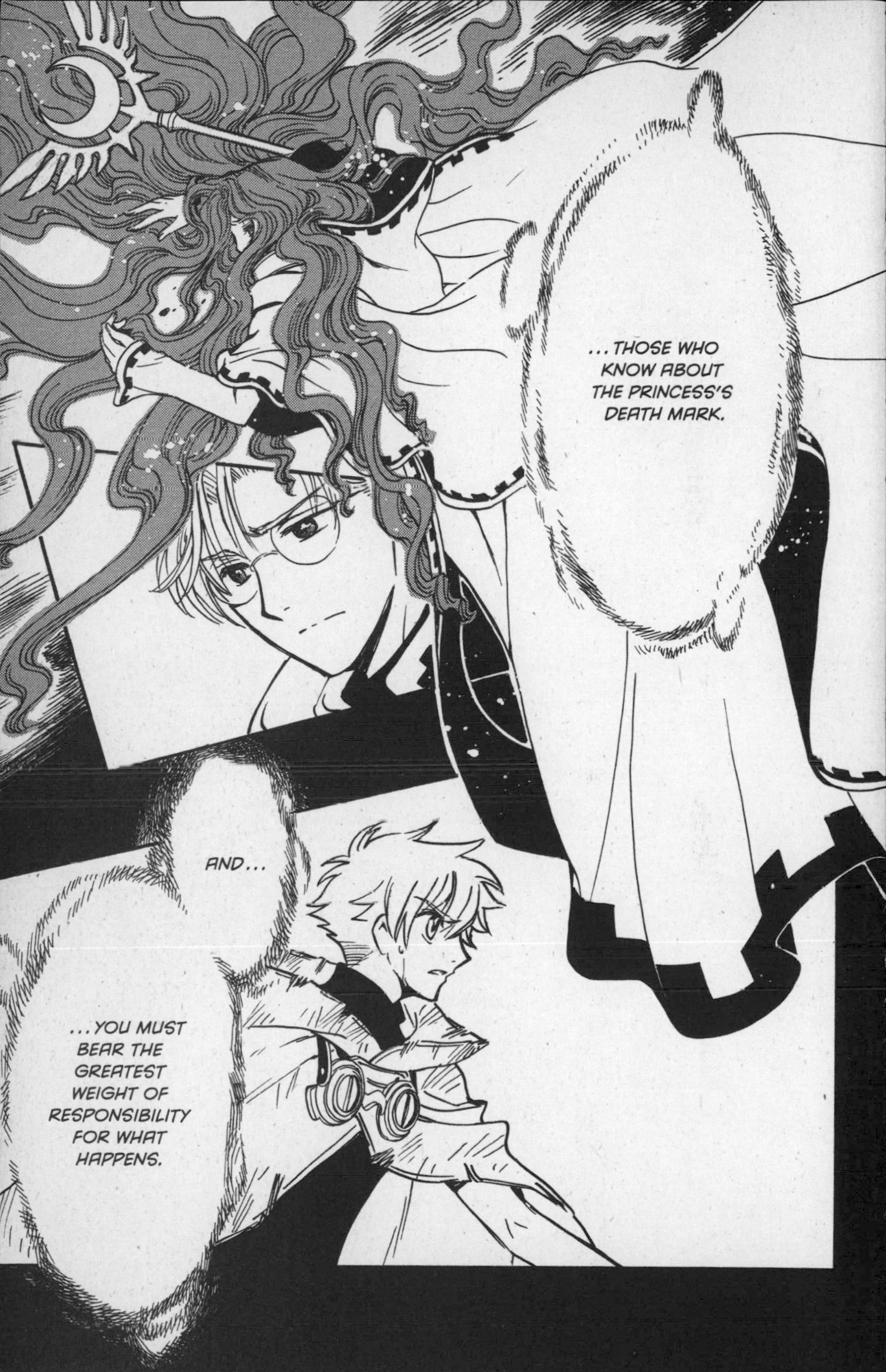
...THOSE WHO KNOW ABOUT THE PRINCESS'S DEATH MARK.
AND...
...YOU MUST BEAR THE GREATEST WEIGHT OF RESPONSIBILITY FOR WHAT HAPPENS.

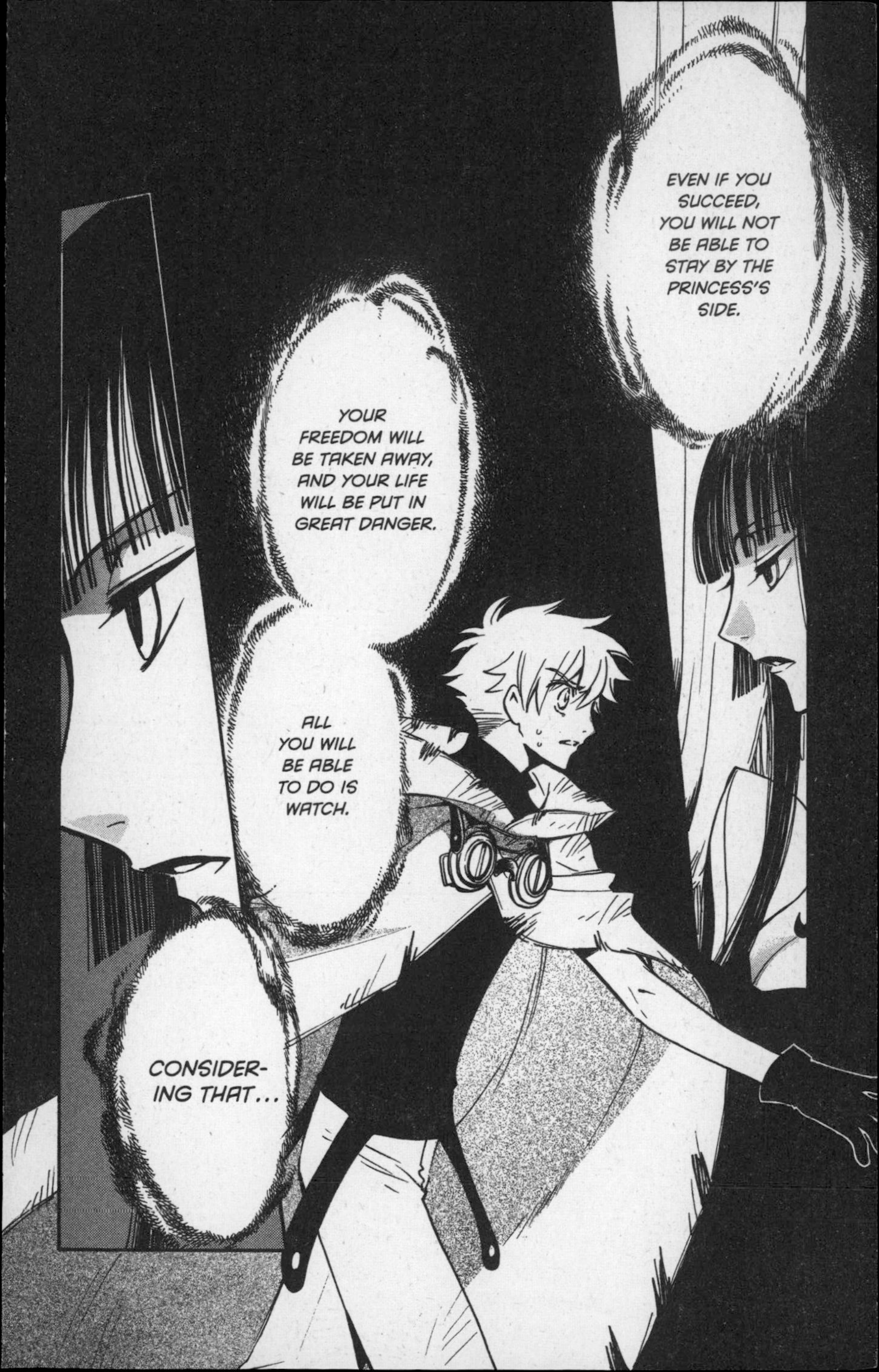
EVEN IF YOU SUCCEED, YOU WILL NOT BE ABLE TO STAY BY THE PRINCESS'S SIDE.
YOUR FREEDOM WILL BE TAKEN AWAY, AND YOUR LIFE WILL BE PUT IN GREAT DANGER.
ALL YOU WILL BE ABLE TO DO IS WATCH.
CONSIDER-ING THAT...

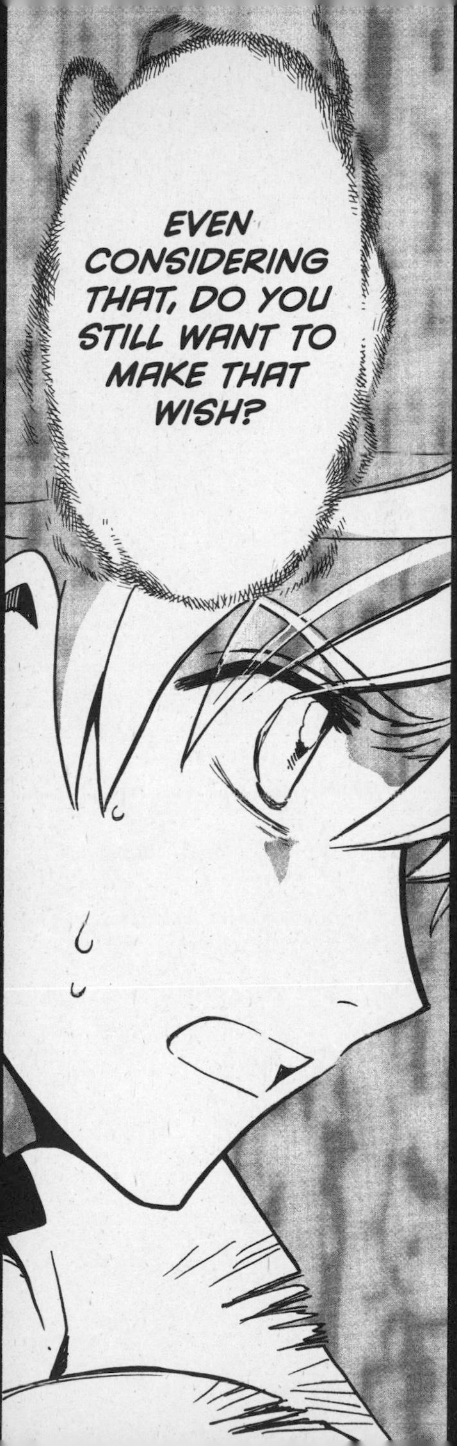
EVEN CONSIDERING THAT, DO YOU STILL WANT TO MAKE THAT WISH?

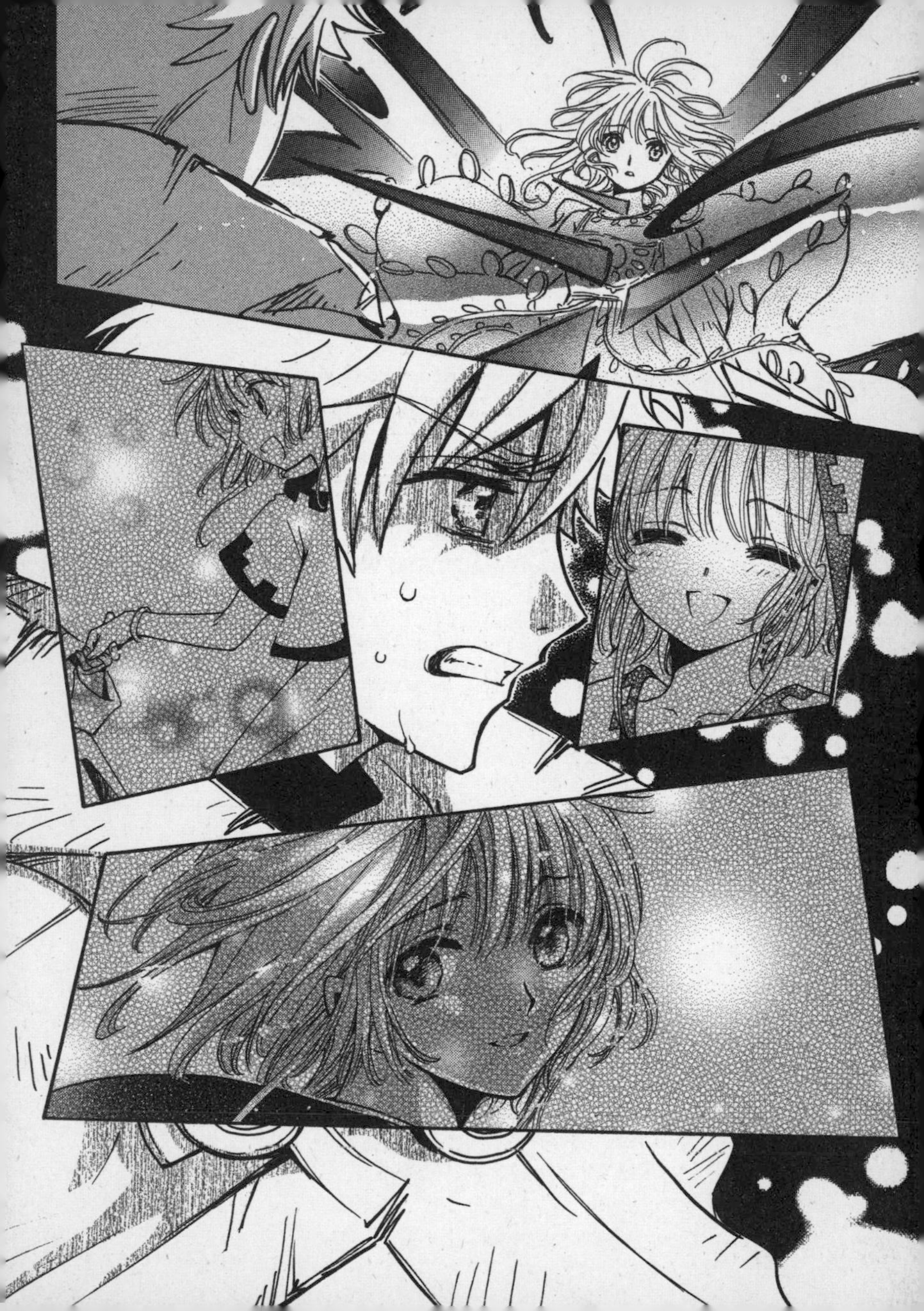

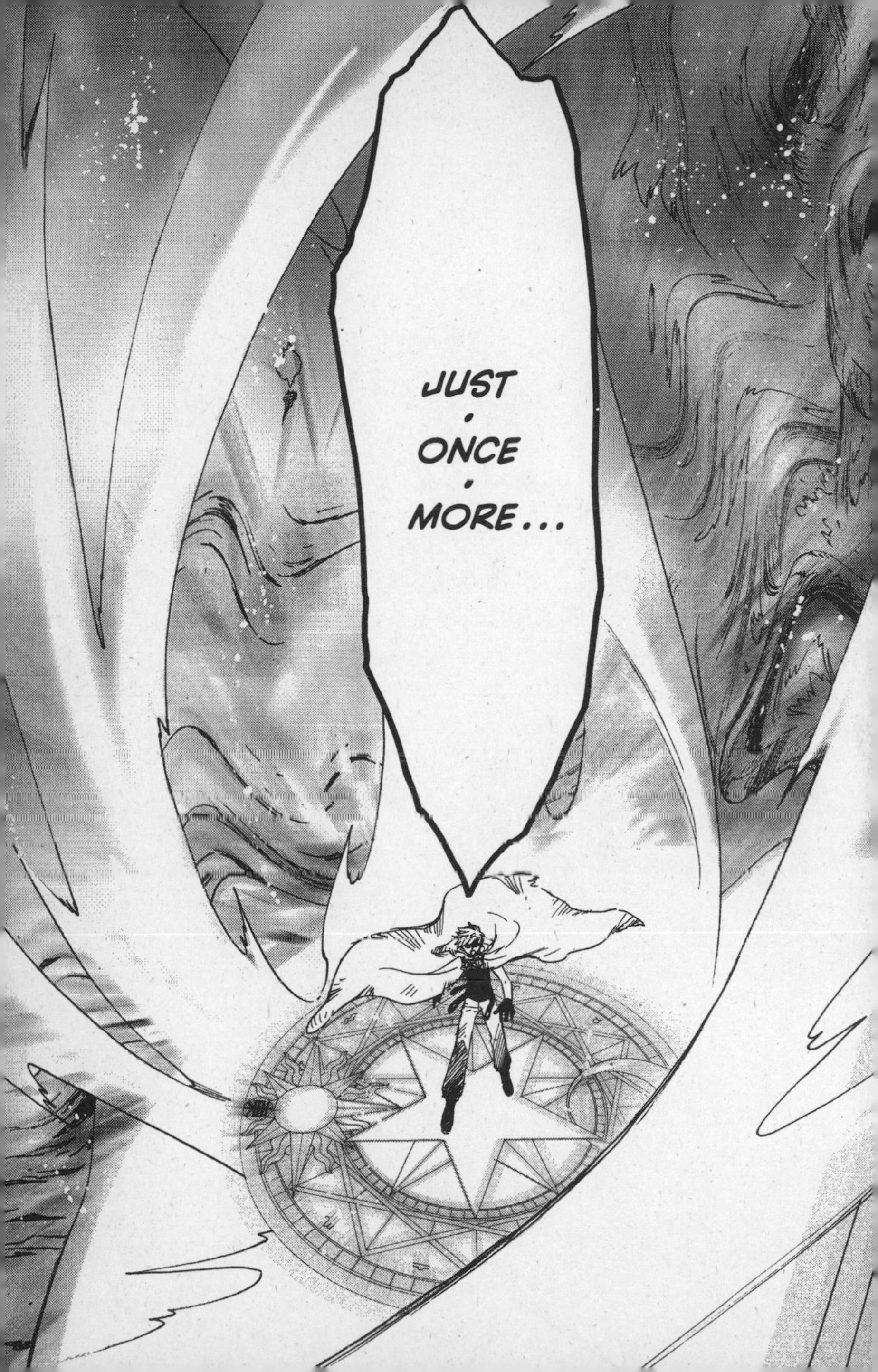
JUST · ONCE · MORE...

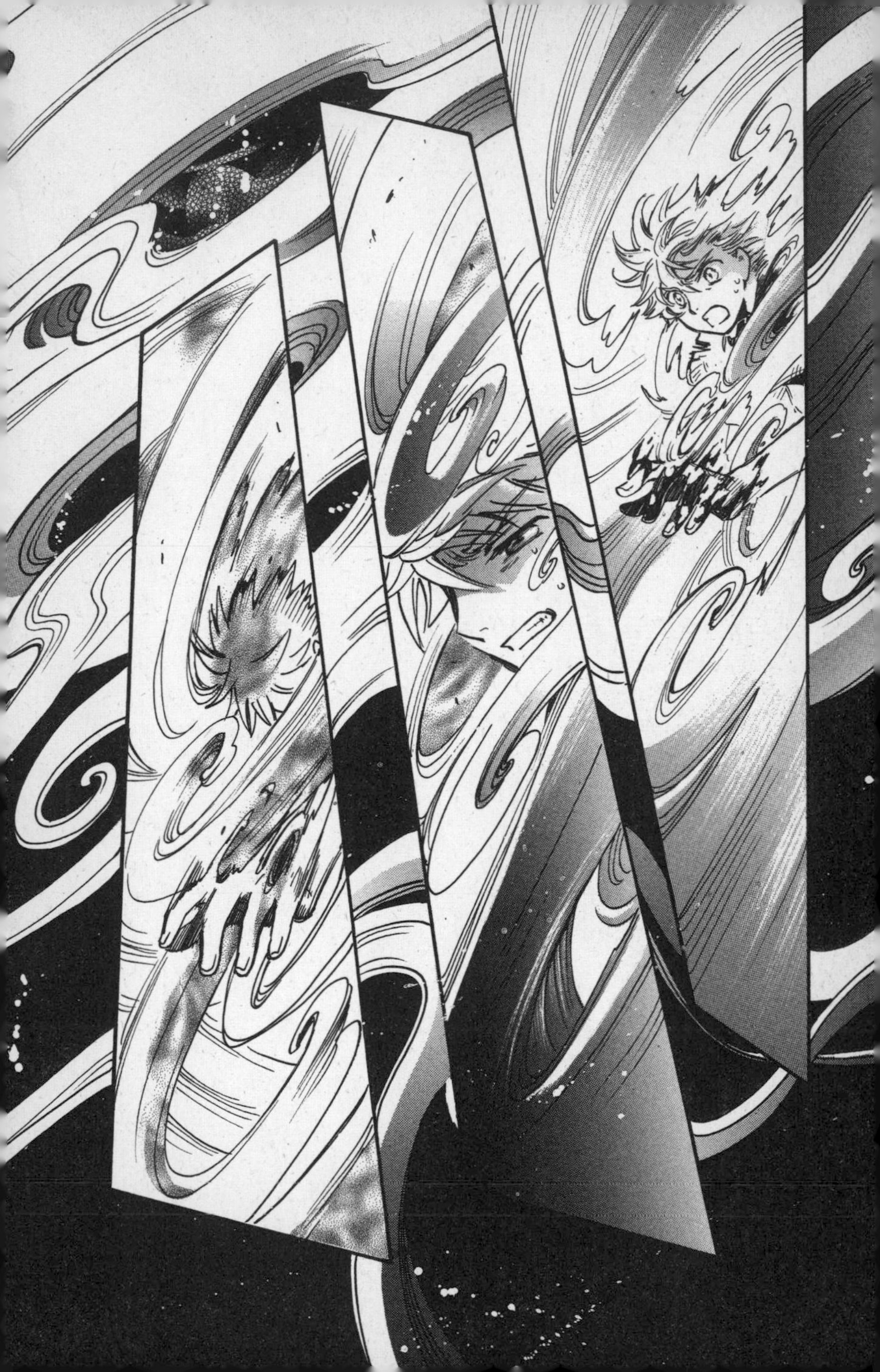

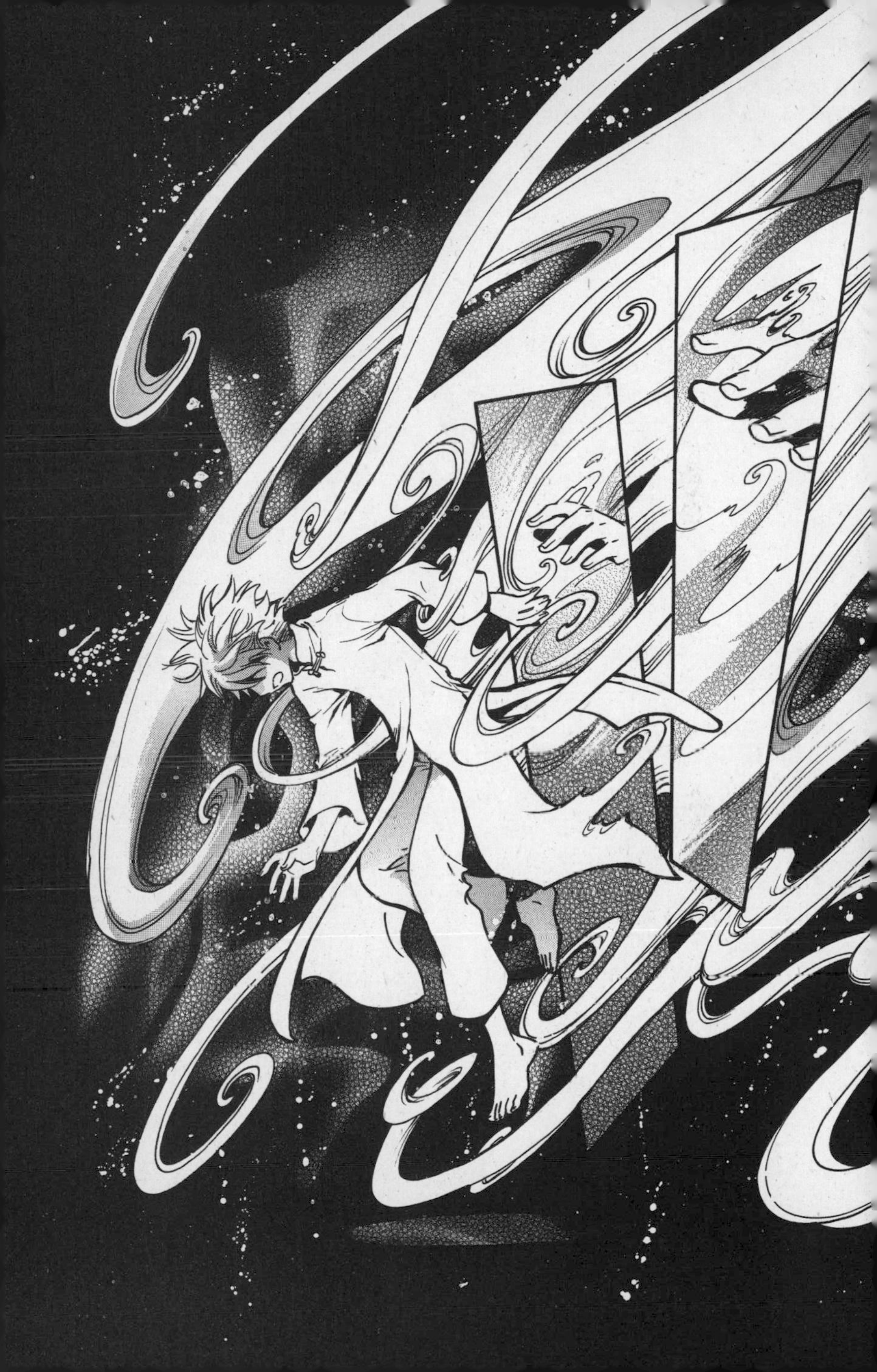

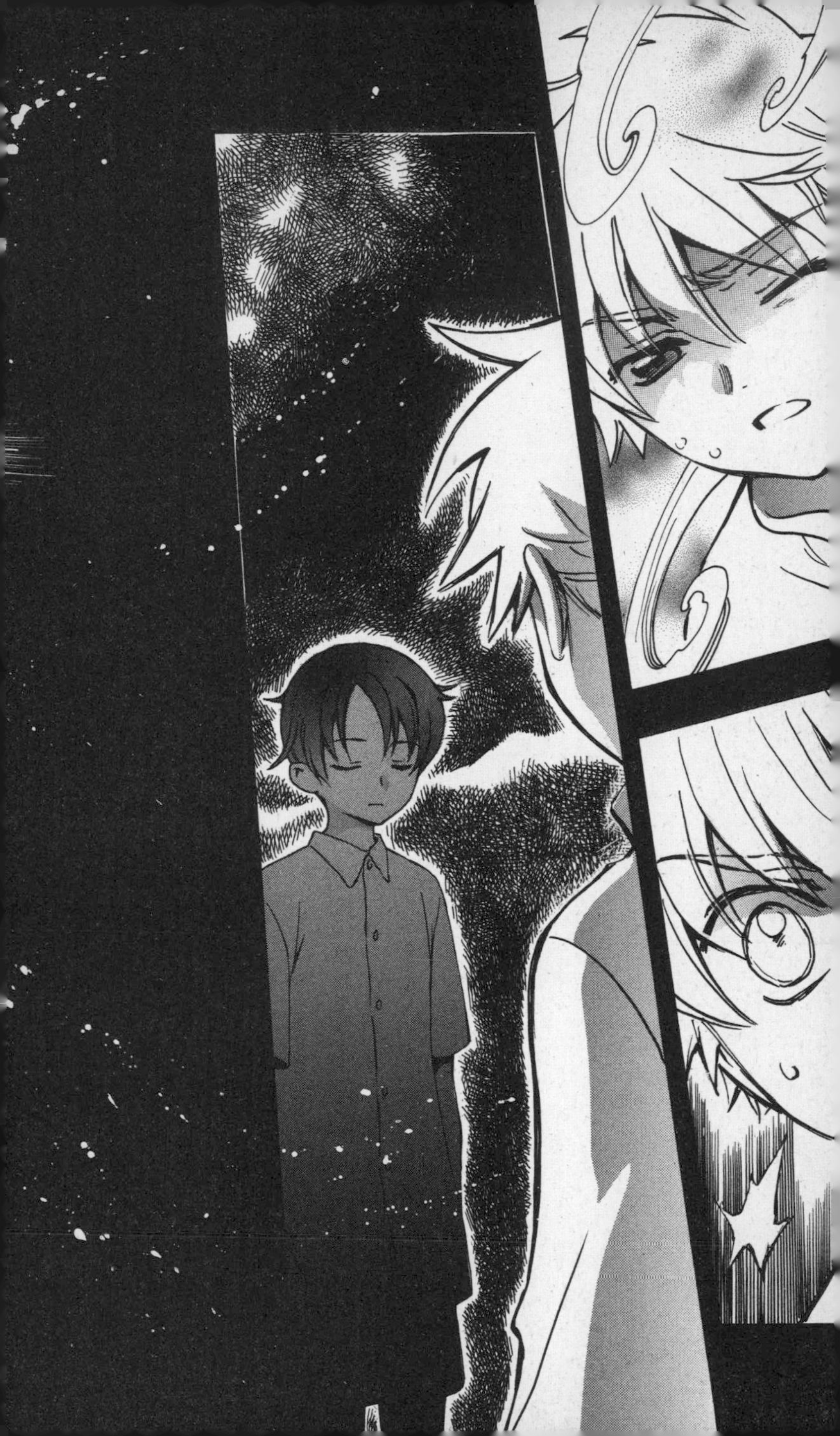

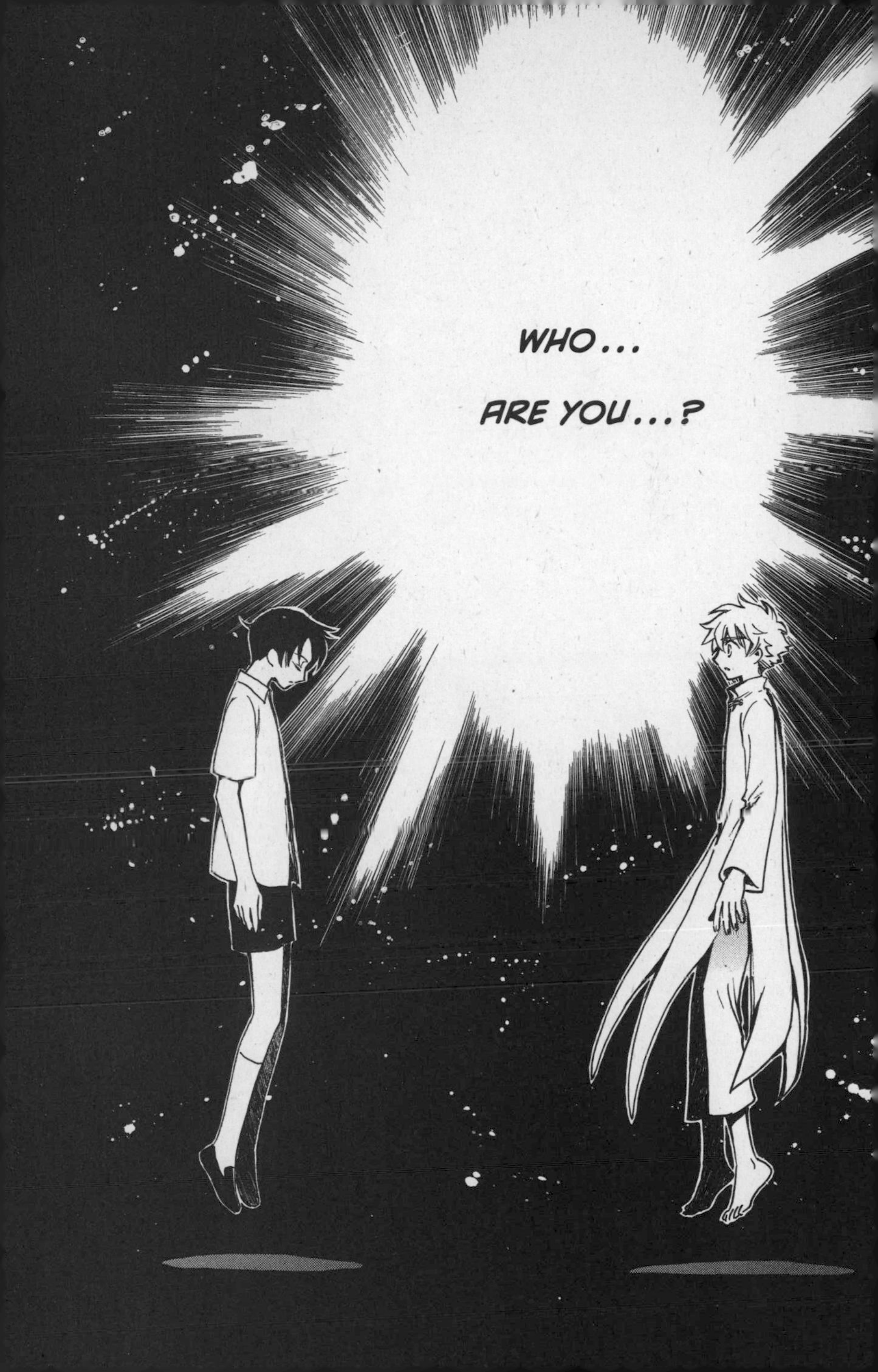
WHO...
ARE YOU...?

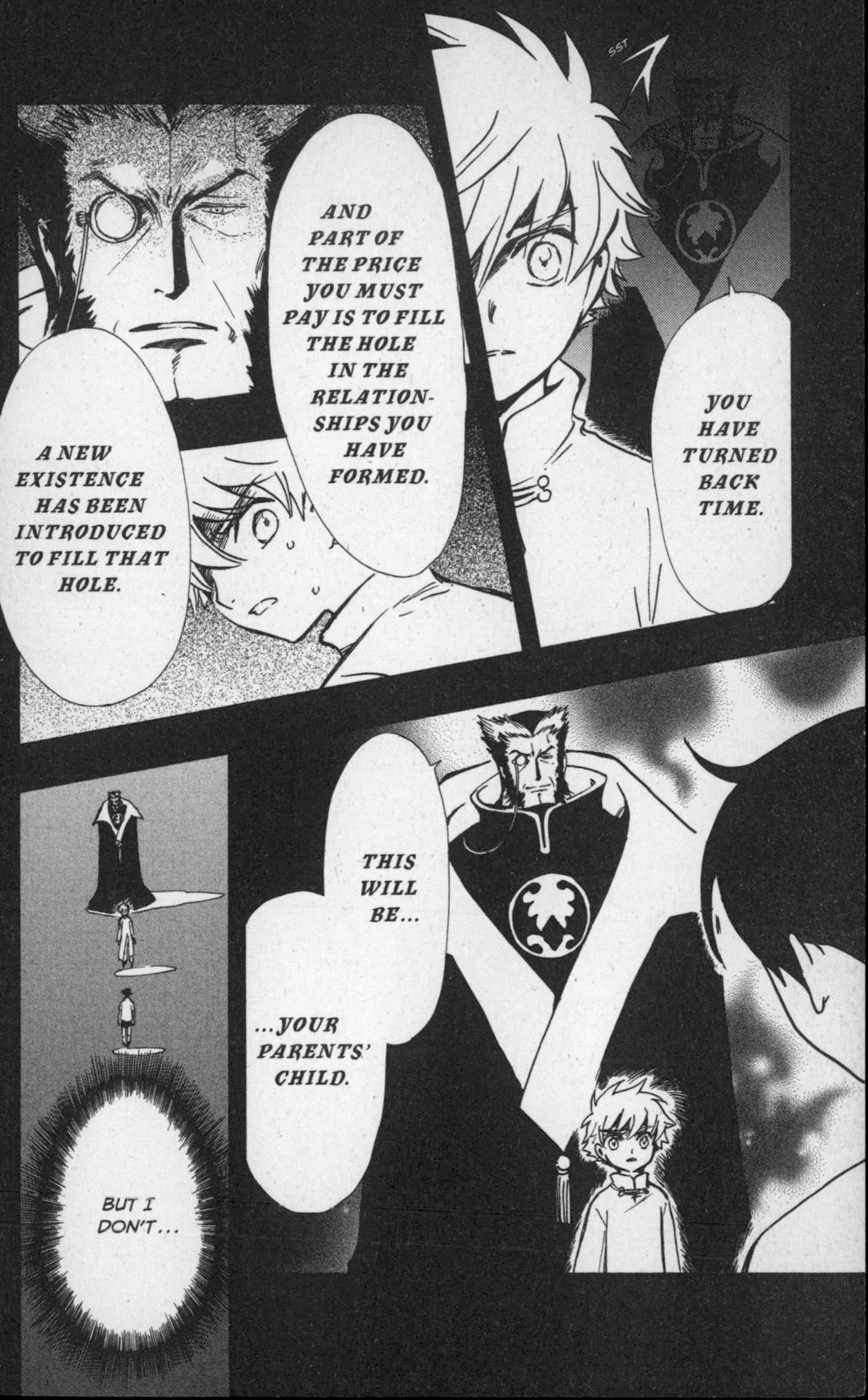
SST
YOU HAVE TURNED BACK TIME.
AND PART OF THE PRICE YOU MUST PAY IS TO FILL THE HOLE IN THE RELATION-SHIPS YOU HAVE FORMED.
A NEW EXISTENCE HAS BEEN INTRODUCED TO FILL THAT HOLE.
THIS WILL BE...
...YOUR PARENTS' CHILD.
BUT I DON'T...

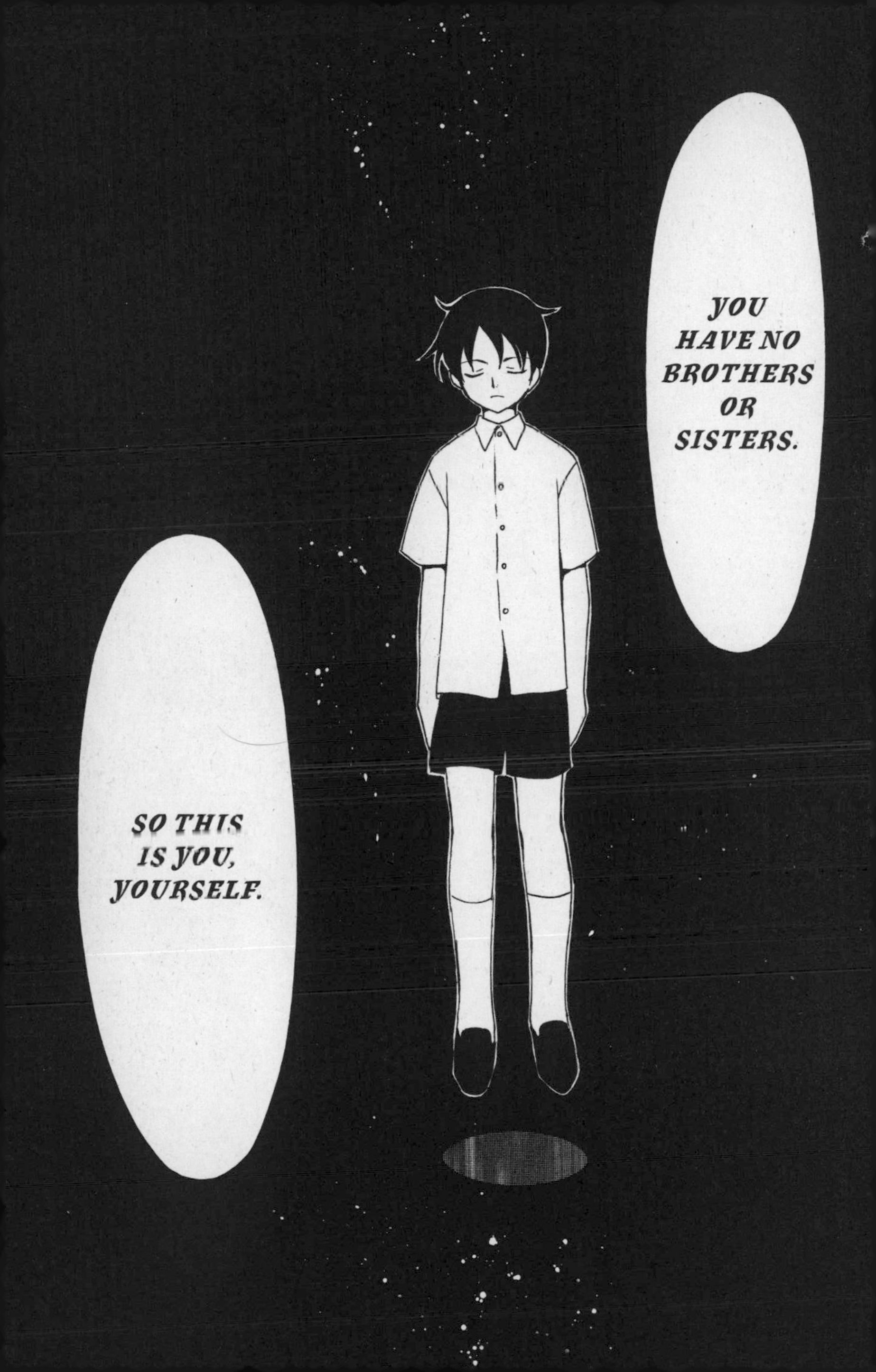
YOU HAVE NO BROTHERS OR SISTERS.
SO THIS IS YOU, YOURSELF.

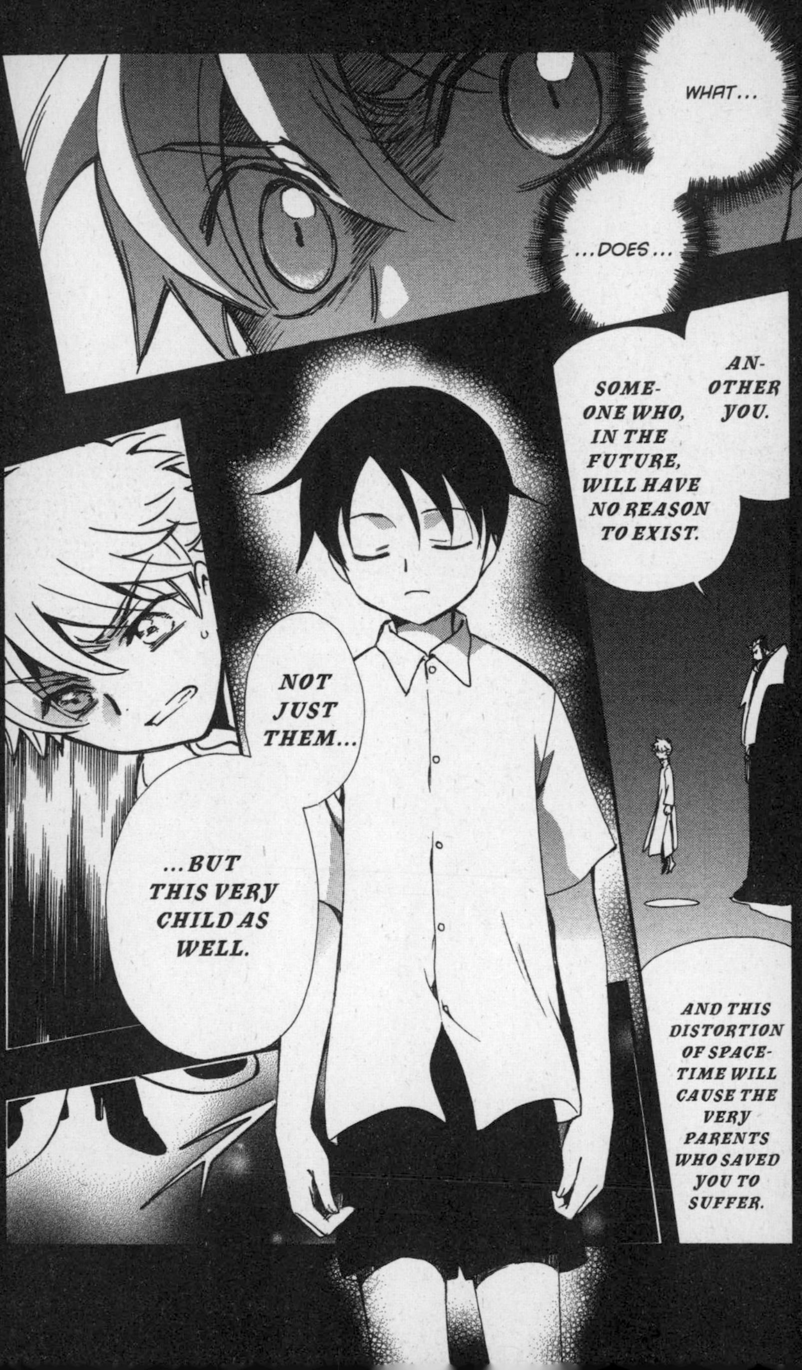
WHAT...
...DOES...
AN-OTHER YOU.
SOME-ONE WHO, IN THE FUTURE, WILL HAVE NO REASON TO EXIST.
NOT JUST THEM...
...BUT THIS VERY CHILD AS WELL.
AND THIS DISTORTION OF SPACE-TIME WILL CAUSE THE VERY PARENTS WHO SAVED YOU TO SUFFER.

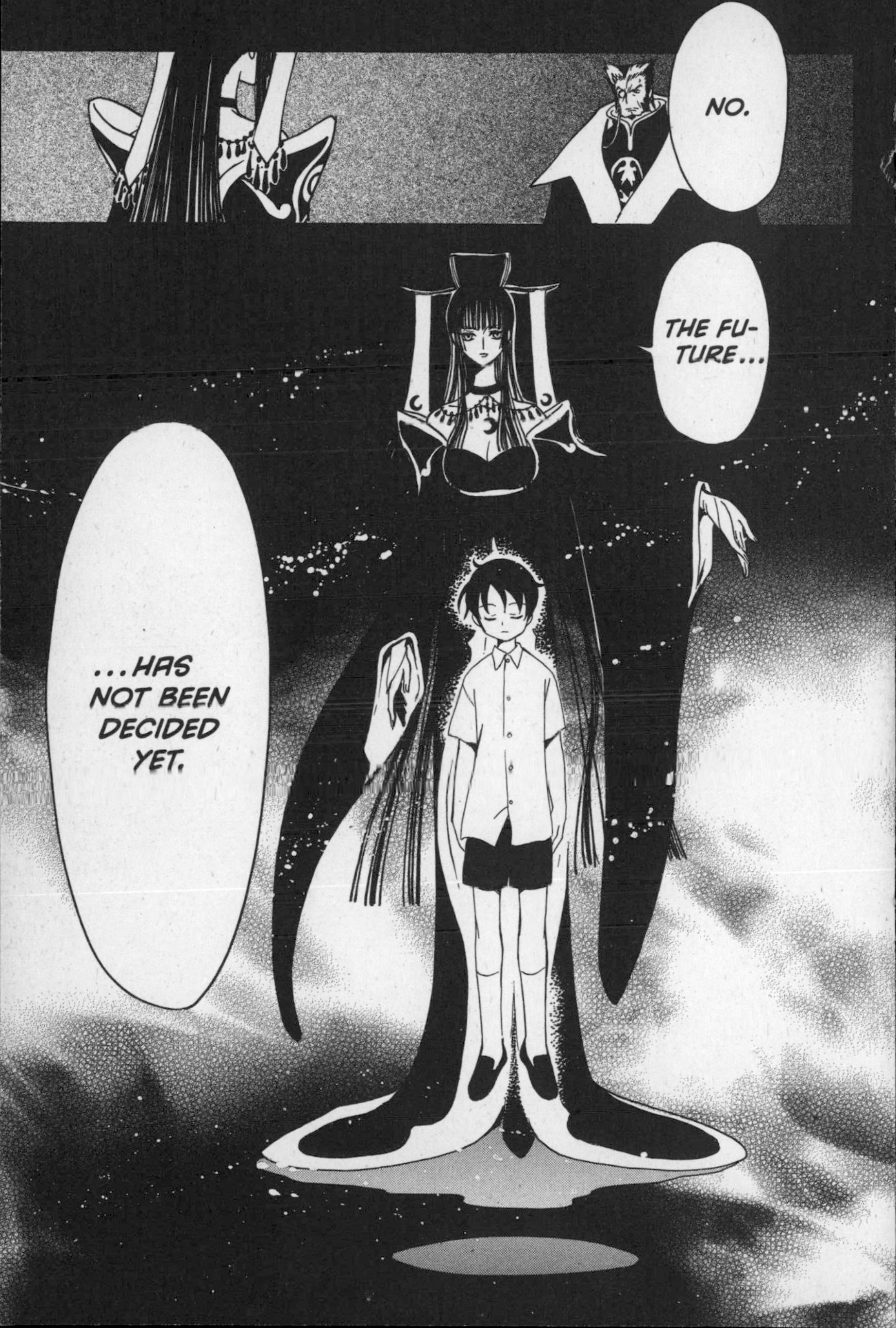
NO.
THE FU-TURE...
...HAS NOT BEEN DECIDED YET.

ツバサ

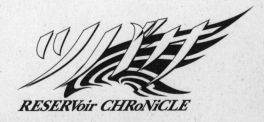

RESERVoir CHRoNiCLE

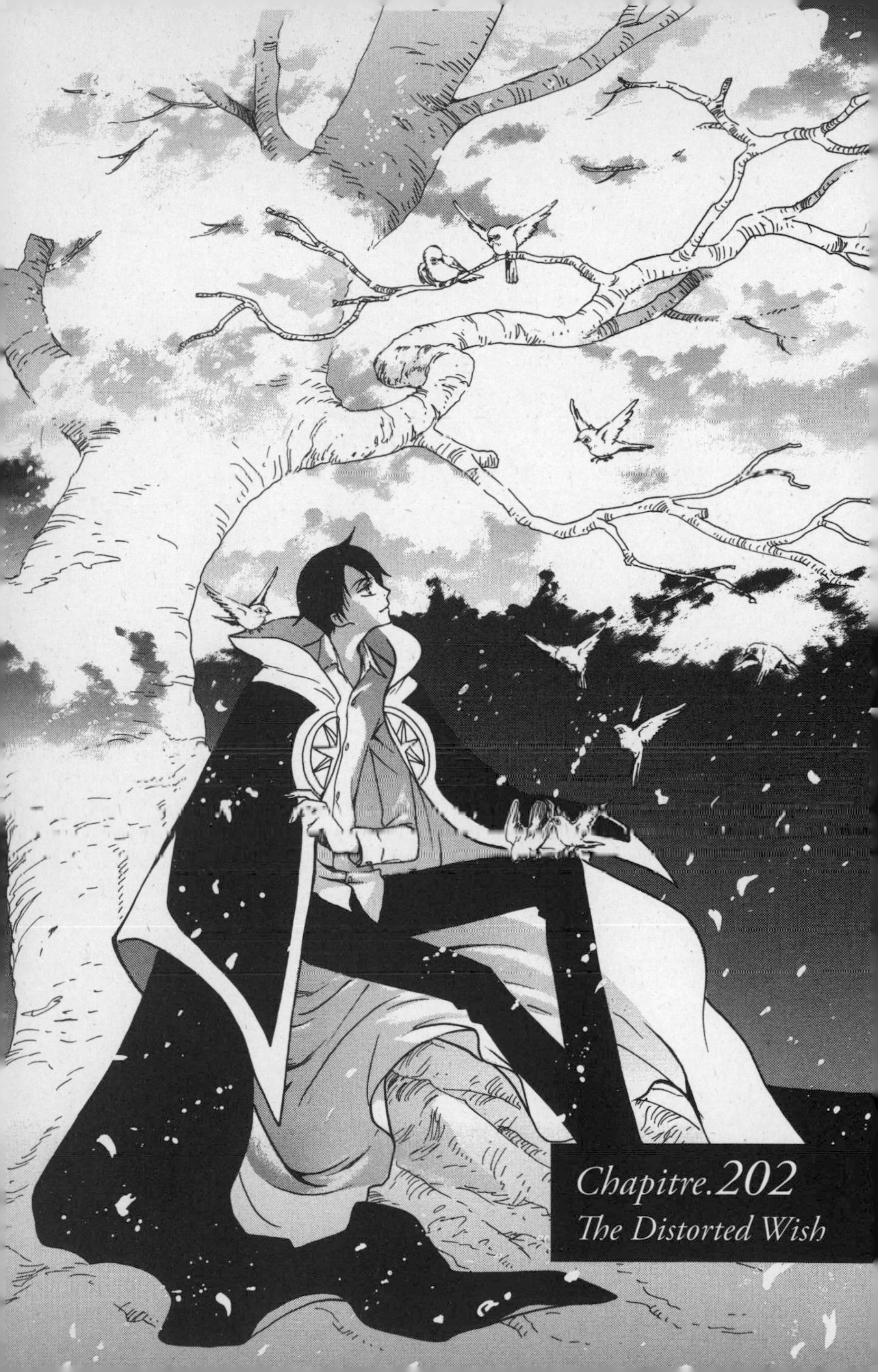
Chapitre.202
The Distorted Wish

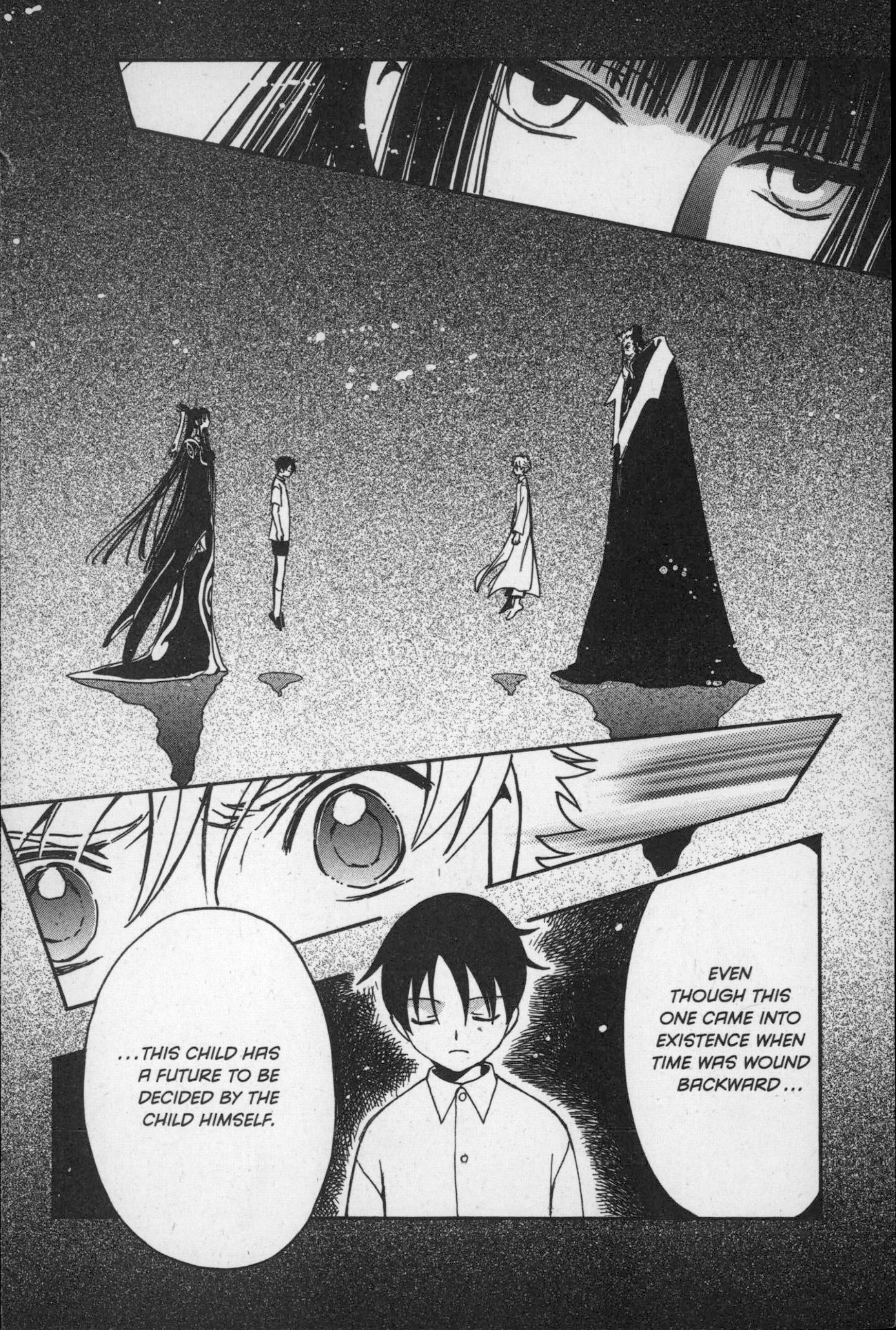
EVEN THOUGH THIS ONE CAME INTO EXISTENCE WHEN TIME WAS WOUND BACKWARD...
...THIS CHILD HAS A FUTURE TO BE DECIDED BY THE CHILD HIMSELF.

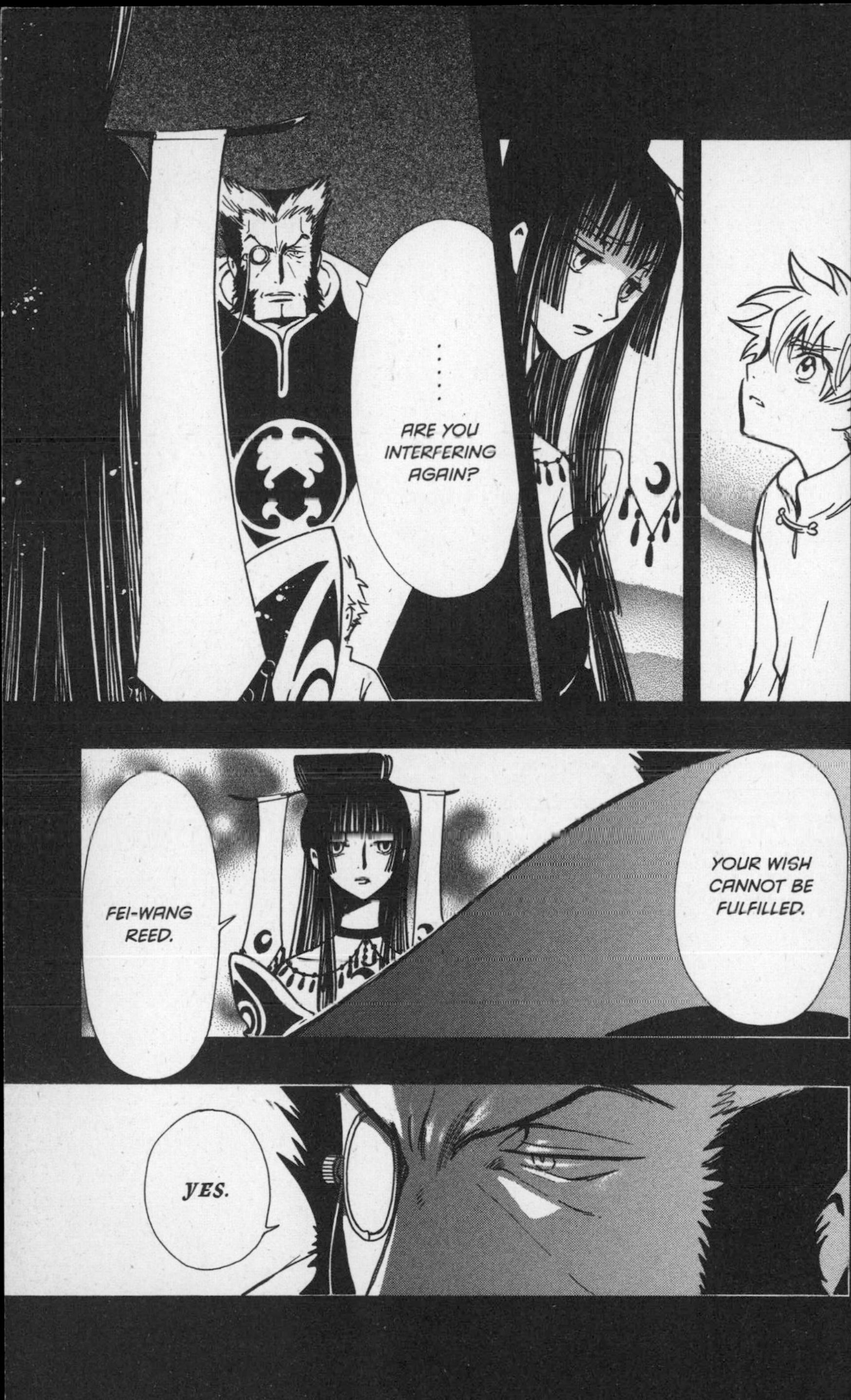

...... ARE YOU INTERFERING AGAIN?
YOUR WISH CANNOT BE FULFILLED.
FEI-WANG REED.
YES.

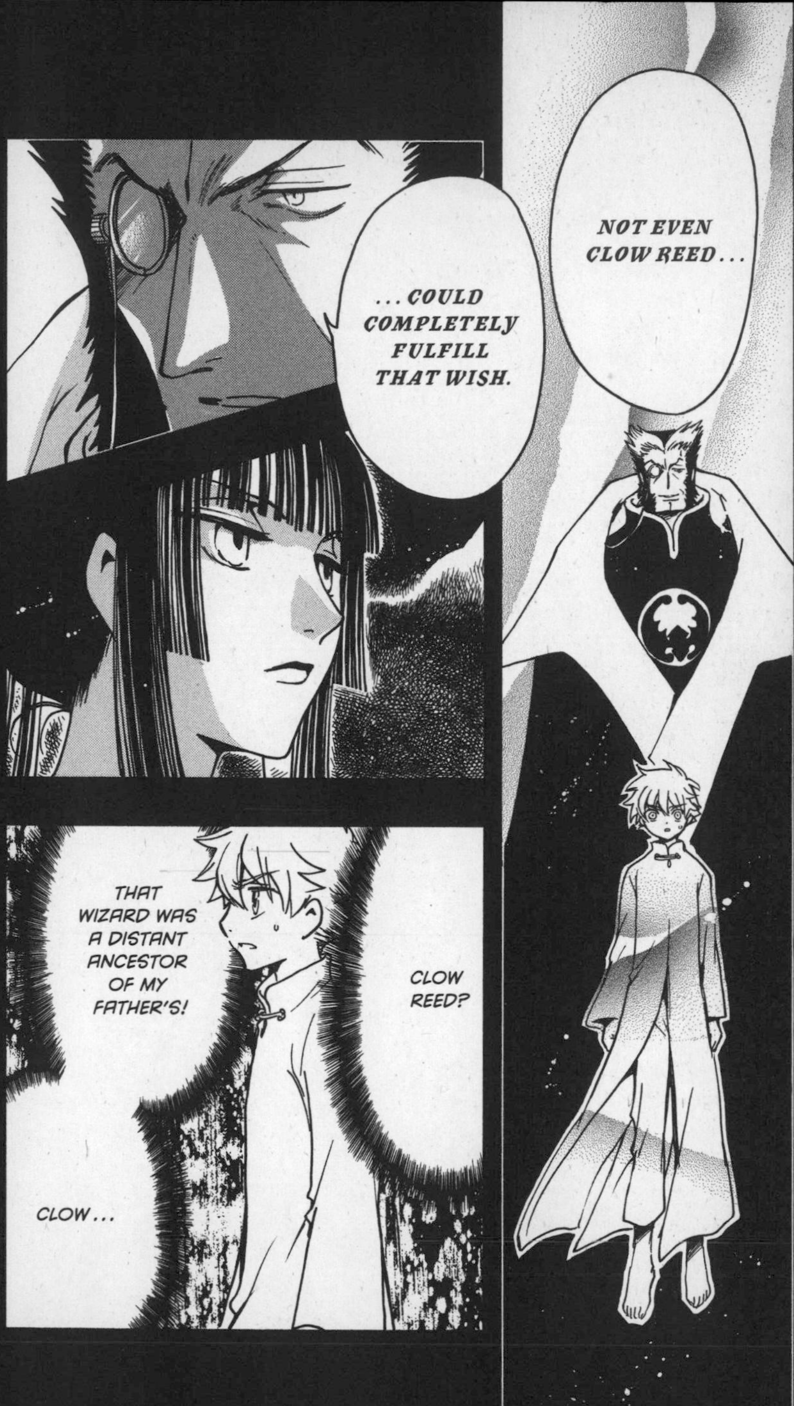
NOT EVEN CLOW REED . . .
. . . COULD COMPLETELY FULFILL THAT WISH.
CLOW REED?
THAT WIZARD WAS A DISTANT ANCESTOR OF MY FATHER'S!
CLOW . . .

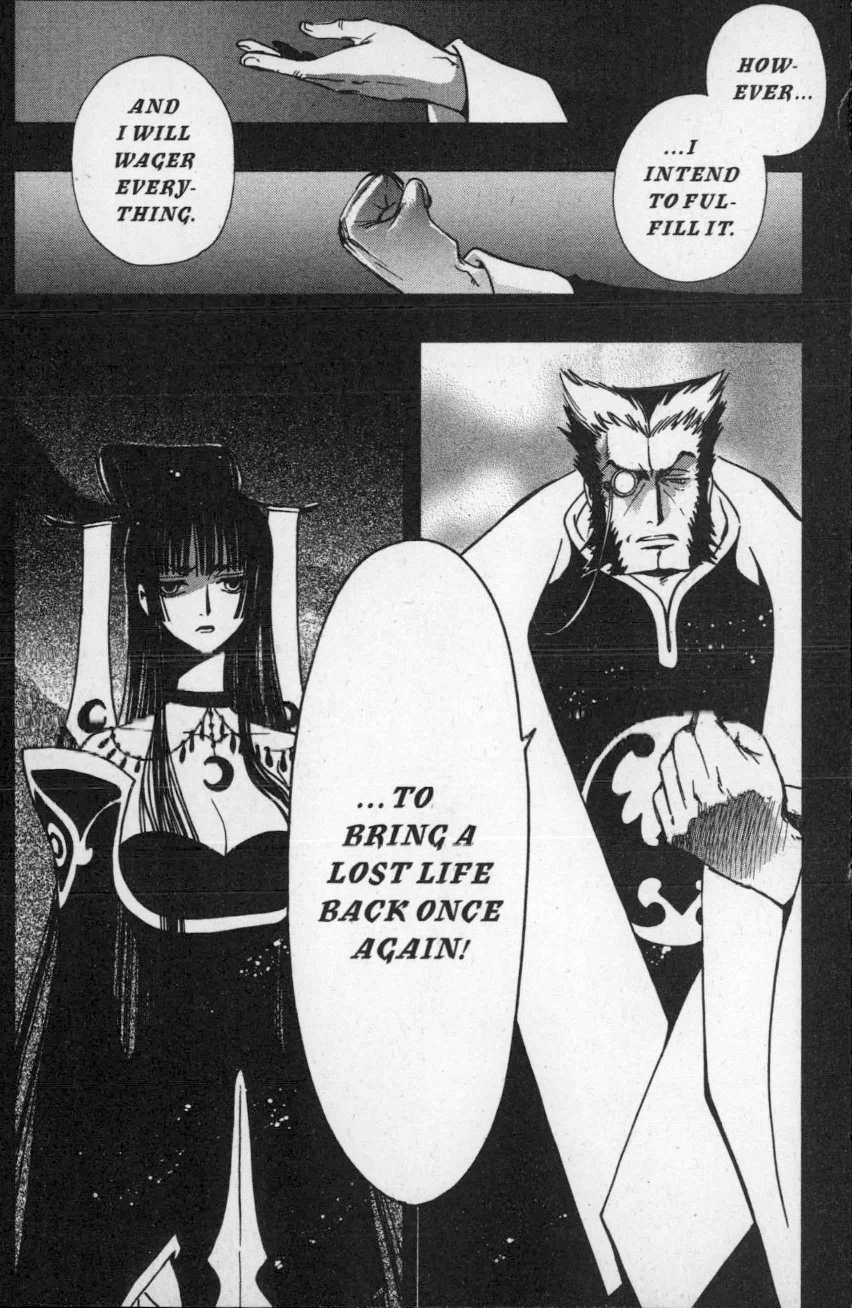
HOW-EVER...
...I INTEND TO FUL-FILL IT.
AND I WILL WAGER EVERY-THING.
...TO BRING A LOST LIFE BACK ONCE AGAIN!

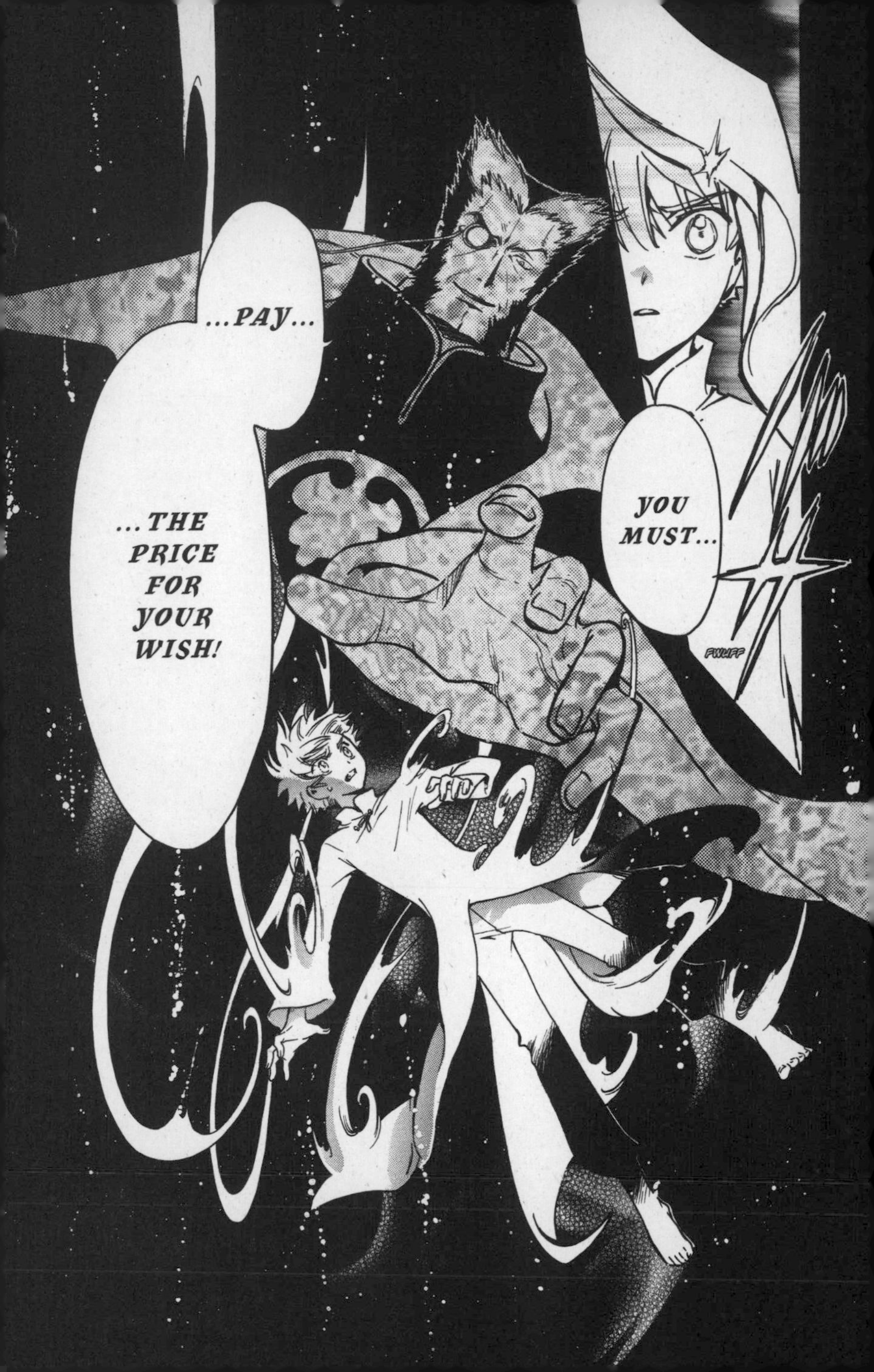
YOU MUST...
FWUFF
...PAY...
...THE PRICE FOR YOUR WISH!

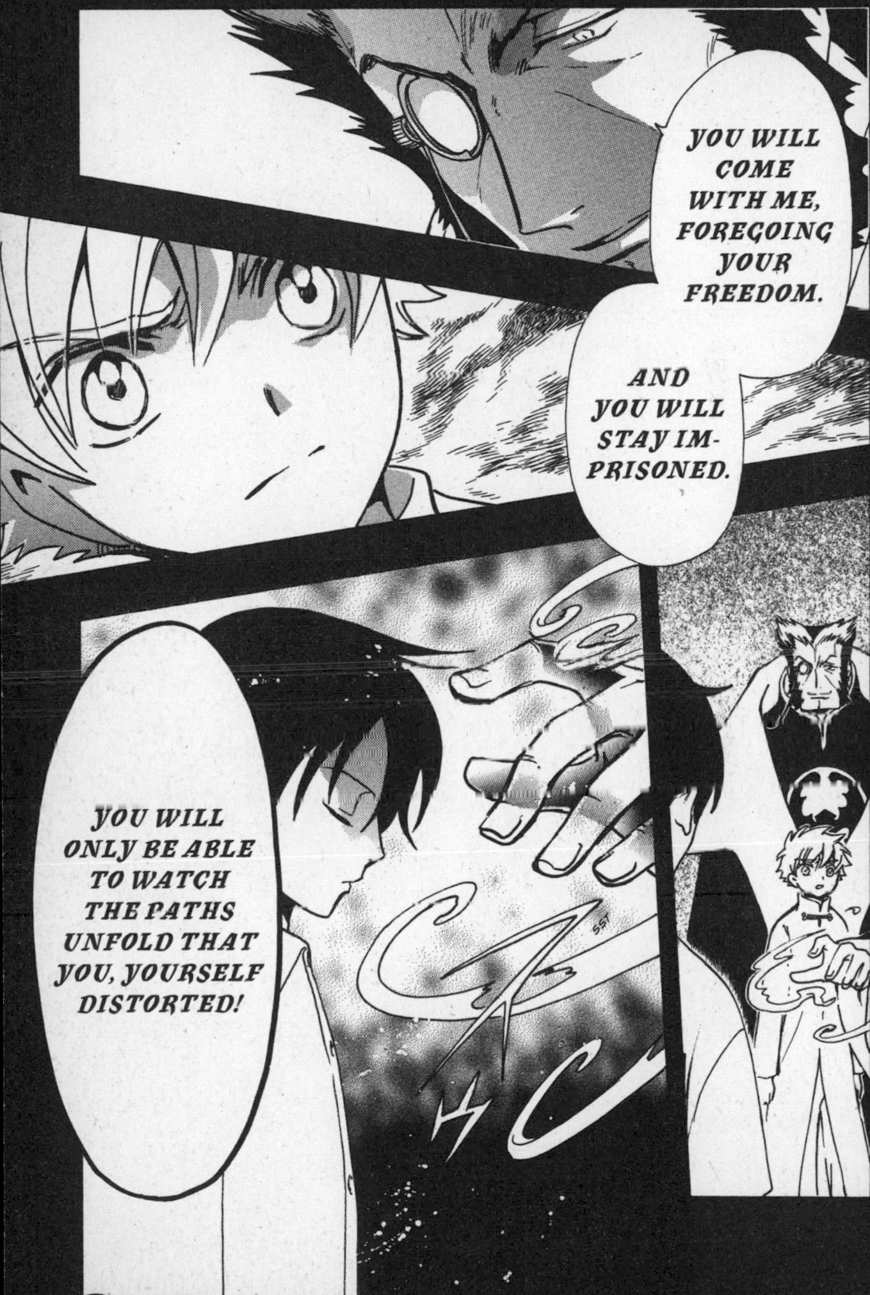
YOU WILL COME WITH ME, FOREGOING YOUR FREEDOM.
AND YOU WILL STAY IM-PRISONED.
YOU WILL ONLY BE ABLE TO WATCH THE PATHS UNFOLD THAT YOU, YOURSELF DISTORTED!

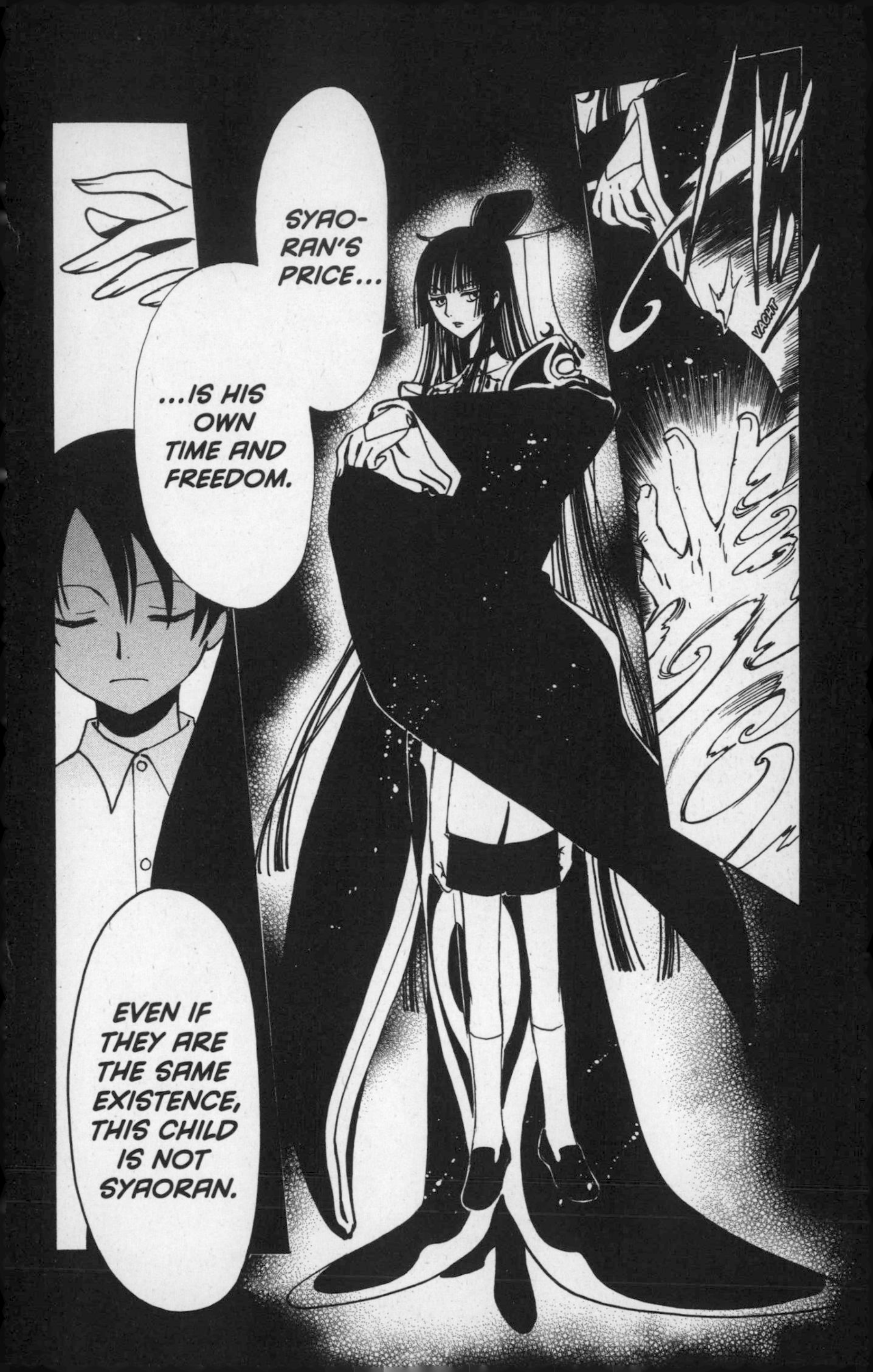
VACHT
SYAO-RAN'S PRICE...
...IS HIS OWN TIME AND FREEDOM.
EVEN IF THEY ARE THE SAME EXISTENCE, THIS CHILD IS NOT SYAORAN.

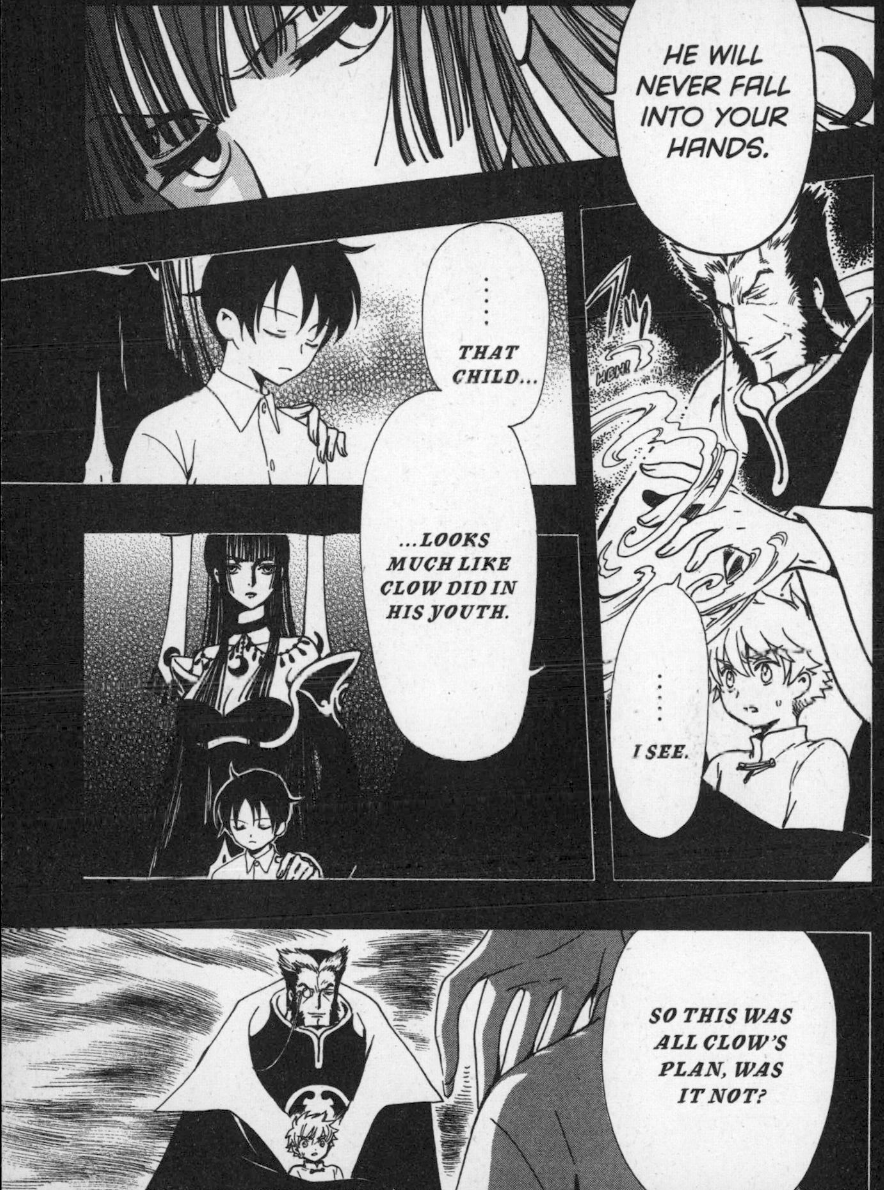
HE WILL NEVER FALL INTO YOUR HANDS.
HEH!
..... I SEE.
..... THAT CHILD...
...LOOKS MUCH LIKE CLOW DID IN HIS YOUTH.
SO THIS WAS ALL CLOW'S PLAN, WAS IT NOT?

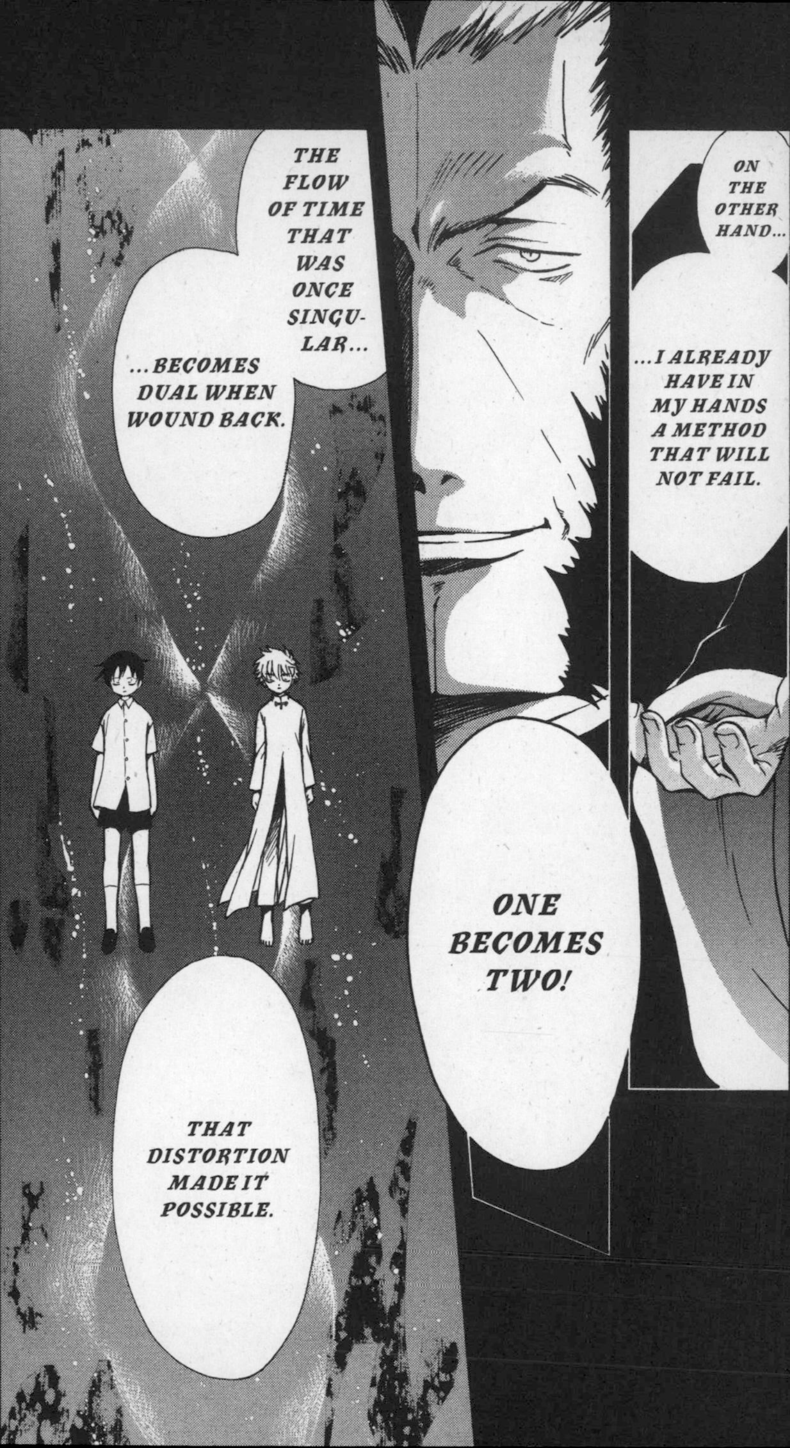
ON THE OTHER HAND...
...I ALREADY HAVE IN MY HANDS A METHOD THAT WILL NOT FAIL.
ONE BECOMES TWO!
THE FLOW OF TIME THAT WAS ONCE SINGU-LAR...
...BECOMES DUAL WHEN WOUND BACK.
THAT DISTORTION MADE IT POSSIBLE.

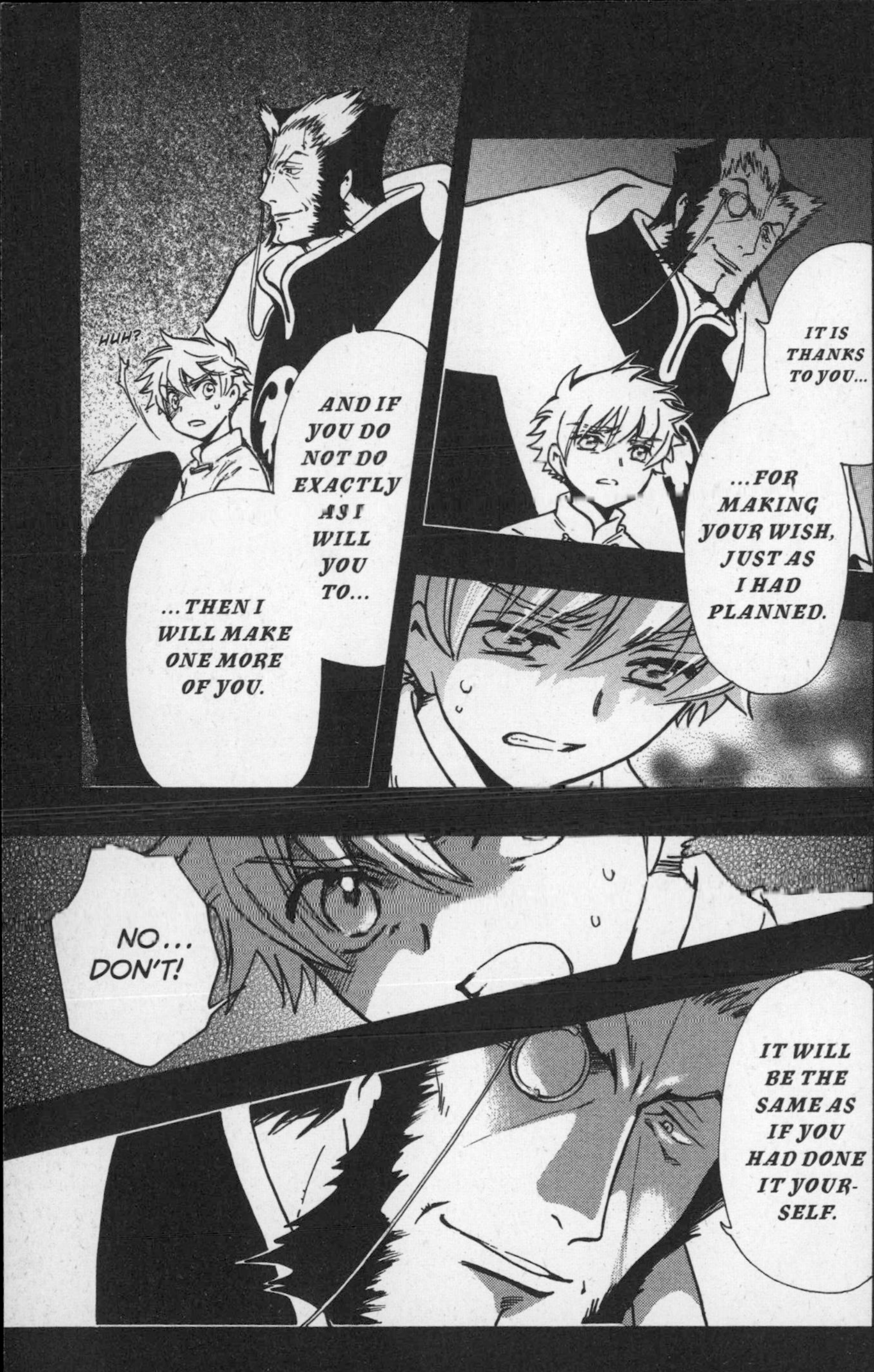
IT IS THANKS TO YOU...
...FOR MAKING YOUR WISH, JUST AS I HAD PLANNED.
HUH?
AND IF YOU DO NOT DO EXACTLY AS I WILL YOU TO...
...THEN I WILL MAKE ONE MORE OF YOU.
NO... DON'T!
IT WILL BE THE SAME AS IF YOU HAD DONE IT YOURSELF.

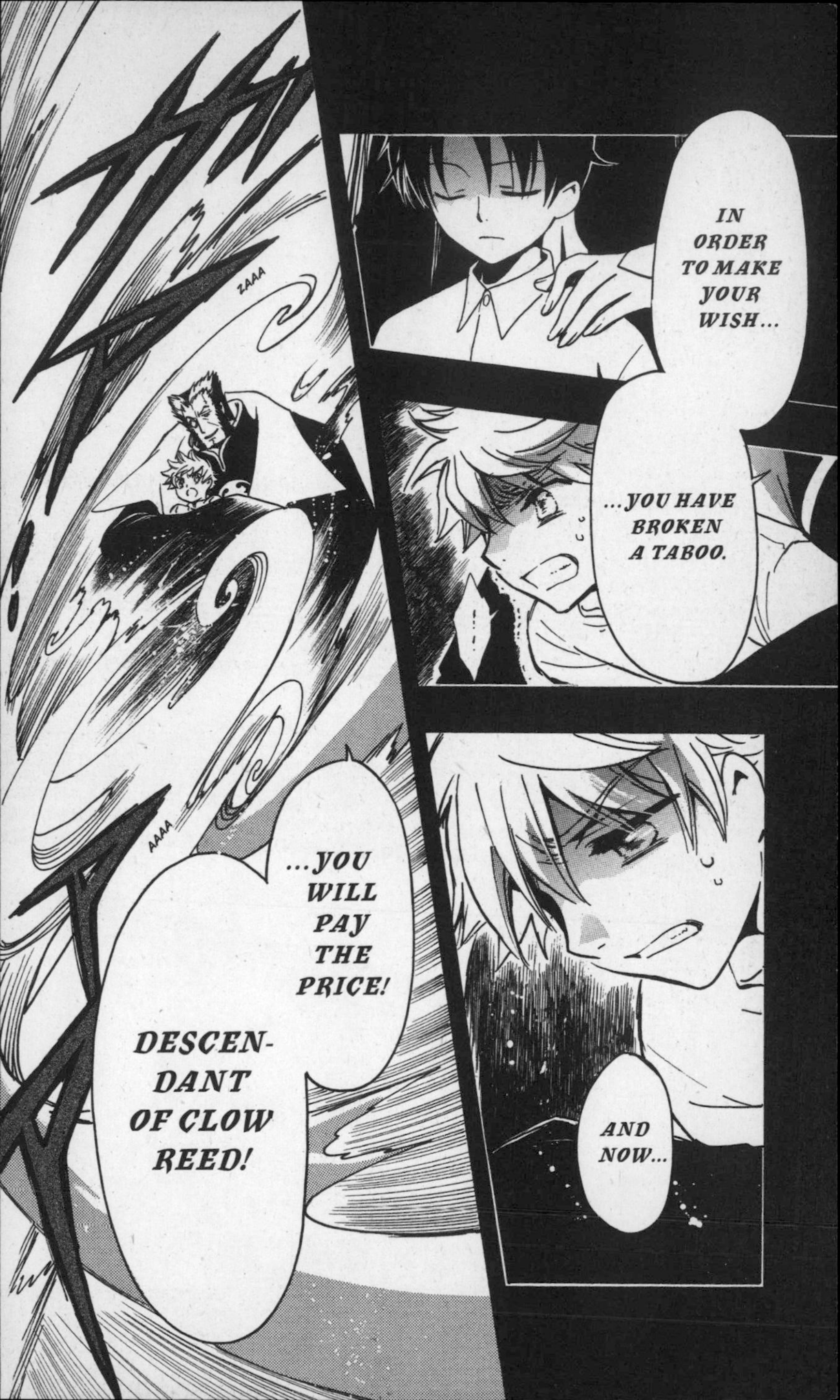
IN ORDER TO MAKE YOUR WISH...
...YOU HAVE BROKEN A TABOO.
AND NOW...
ZAAA
...YOU WILL PAY THE PRICE!
AAAA
DESCEN-DANT OF CLOW REED!

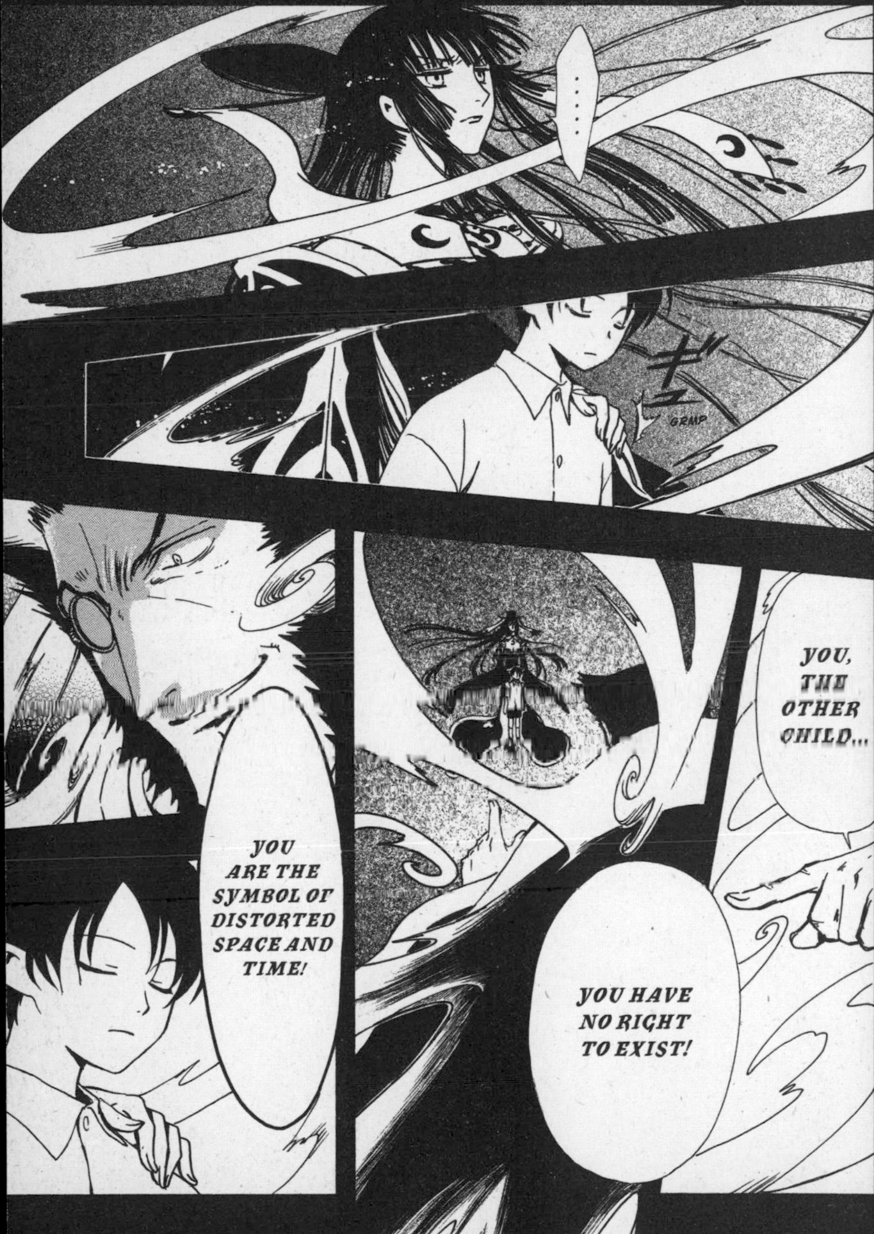
.....
ギュ
GRMP
YOU, THE OTHER CHILD...
YOU ARE THE SYMBOL OF DISTORTED SPACE AND TIME!
YOU HAVE NO RIGHT TO EXIST!

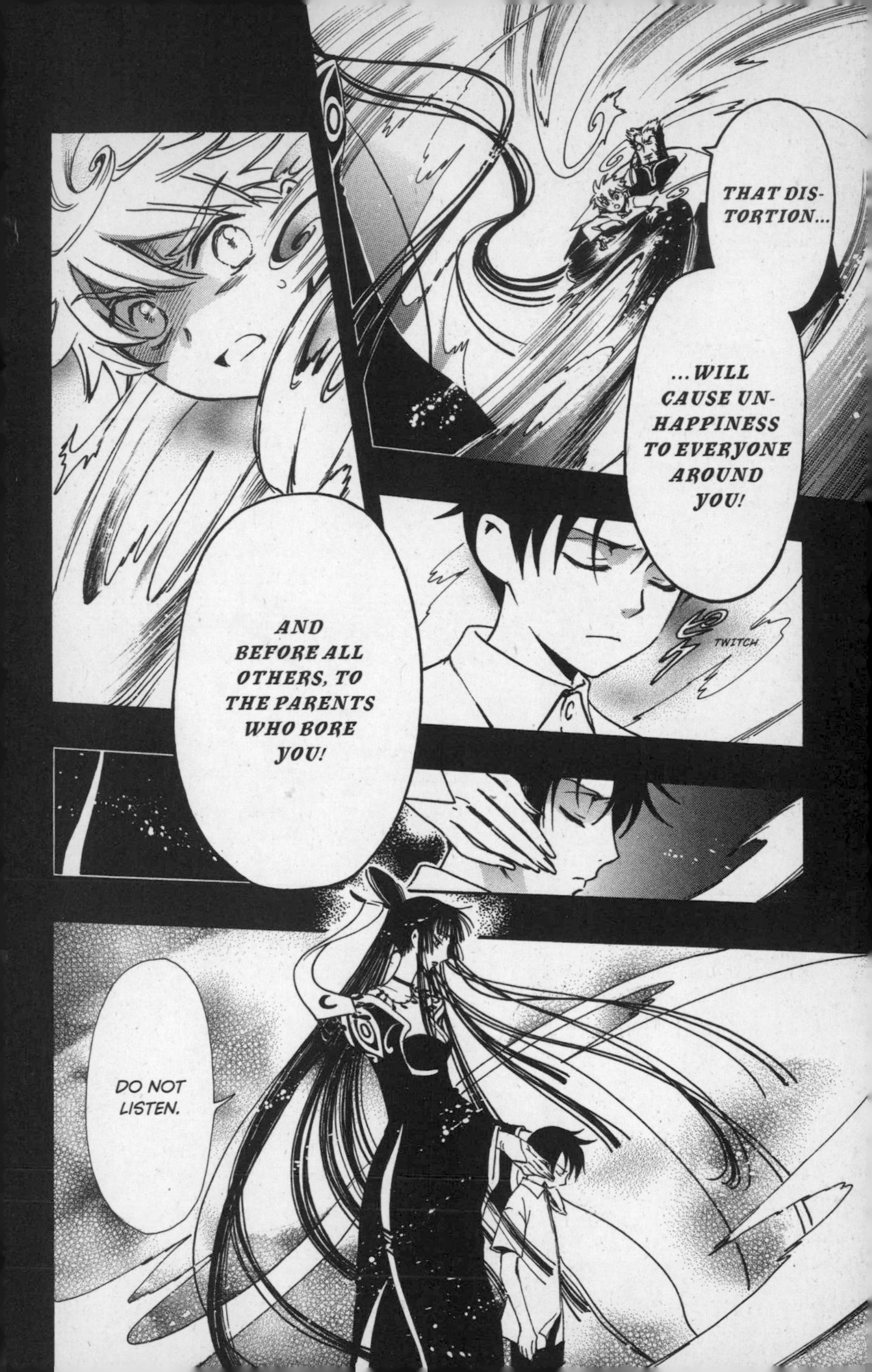
THAT DIS-TORTION...
...WILL CAUSE UN-HAPPINESS TO EVERYONE AROUND YOU!
TWITCH
AND BEFORE ALL OTHERS, TO THE PARENTS WHO BORE YOU!
DO NOT LISTEN.

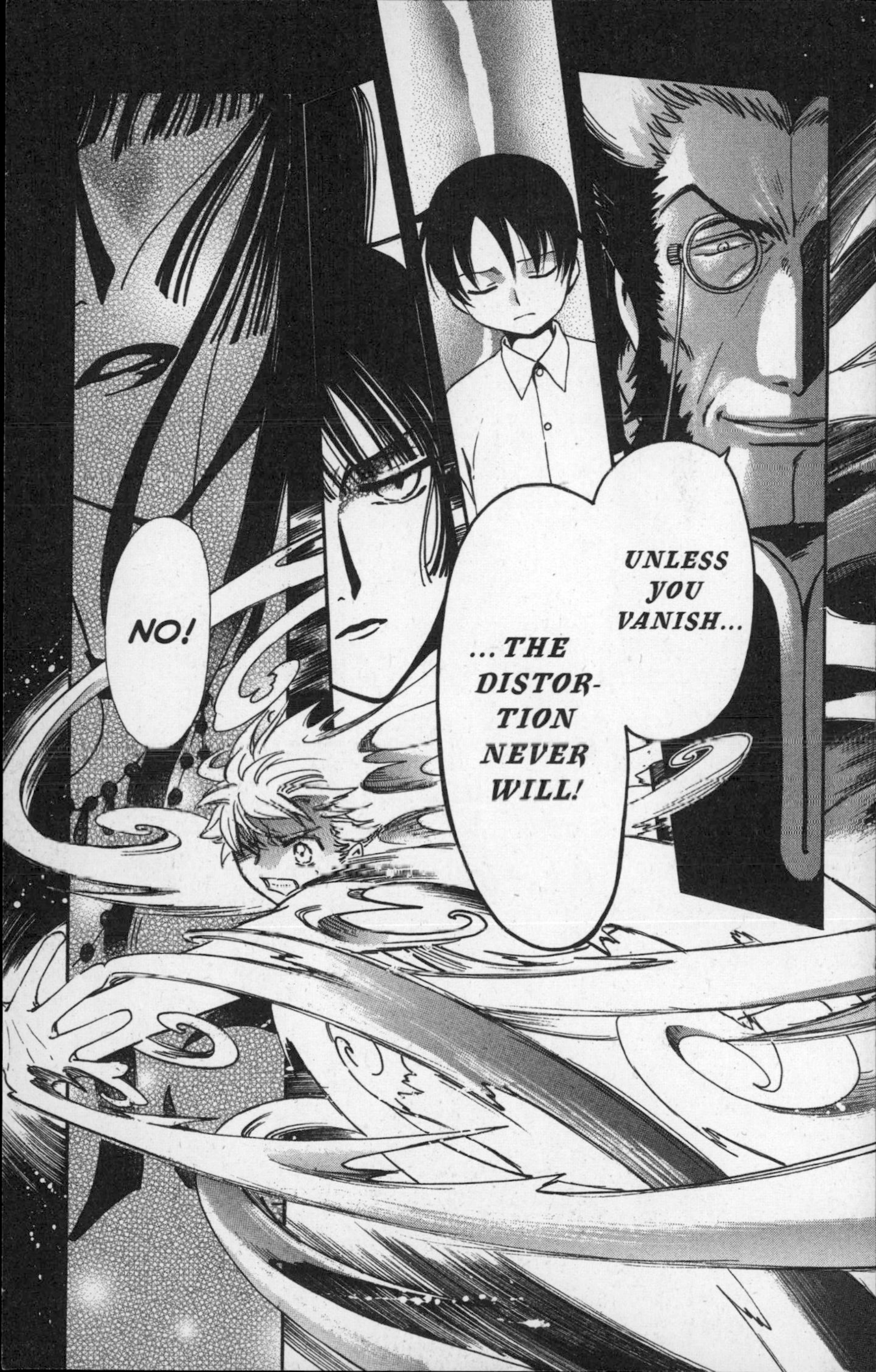
UNLESS YOU VANISH...
...THE DISTORTION NEVER WILL!
NO!

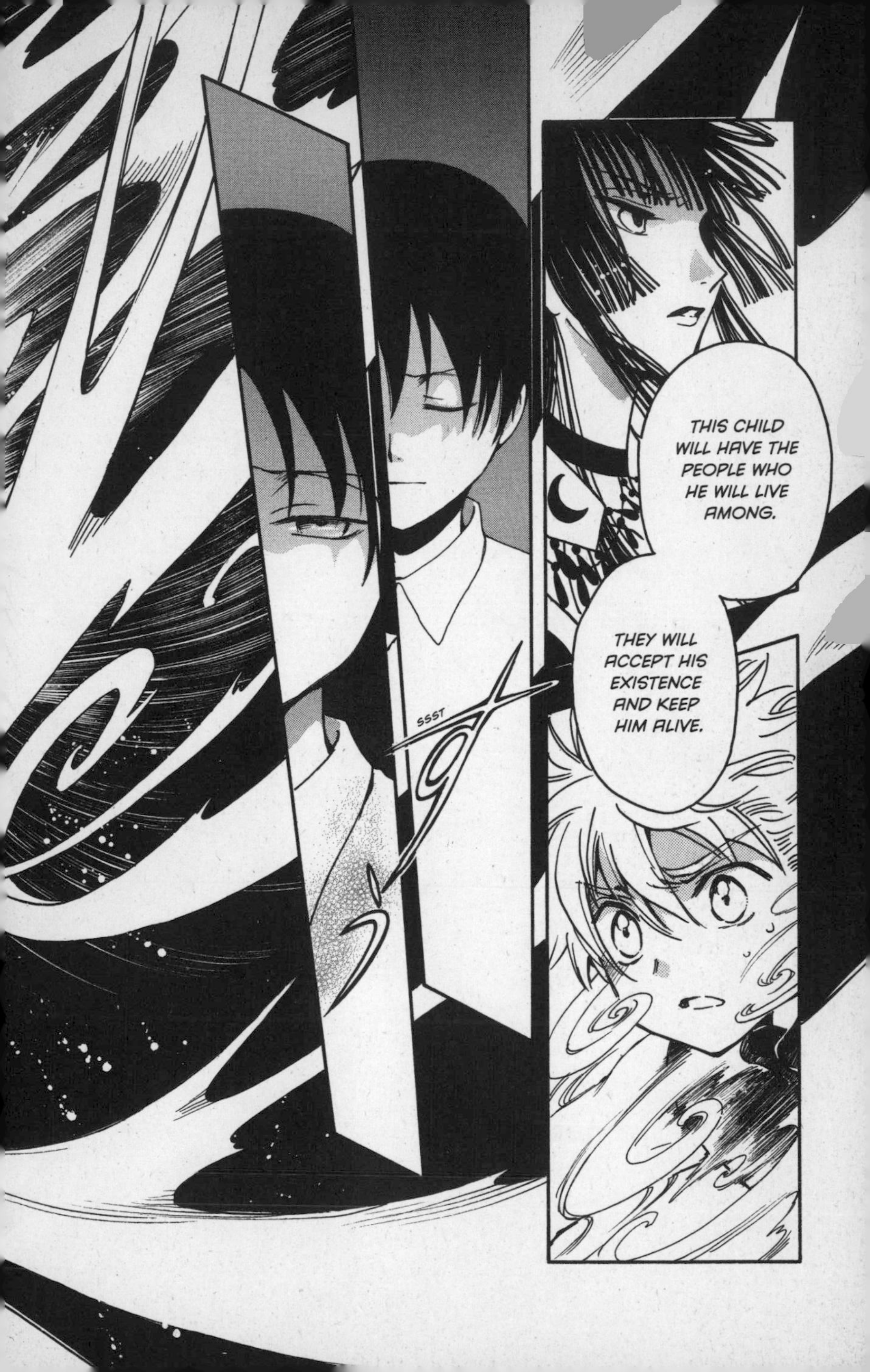
THIS CHILD WILL HAVE THE PEOPLE WHO HE WILL LIVE AMONG.
THEY WILL ACCEPT HIS EXISTENCE AND KEEP HIM ALIVE.
SSST

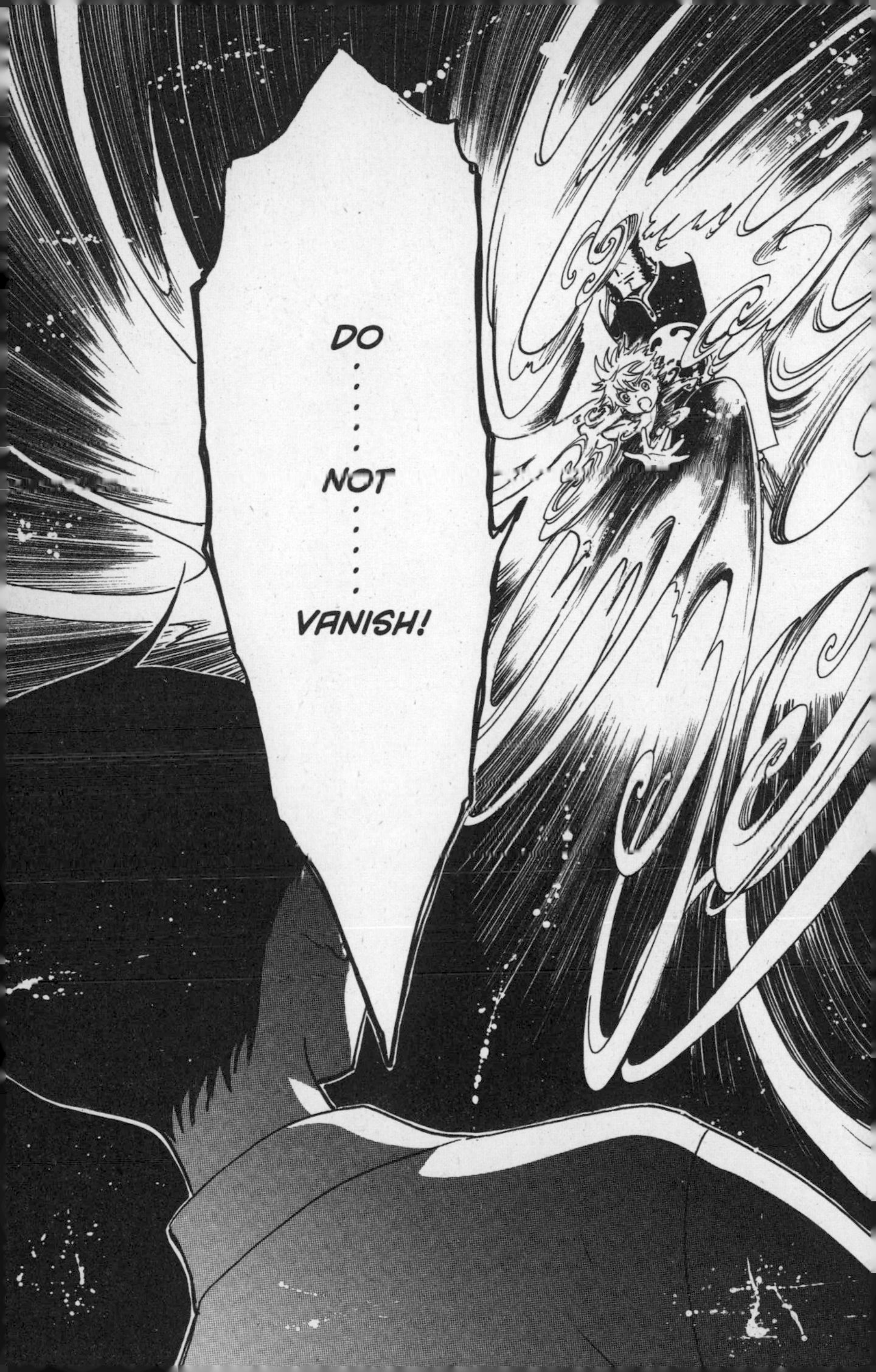
DO ... NOT ... VANISH!

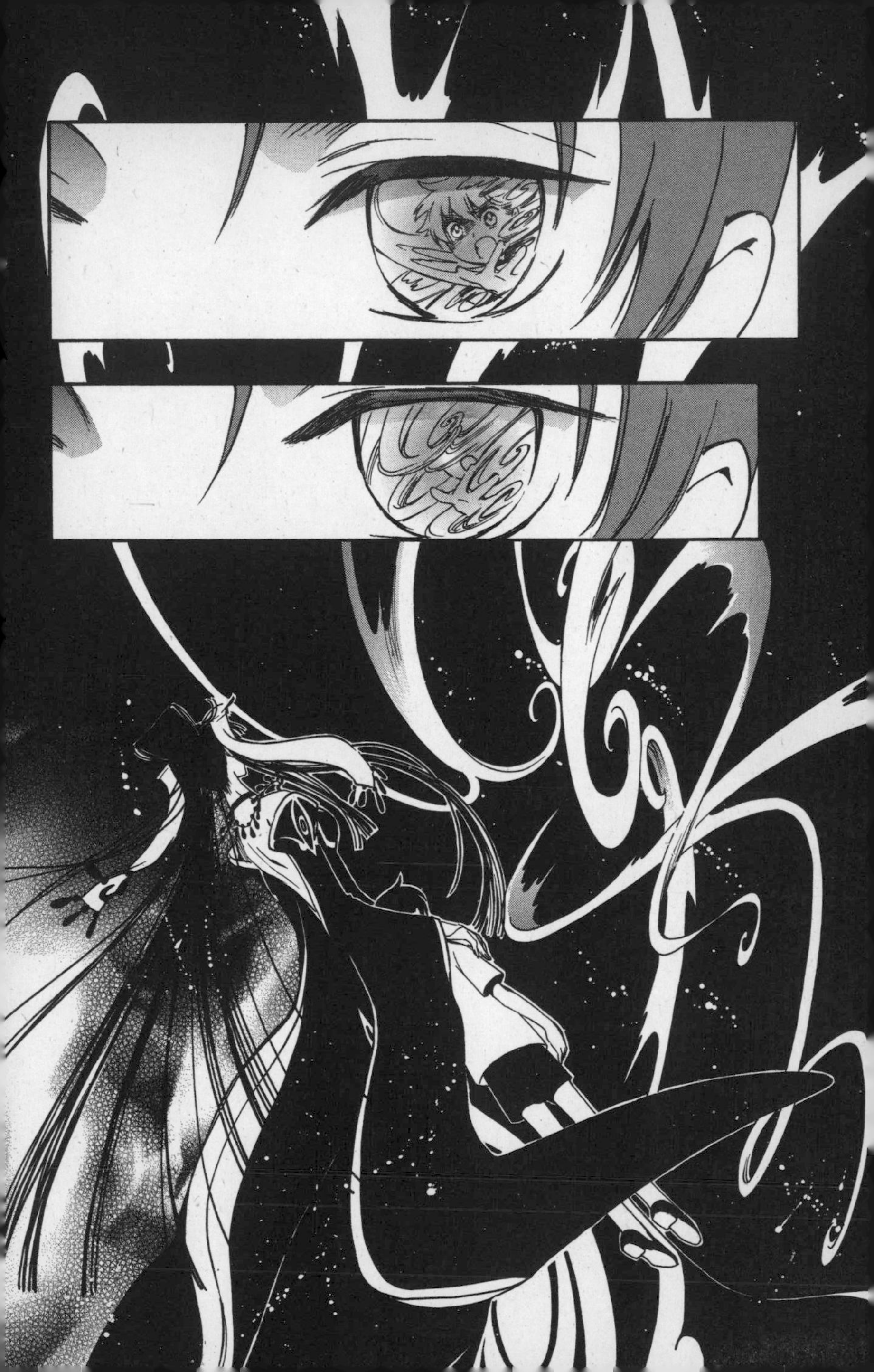

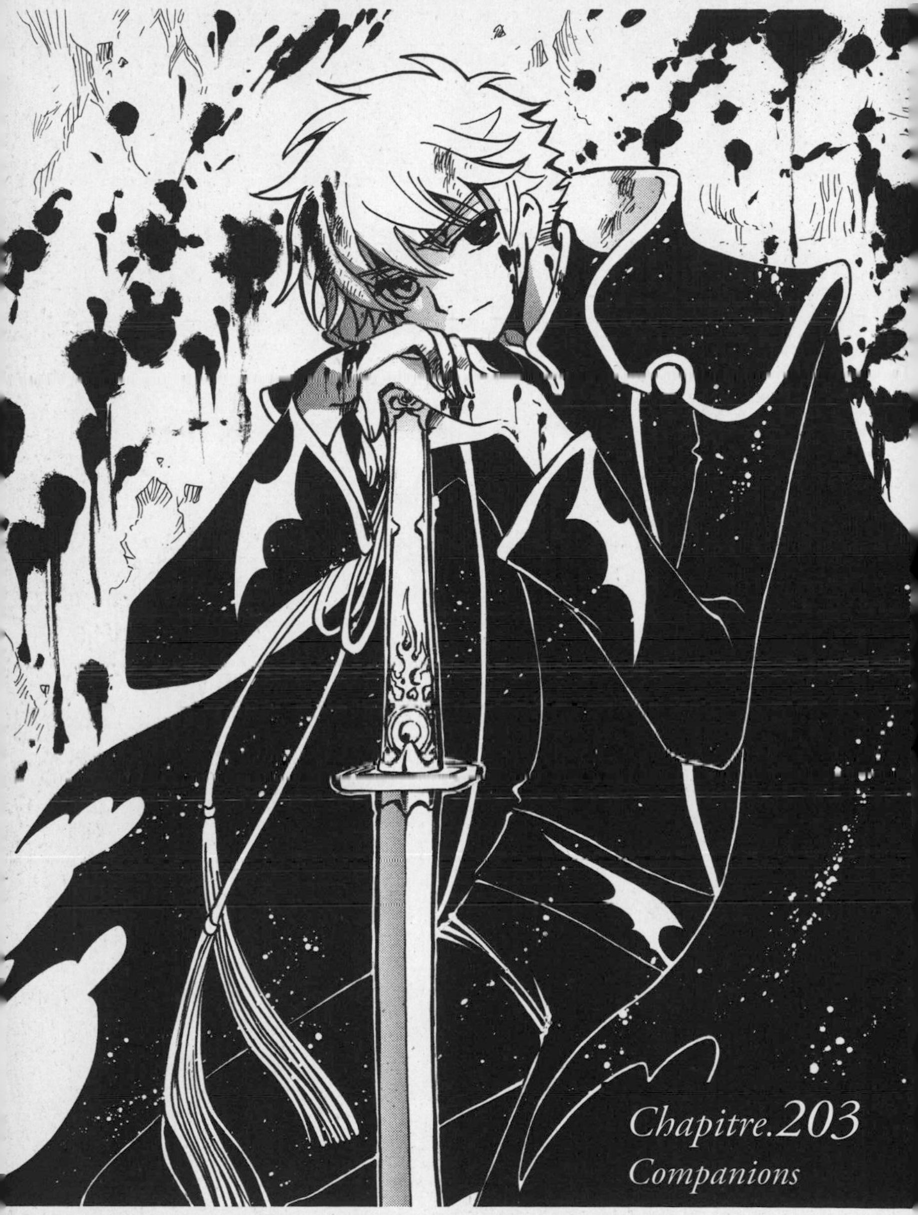
Chapitre.203
Companions

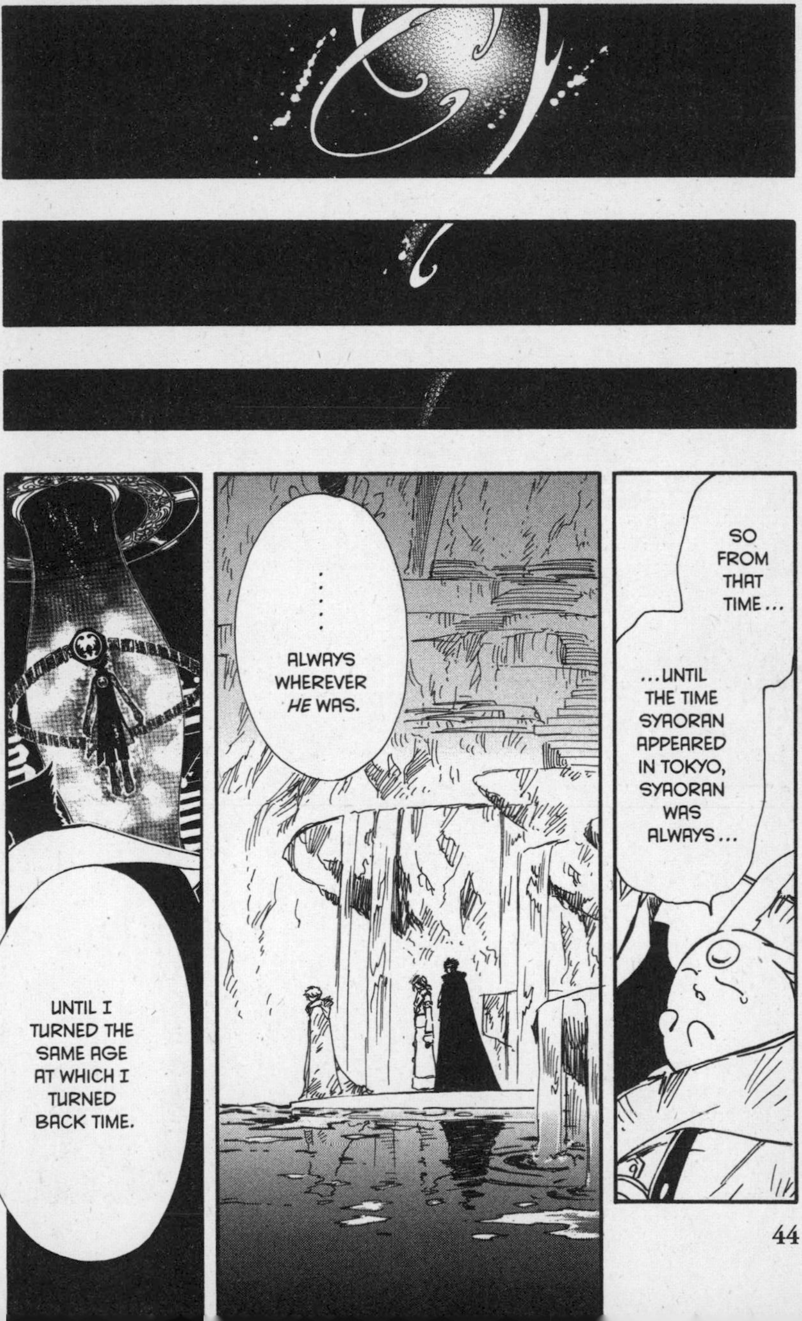
SO FROM THAT TIME...
...UNTIL THE TIME SYAORAN APPEARED IN TOKYO, SYAORAN WAS ALWAYS...
......
ALWAYS WHEREVER *HE* WAS.
UNTIL I TURNED THE SAME AGE AT WHICH I TURNED BACK TIME.

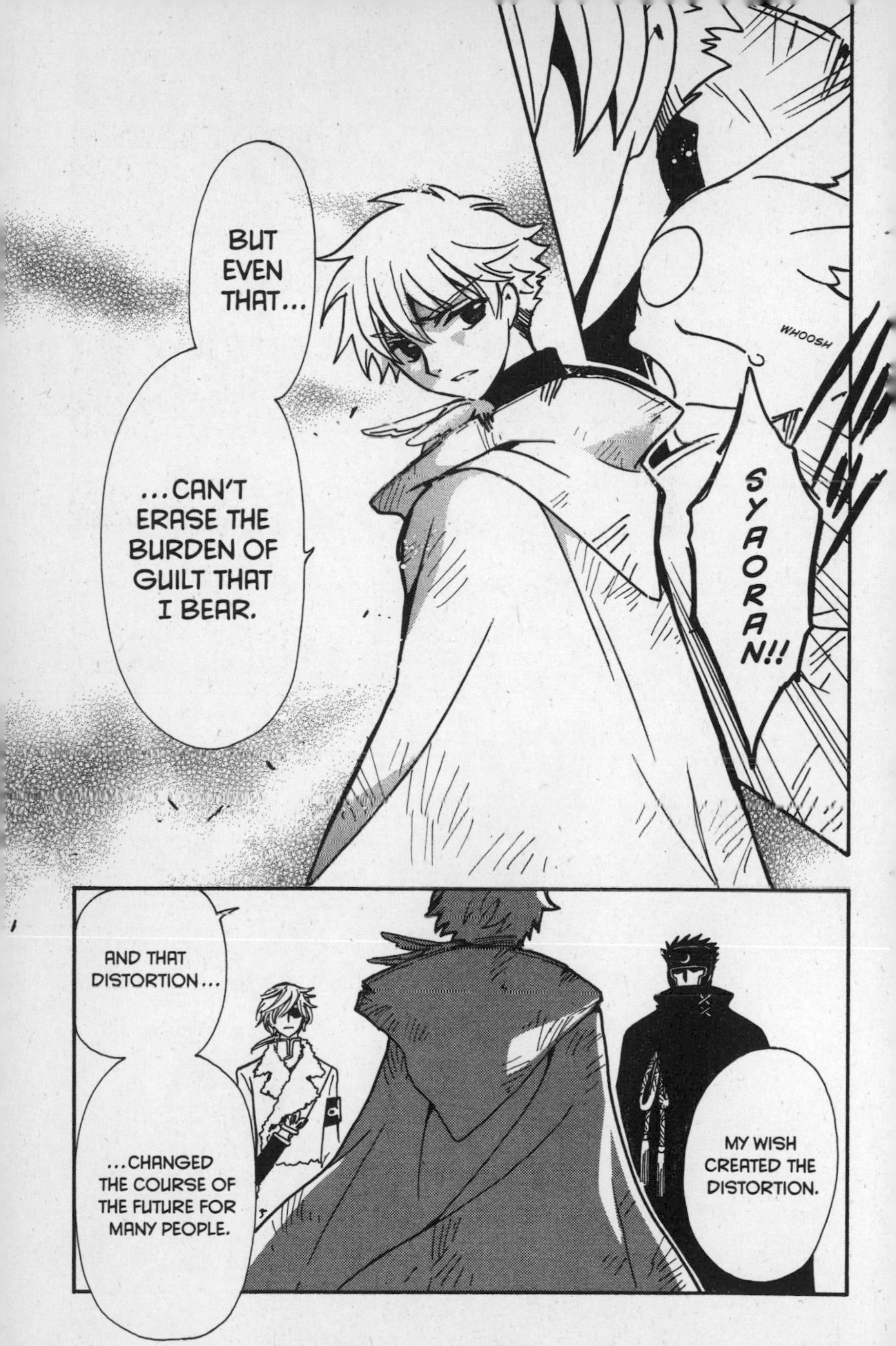
WHOOSH
SYAORAN!!
BUT EVEN THAT...
...CAN'T ERASE THE BURDEN OF GUILT THAT I BEAR.
MY WISH CREATED THE DISTORTION.
AND THAT DISTORTION...
...CHANGED THE COURSE OF THE FUTURE FOR MANY PEOPLE.

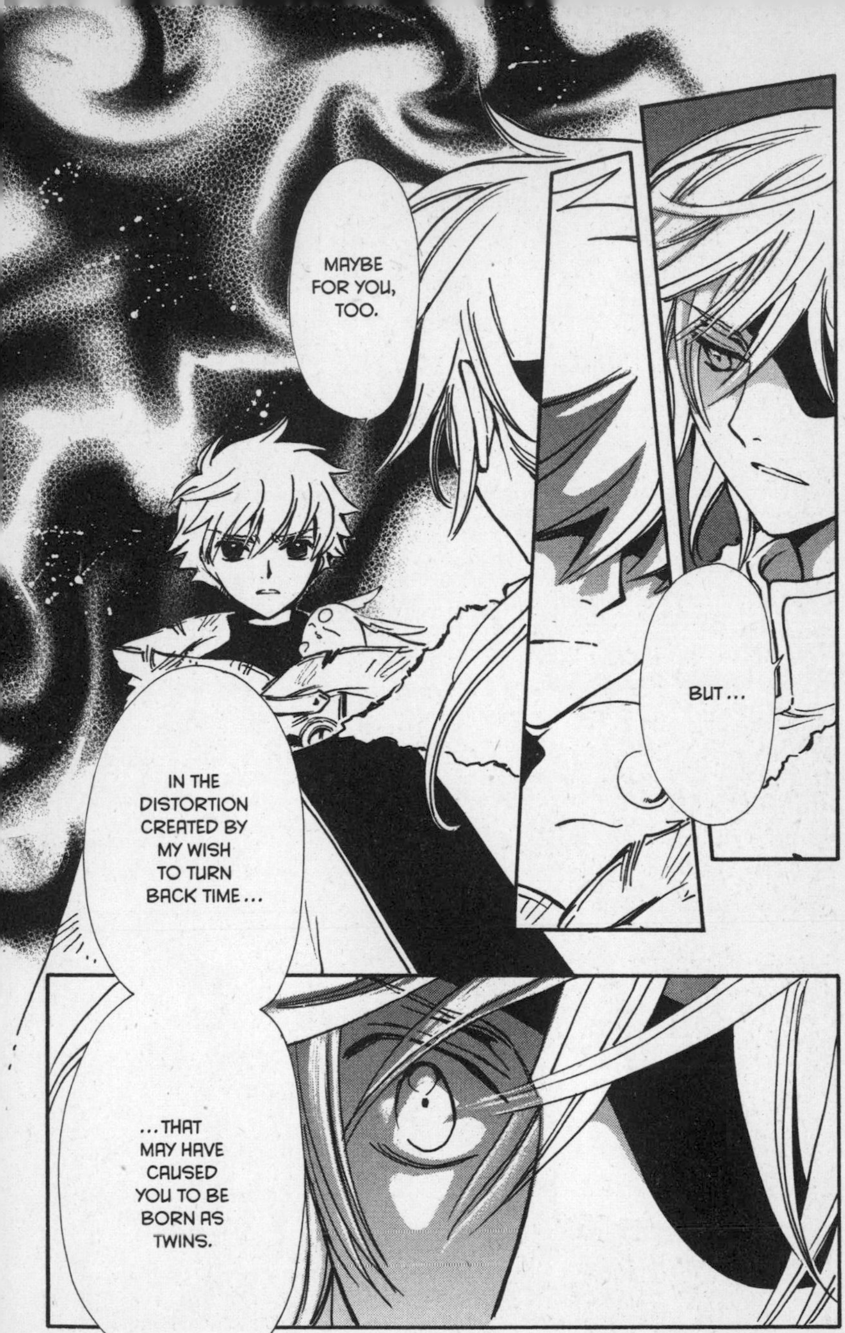
MAYBE FOR YOU, TOO.
BUT...
IN THE DISTORTION CREATED BY MY WISH TO TURN BACK TIME...
...THAT MAY HAVE CAUSED YOU TO BE BORN AS TWINS.

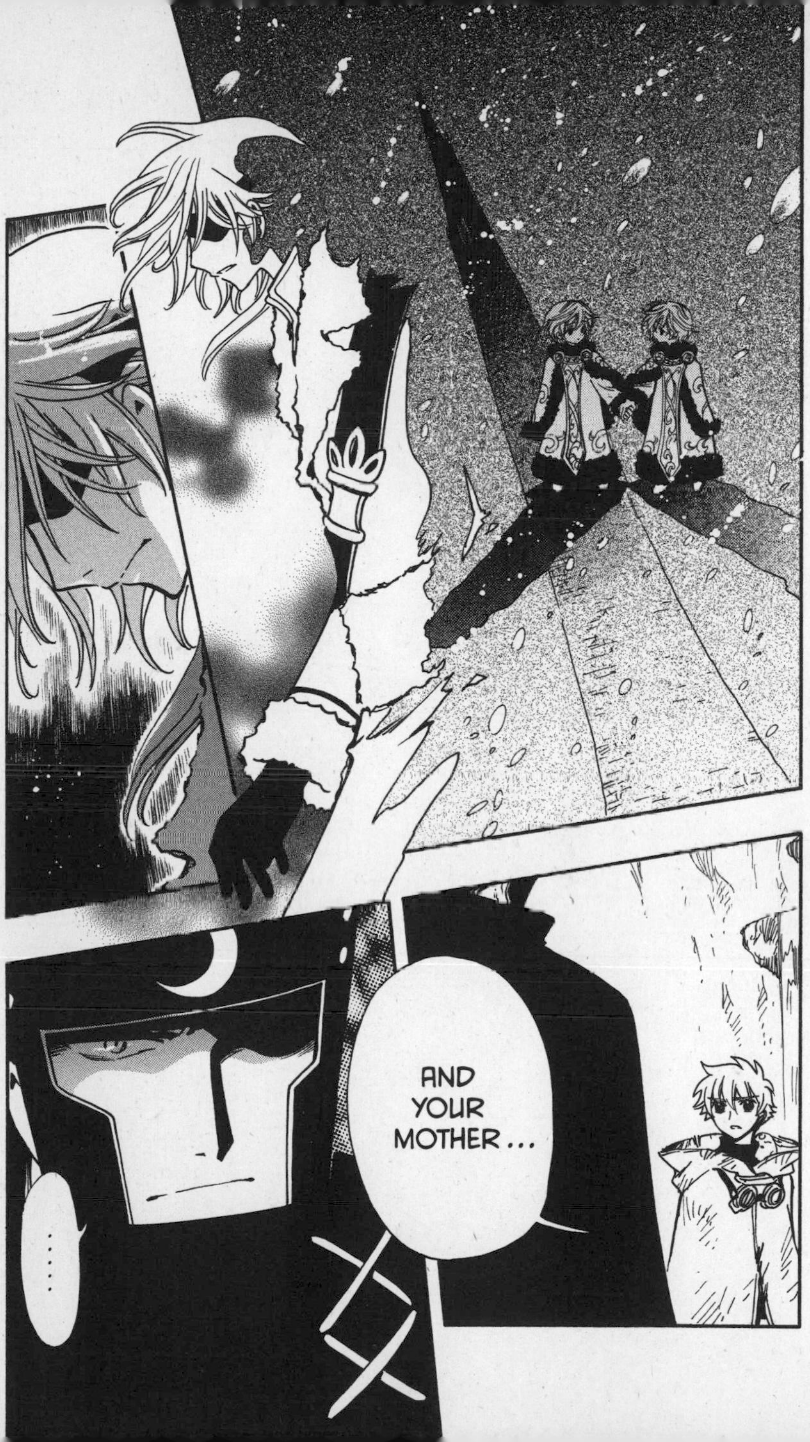
AND YOUR MOTHER...
......

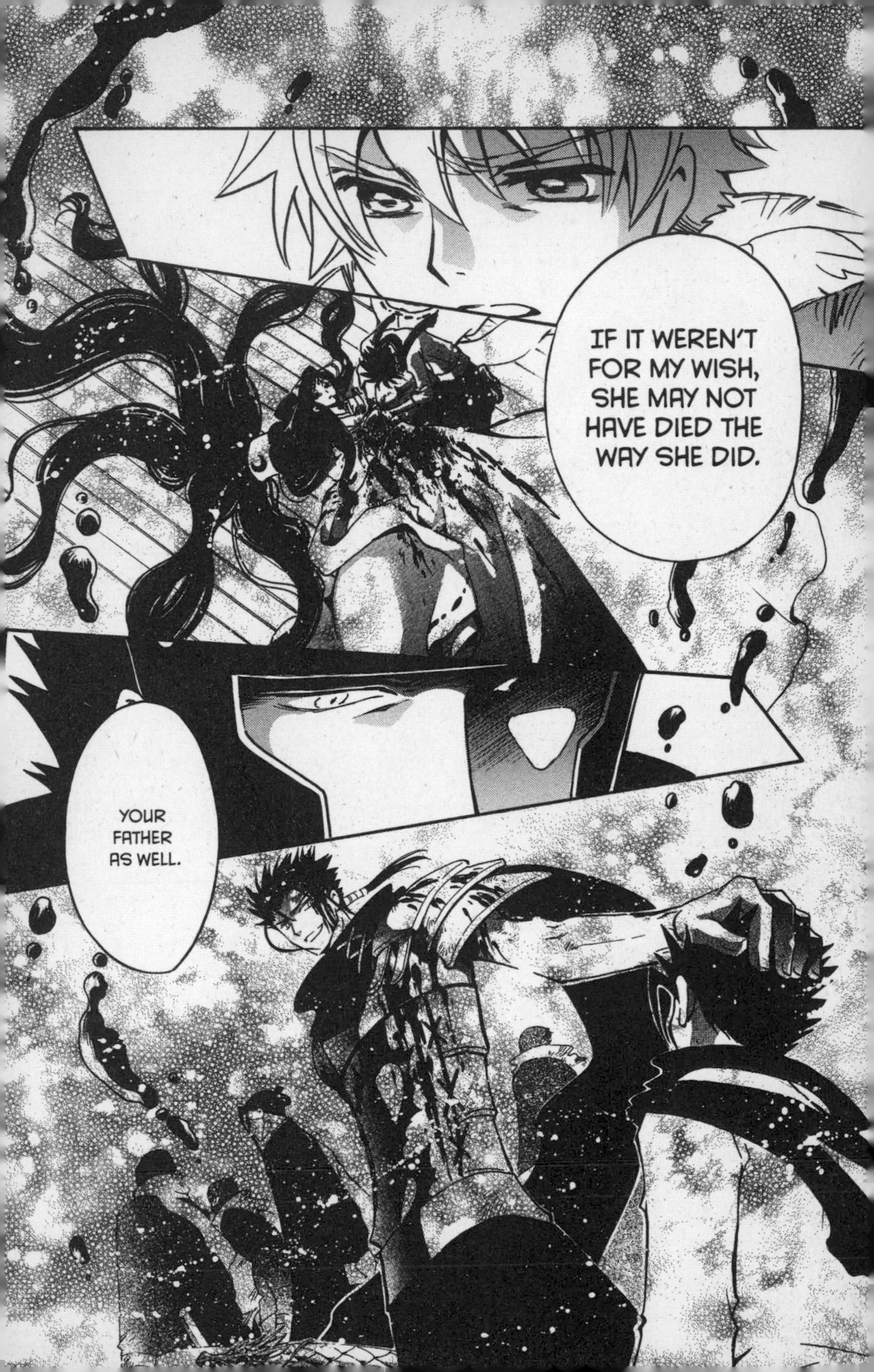
IF IT WEREN'T FOR MY WISH, SHE MAY NOT HAVE DIED THE WAY SHE DID.
YOUR FATHER AS WELL.

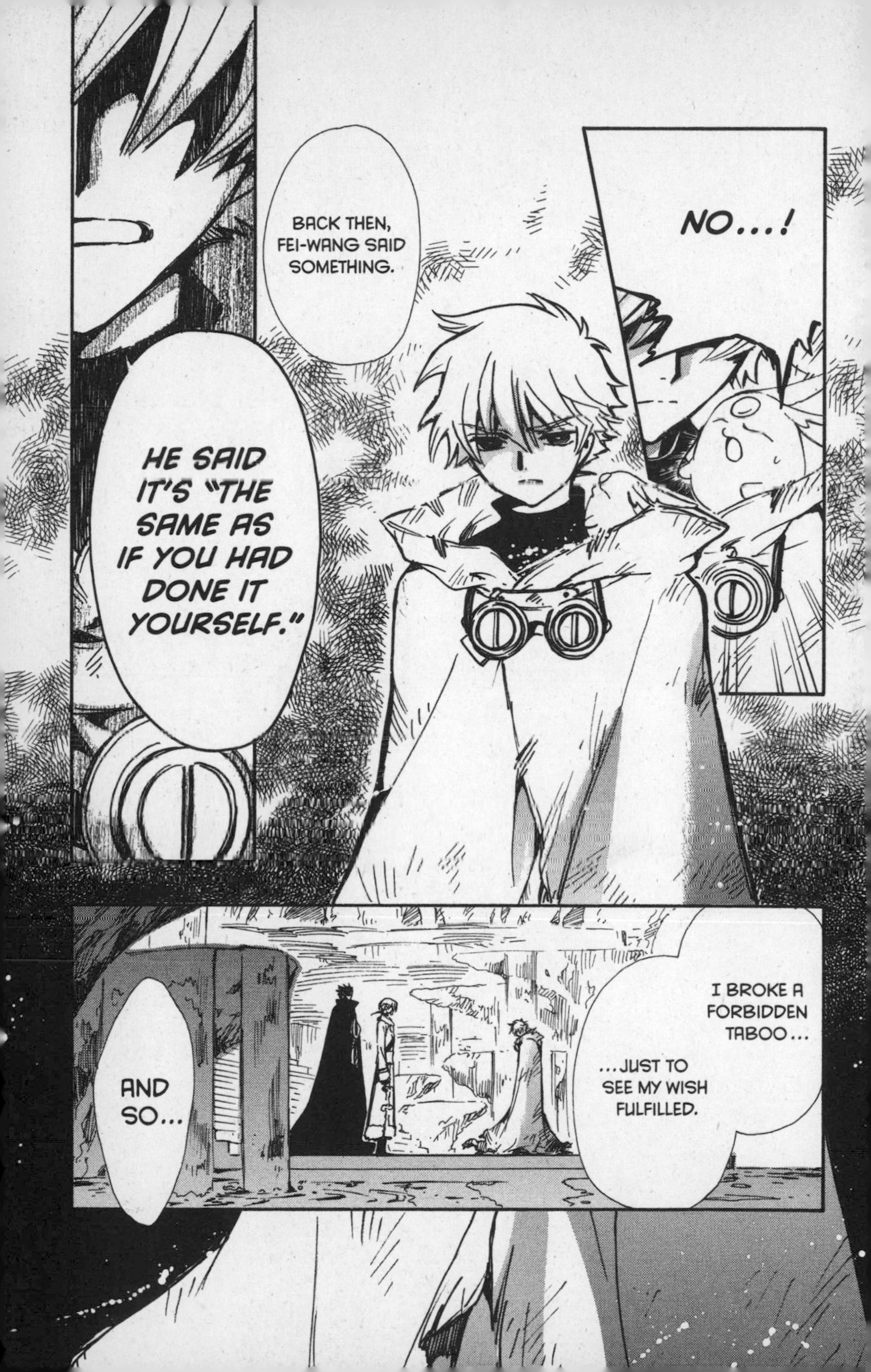
NO...!
BACK THEN, FEI-WANG SAID SOMETHING.
HE SAID IT'S "THE SAME AS IF YOU HAD DONE IT YOURSELF."
I BROKE A FORBIDDEN TABOO...
...JUST TO SEE MY WISH FULFILLED.
AND SO...

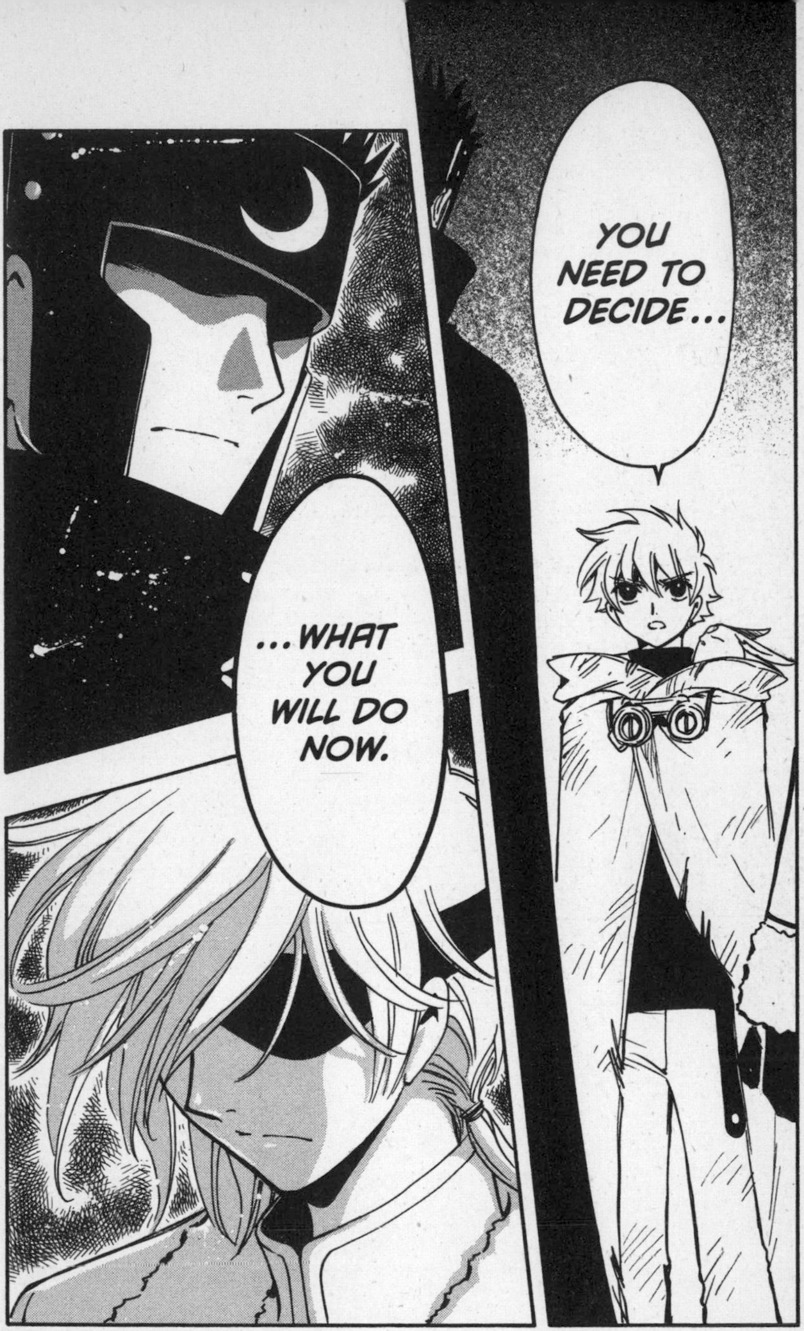
YOU NEED TO DECIDE...
...WHAT YOU WILL DO NOW.

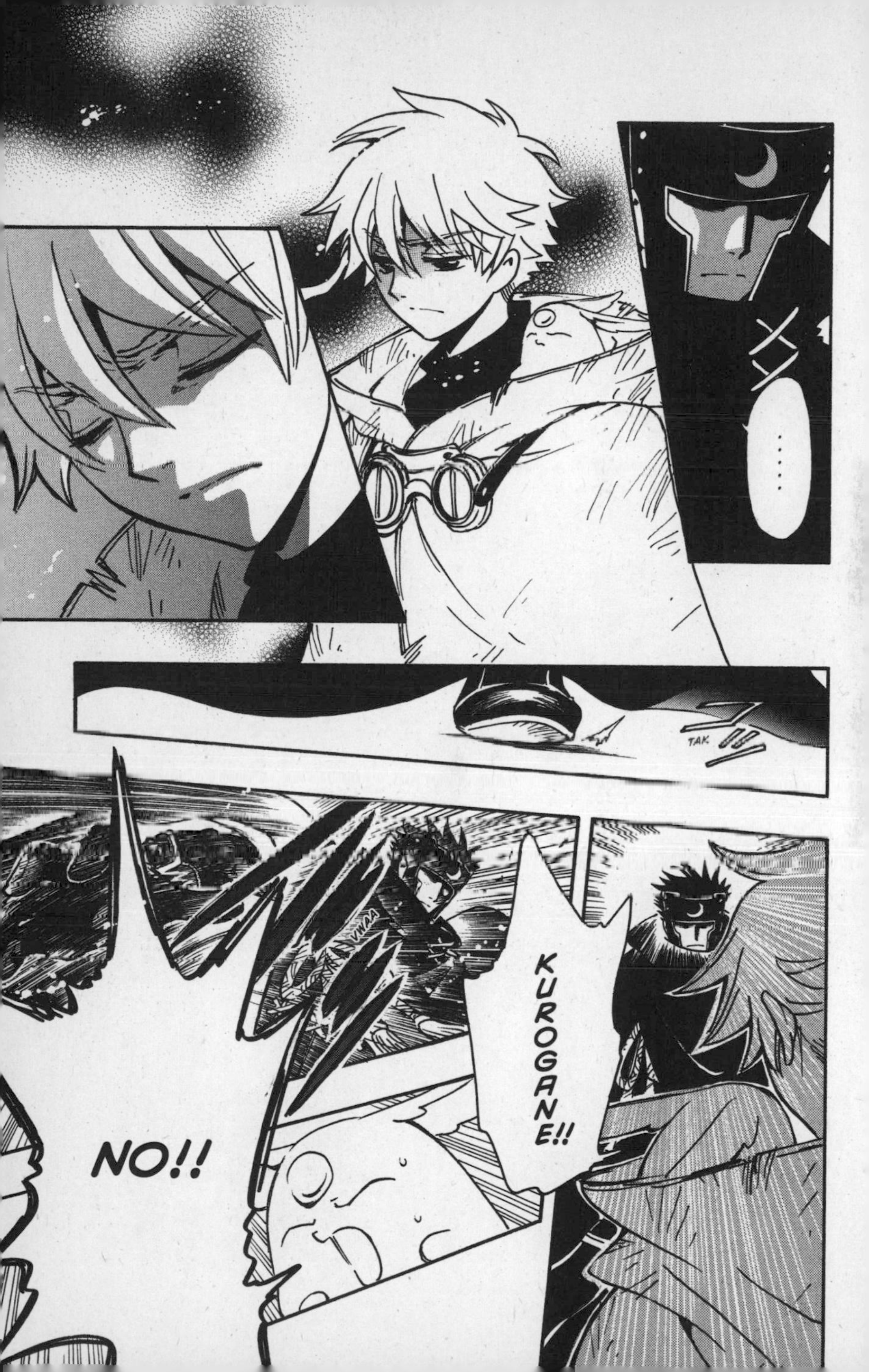
....
TAK
KUROGANE!!
VWAA
NO!!

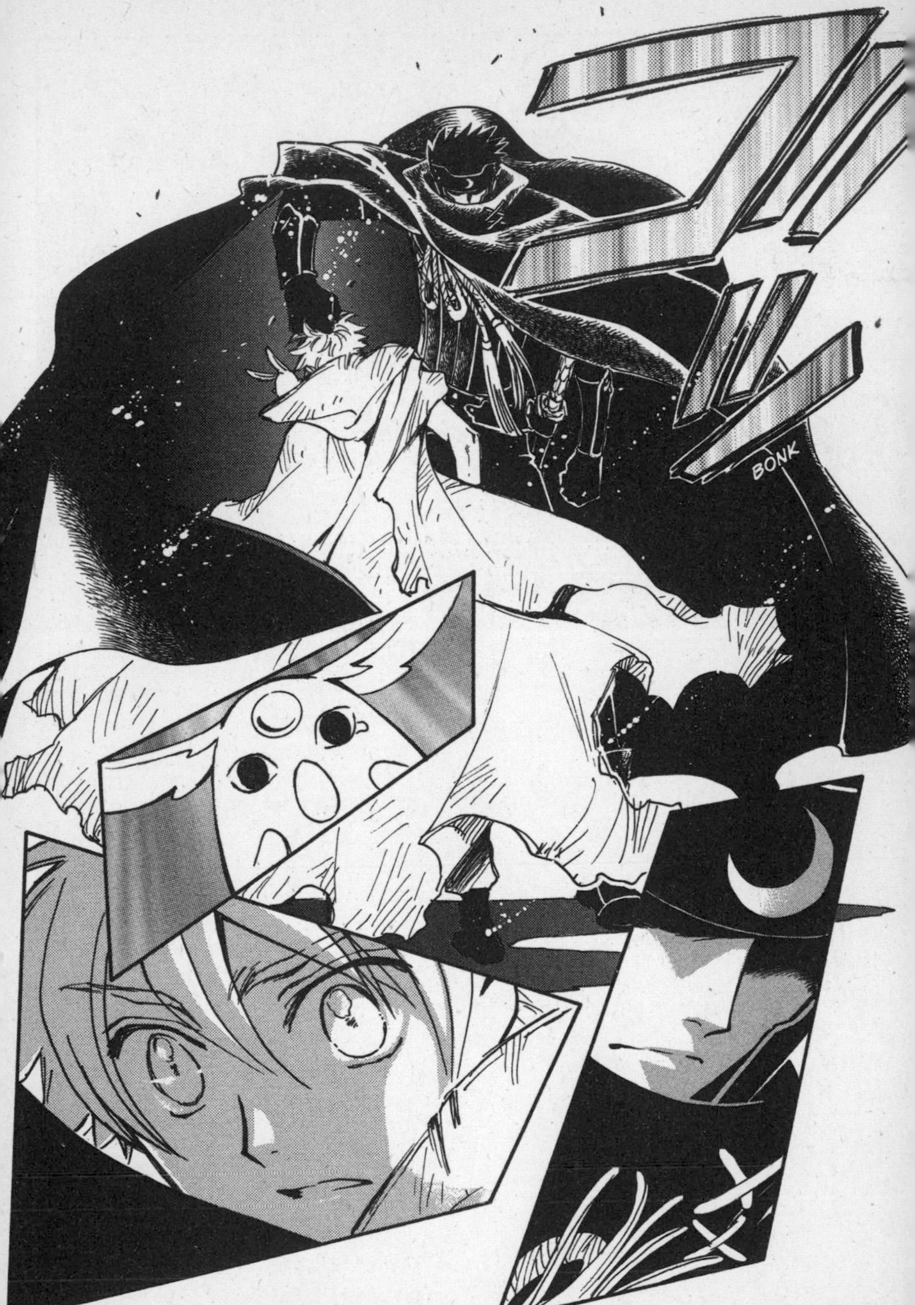
BONK

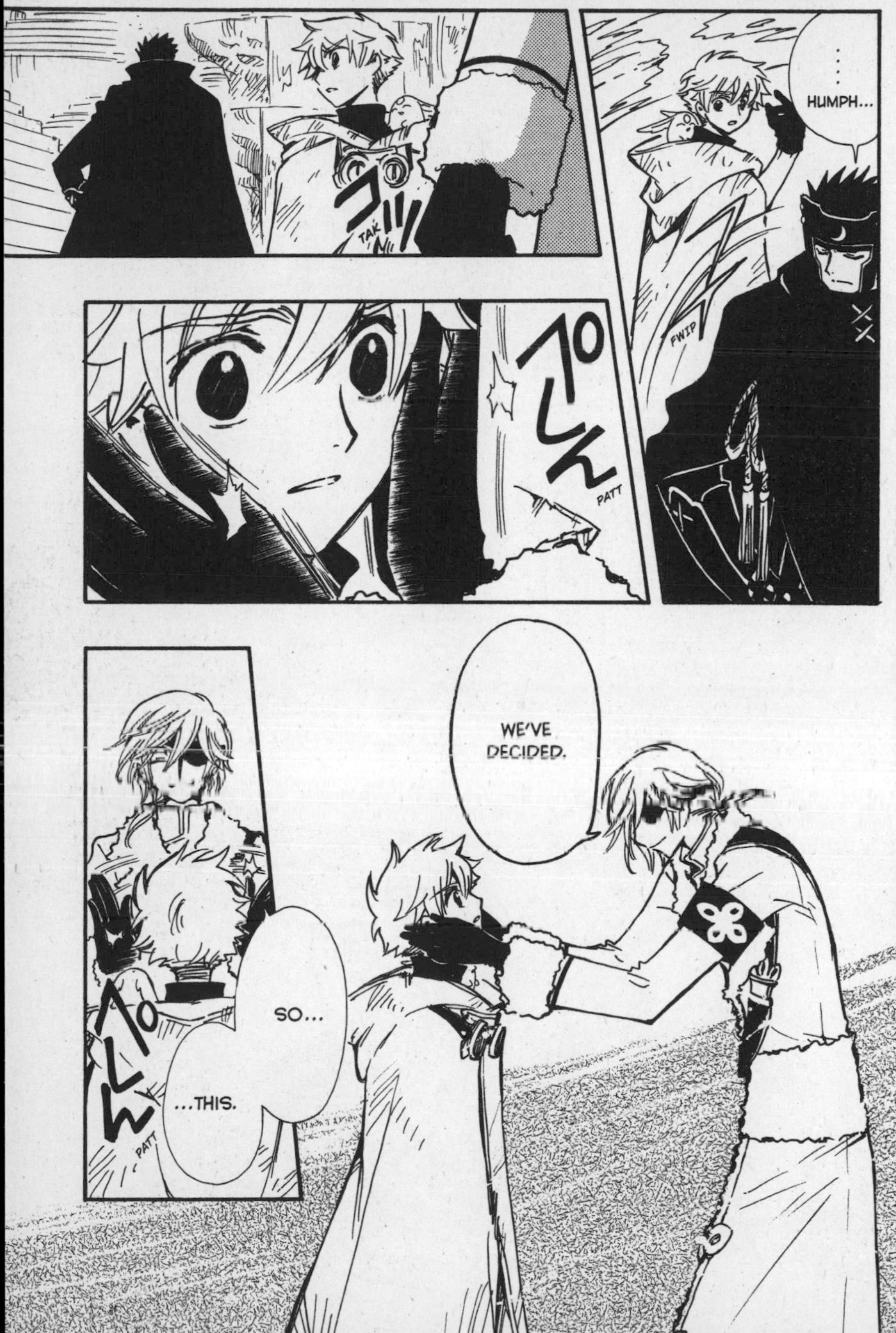

......
HUMPH...
FWIP
TAK
PATT
WE'VE DECIDED.
SO...
...THIS.
PATT

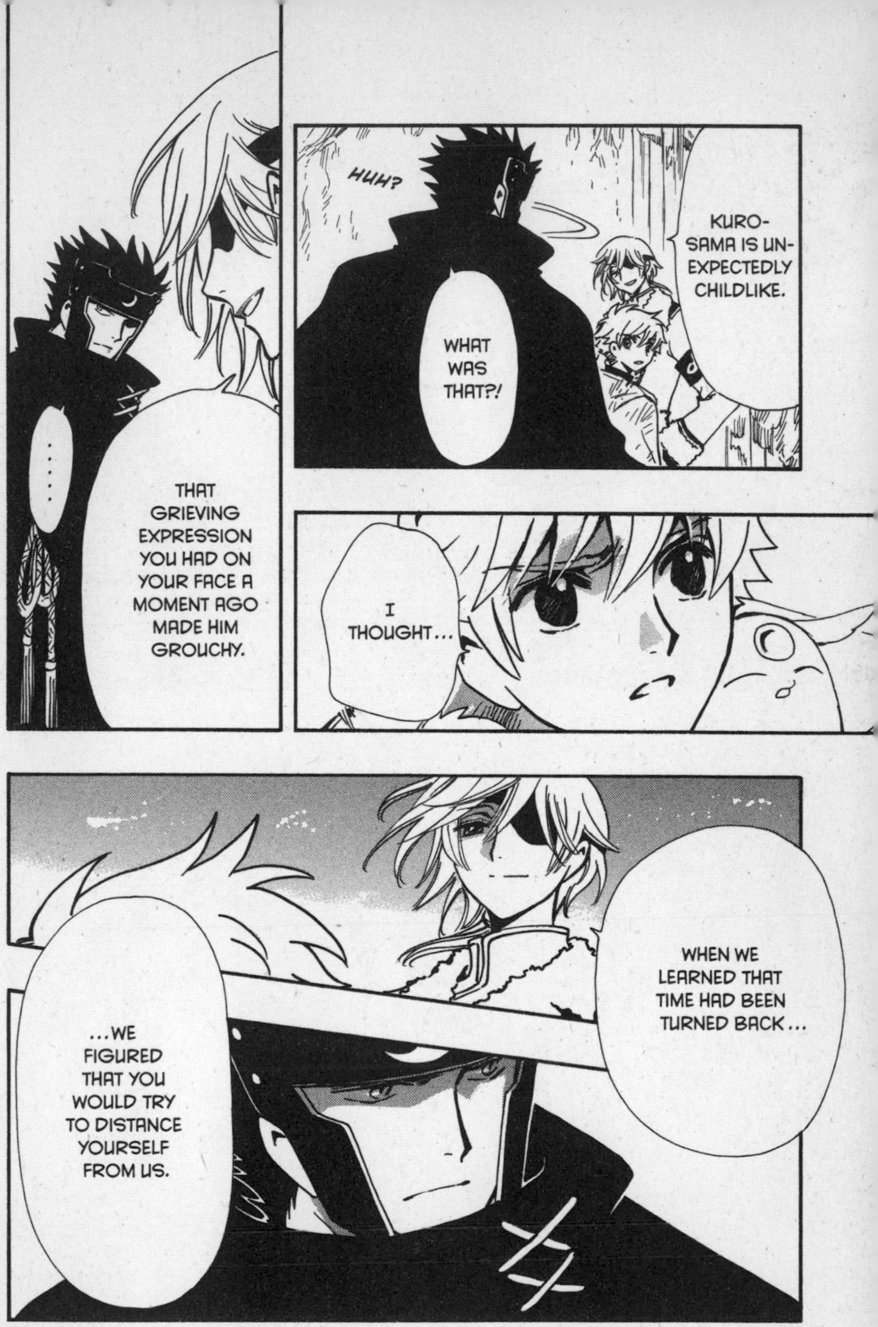
KURO-SAMA IS UN-EXPECTEDLY CHILDLIKE.
HUH?
WHAT WAS THAT?!
I THOUGHT...
THAT GRIEVING EXPRESSION YOU HAD ON YOUR FACE A MOMENT AGO MADE HIM GROUCHY.
.....
WHEN WE LEARNED THAT TIME HAD BEEN TURNED BACK...
...WE FIGURED THAT YOU WOULD TRY TO DISTANCE YOURSELF FROM US.

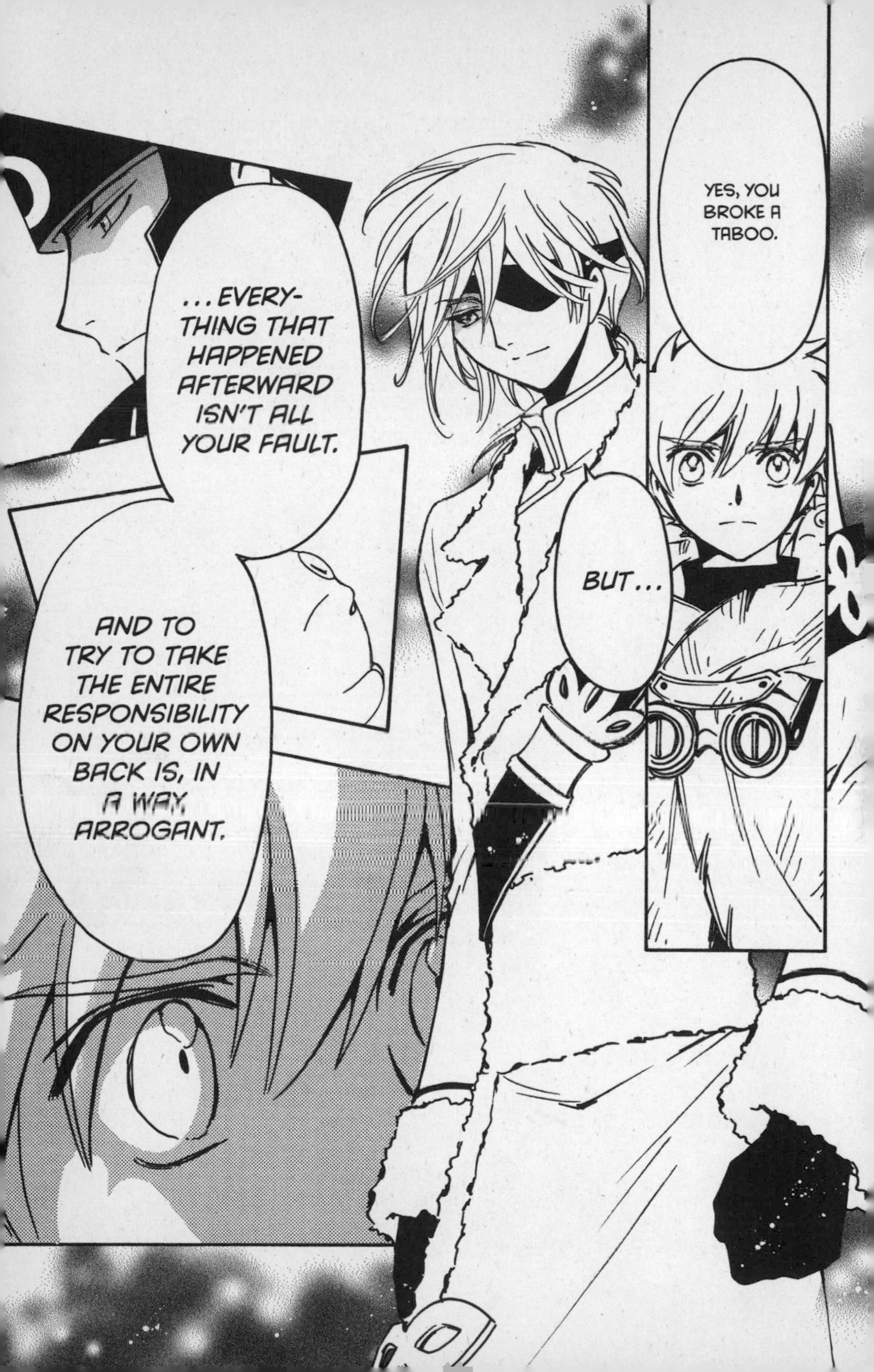
YES, YOU BROKE A TABOO.
BUT...
...EVERY-THING THAT HAPPENED AFTERWARD ISN'T ALL YOUR FAULT.
AND TO TRY TO TAKE THE ENTIRE RESPONSIBILITY ON YOUR OWN BACK IS, IN A WAY, ARROGANT.

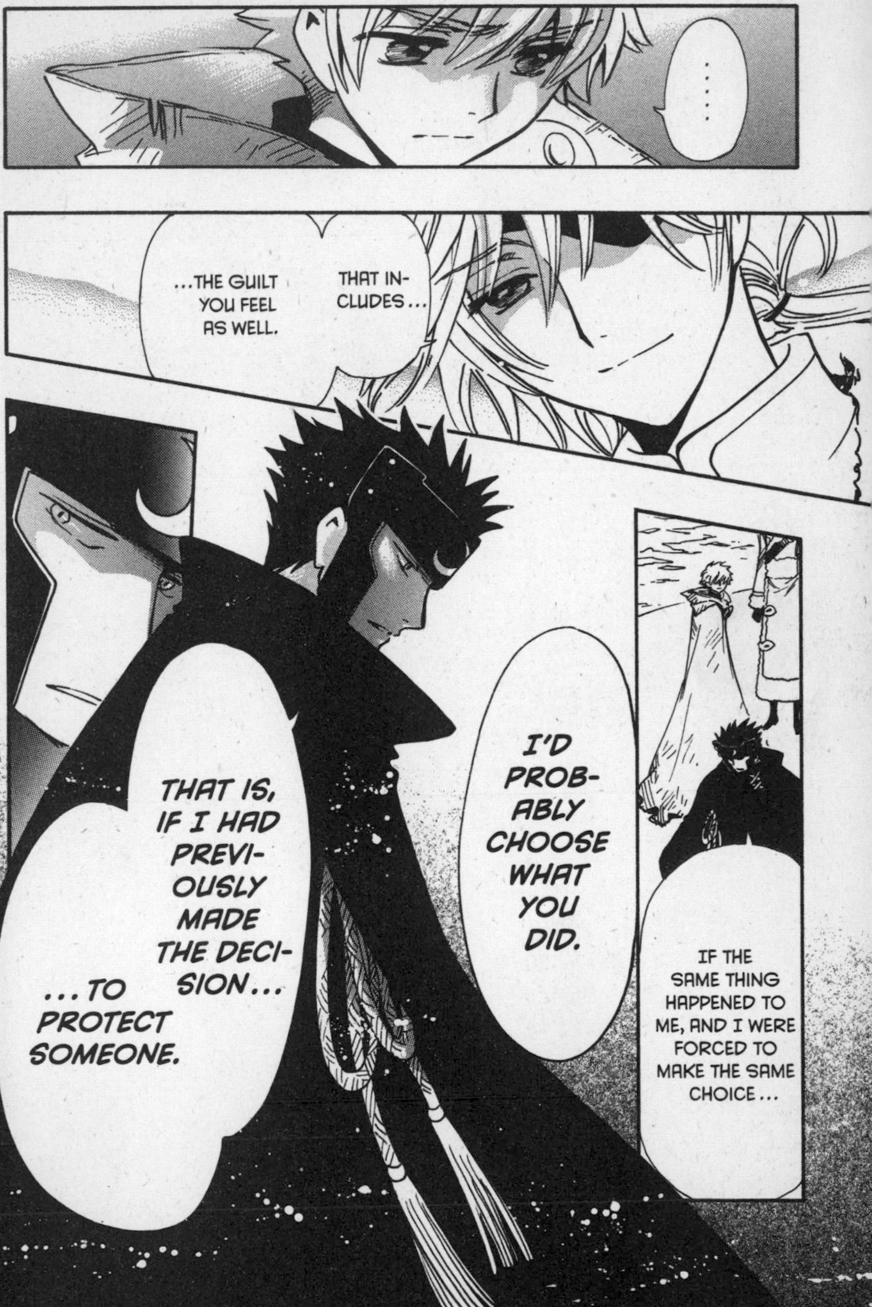
......
THAT IN-CLUDES...
...THE GUILT YOU FEEL AS WELL.
IF THE SAME THING HAPPENED TO ME, AND I WERE FORCED TO MAKE THE SAME CHOICE...
I'D PROB-ABLY CHOOSE WHAT YOU DID.
THAT IS, IF I HAD PREVI-OUSLY MADE THE DECI-SION...
...TO PROTECT SOMEONE.

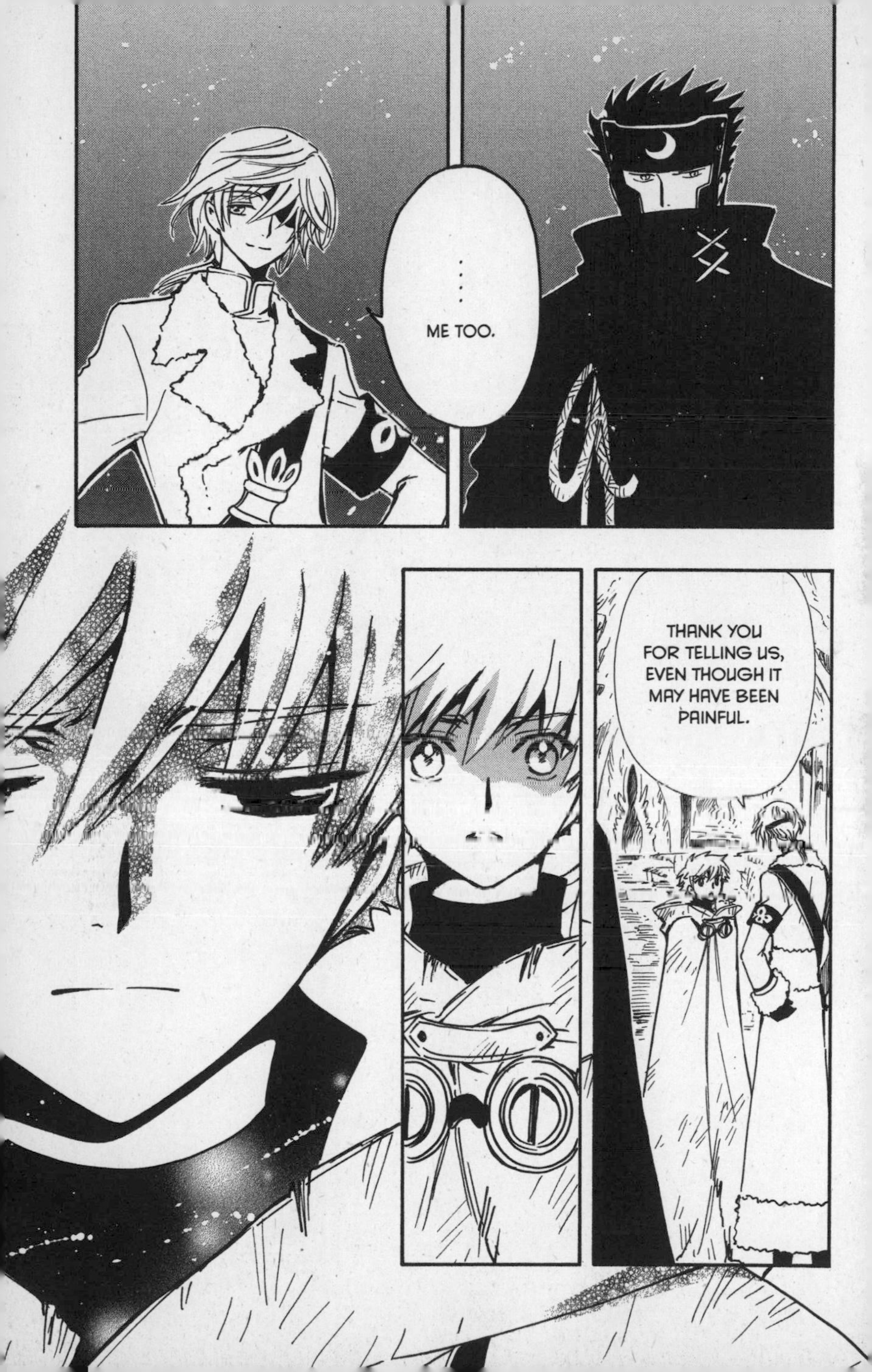
......
ME TOO.
THANK YOU FOR TELLING US, EVEN THOUGH IT MAY HAVE BEEN PAINFUL.

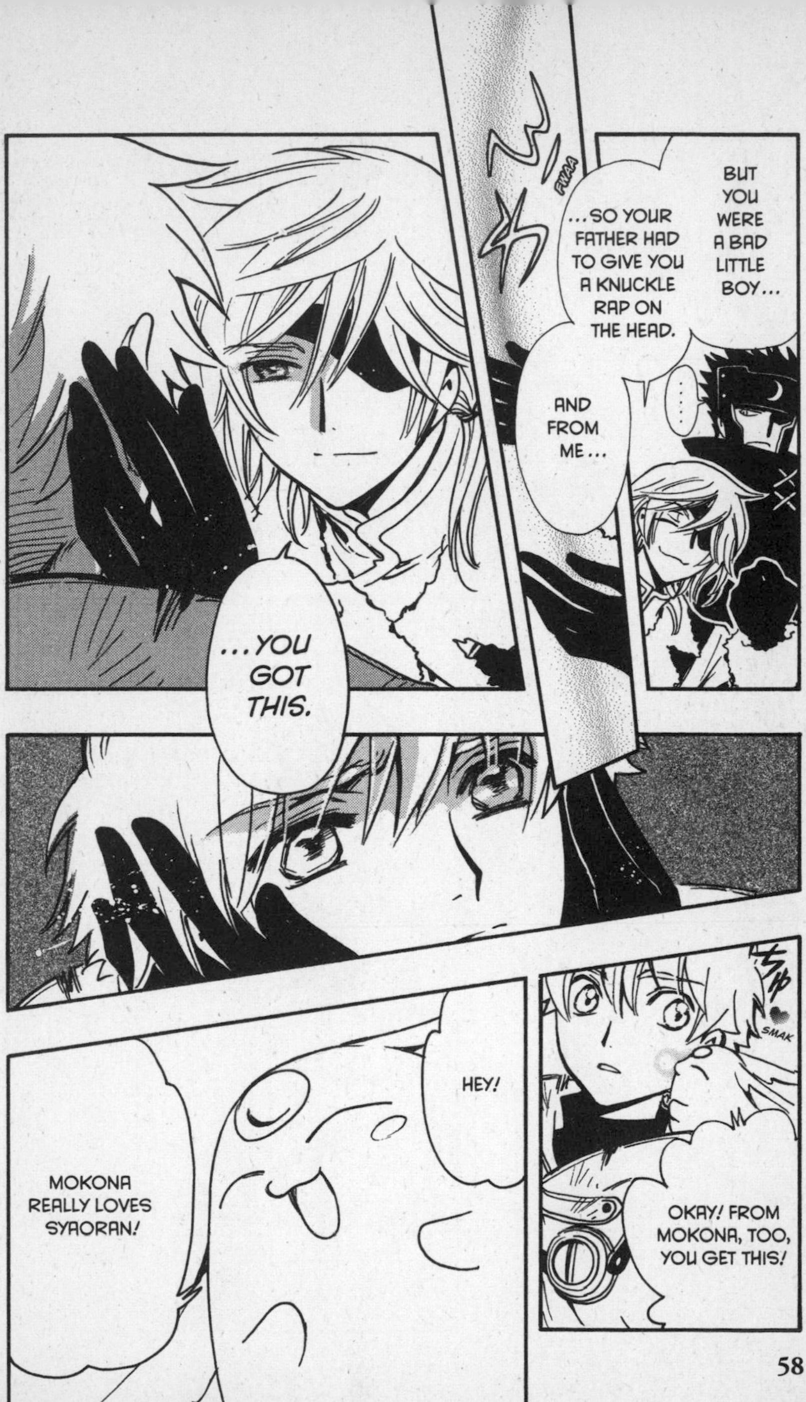
BUT YOU WERE A BAD LITTLE BOY...
...SO YOUR FATHER HAD TO GIVE YOU A KNUCKLE RAP ON THE HEAD.
FWAA
...
AND FROM ME...
...YOU GOT THIS.
SMAK
OKAY! FROM MOKONA, TOO, YOU GET THIS!
HEY!
MOKONA REALLY LOVES SYAORAN!

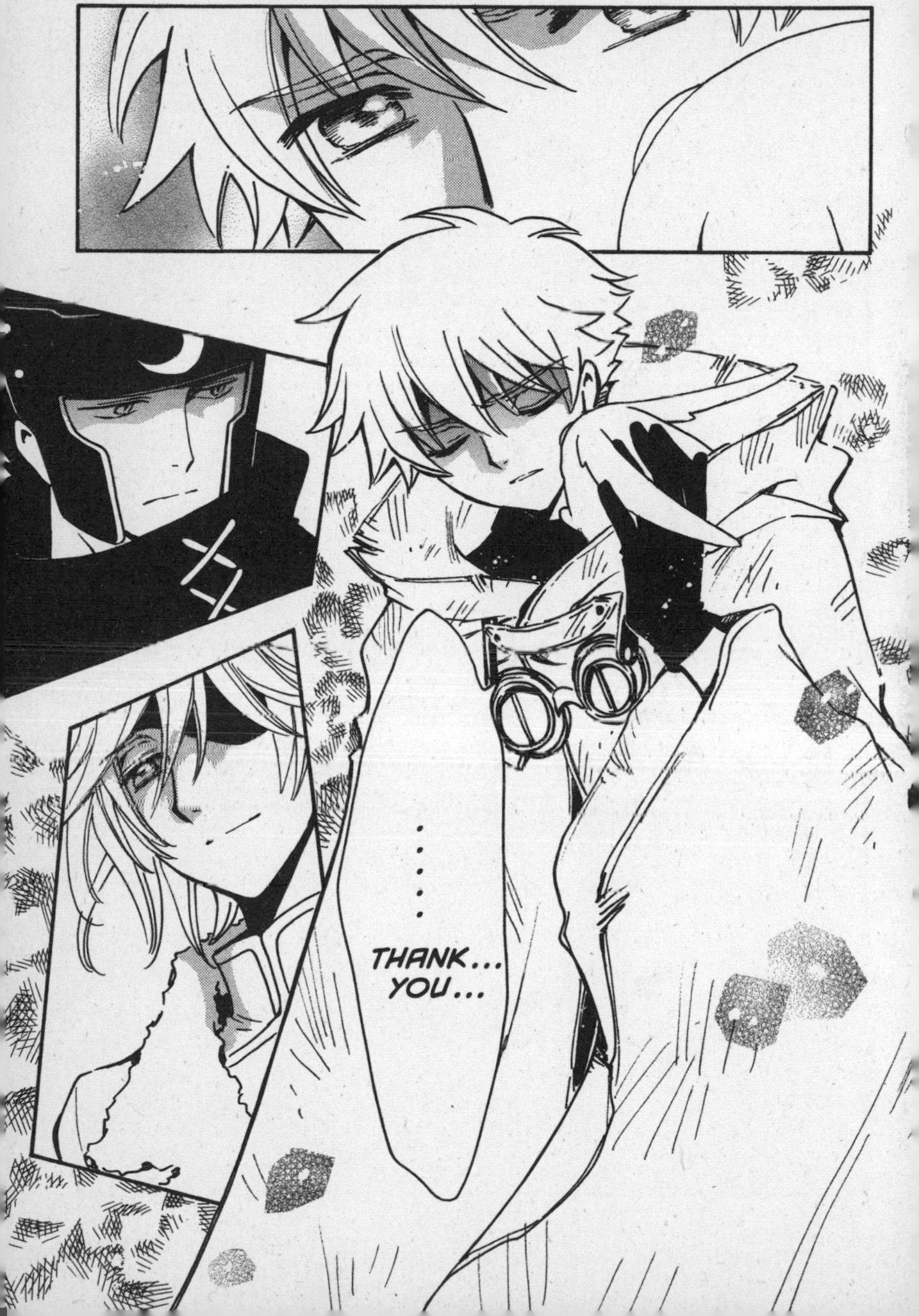
.....
THANK... YOU...

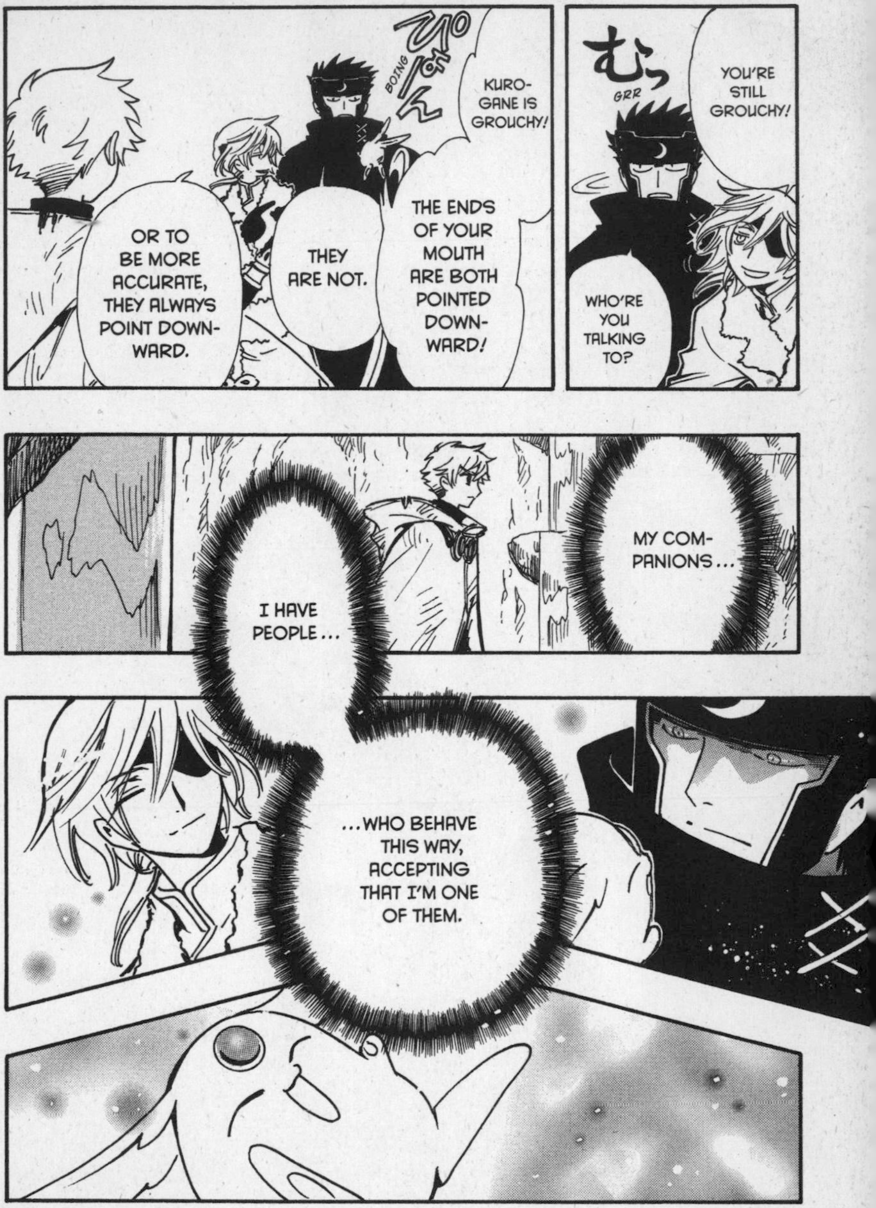
YOU'RE STILL GROUCHY!
むっ
GRR
WHO'RE YOU TALKING TO?
KURO-GANE IS GROUCHY!
ぴょん
BOING
THE ENDS OF YOUR MOUTH ARE BOTH POINTED DOWN-WARD!
THEY ARE NOT.
OR TO BE MORE ACCURATE, THEY ALWAYS POINT DOWN-WARD.
MY COM-PANIONS...
I HAVE PEOPLE...
...WHO BEHAVE THIS WAY, ACCEPTING THAT I'M ONE OF THEM.

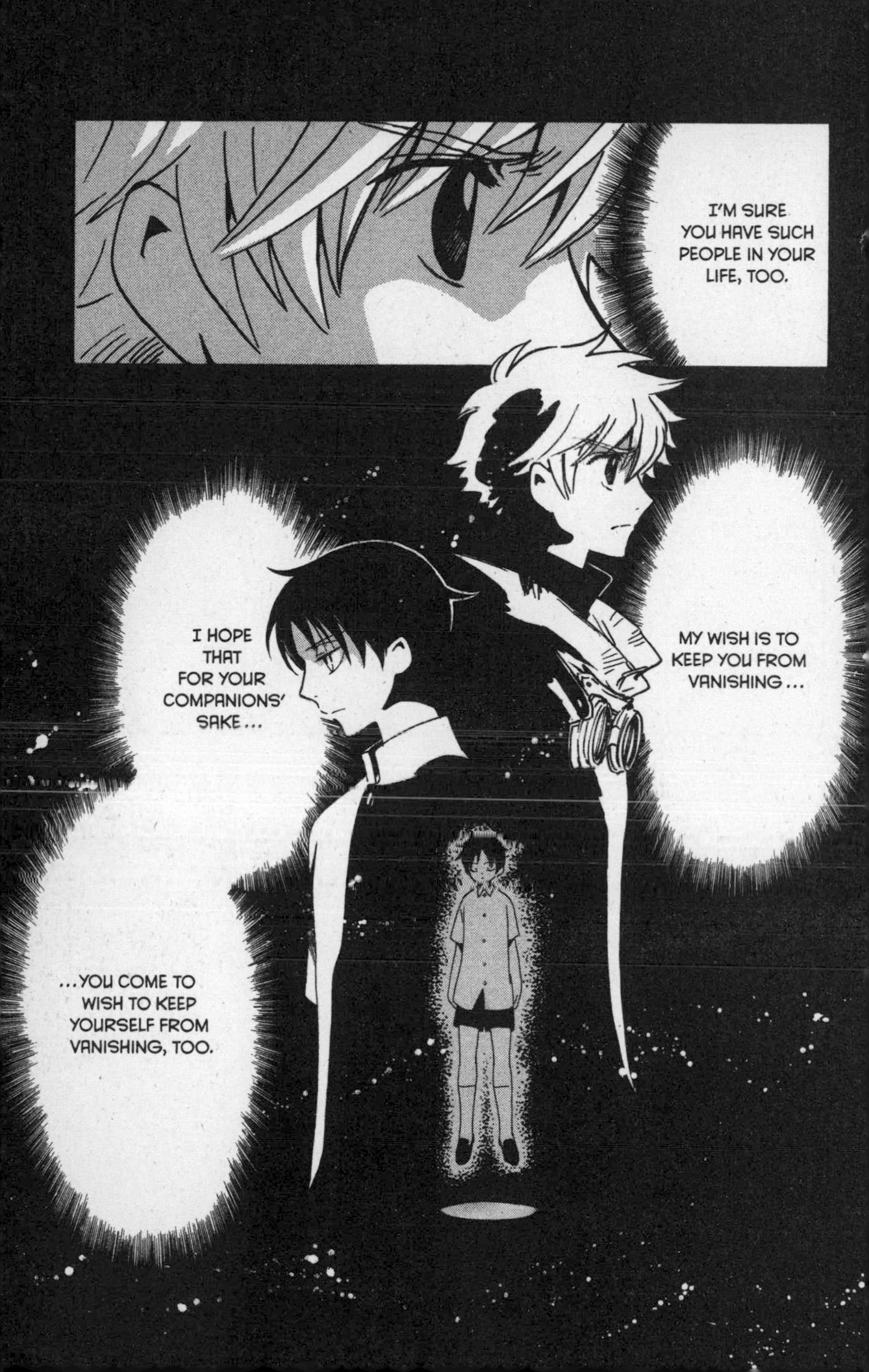
I'M SURE YOU HAVE SUCH PEOPLE IN YOUR LIFE, TOO.
MY WISH IS TO KEEP YOU FROM VANISHING...
I HOPE THAT FOR YOUR COMPANIONS' SAKE...
...YOU COME TO WISH TO KEEP YOURSELF FROM VANISHING, TOO.

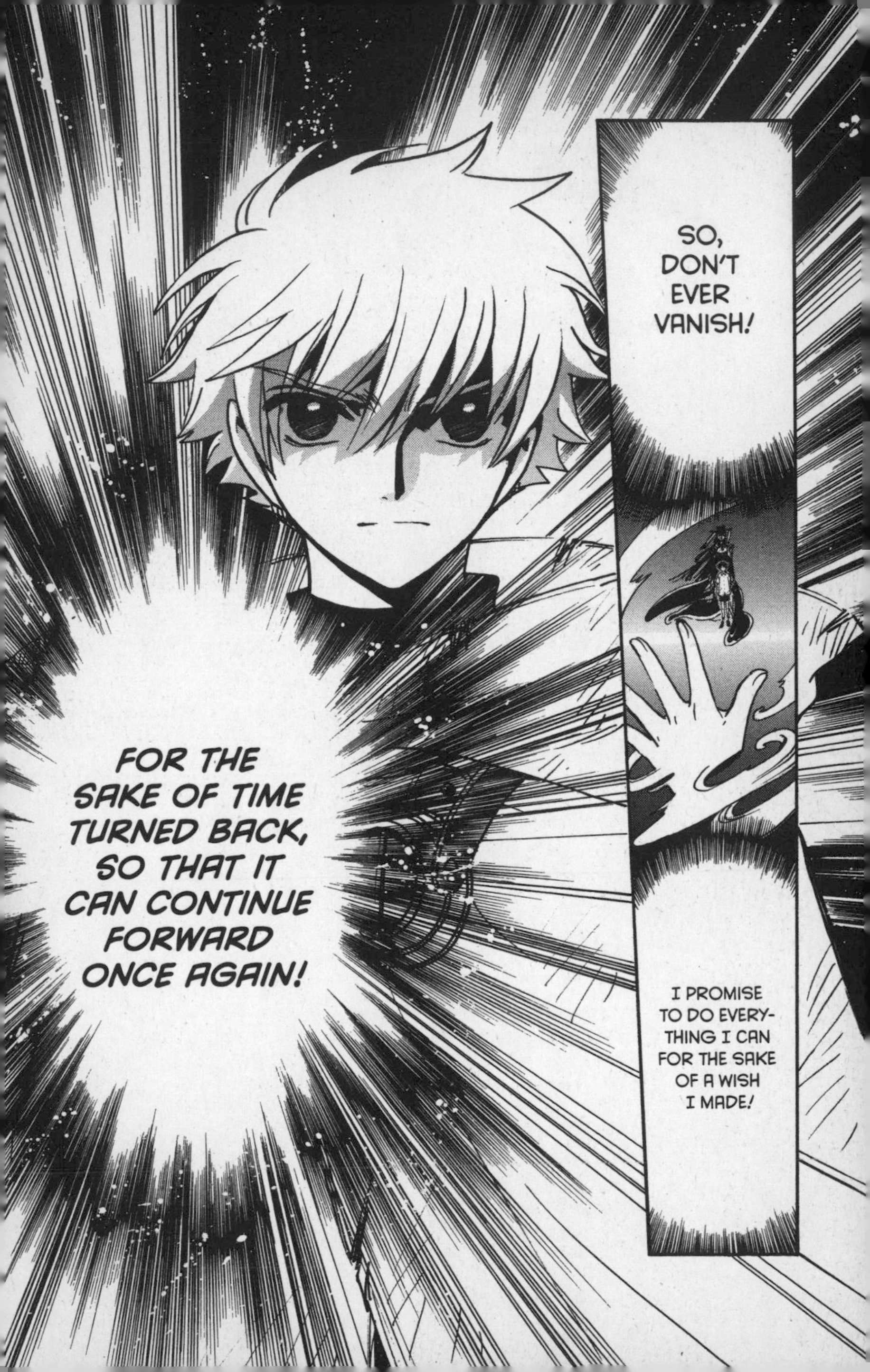
SO, DON'T EVER VANISH!
I PROMISE TO DO EVERY-THING I CAN FOR THE SAKE OF A WISH I MADE!
FOR THE SAKE OF TIME TURNED BACK, SO THAT IT CAN CONTINUE FORWARD ONCE AGAIN!

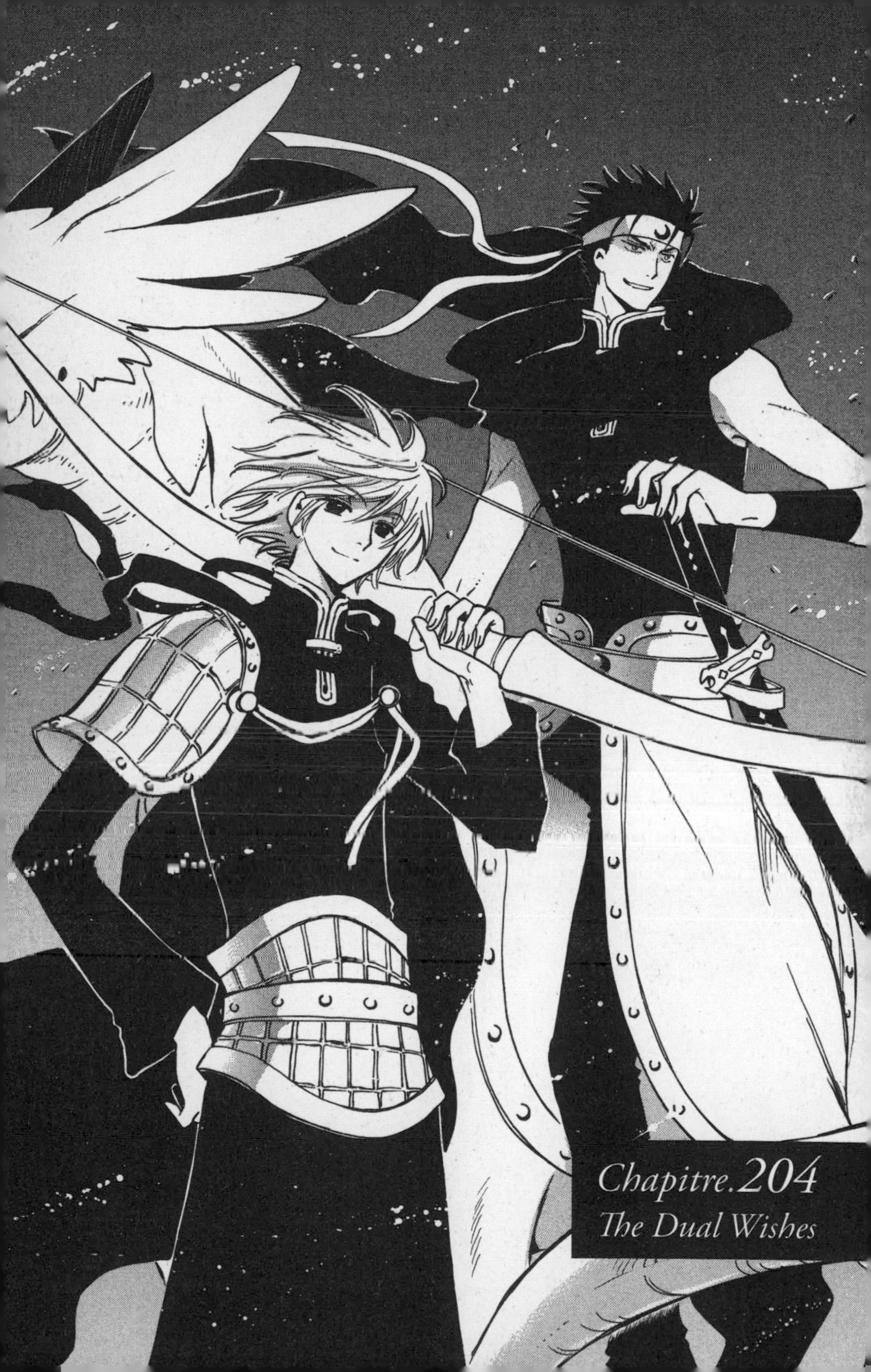
Chapitre.204
The Dual Wishes

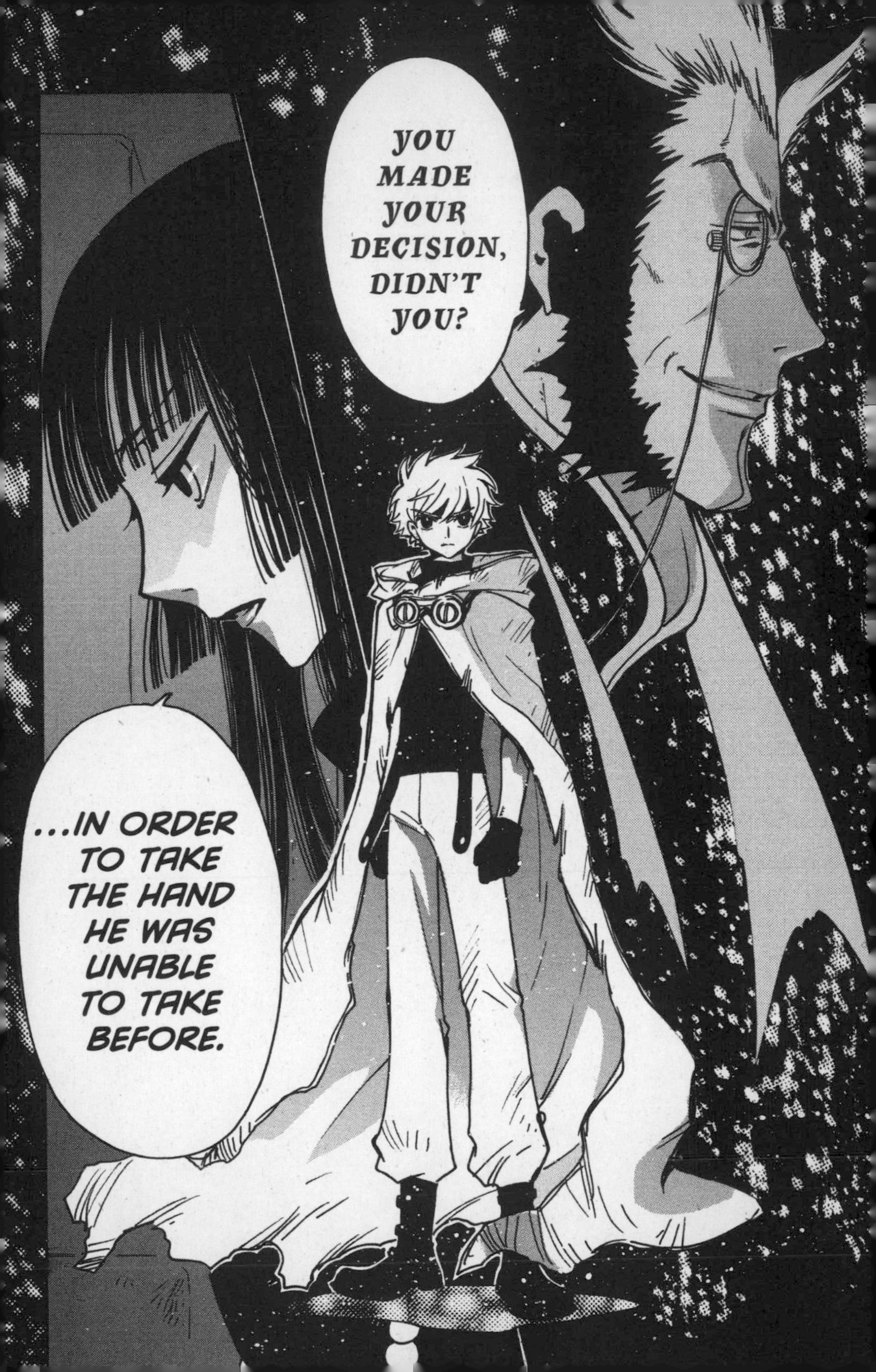
YOU MADE YOUR DECISION, DIDN'T YOU?
...IN ORDER TO TAKE THE HAND HE WAS UNABLE TO TAKE BEFORE.

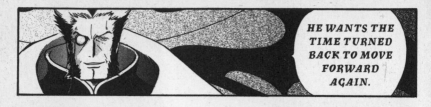

HE WANTS THE TIME TURNED BACK TO MOVE FORWARD AGAIN.

AND WATANUKI HAS MADE A DECISION AS WELL.

TAK

TO MOVE FORWARD.

SO THAT HE WILL NOT VANISH.

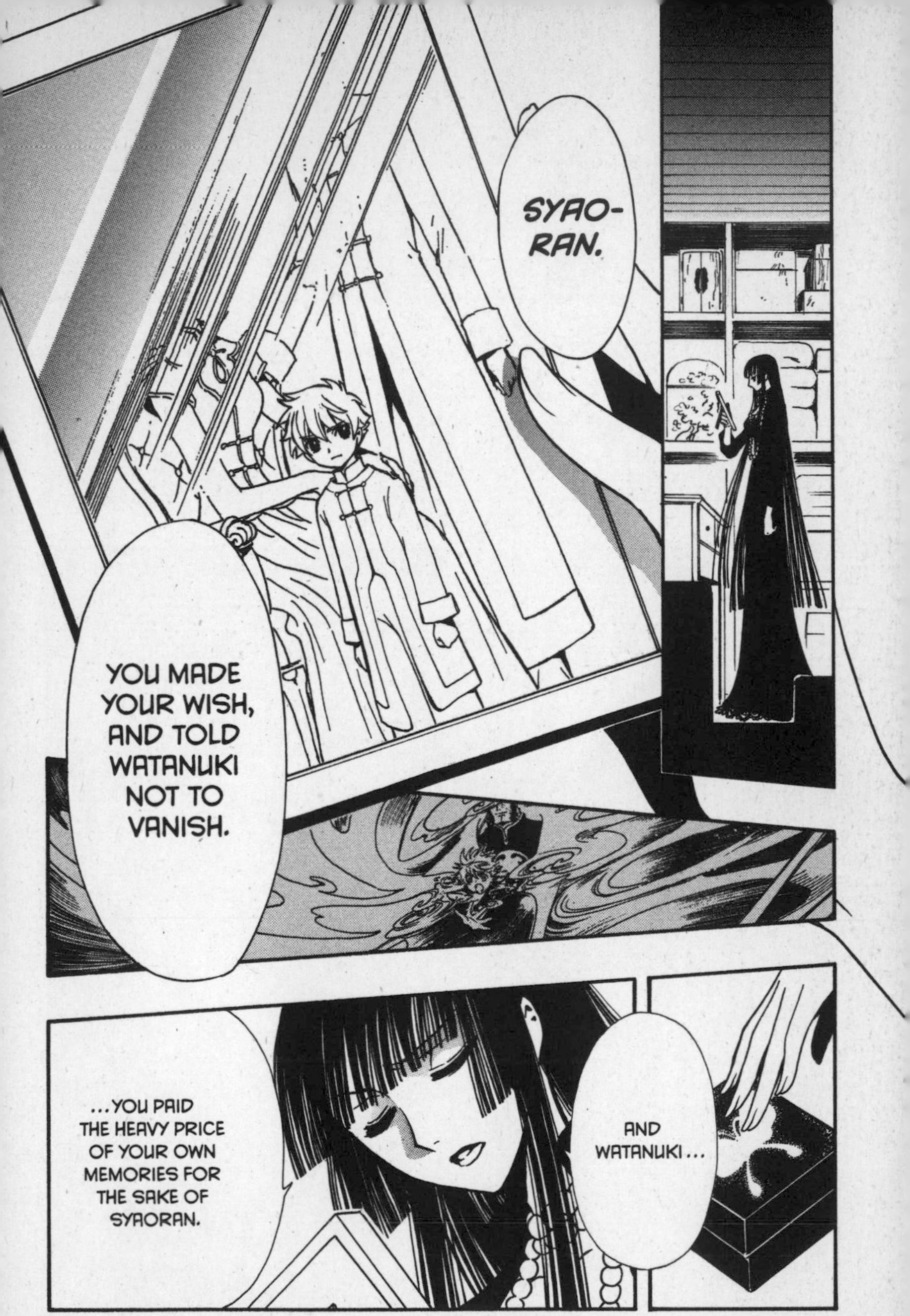
SYAO-RAN.
YOU MADE YOUR WISH, AND TOLD WATANUKI NOT TO VANISH.
AND WATANUKI...
...YOU PAID THE HEAVY PRICE OF YOUR OWN MEMORIES FOR THE SAKE OF SYAORAN.

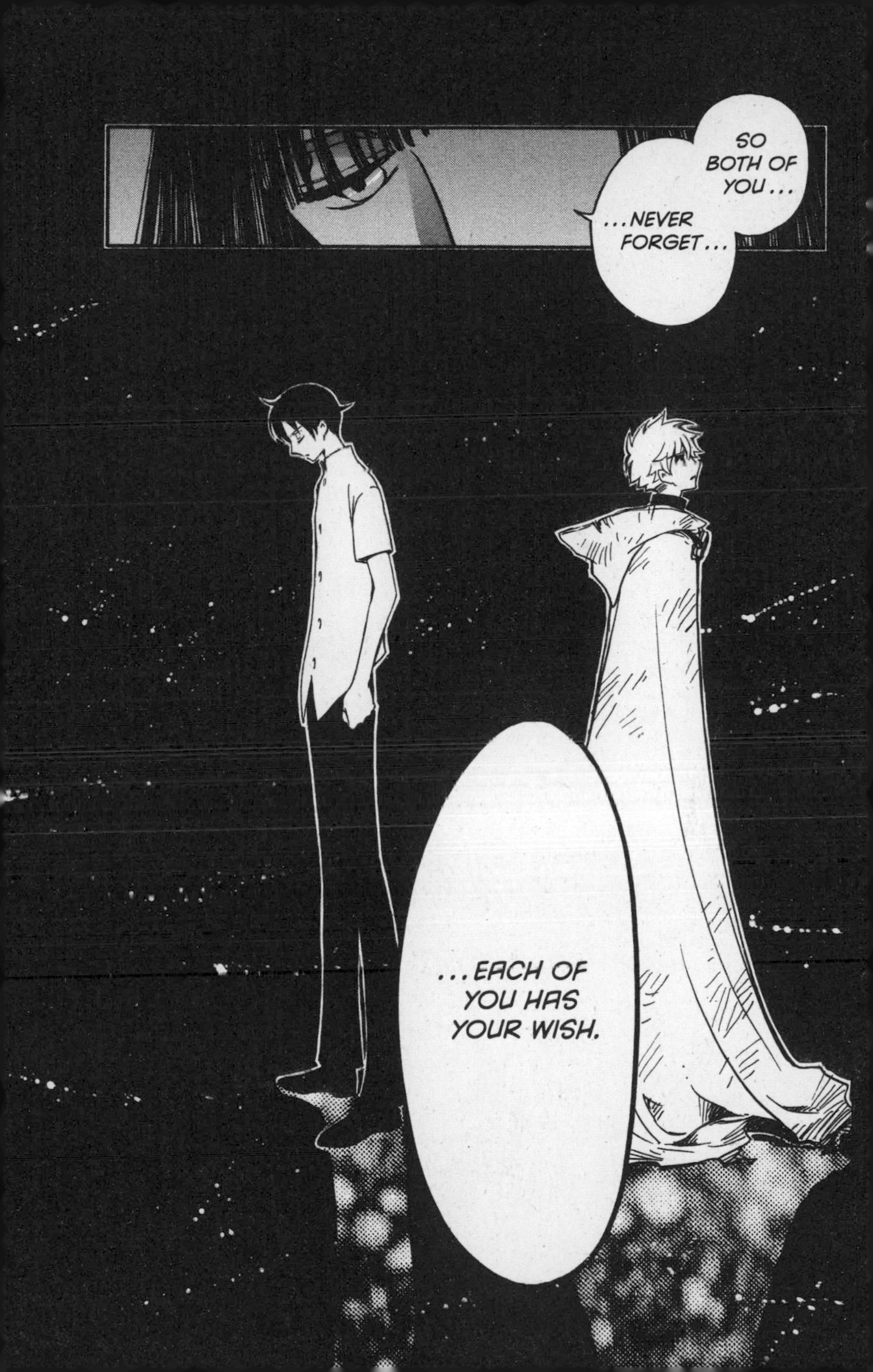
SO BOTH OF YOU...
...NEVER FORGET...
...EACH OF YOU HAS YOUR WISH.

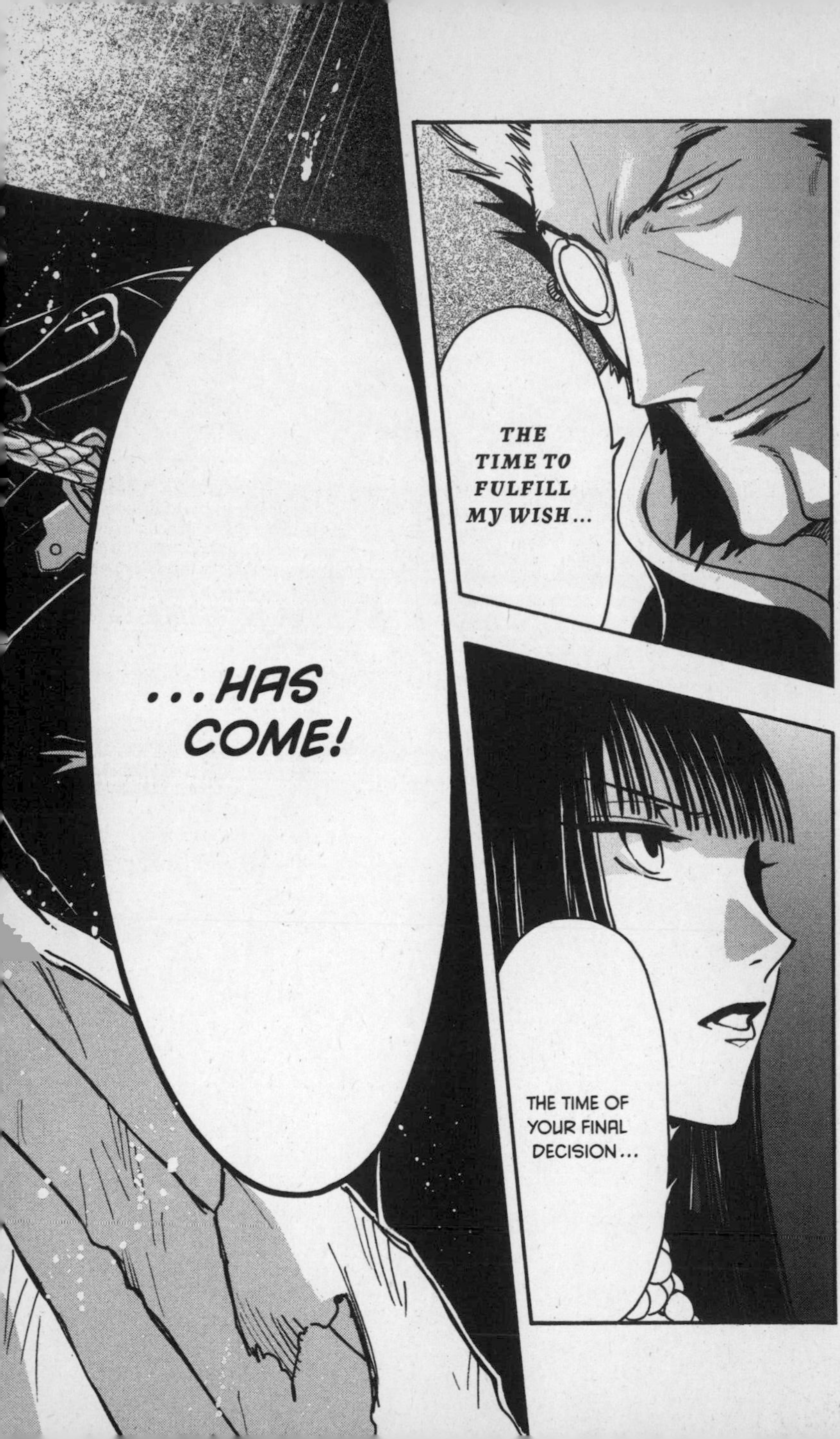
THE TIME TO FULFILL MY WISH...
THE TIME OF YOUR FINAL DECISION...
...HAS COME!

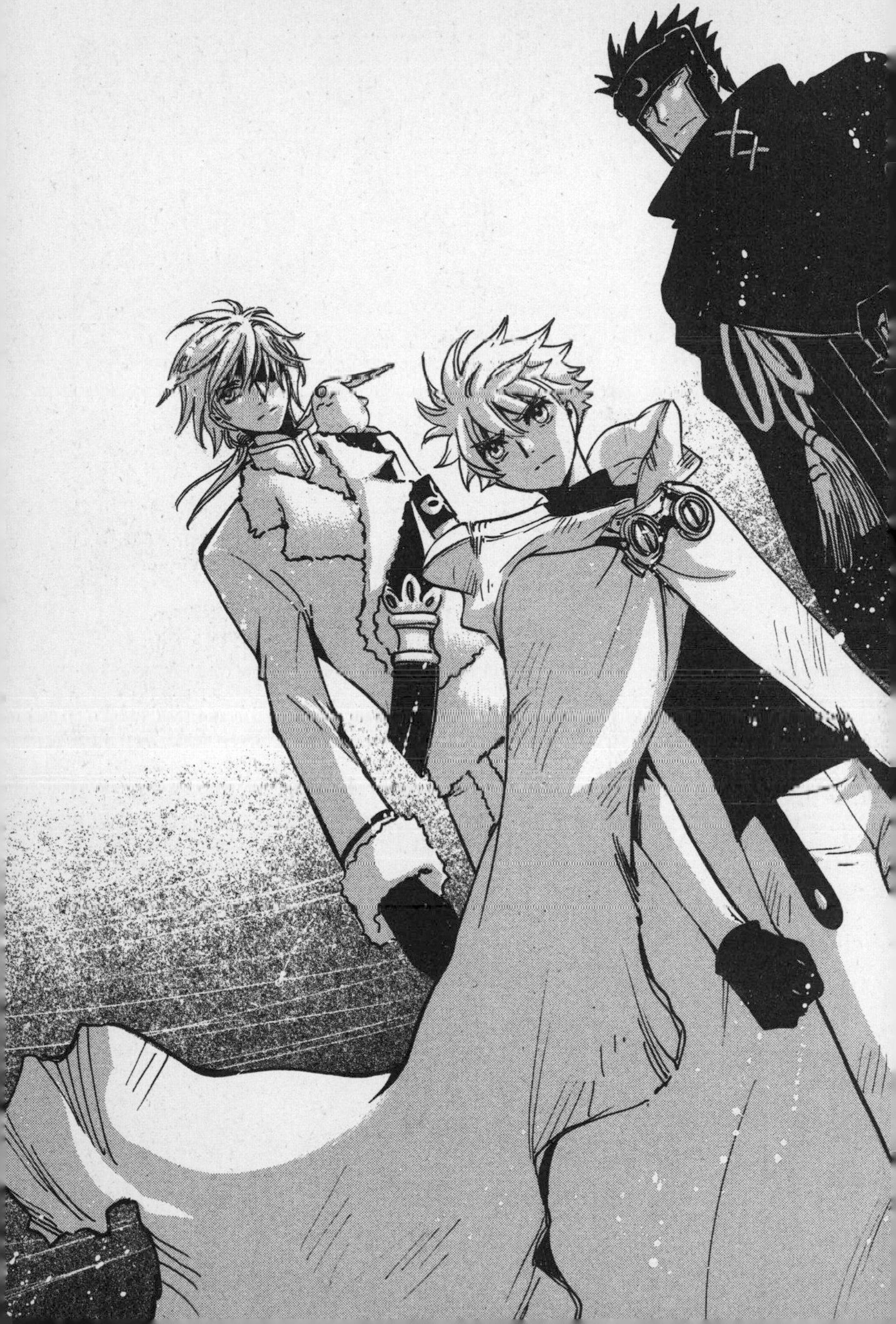

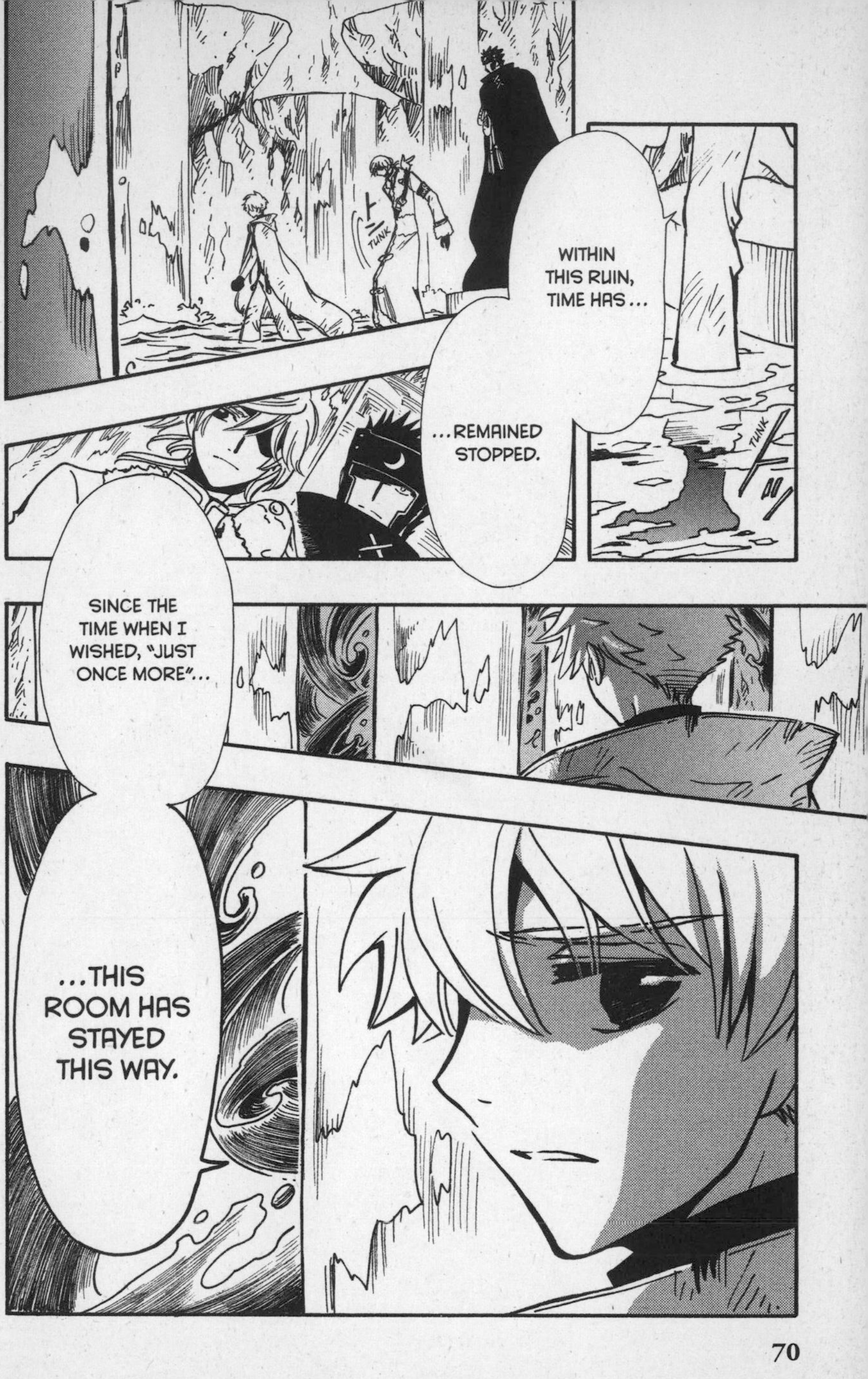
TUNK
WITHIN THIS RUIN, TIME HAS...
...REMAINED STOPPED.
TUNK
SINCE THE TIME WHEN I WISHED, "JUST ONCE MORE"...
...THIS ROOM HAS STAYED THIS WAY.

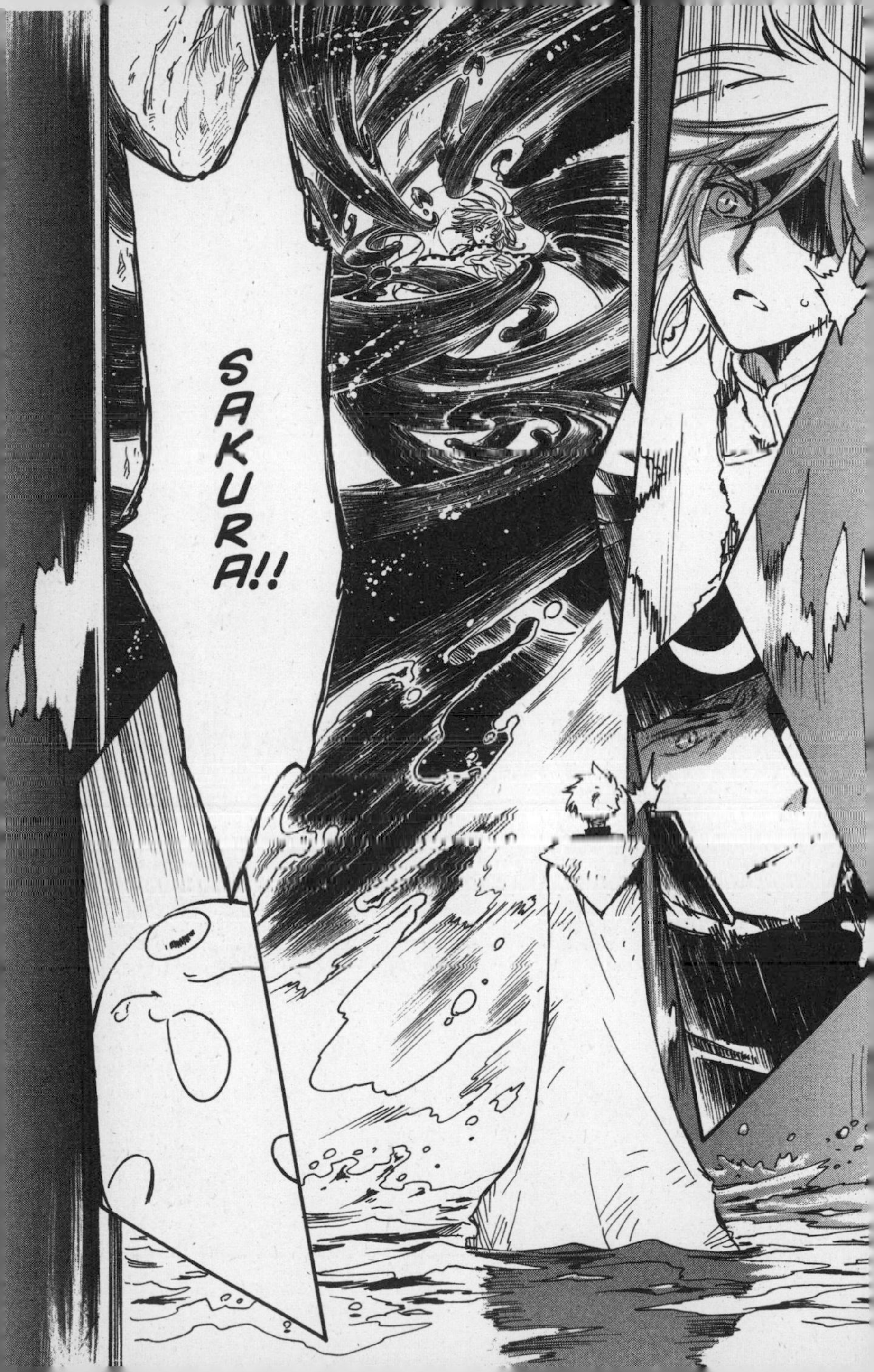
SAKURA!!

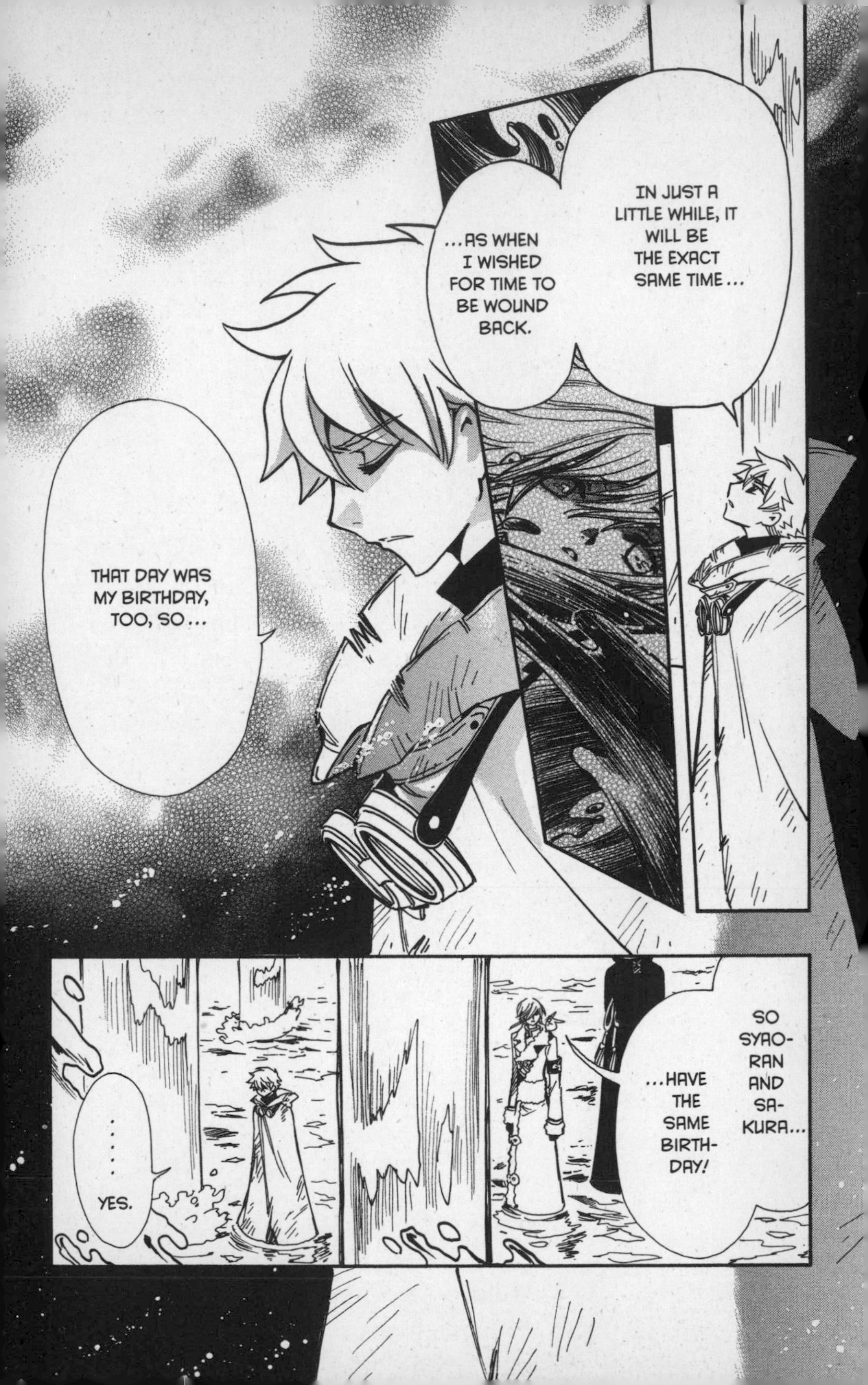
IN JUST A LITTLE WHILE, IT WILL BE THE EXACT SAME TIME...
...AS WHEN I WISHED FOR TIME TO BE WOUND BACK.
THAT DAY WAS MY BIRTHDAY, TOO, SO...
SO SYAORAN AND SAKURA...
...HAVE THE SAME BIRTHDAY!
..... YES.

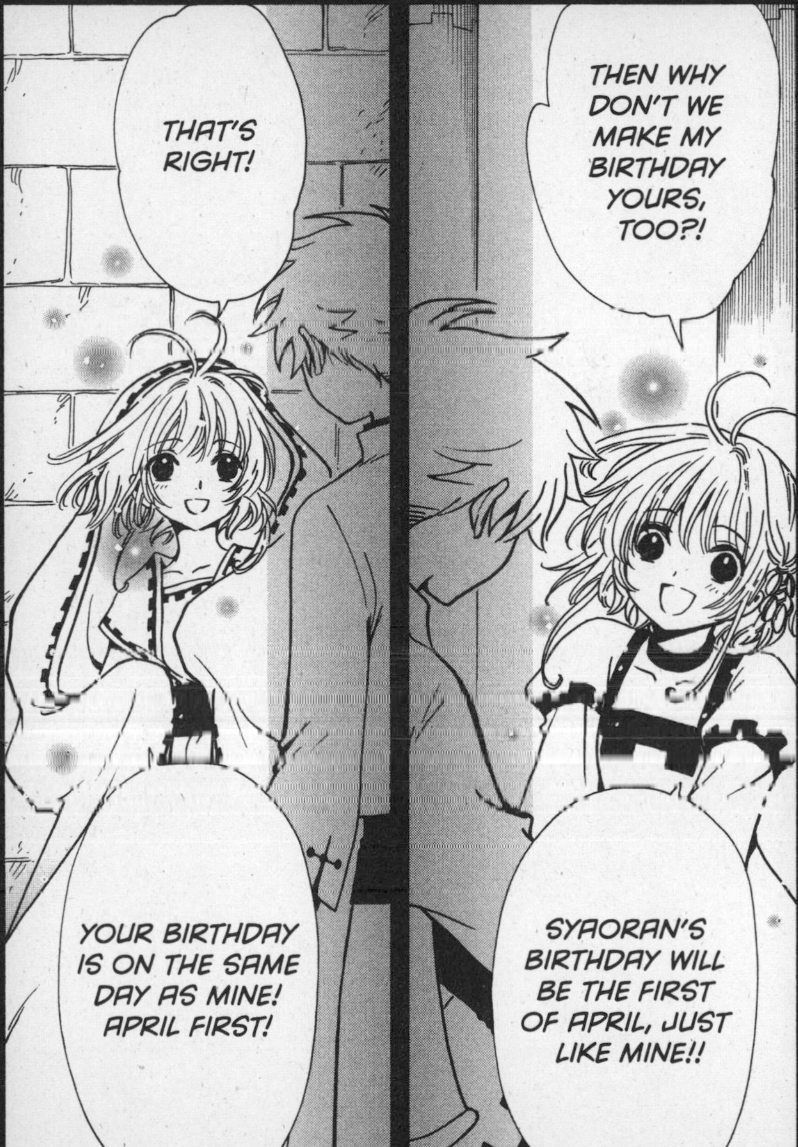
THEN WHY DON'T WE MAKE MY BIRTHDAY YOURS, TOO?!
SYAORAN'S BIRTHDAY WILL BE THE FIRST OF APRIL, JUST LIKE MINE!!
THAT'S RIGHT!
YOUR BIRTHDAY IS ON THE SAME DAY AS MINE! APRIL FIRST!

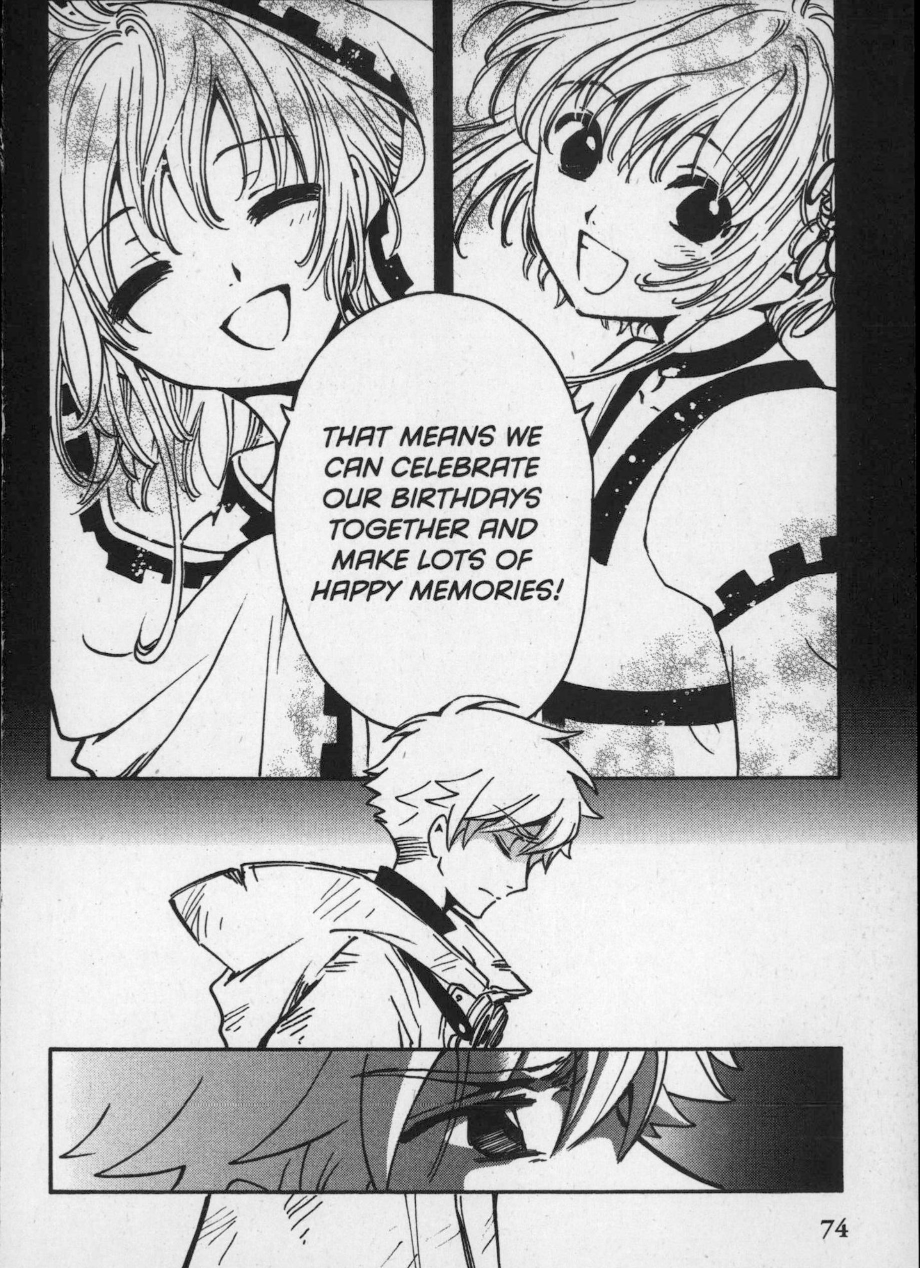
THAT MEANS WE CAN CELEBRATE OUR BIRTHDAYS TOGETHER AND MAKE LOTS OF HAPPY MEMORIES!

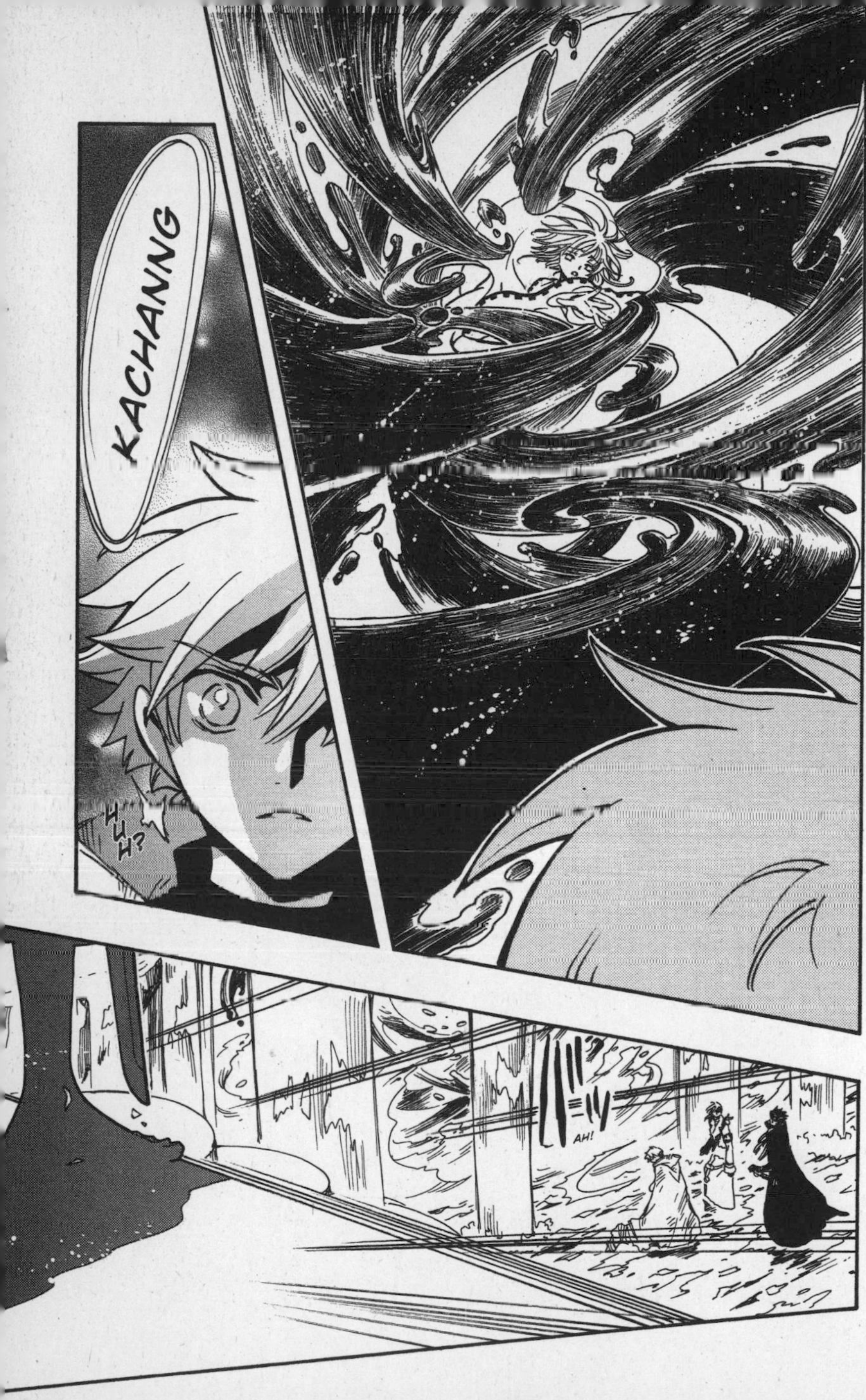
KACHANNG
HUH?
AH!

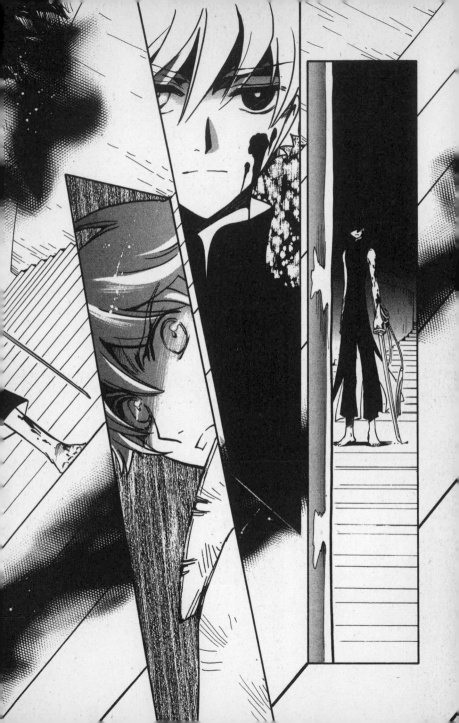

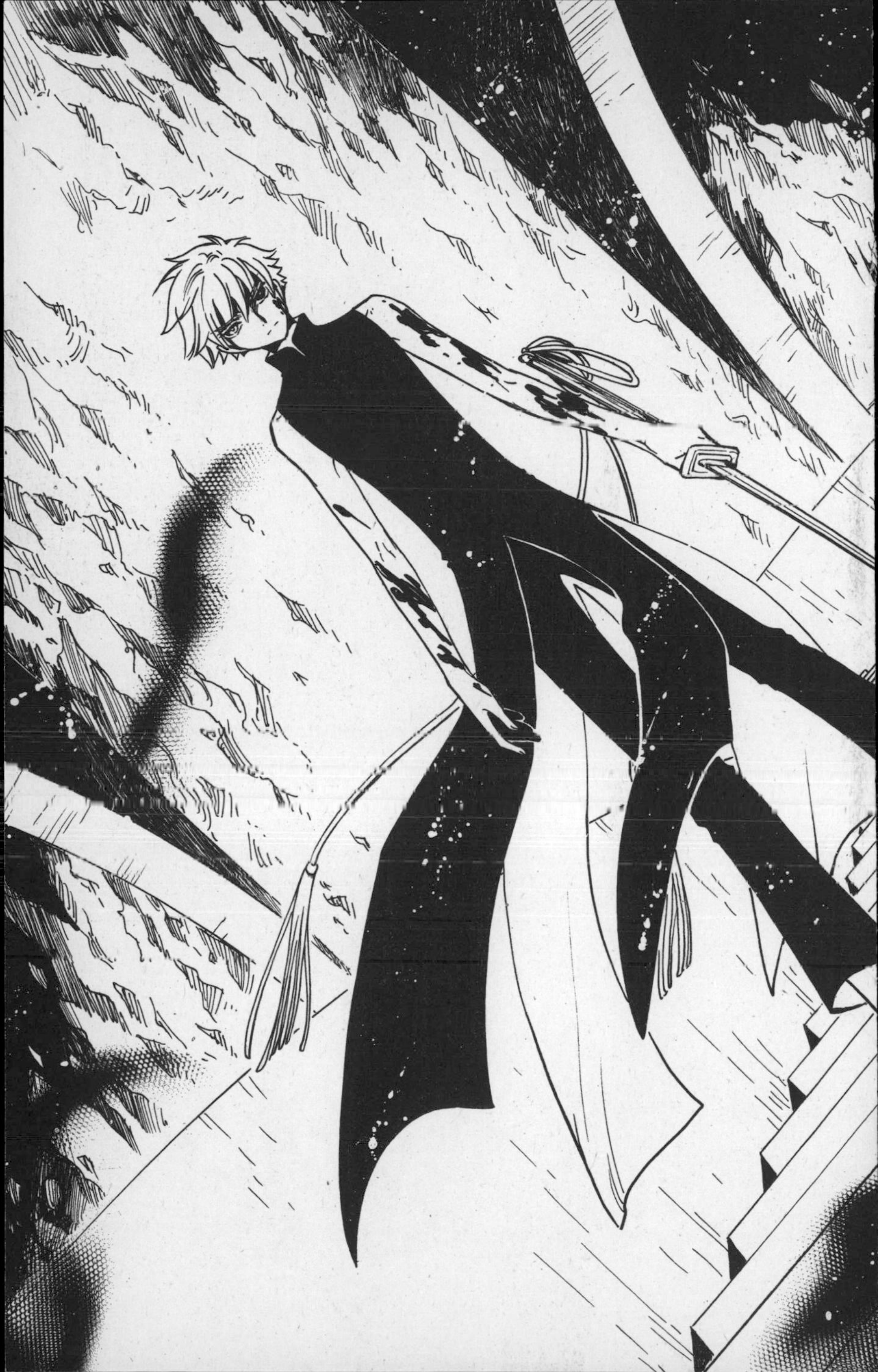

RESERVoir CHRoNiCLE

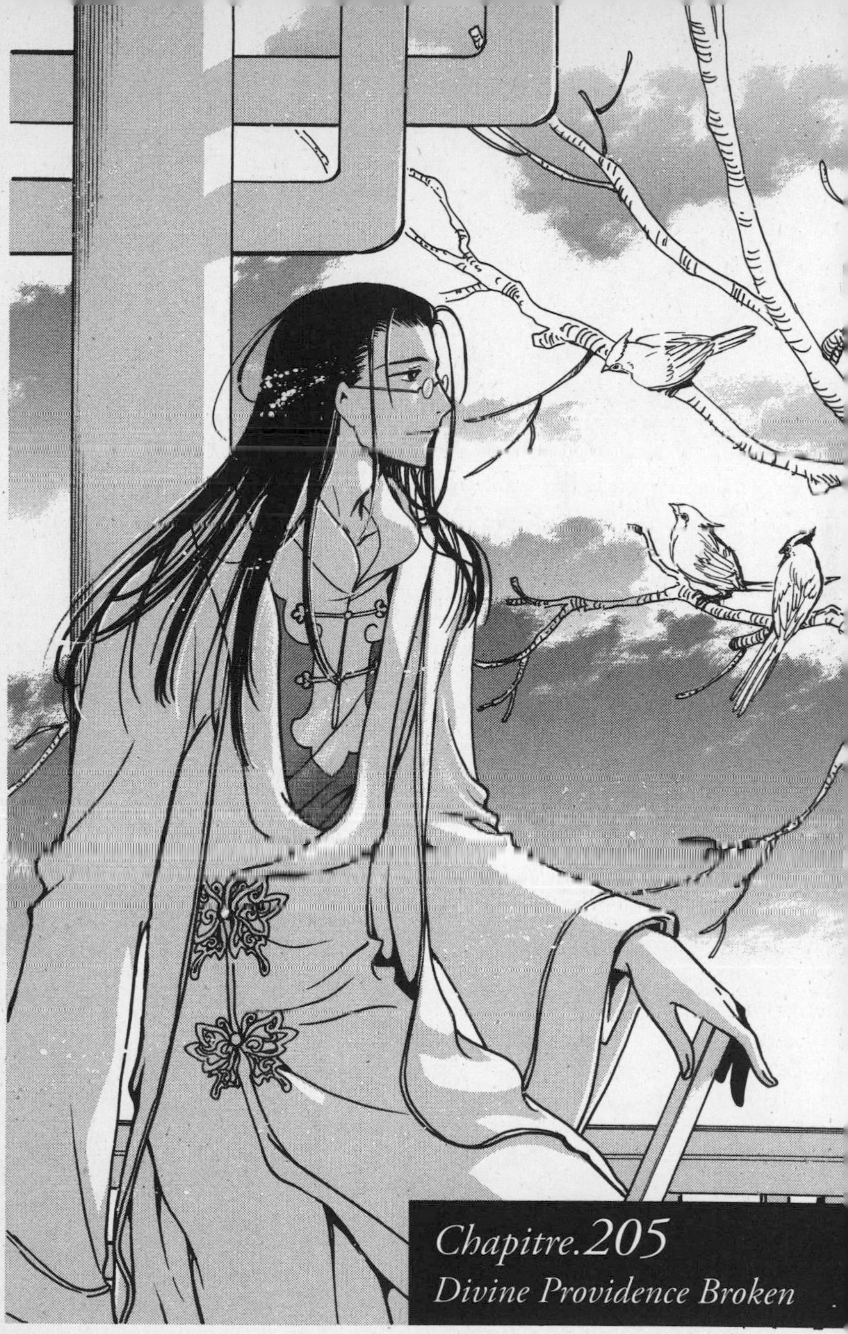

Chapitre. 205
Divine Providence Broken

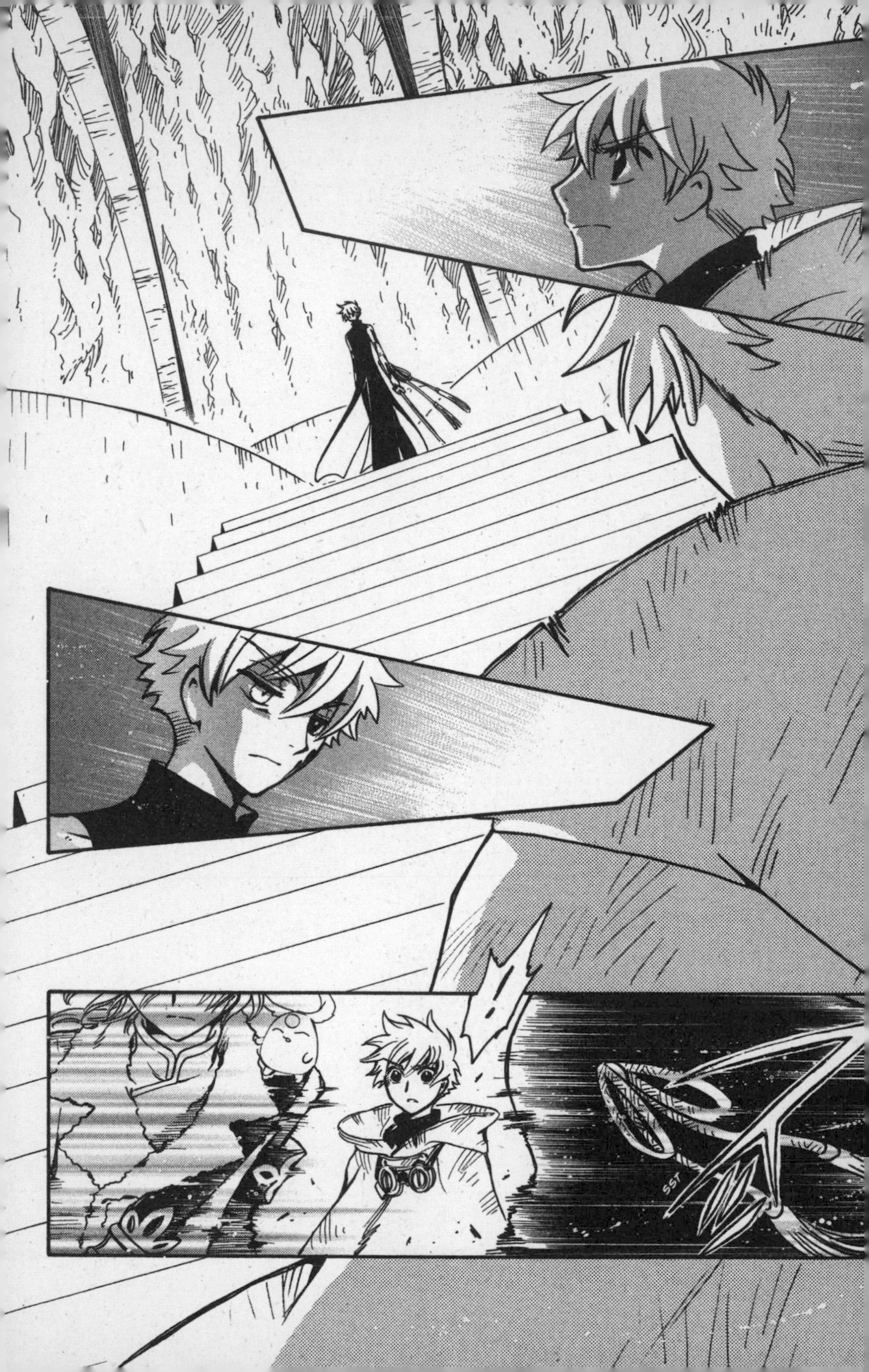
SST

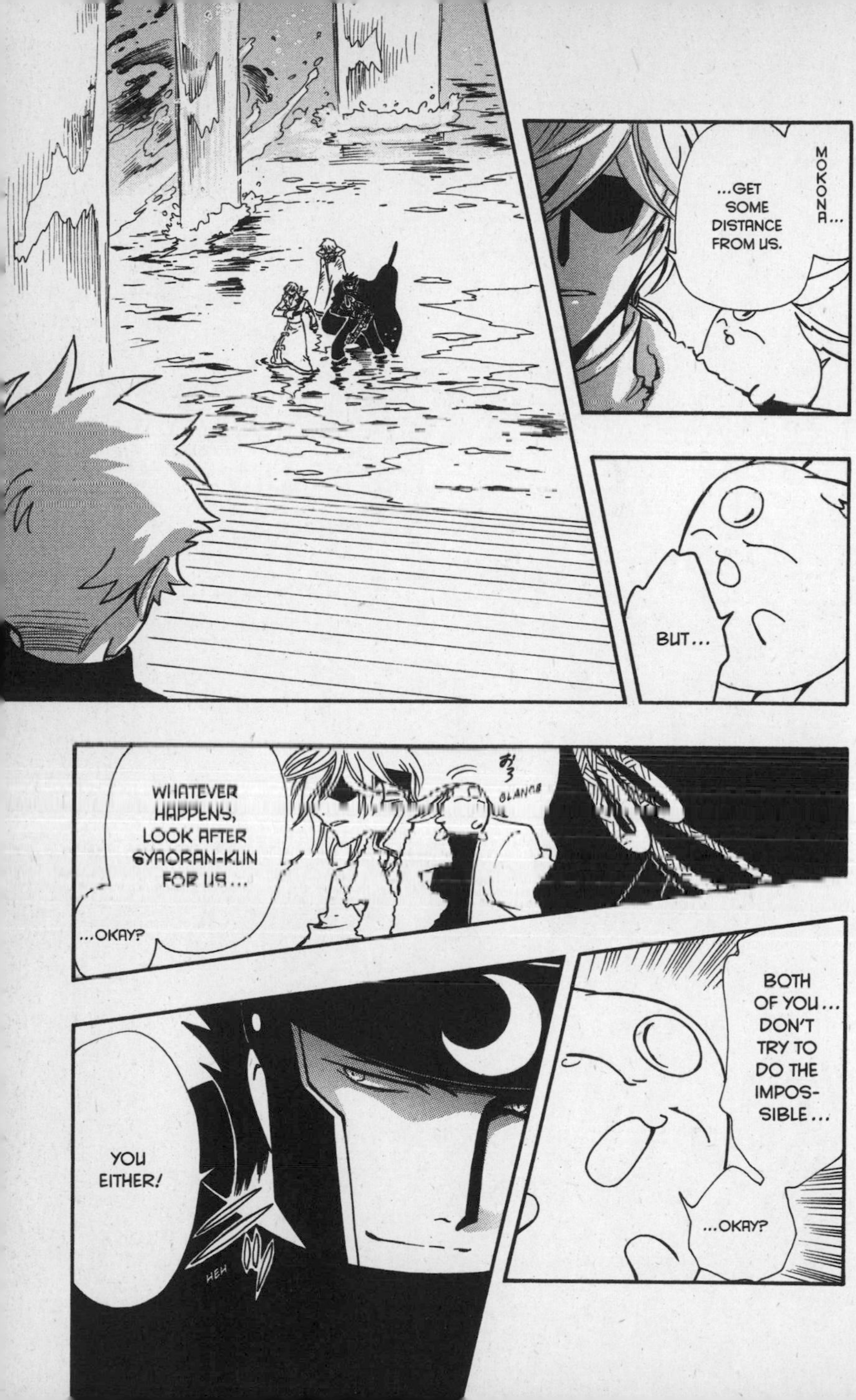
MOKONA...
...GET SOME DISTANCE FROM US.
BUT...
GLANCE
WHATEVER HAPPENS, LOOK AFTER SYAORAN-KUN FOR US...
...OKAY?
BOTH OF YOU... DON'T TRY TO DO THE IMPOSSIBLE...
...OKAY?
YOU EITHER!
HEH

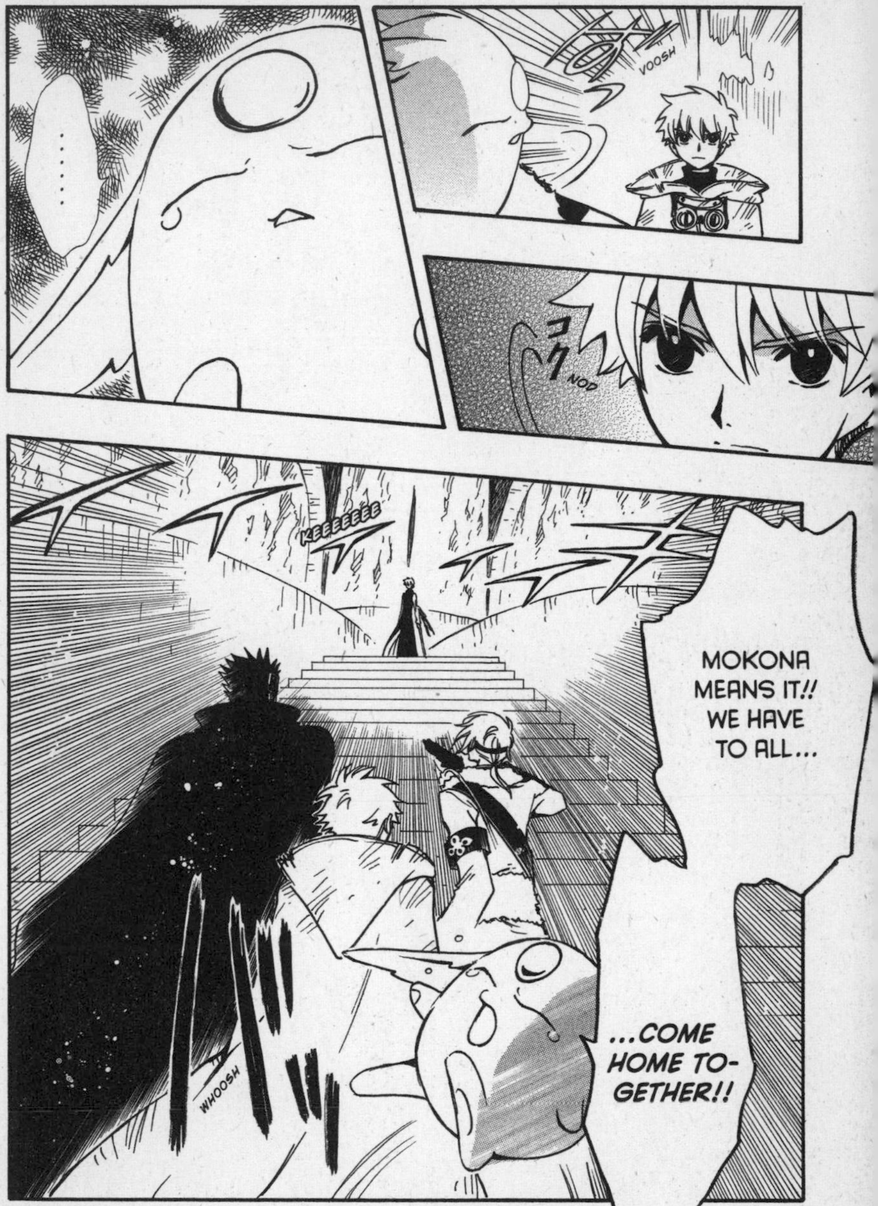
VOOSH
NOD
......
KEEEEEEE
MOKONA MEANS IT!! WE HAVE TO ALL...
...COME HOME TO-GETHER!!
WHOOSH

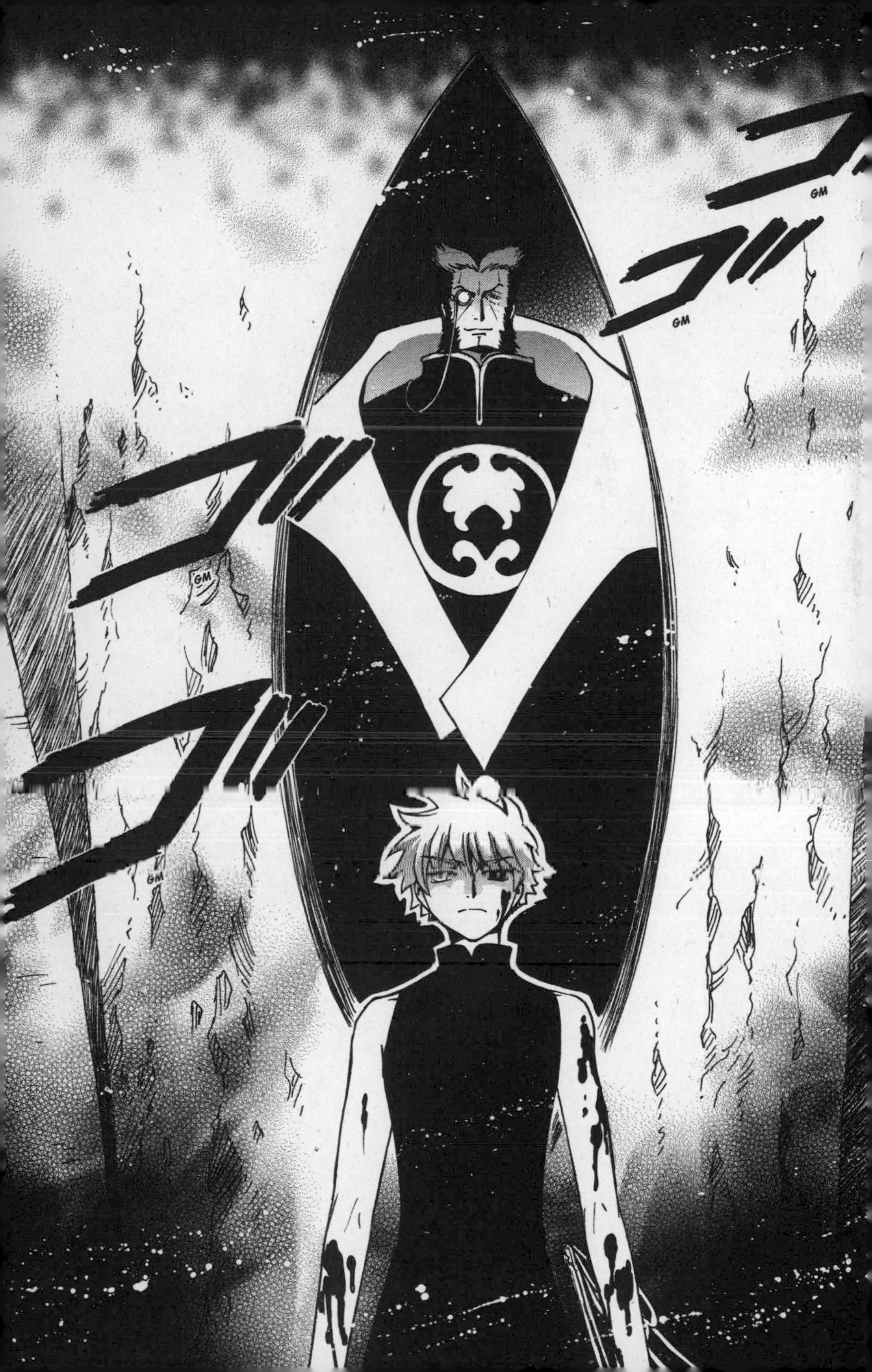
ゴゴ
GM
GM
ゴゴ
GM
GM

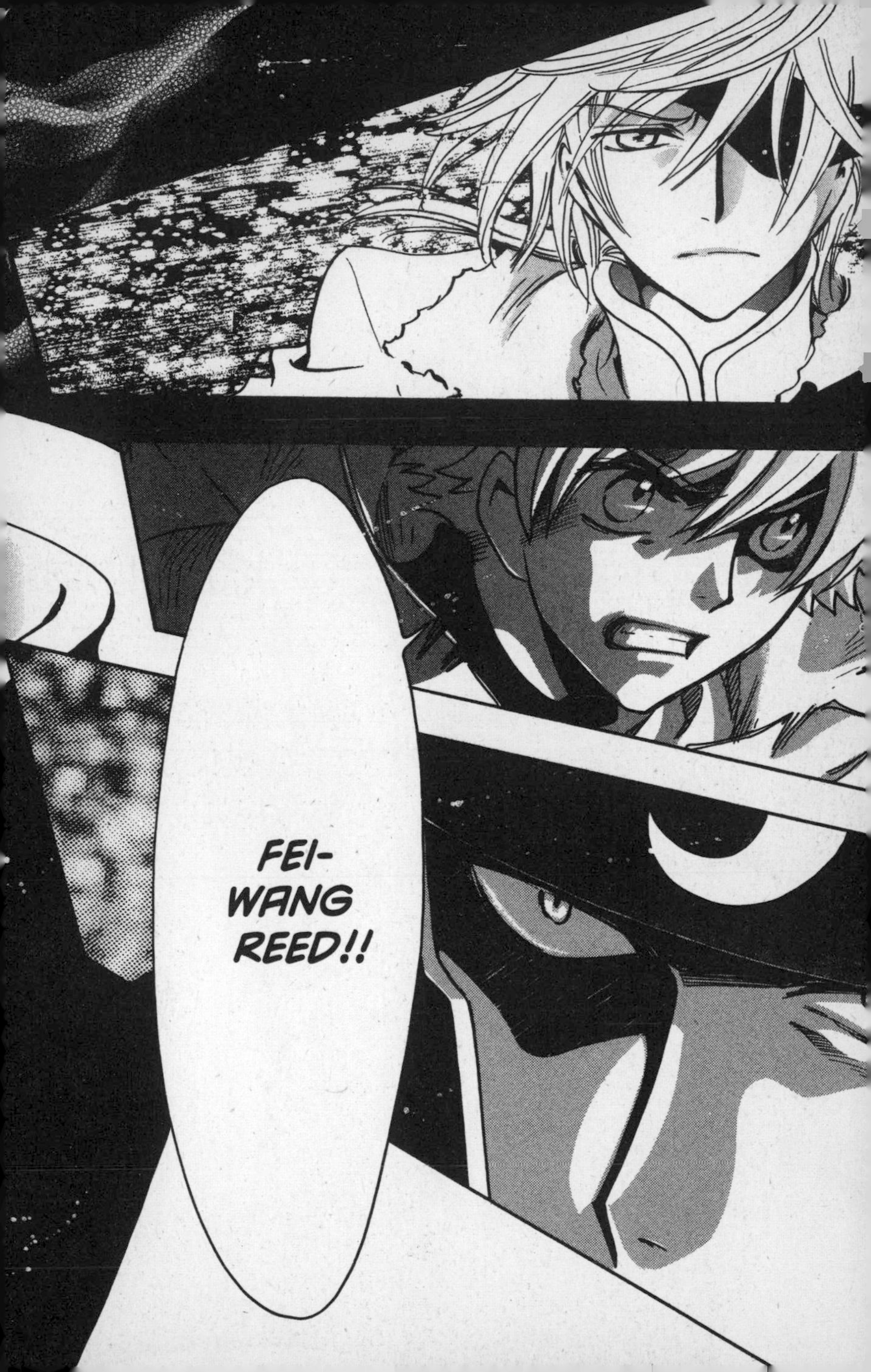
FEI-WANG REED!!

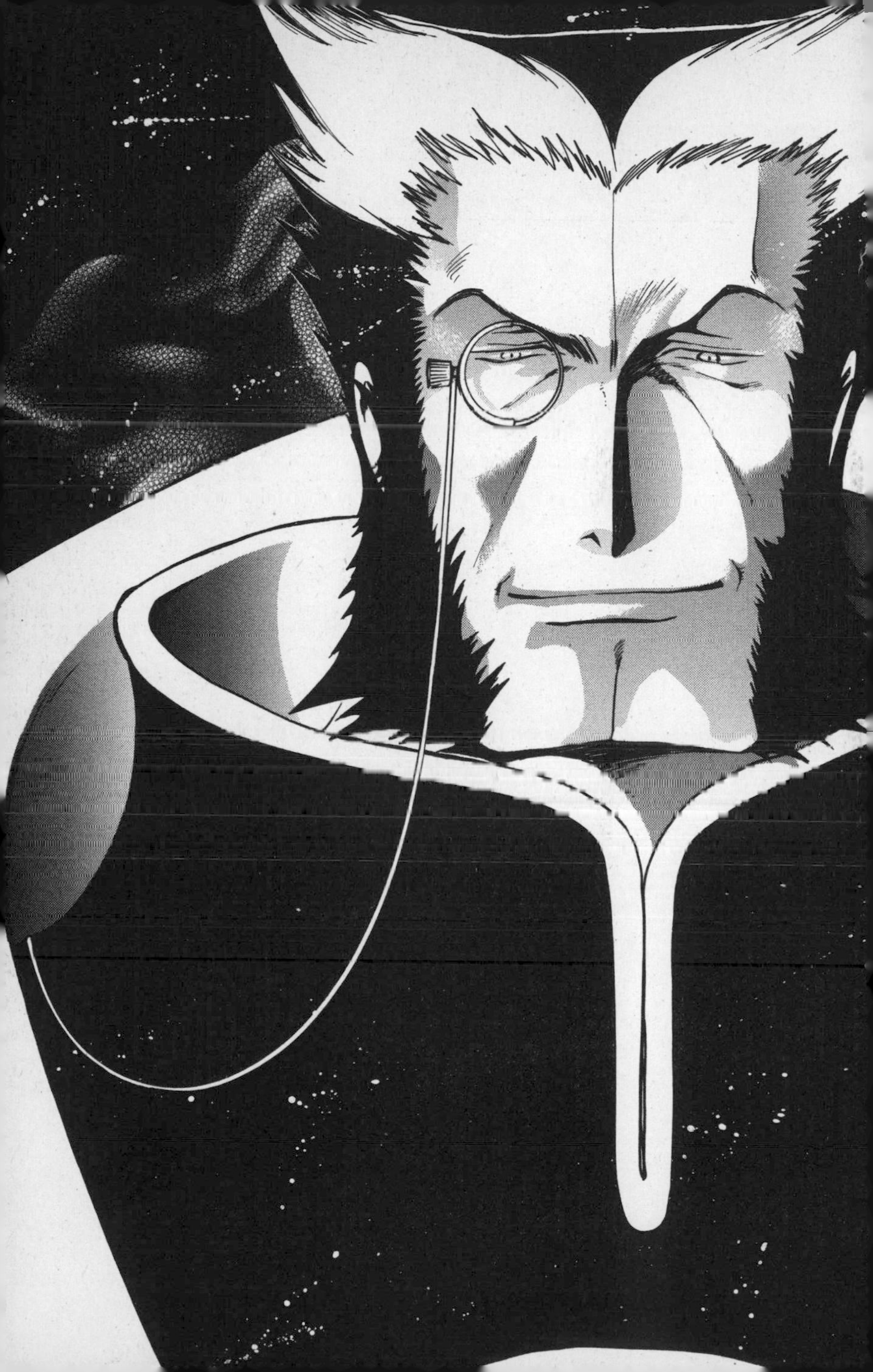

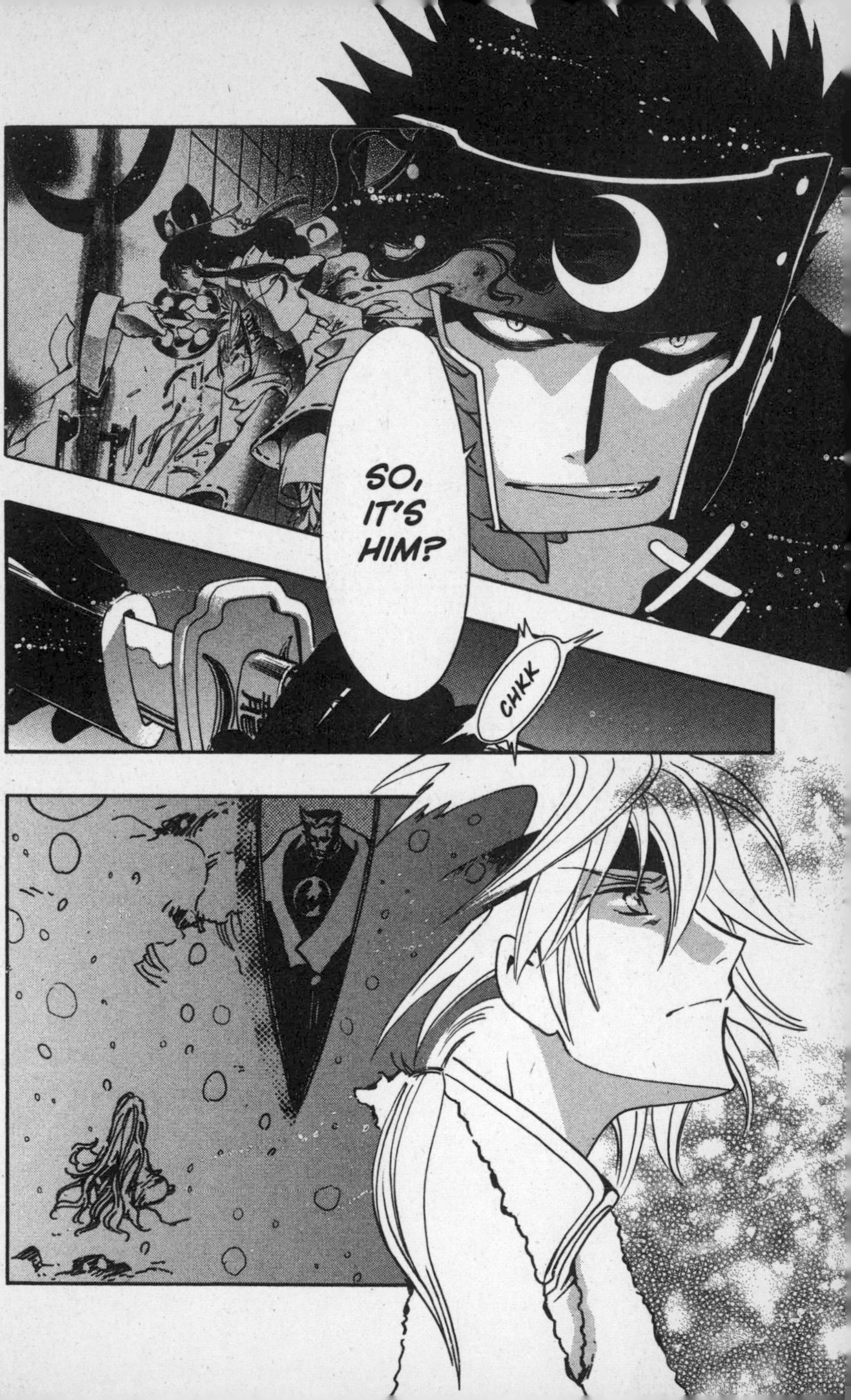
SO, IT'S HIM?
CHKK

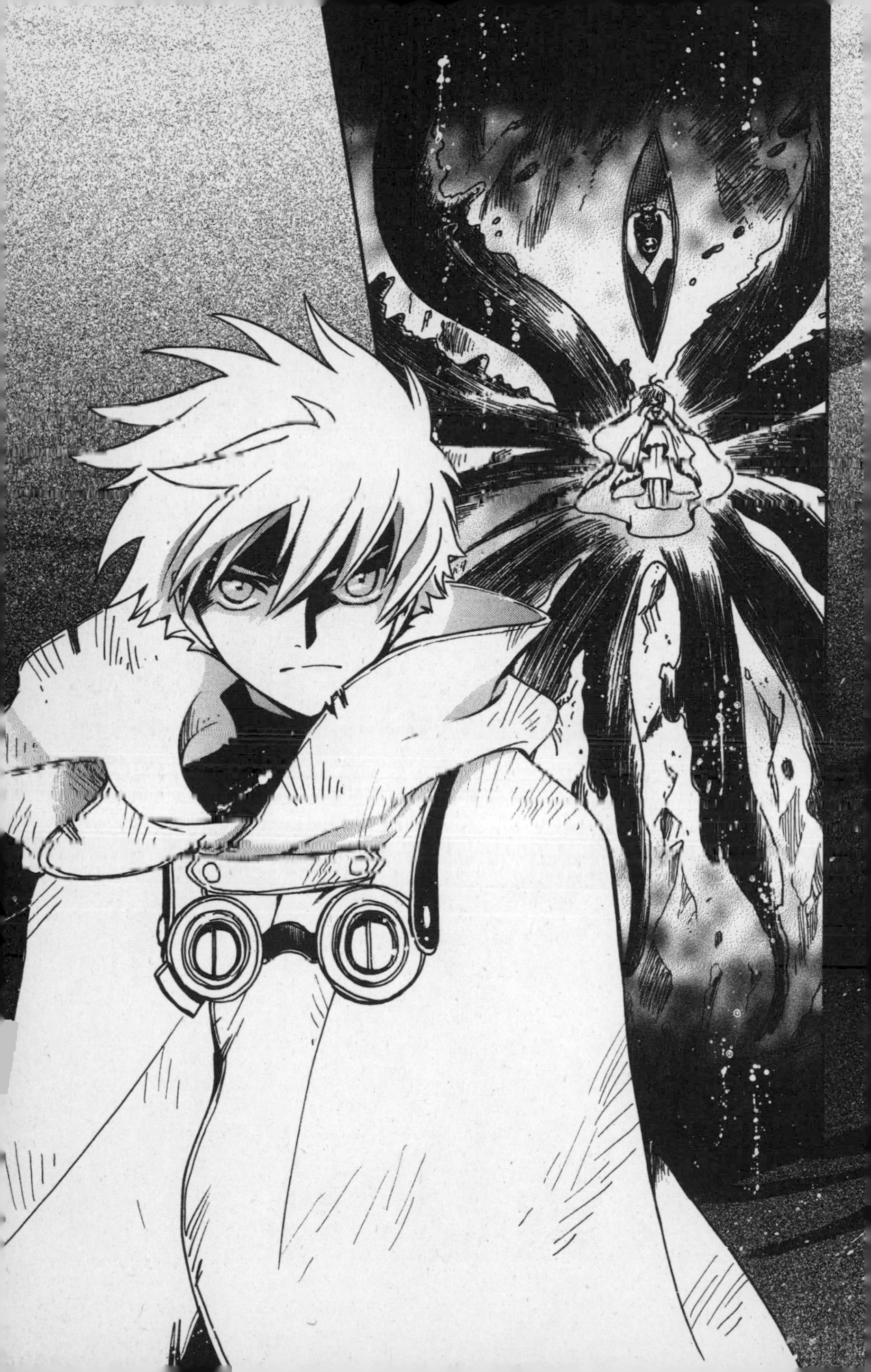

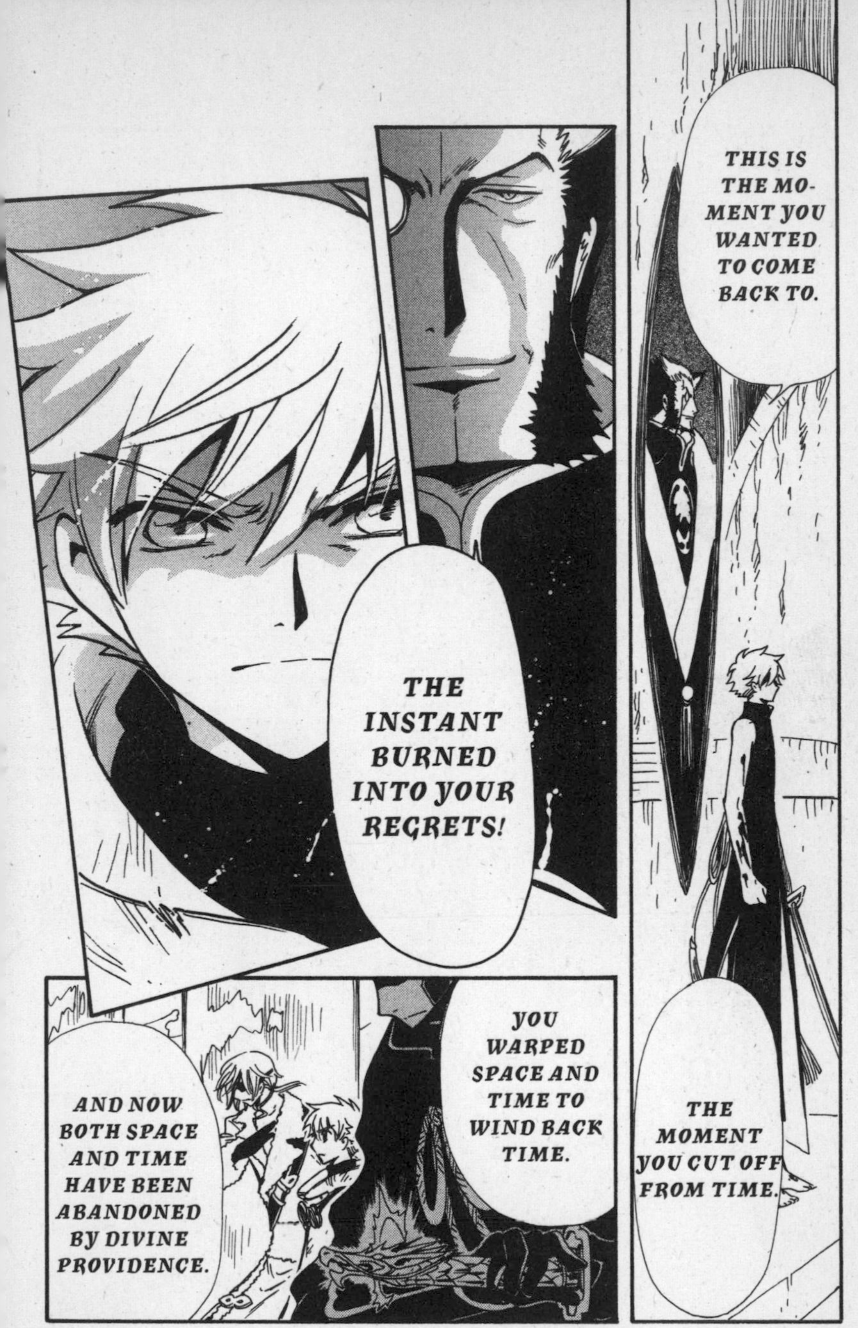
THIS IS THE MOMENT YOU WANTED TO COME BACK TO.
THE MOMENT YOU CUT OFF FROM TIME.
THE INSTANT BURNED INTO YOUR REGRETS!
YOU WARPED SPACE AND TIME TO WIND BACK TIME.
AND NOW BOTH SPACE AND TIME HAVE BEEN ABANDONED BY DIVINE PROVIDENCE.

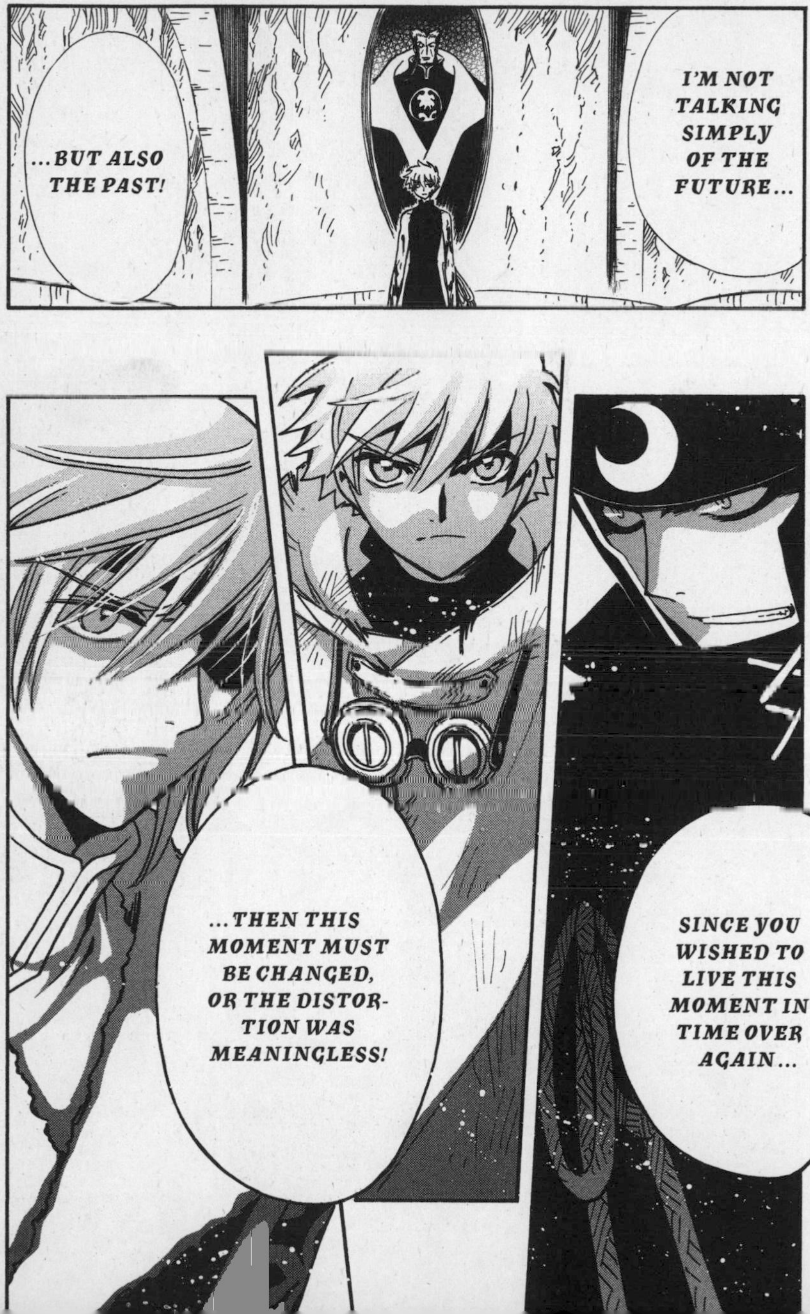
I'M NOT TALKING SIMPLY OF THE FUTURE...
...BUT ALSO THE PAST!
SINCE YOU WISHED TO LIVE THIS MOMENT IN TIME OVER AGAIN...
...THEN THIS MOMENT MUST BE CHANGED, OR THE DISTORTION WAS MEANINGLESS!

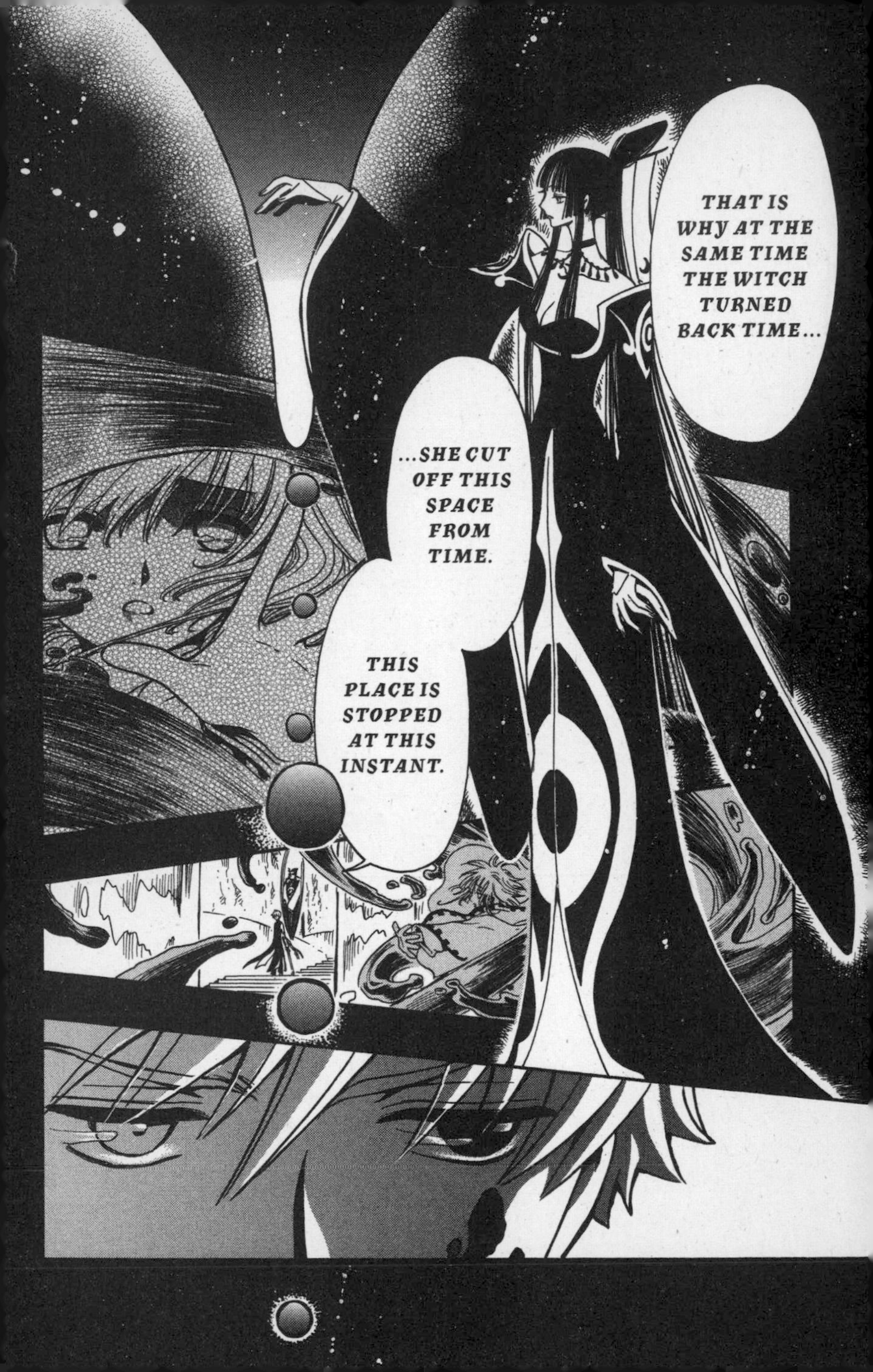
THAT IS WHY AT THE SAME TIME THE WITCH TURNED BACK TIME...
...SHE CUT OFF THIS SPACE FROM TIME.
THIS PLACE IS STOPPED AT THIS INSTANT.

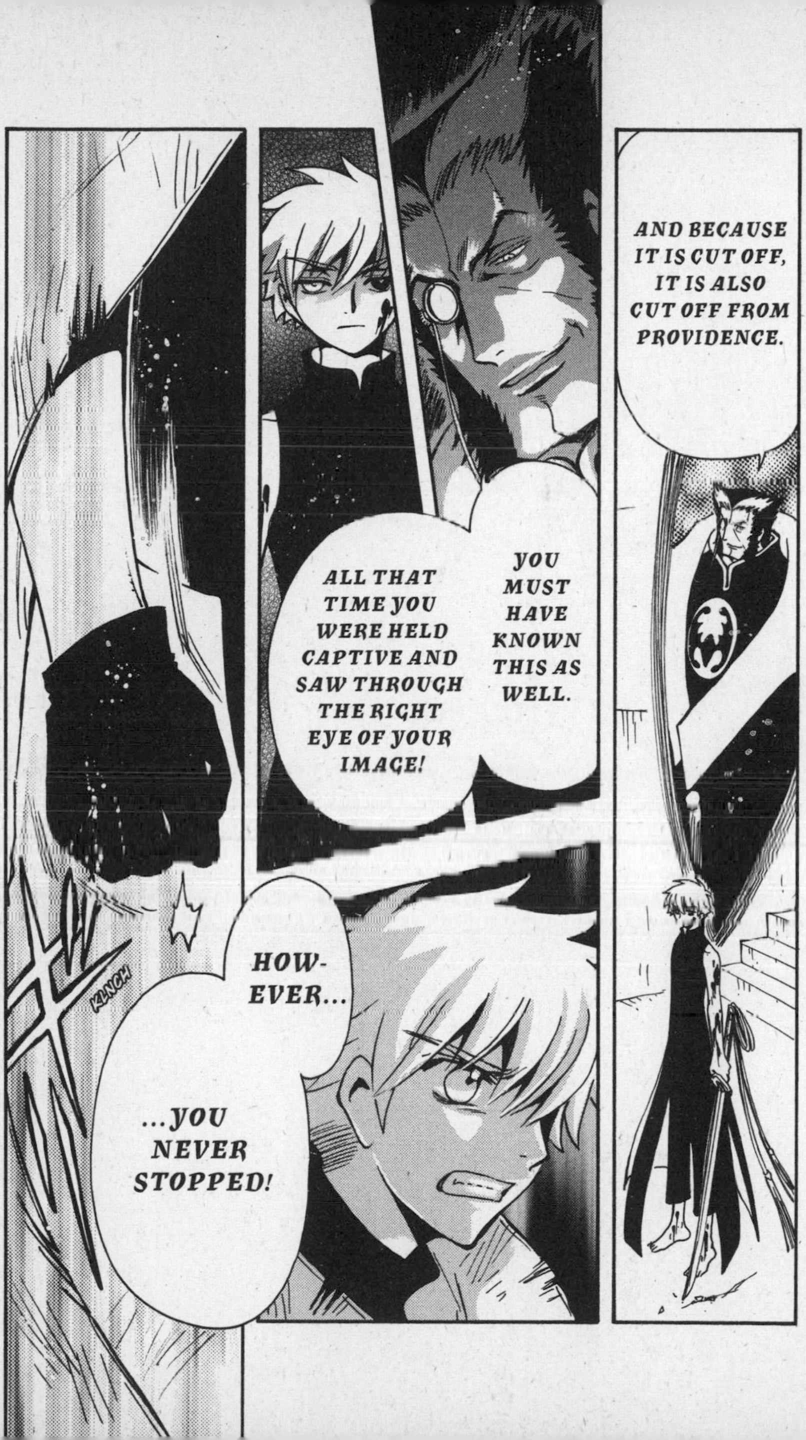
AND BECAUSE IT IS CUT OFF, IT IS ALSO CUT OFF FROM PROVIDENCE.
YOU MUST HAVE KNOWN THIS AS WELL.
ALL THAT TIME YOU WERE HELD CAPTIVE AND SAW THROUGH THE RIGHT EYE OF YOUR IMAGE!
HOW-EVER...
...YOU NEVER STOPPED!
KLNCH

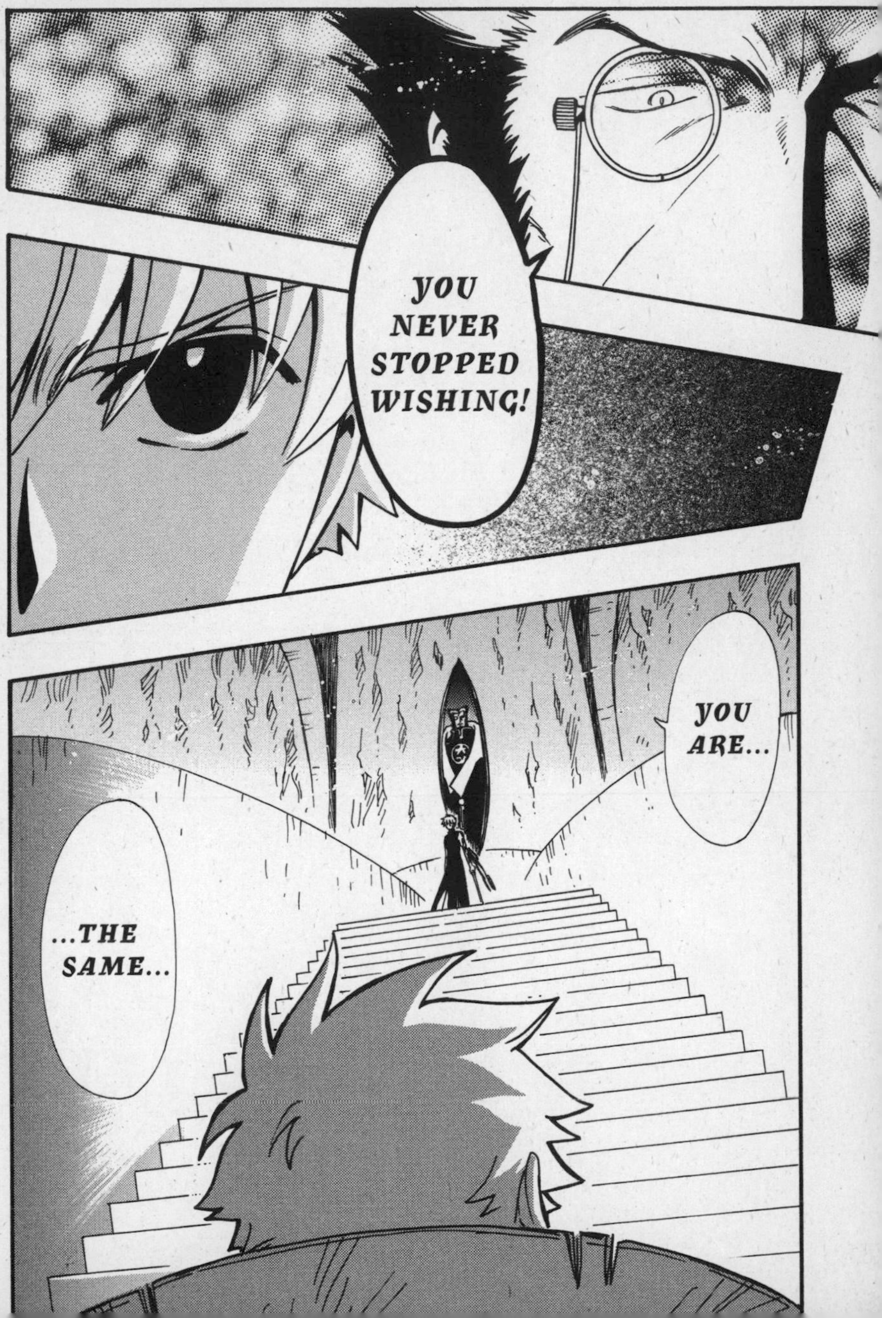
YOU NEVER STOPPED WISHING!
YOU ARE...
...THE SAME...

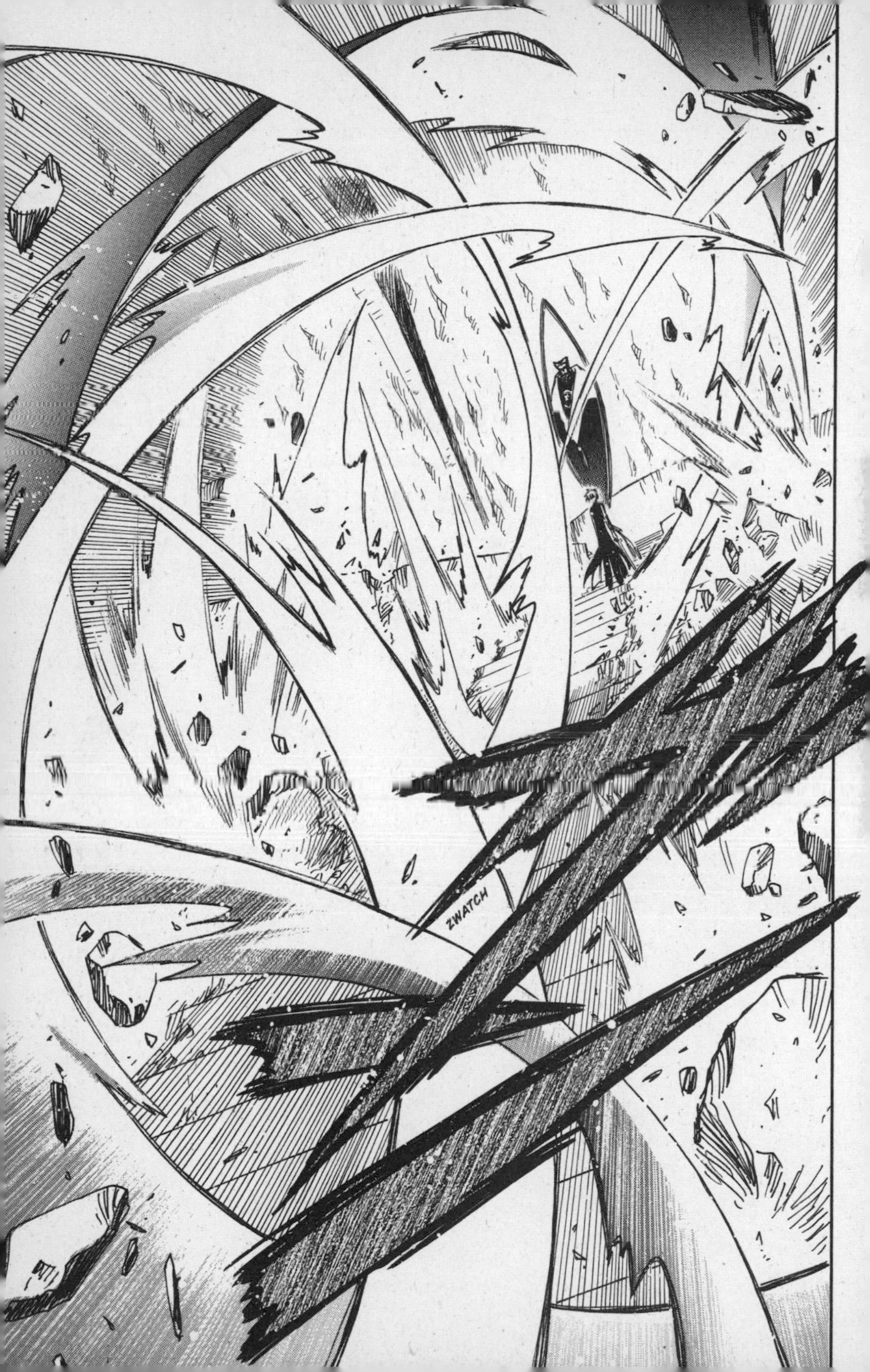
ZWATCH

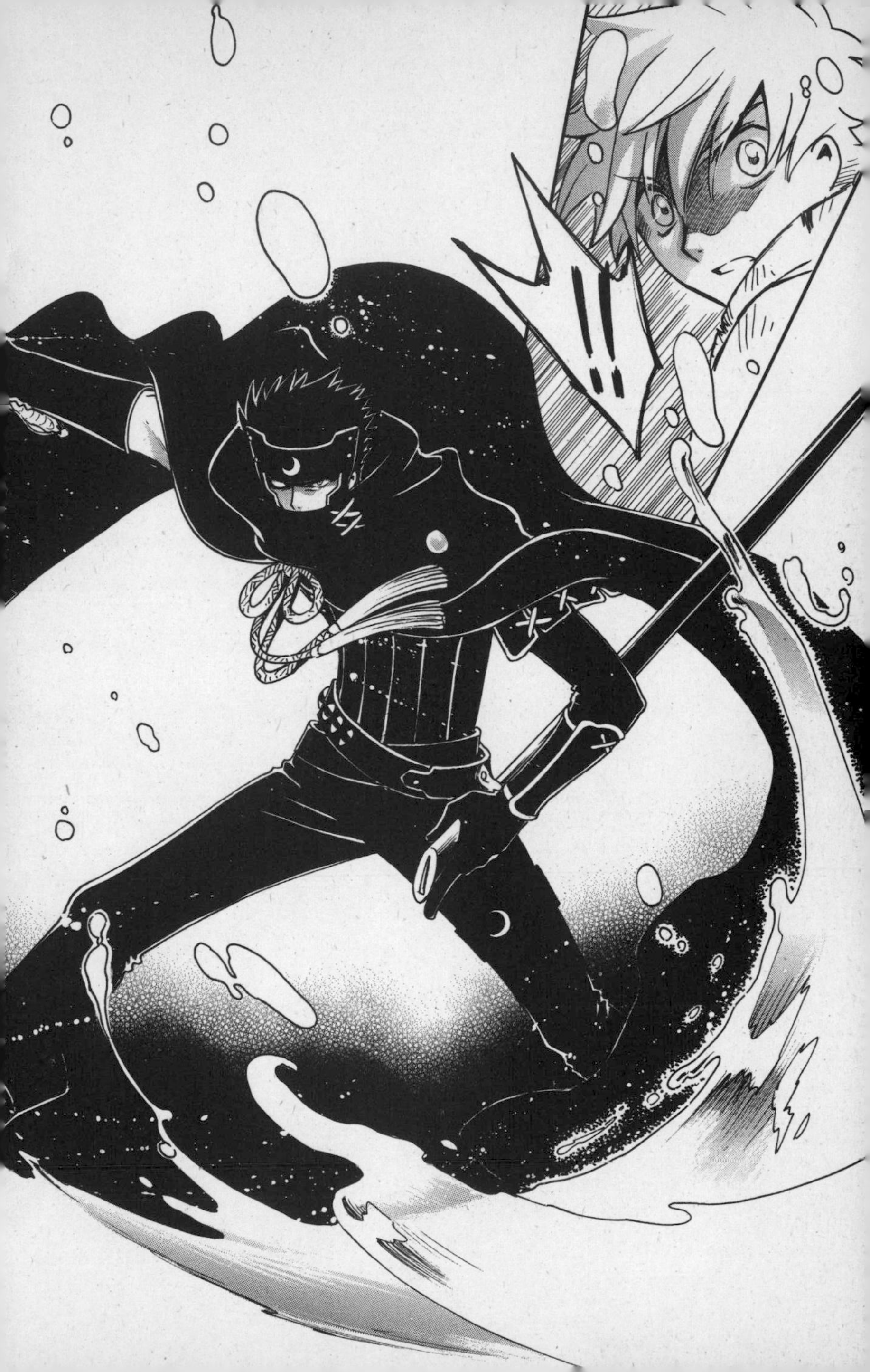
!!

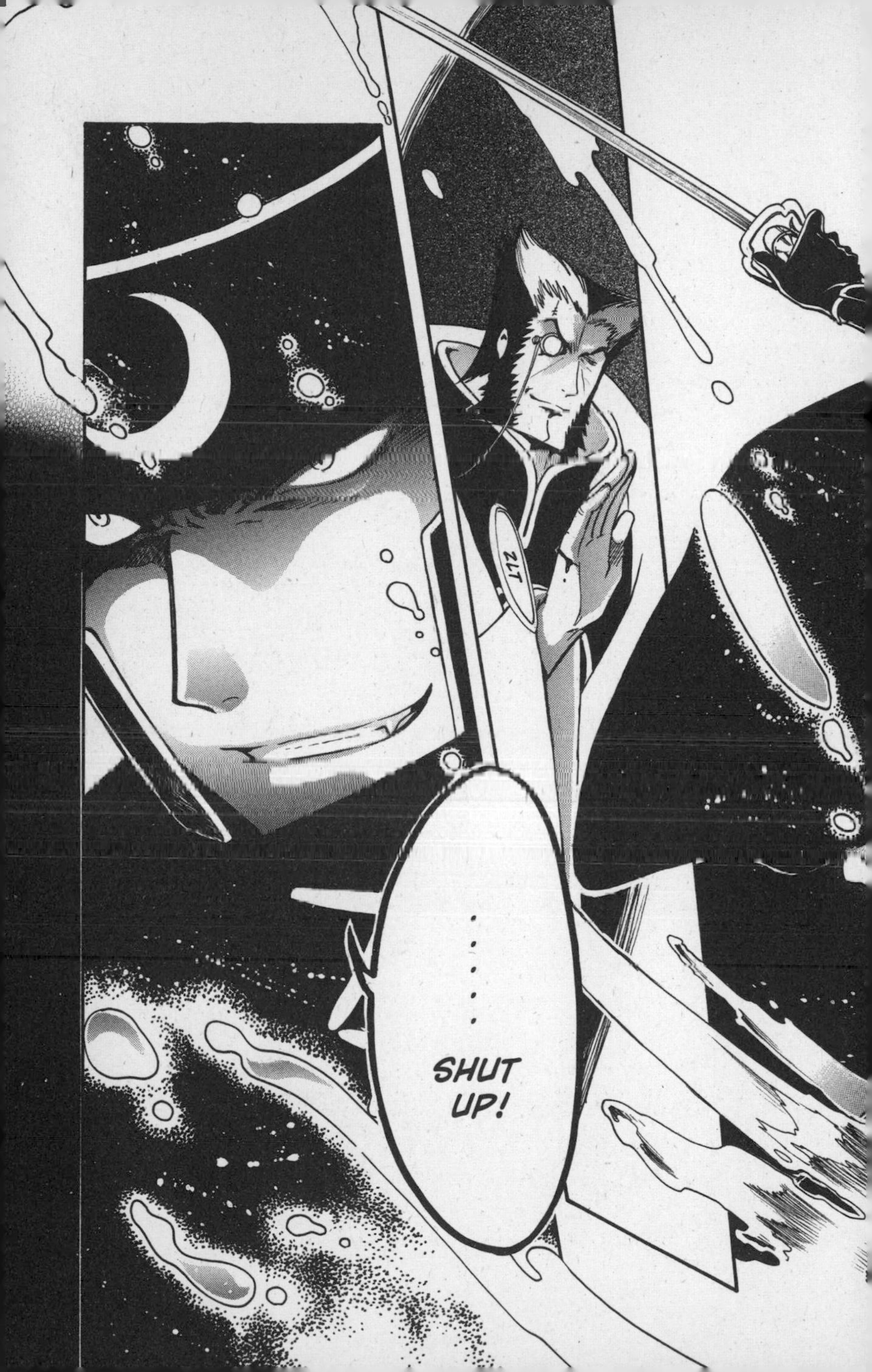
...... SHUT UP!

RESERVoir CHRoNiCLE

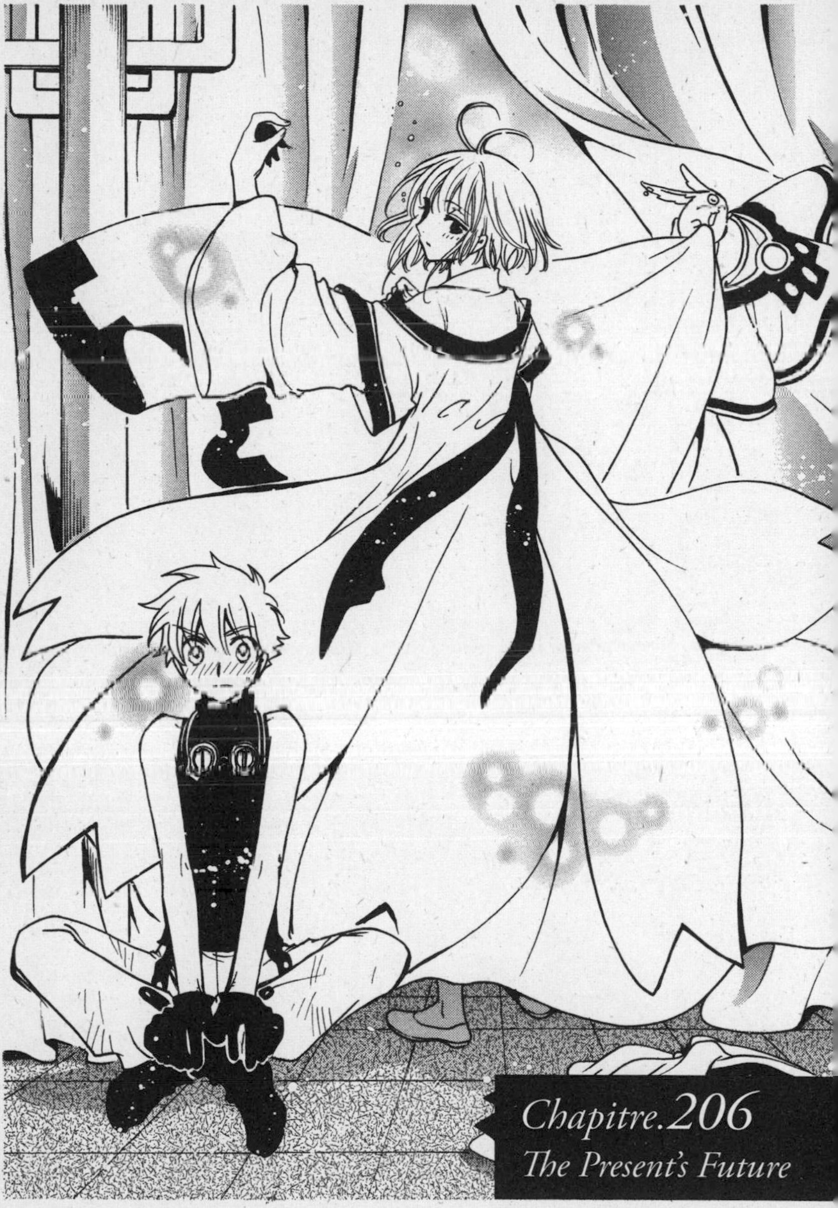
Chapitre.206
The Present's Future

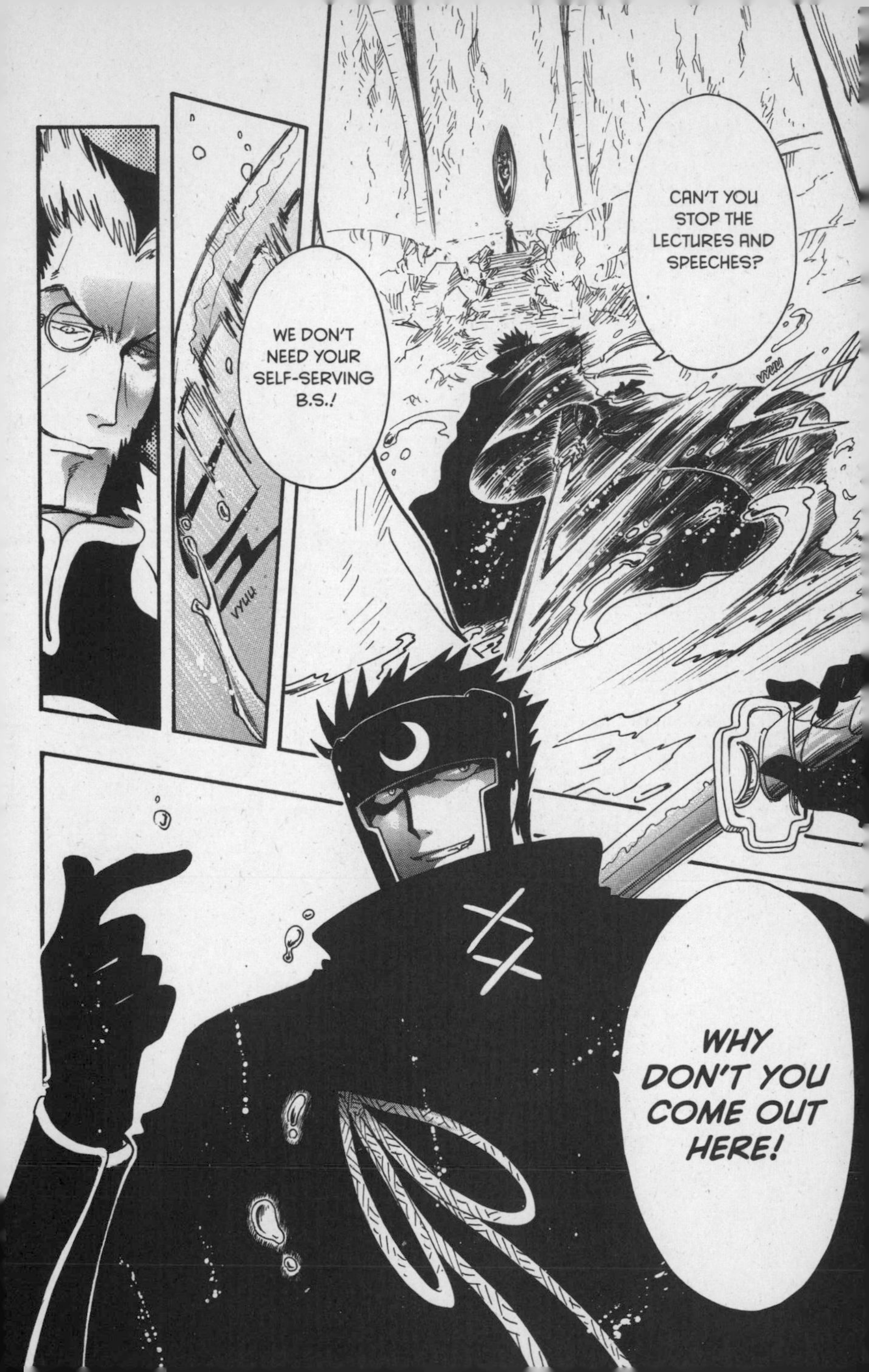
CAN'T YOU STOP THE LECTURES AND SPEECHES?
WE DON'T NEED YOUR SELF-SERVING B.S.!
VYUH
VYUH
WHY DON'T YOU COME OUT HERE!

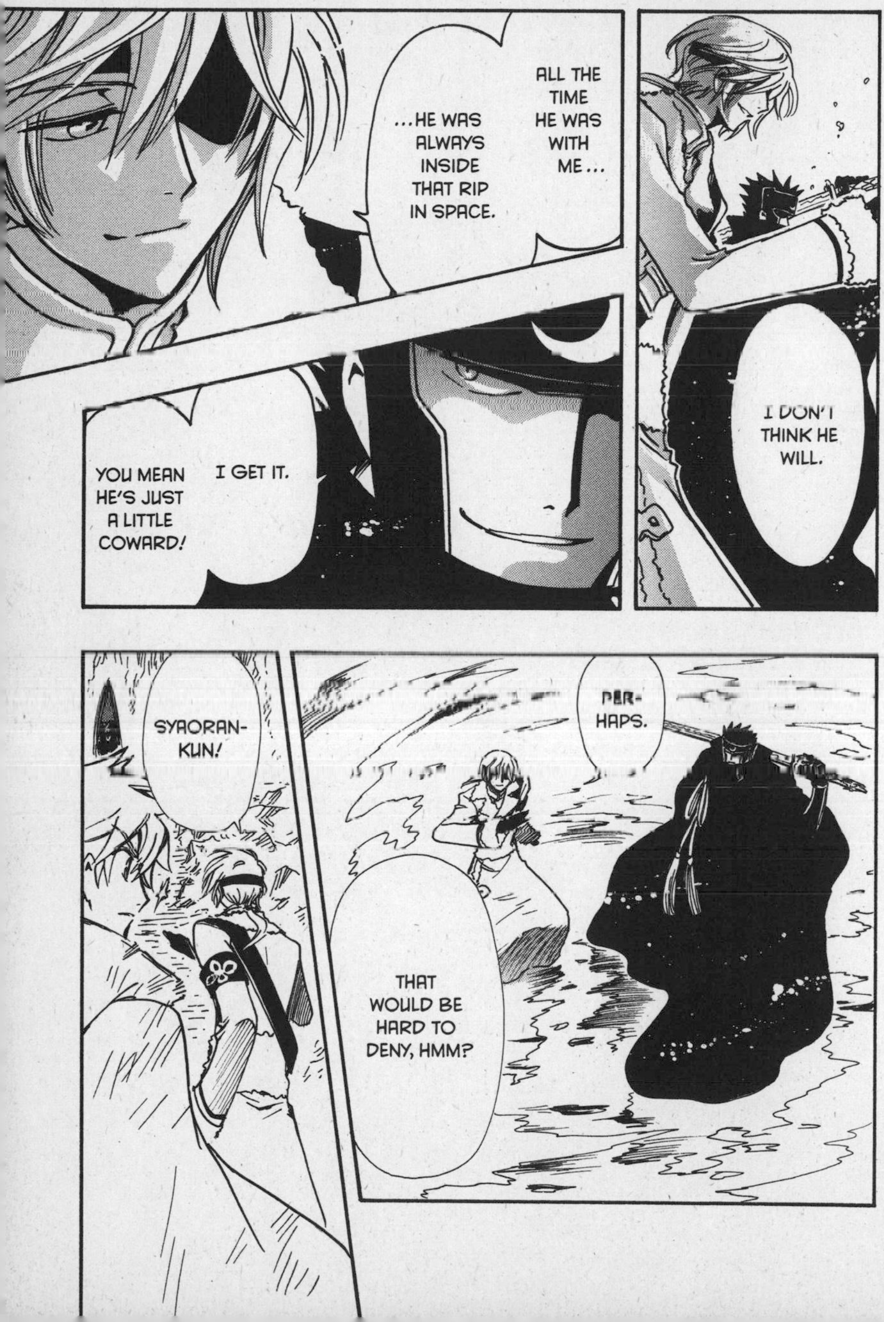
I DON'T THINK HE WILL.
ALL THE TIME HE WAS WITH ME...
...HE WAS ALWAYS INSIDE THAT RIP IN SPACE.
I GET IT.
YOU MEAN HE'S JUST A LITTLE COWARD!
PER-HAPS.
THAT WOULD BE HARD TO DENY, HMM?
SYAORAN-KUN!

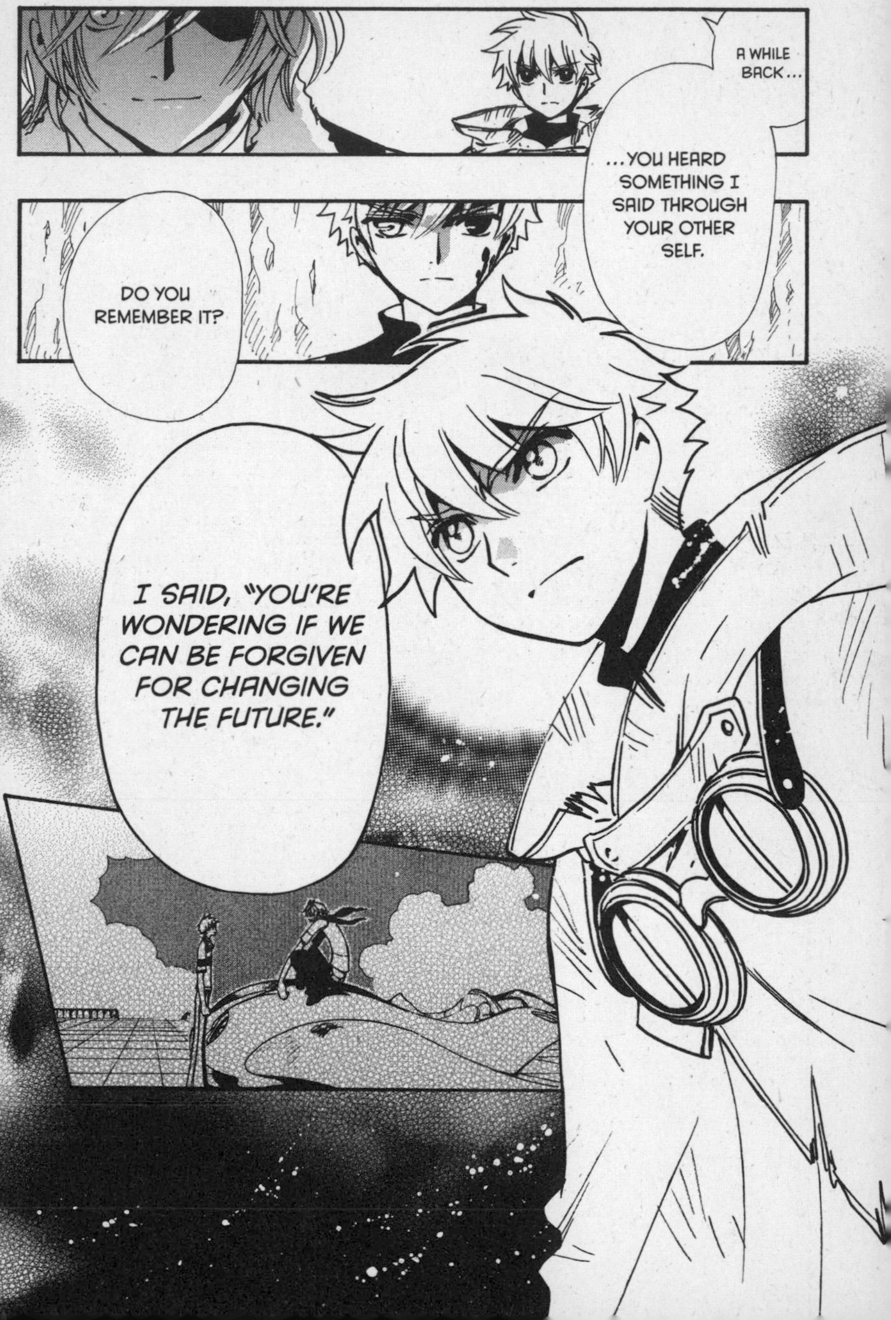
A WHILE BACK...
...YOU HEARD SOMETHING I SAID THROUGH YOUR OTHER SELF.
DO YOU REMEMBER IT?
I SAID, "YOU'RE WONDERING IF WE CAN BE FORGIVEN FOR CHANGING THE FUTURE."

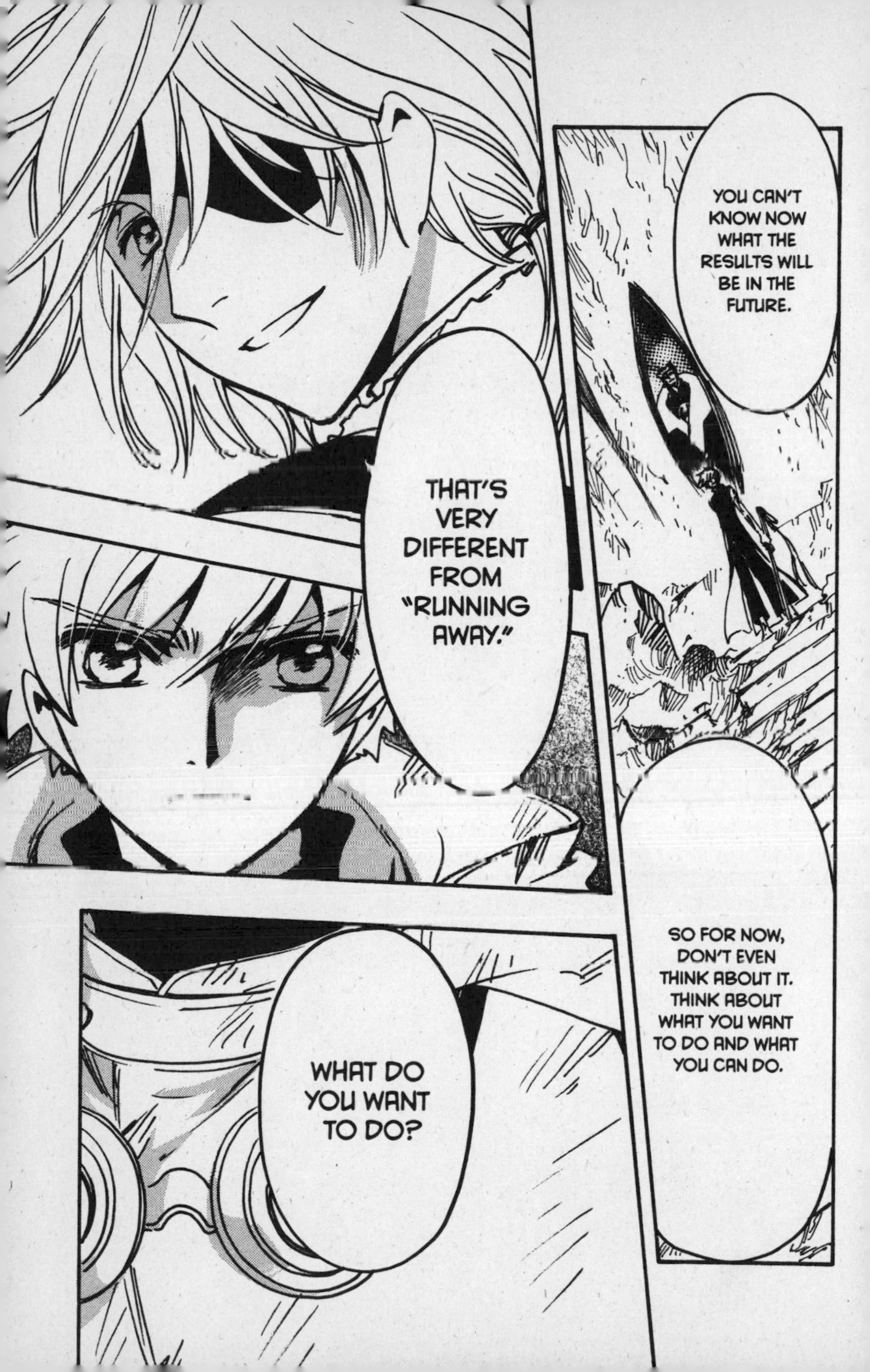
YOU CAN'T KNOW NOW WHAT THE RESULTS WILL BE IN THE FUTURE.
SO FOR NOW, DON'T EVEN THINK ABOUT IT. THINK ABOUT WHAT YOU WANT TO DO AND WHAT YOU CAN DO.
THAT'S VERY DIFFERENT FROM "RUNNING AWAY."
WHAT DO YOU WANT TO DO?

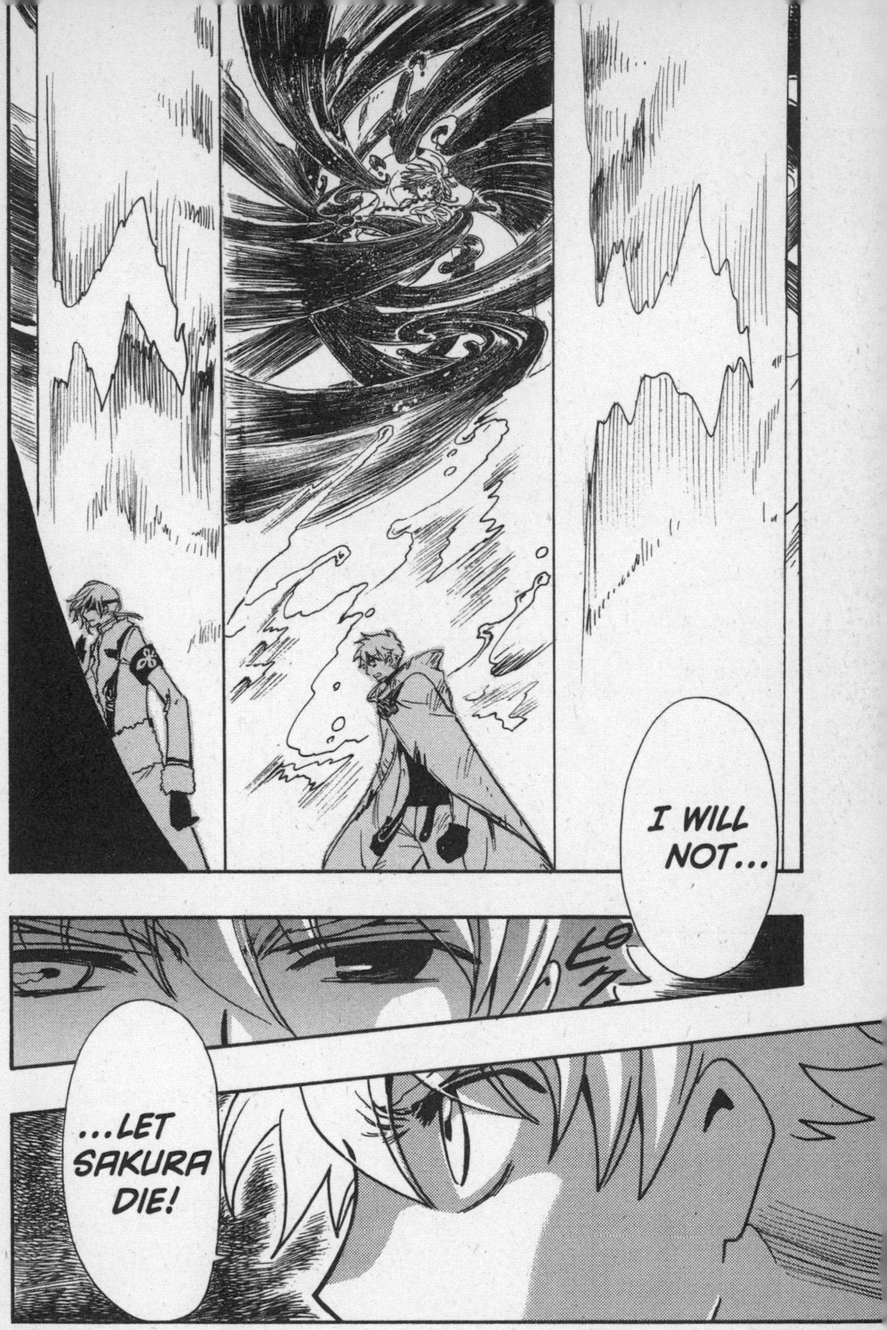
I WILL NOT...
...LET SAKURA DIE!

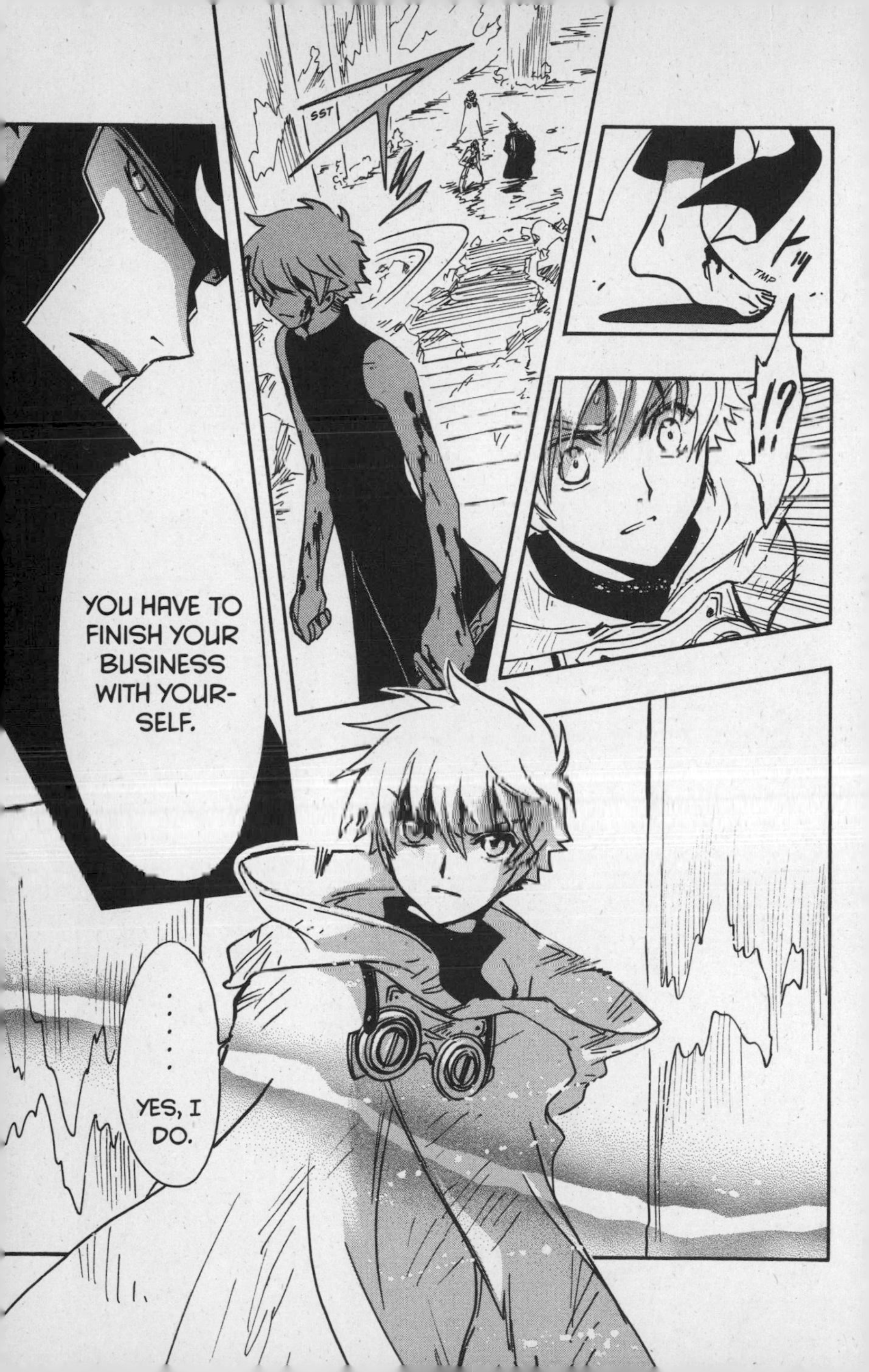
TMP
!?
SST
YOU HAVE TO FINISH YOUR BUSINESS WITH YOUR-SELF.
.....
YES, I DO.

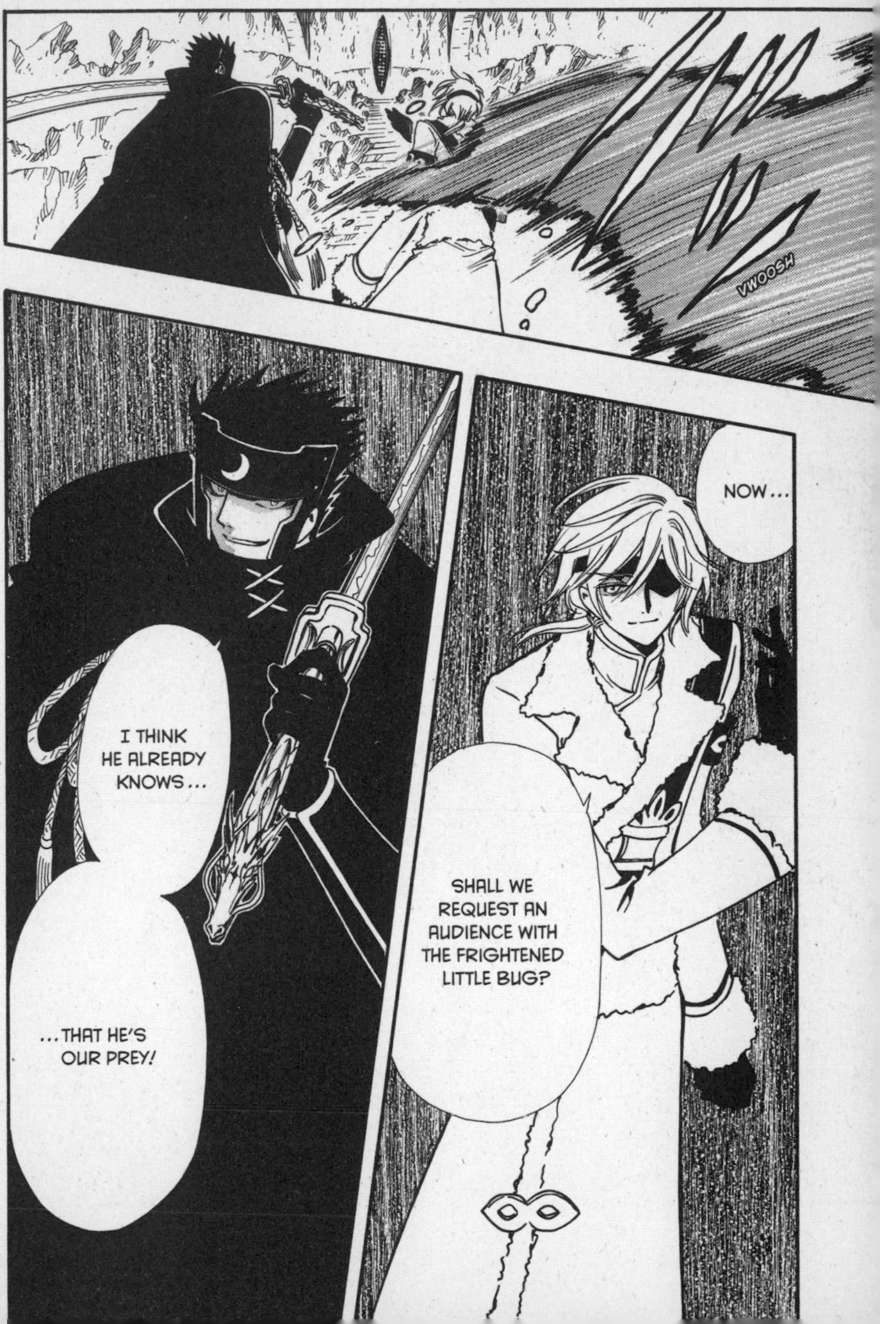
VWOOSH
NOW...
SHALL WE REQUEST AN AUDIENCE WITH THE FRIGHTENED LITTLE BUG?
I THINK HE ALREADY KNOWS...
...THAT HE'S OUR PREY!

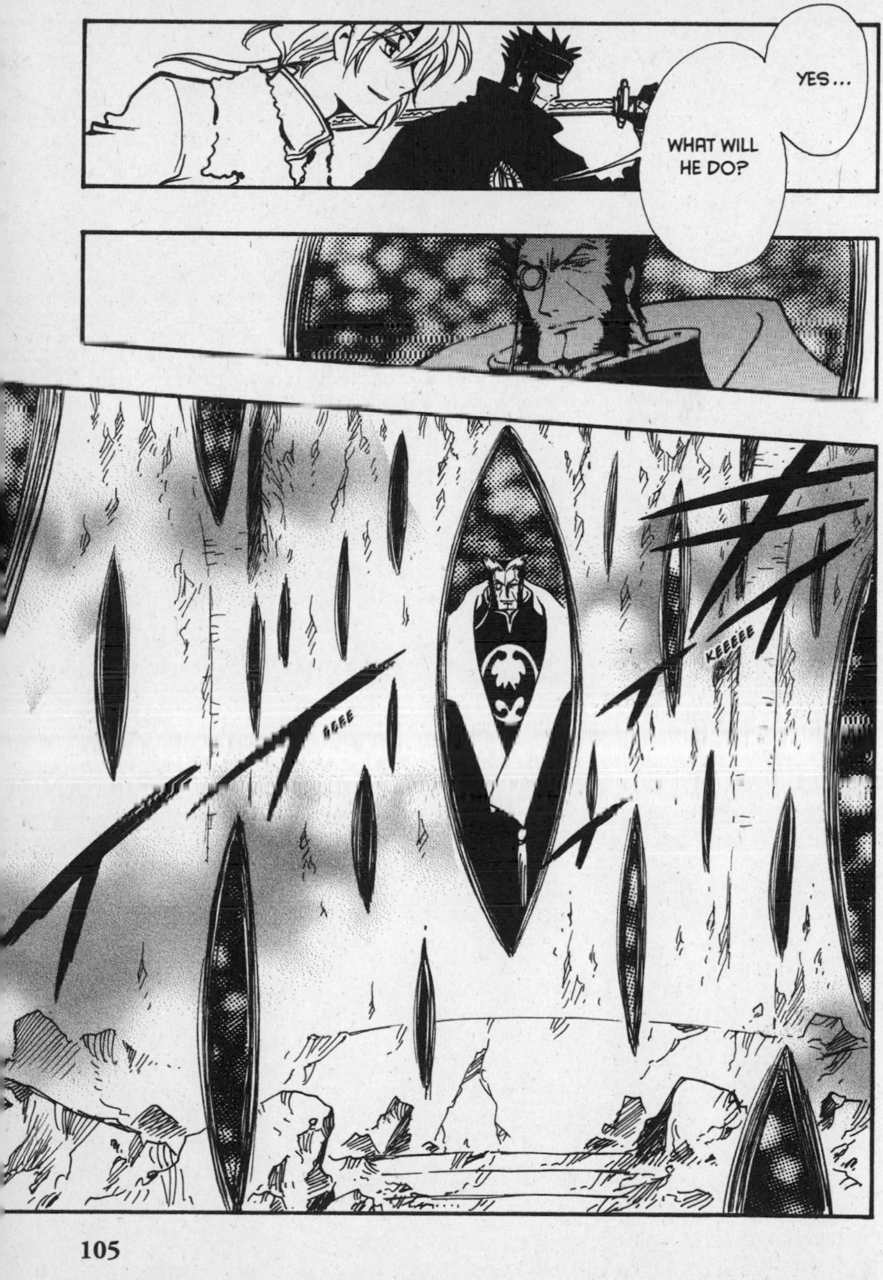
YES... WHAT WILL HE DO?
KEEEEE

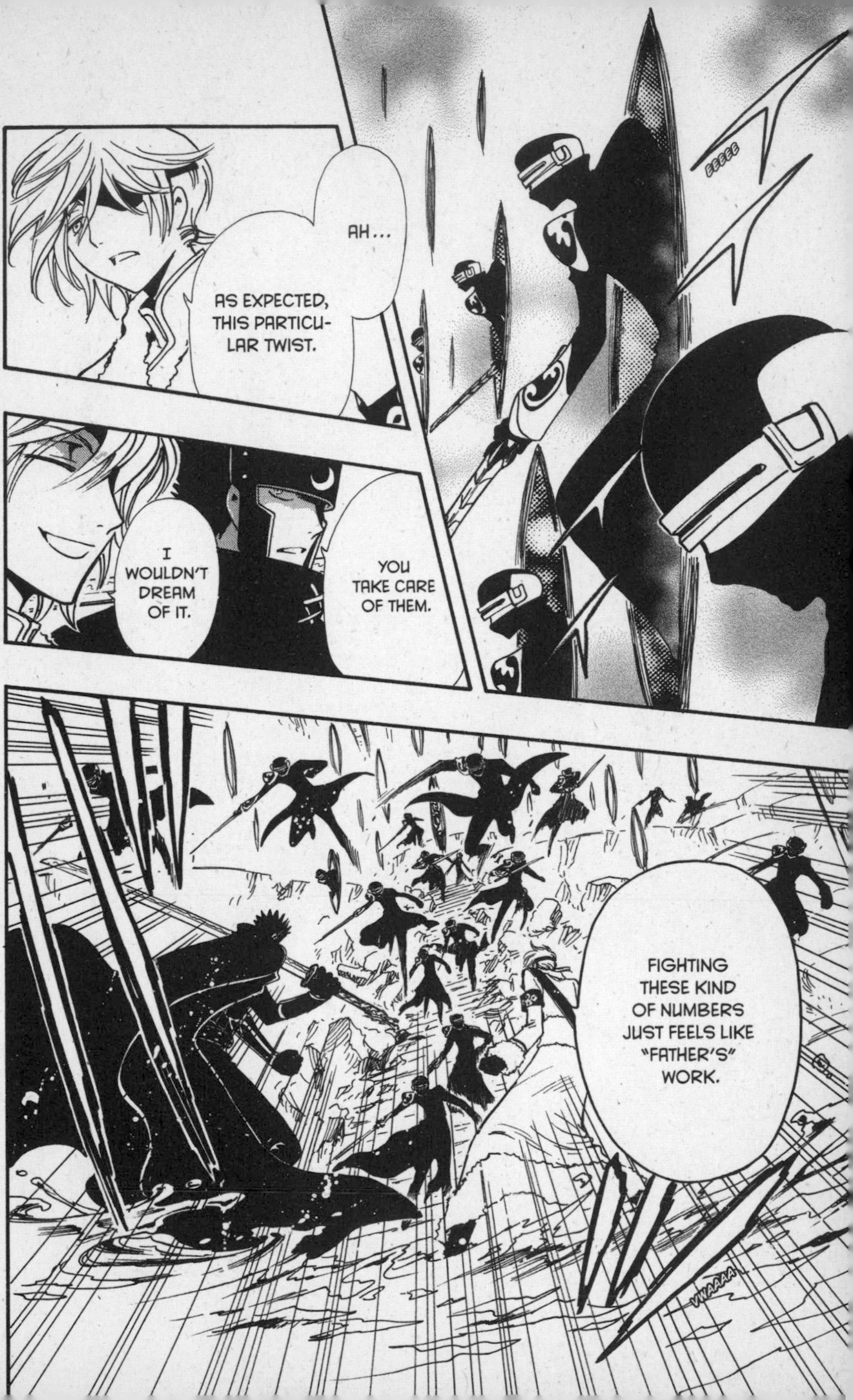
EEEEE
AH...
AS EXPECTED, THIS PARTICULAR TWIST.
YOU TAKE CARE OF THEM.
I WOULDN'T DREAM OF IT.
FIGHTING THESE KIND OF NUMBERS JUST FEELS LIKE "FATHER'S" WORK.
VWAAAA

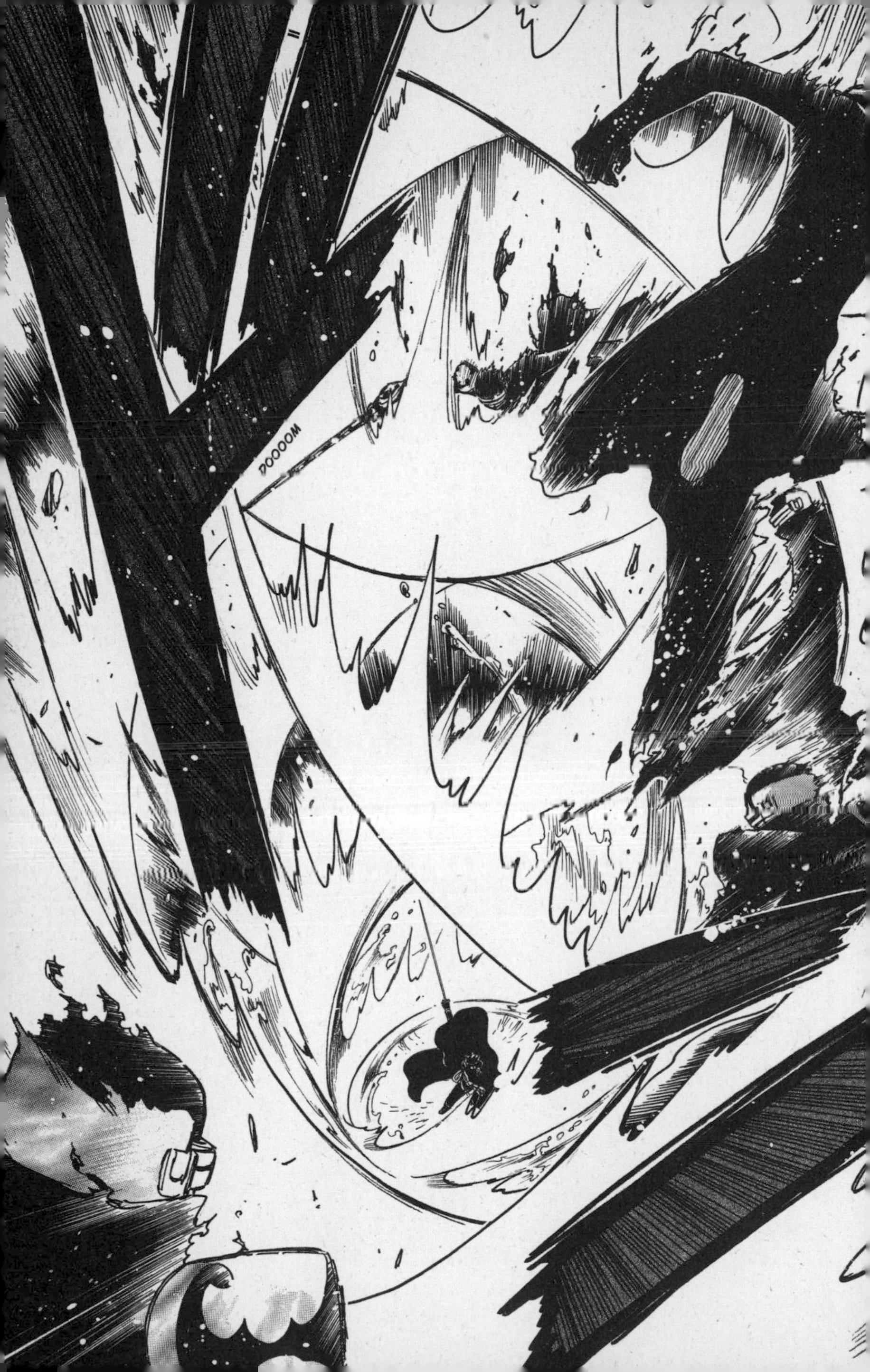
DOOOOM

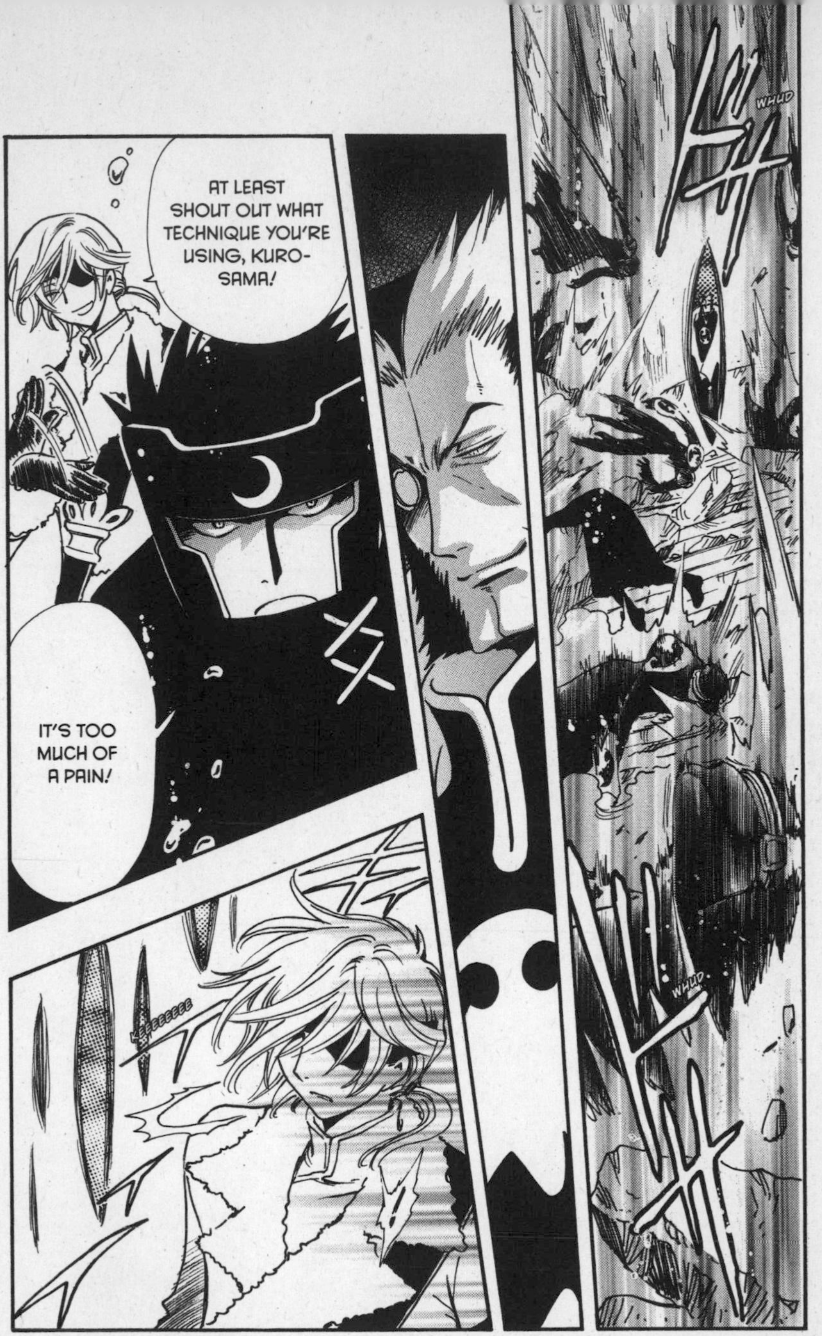
WHUD
WHUD
AT LEAST SHOUT OUT WHAT TECHNIQUE YOU'RE USING, KURO-SAMA!
IT'S TOO MUCH OF A PAIN!
KEEEEEEEEE

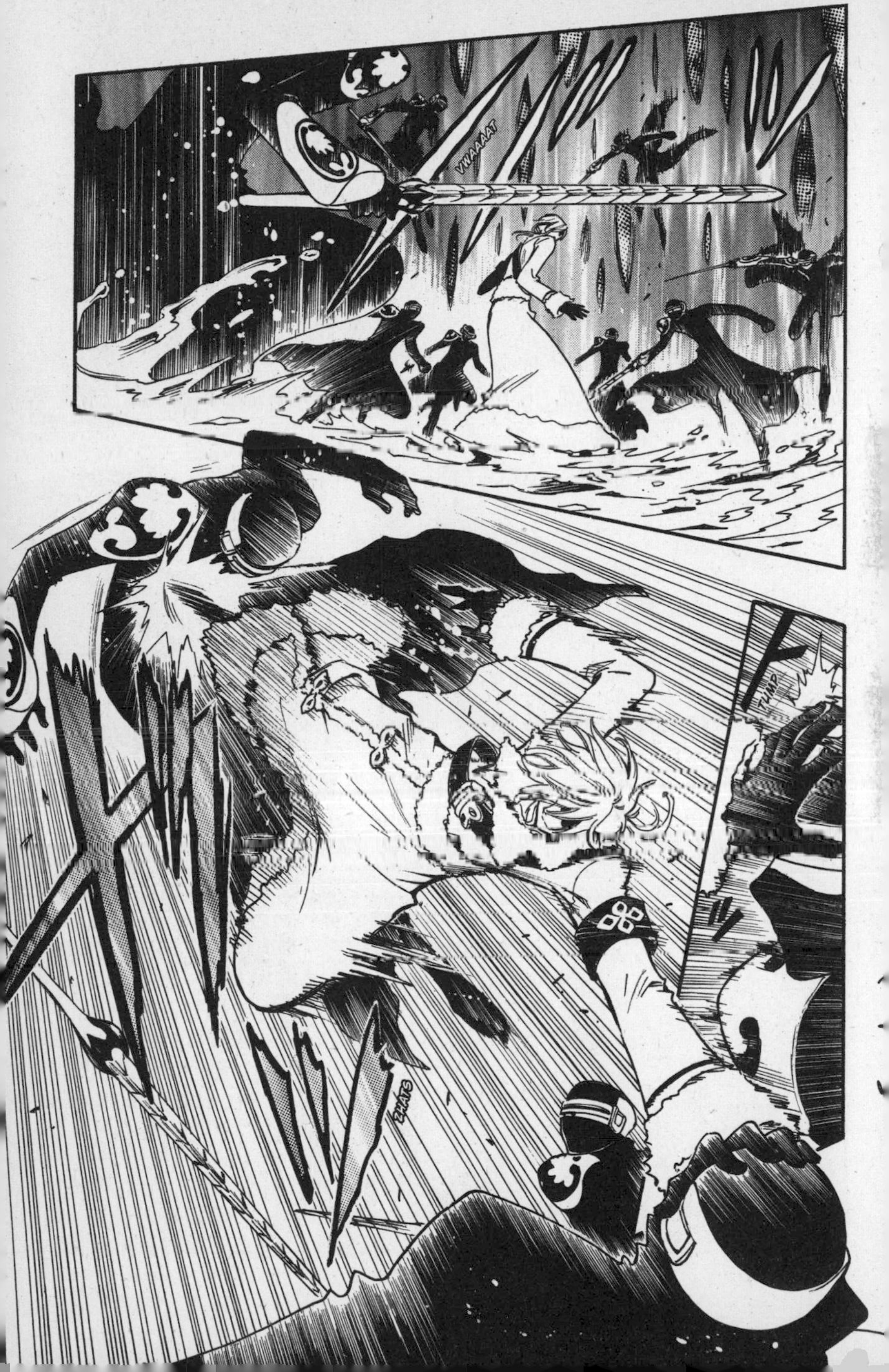
VWAAAAT
TUMP
ZHATS

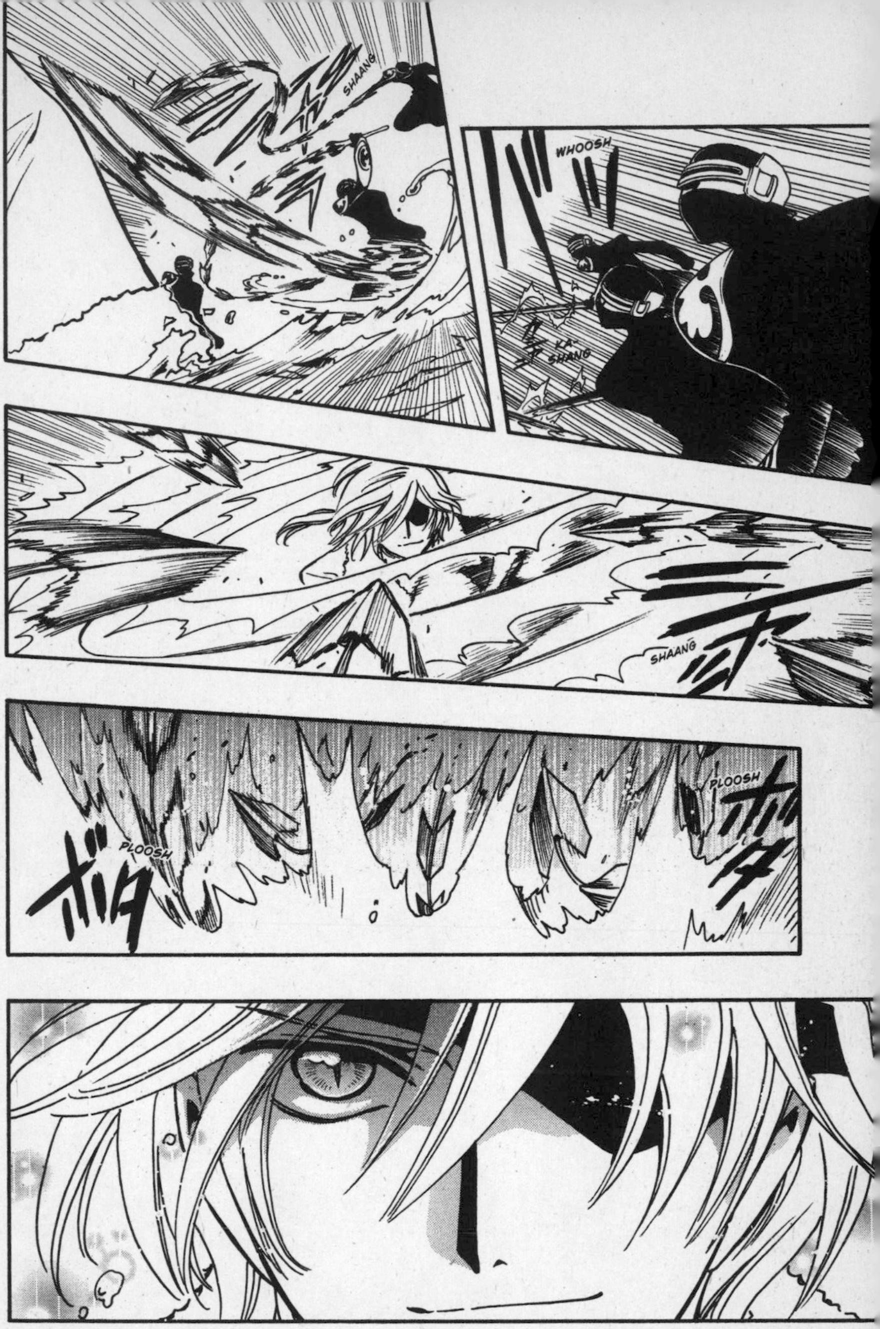
WHOOSH
KA-SHANG
SHAANG
SHAANG
PLOOSH
PLOOSH

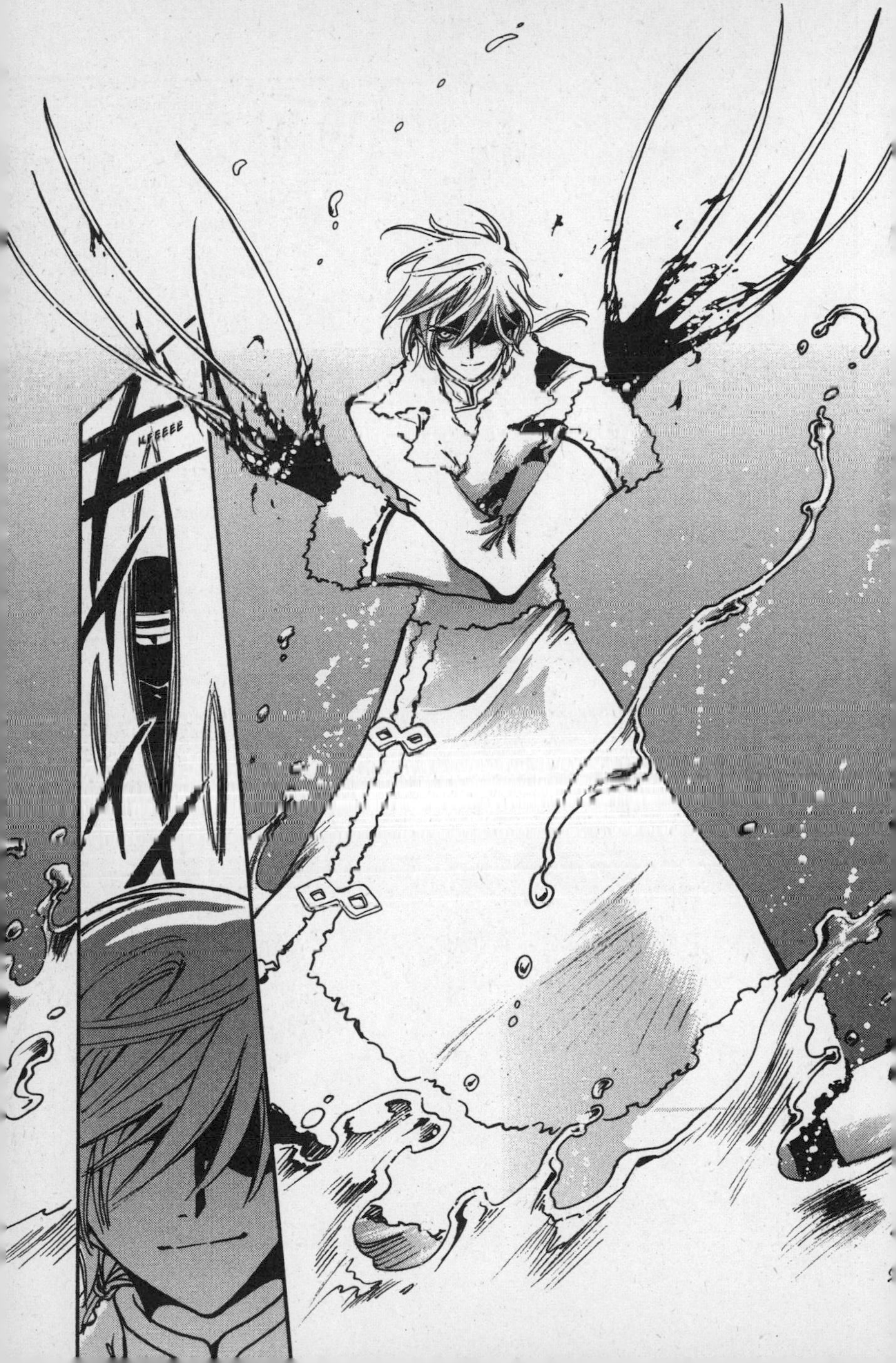

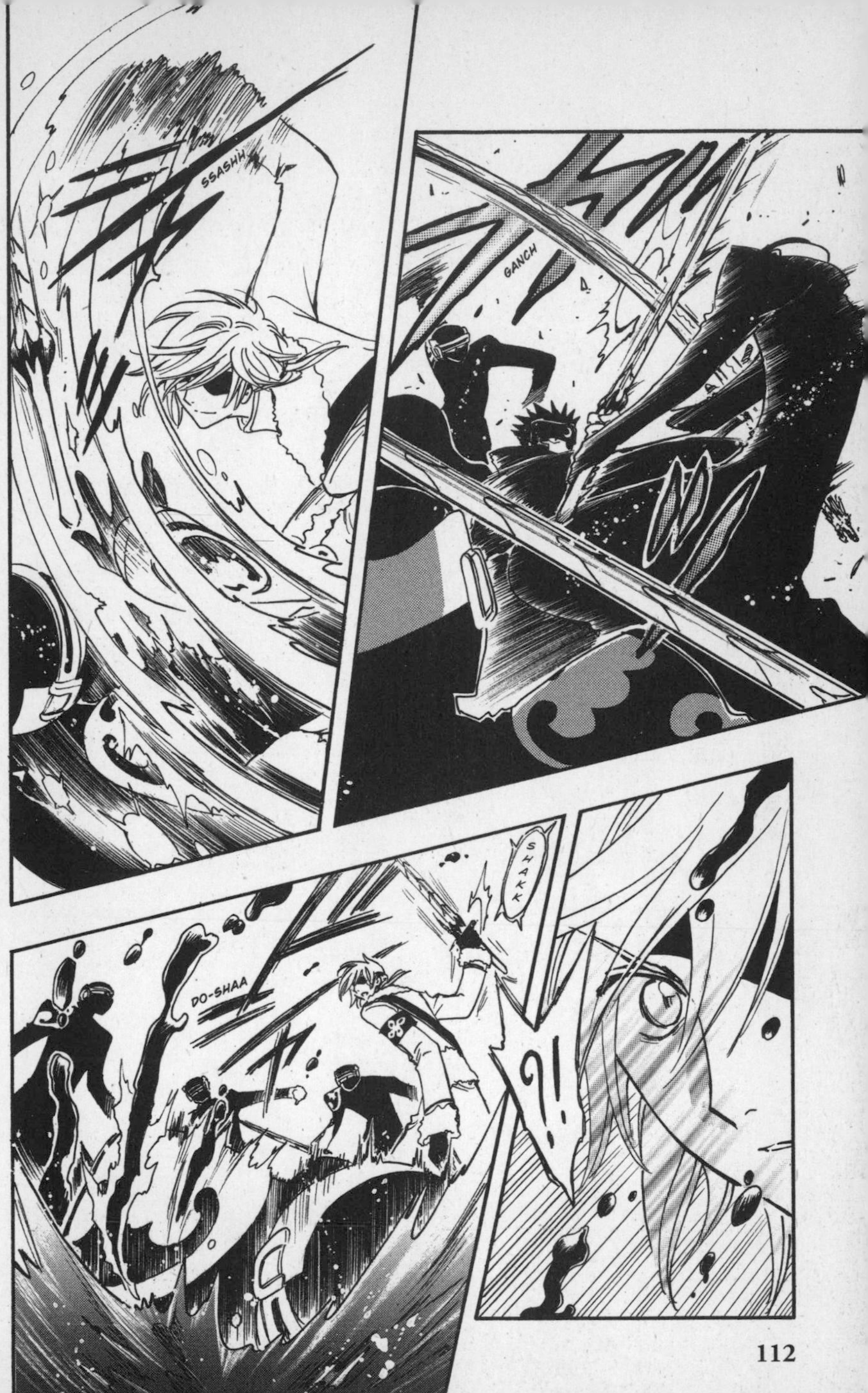
GANCH
SSASHH
SHAKK
?!
DO-SHAA

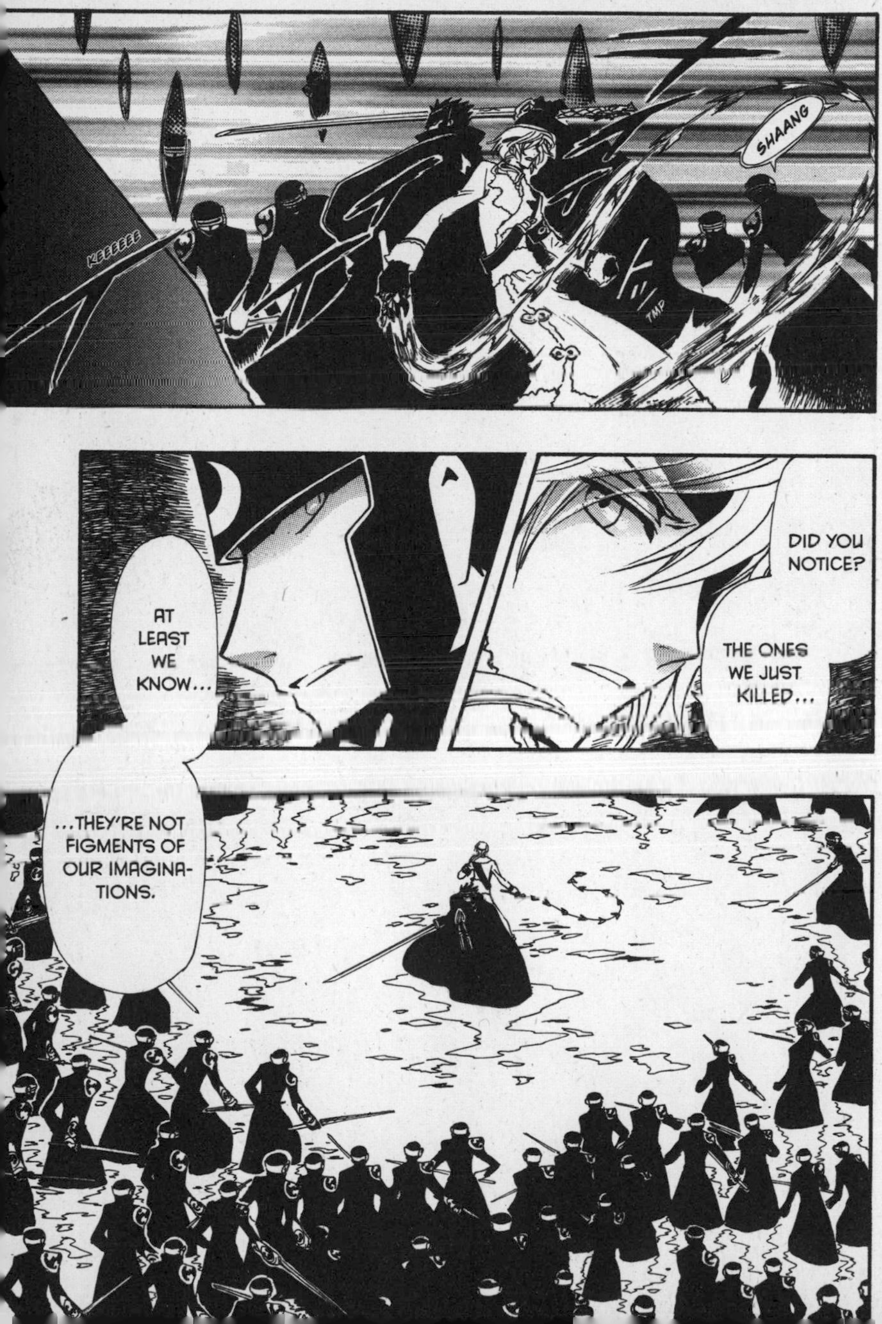
SHAANG
TMP
KEEEEEE
DID YOU NOTICE?
THE ONES WE JUST KILLED...
AT LEAST WE KNOW...
...THEY'RE NOT FIGMENTS OF OUR IMAGINATIONS.

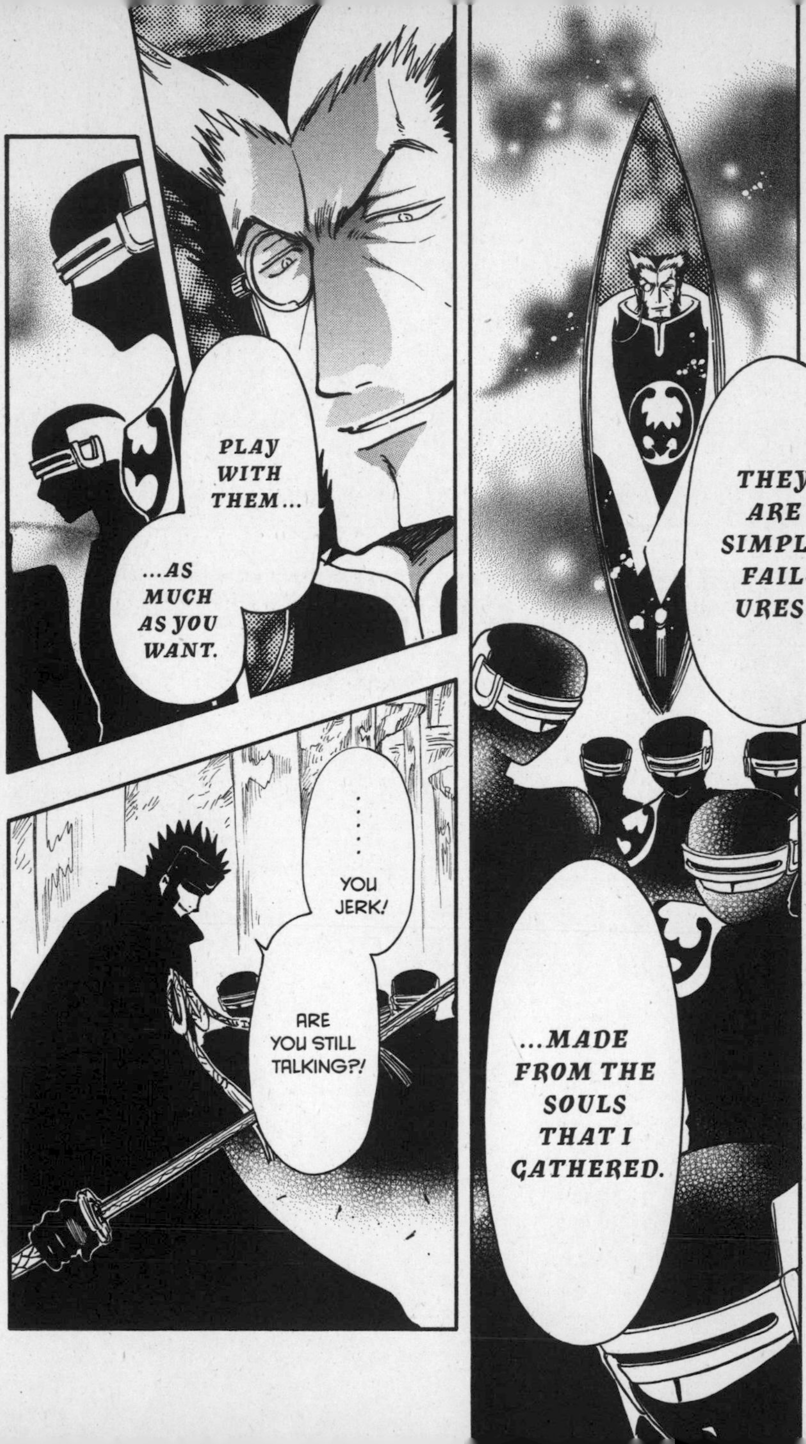
THEY ARE SIMPLY FAIL-URES...
...MADE FROM THE SOULS THAT I GATHERED.
PLAY WITH THEM...
...AS MUCH AS YOU WANT.
.....
YOU JERK!
ARE YOU STILL TALKING?!

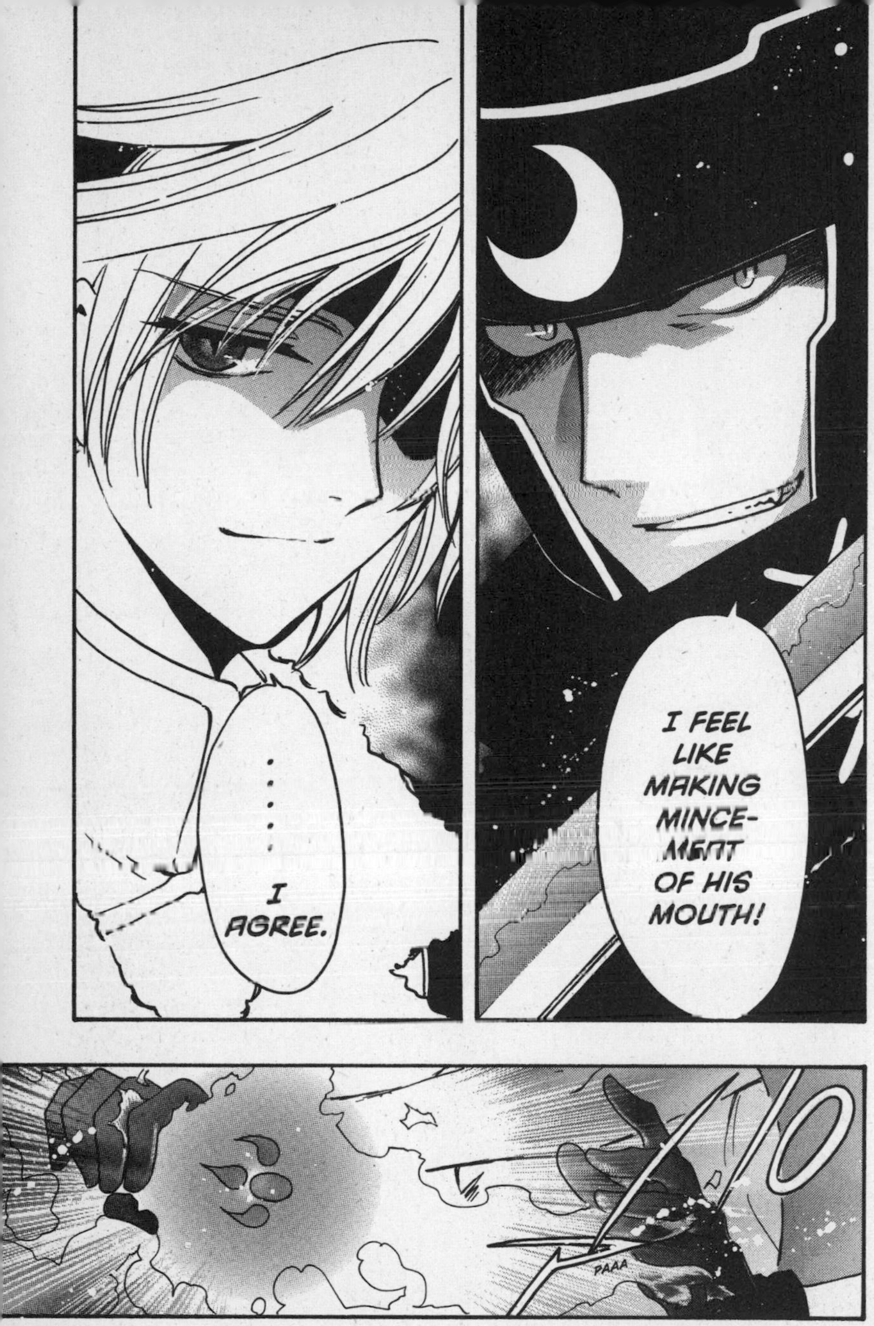
I FEEL LIKE MAKING MINCE-MEAT OF HIS MOUTH!
...... I AGREE.
PAAA

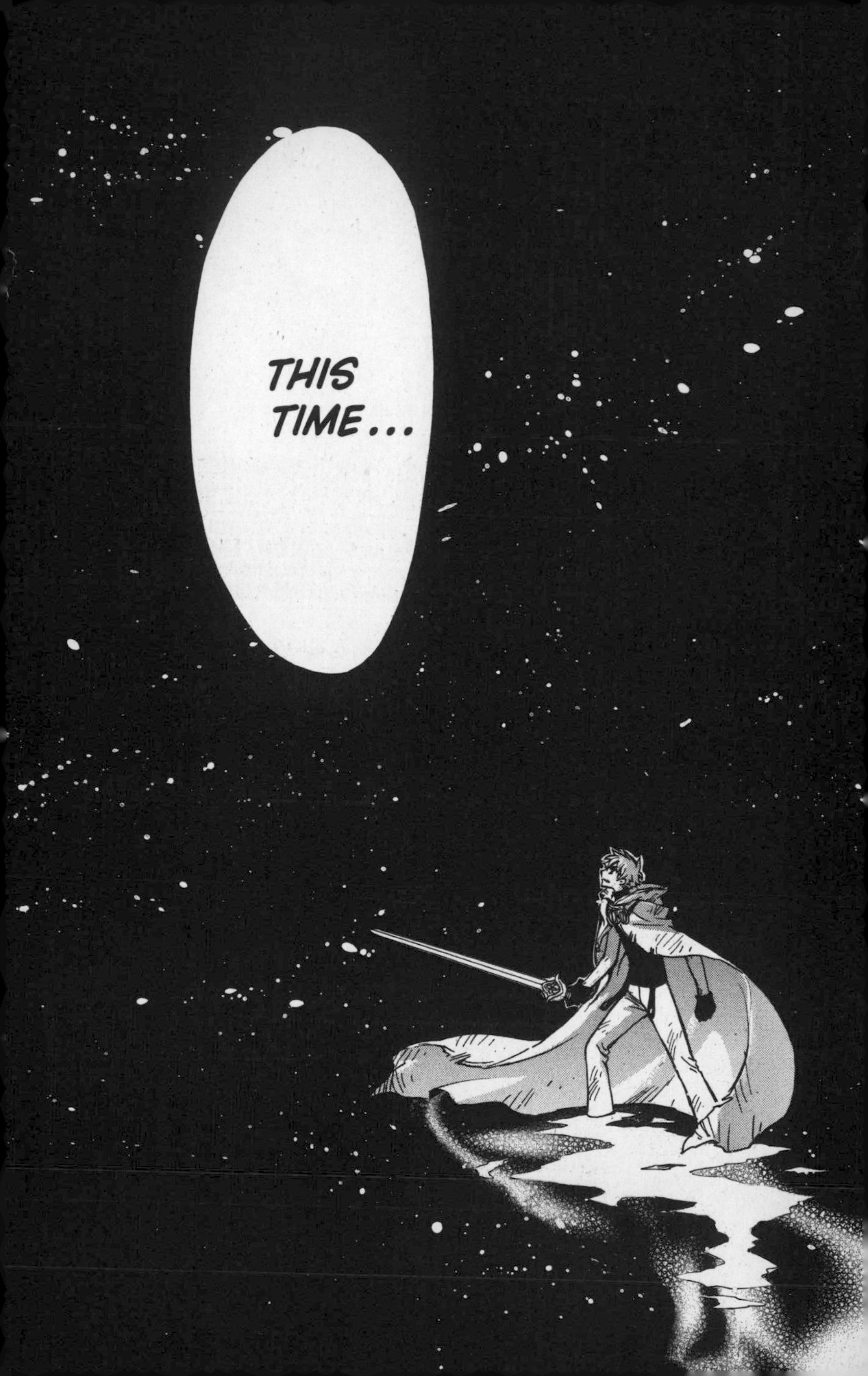
THIS TIME...

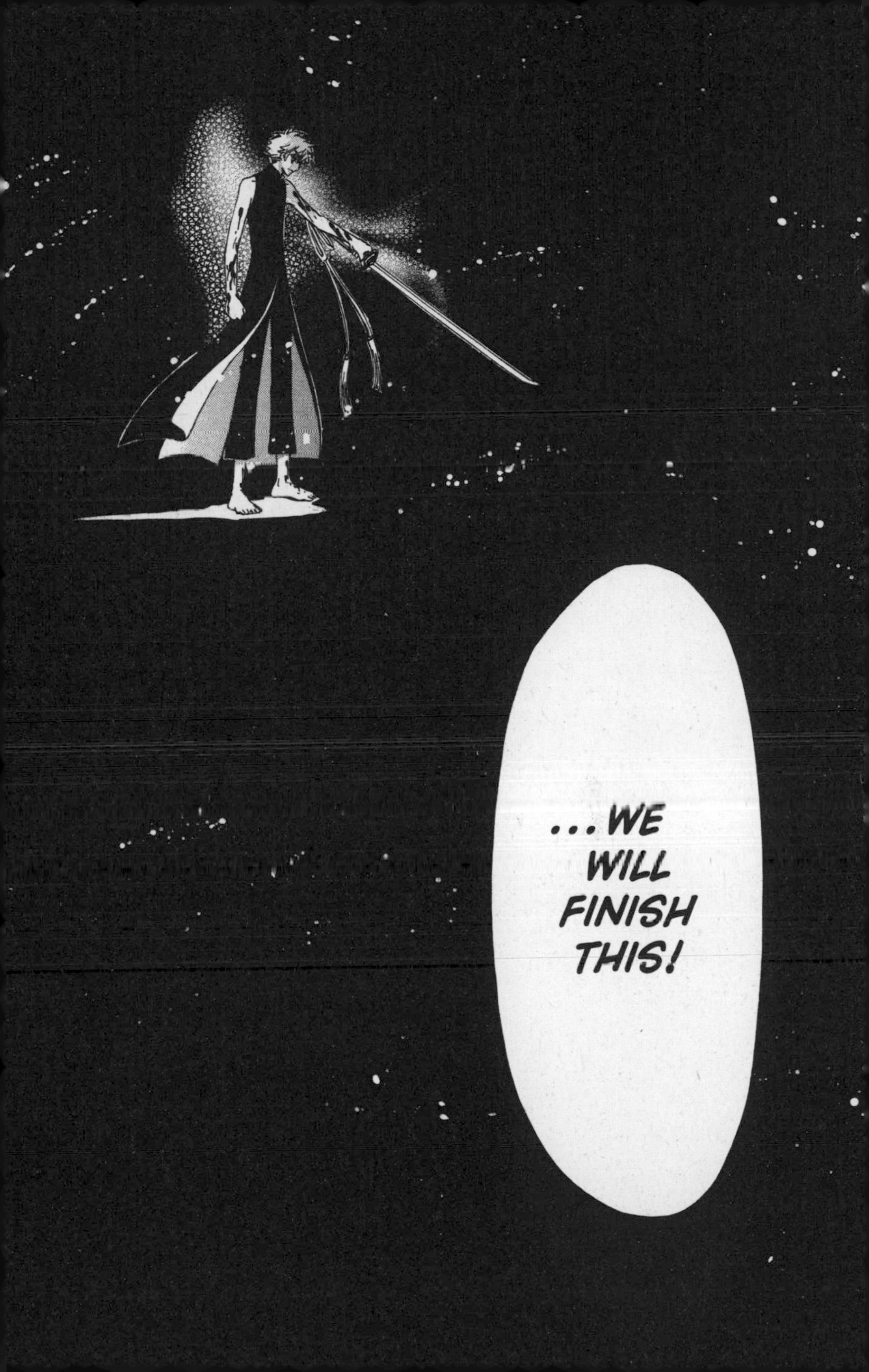
...WE WILL FINISH THIS!

ツバサ

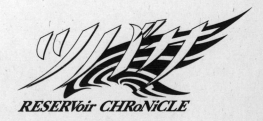

RESERVoir CHRoNiCLE

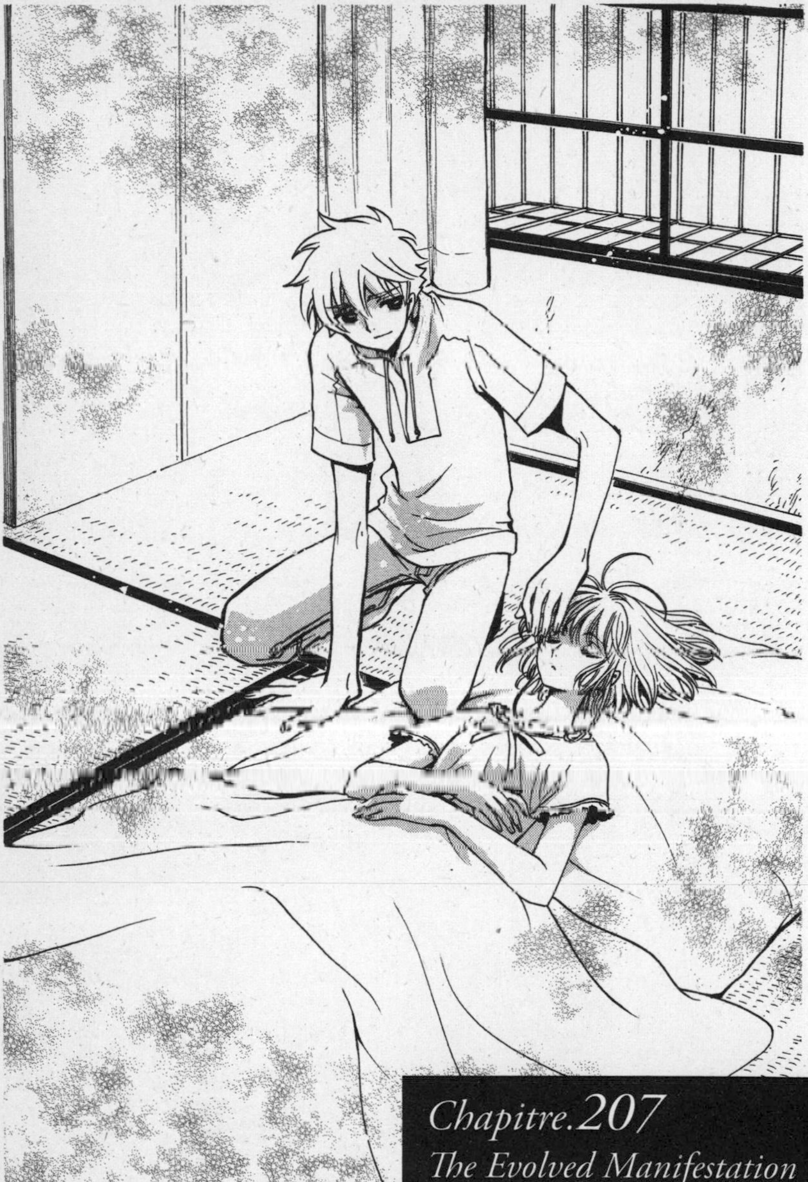

Chapitre.207
The Evolved Manifestation

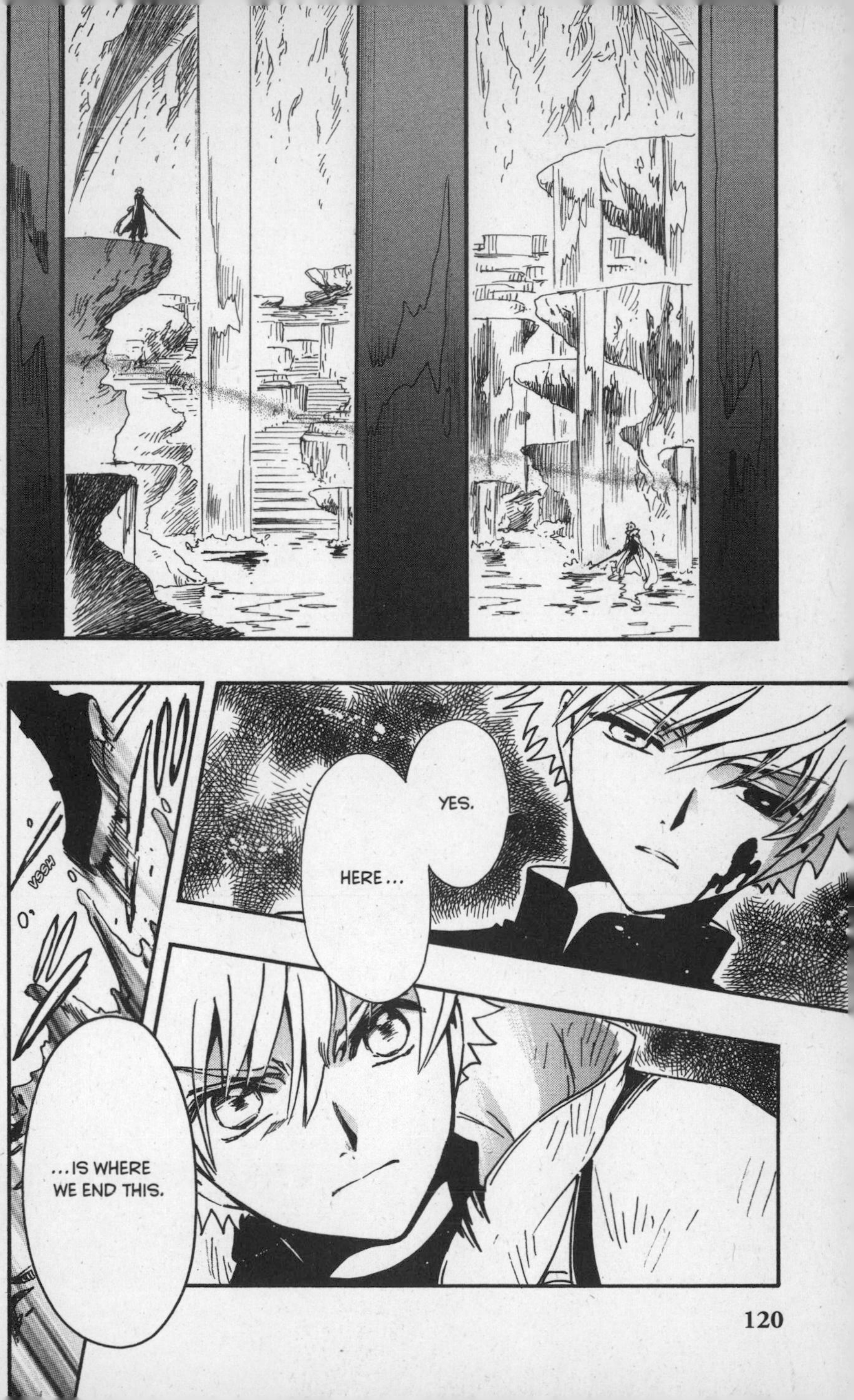
YES.
HERE...
...IS WHERE WE END THIS.

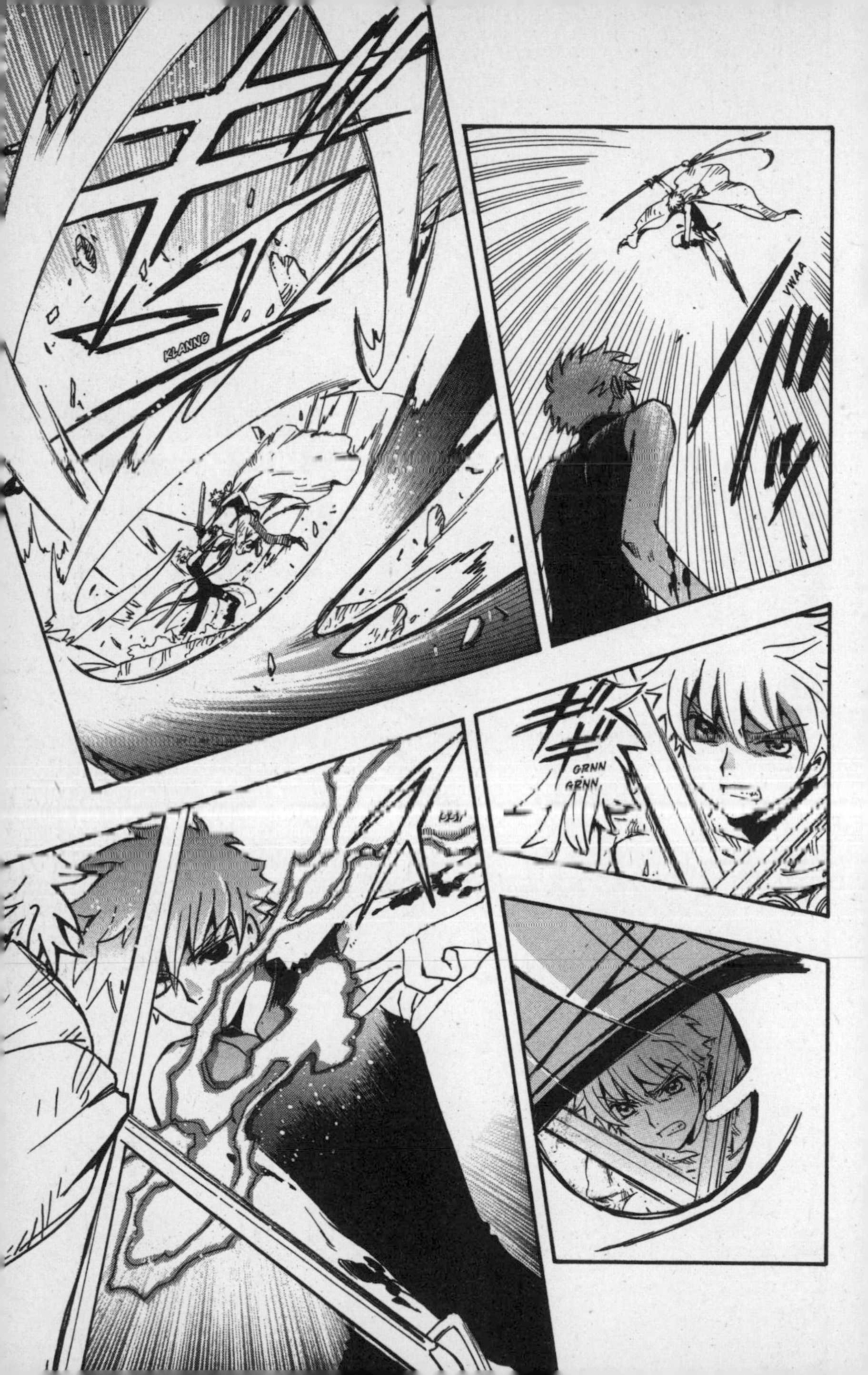
VWAA
KLANNG
GRNN
GRNN

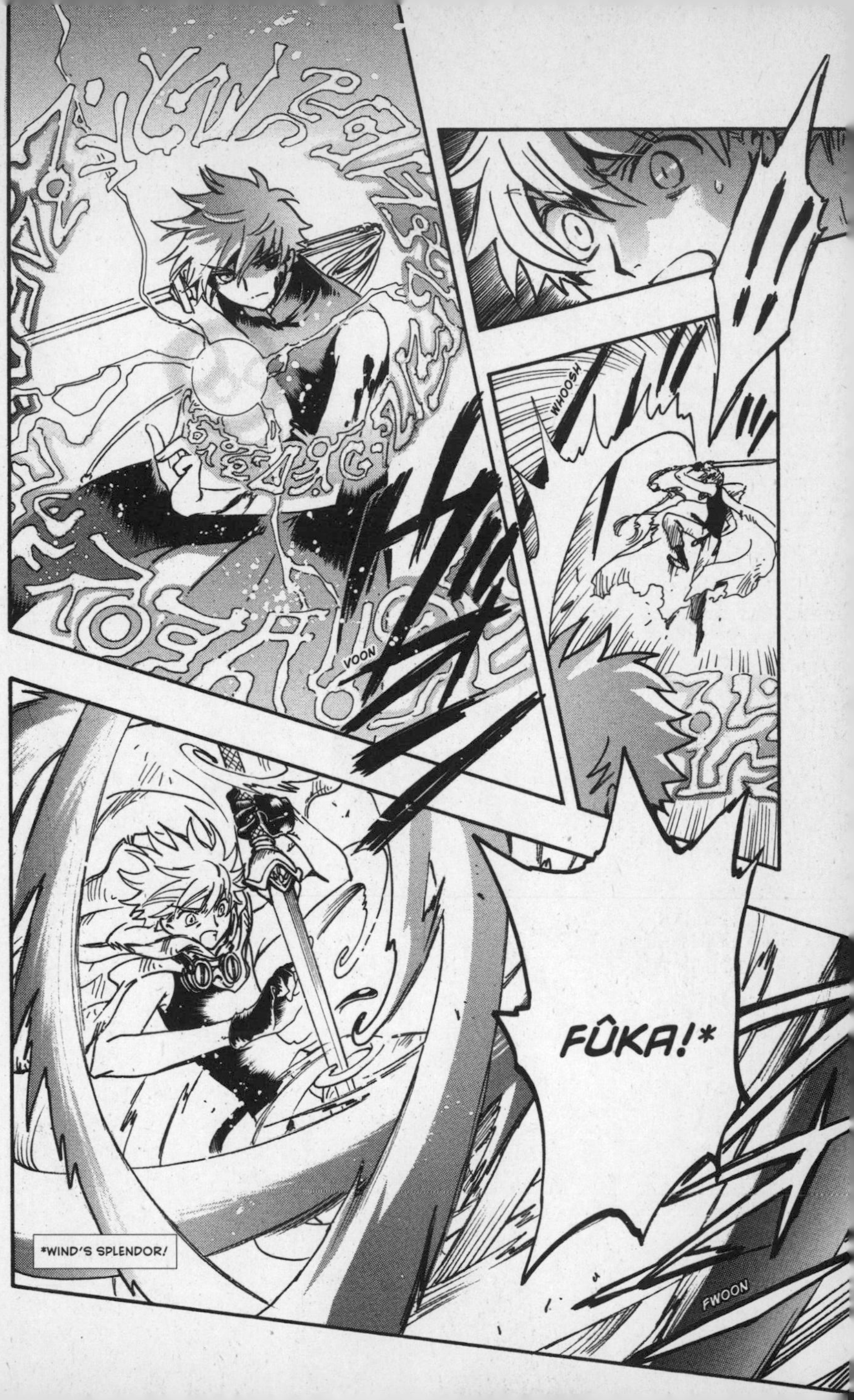
WHOOSH
VOON
FÛKA!*
FWOON
*WIND'S SPLENDOR!

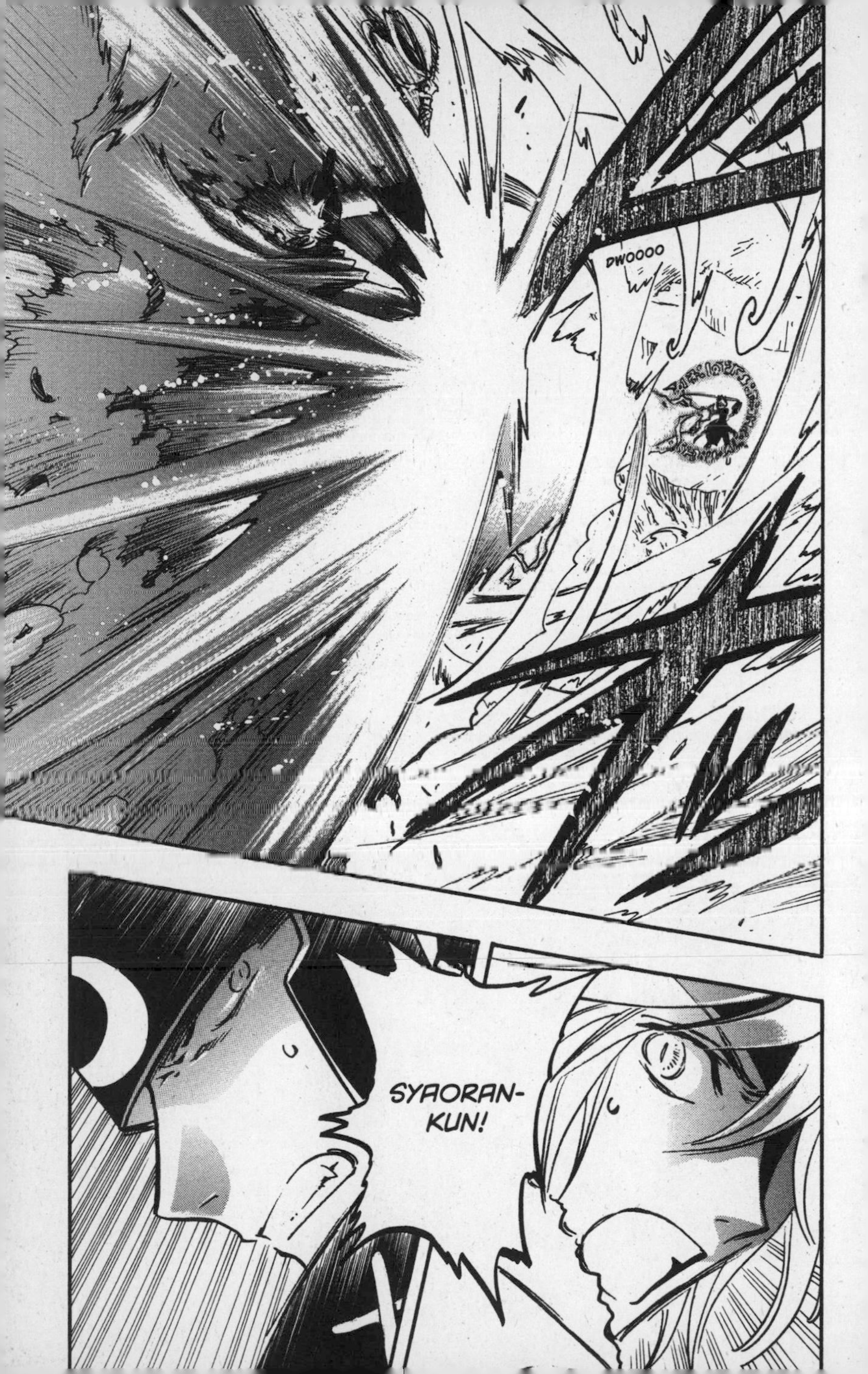
DWOOOO
SYAORAN-
KUN!

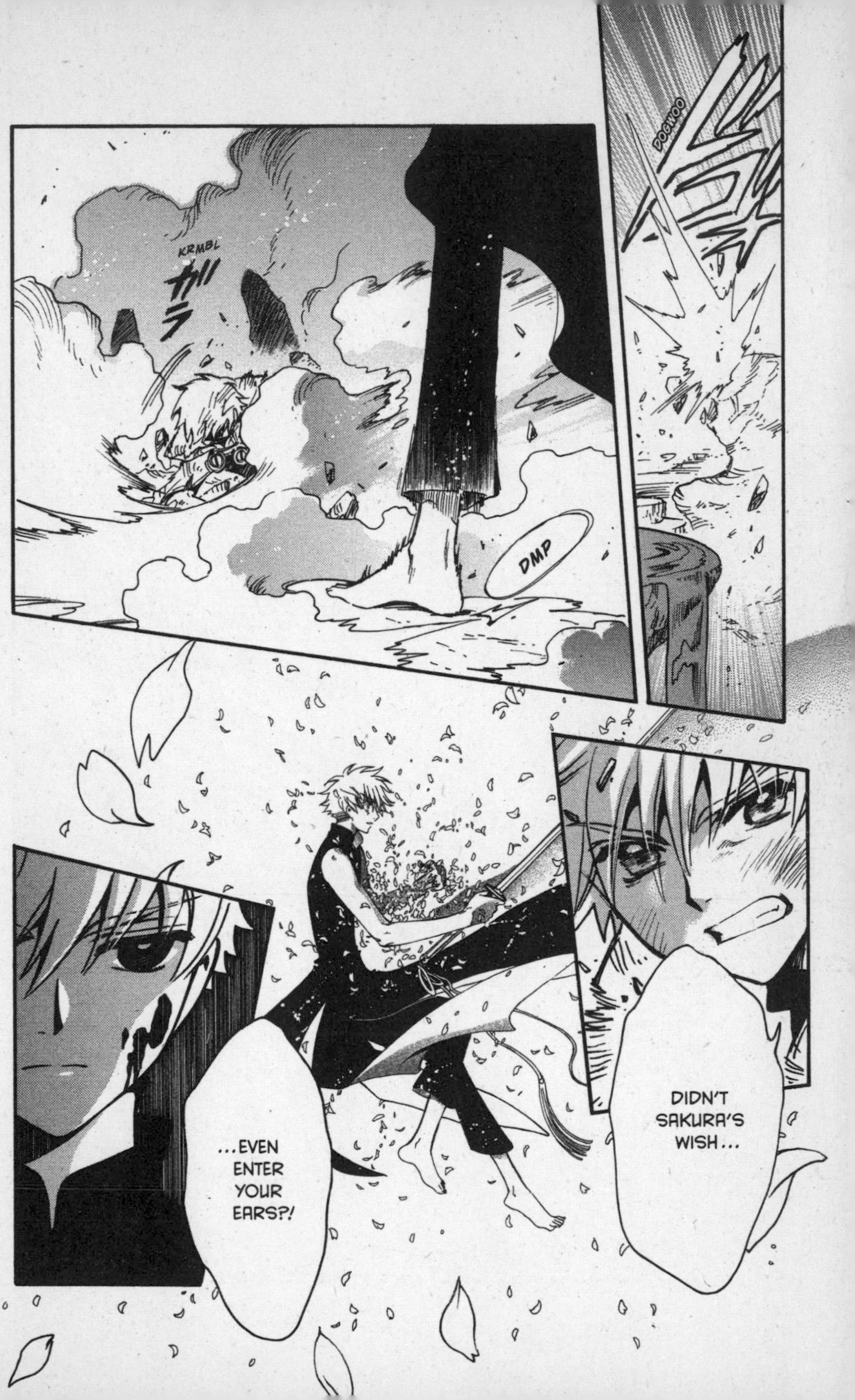
DOGWOO
KRMBL
ガラ
DMP
DIDN'T SAKURA'S WISH...
...EVEN ENTER YOUR EARS?!

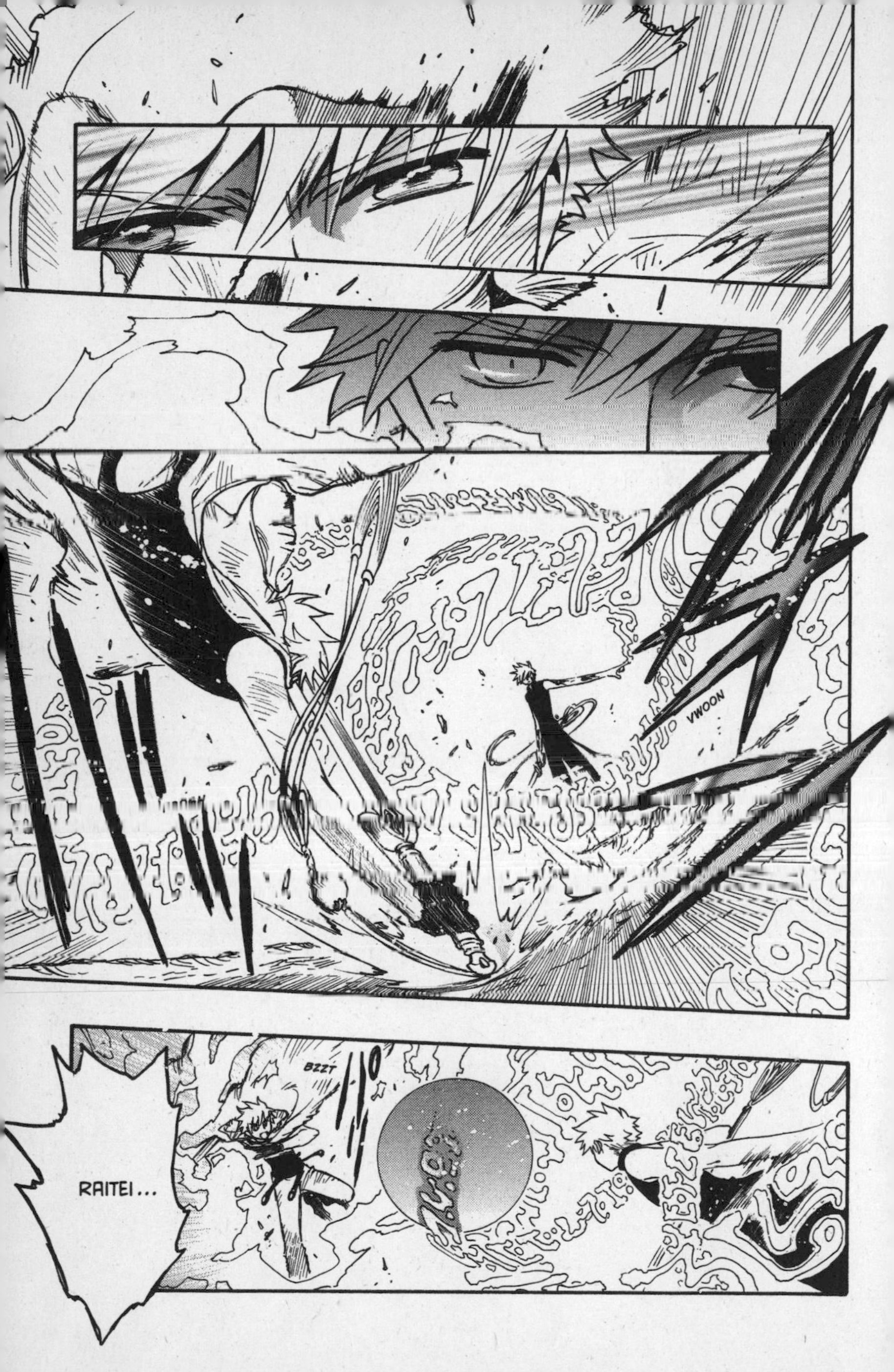
VWOON
BZZT
RAITEI...

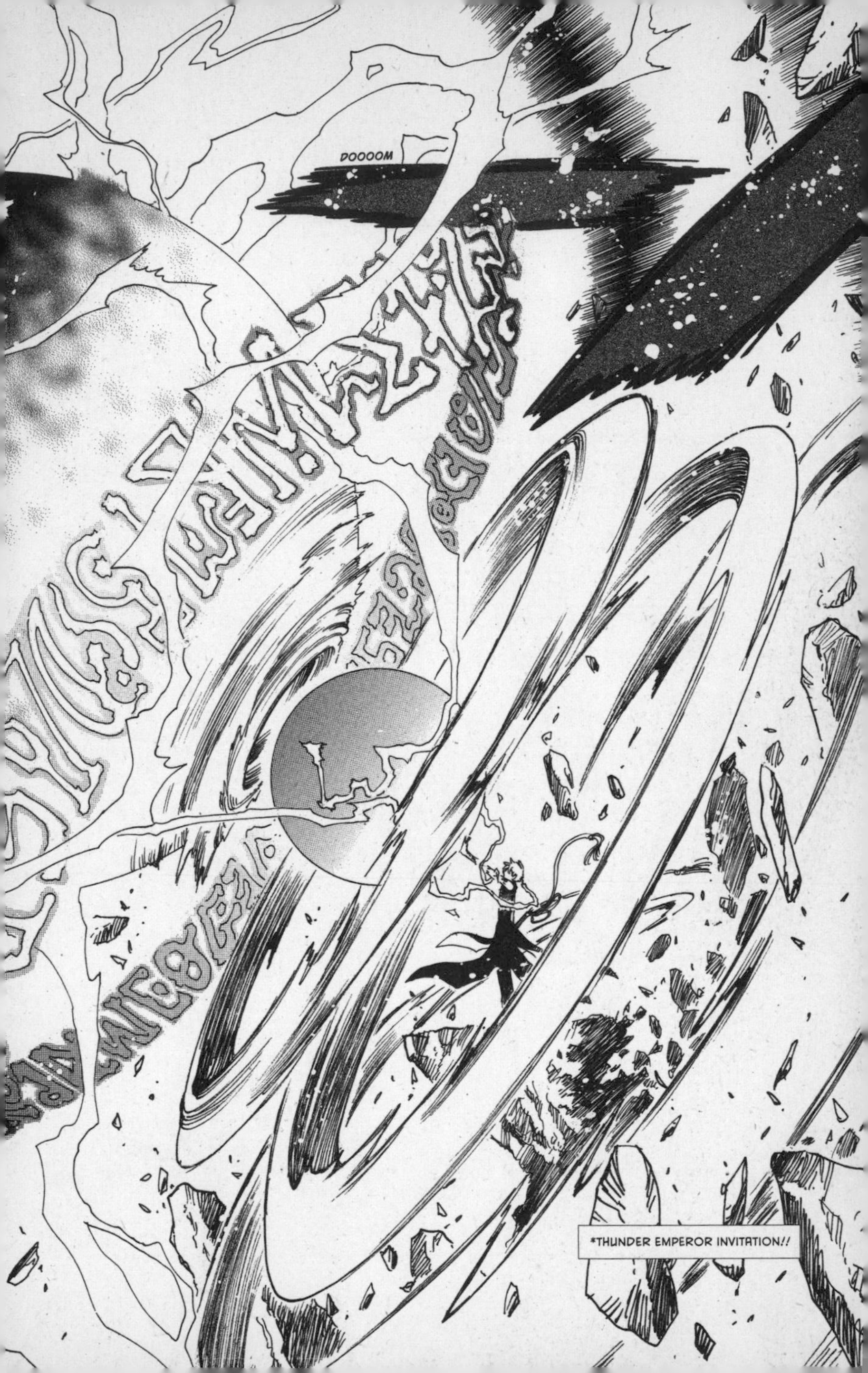
DOOOM
*THUNDER EMPEROR INVITATION!!

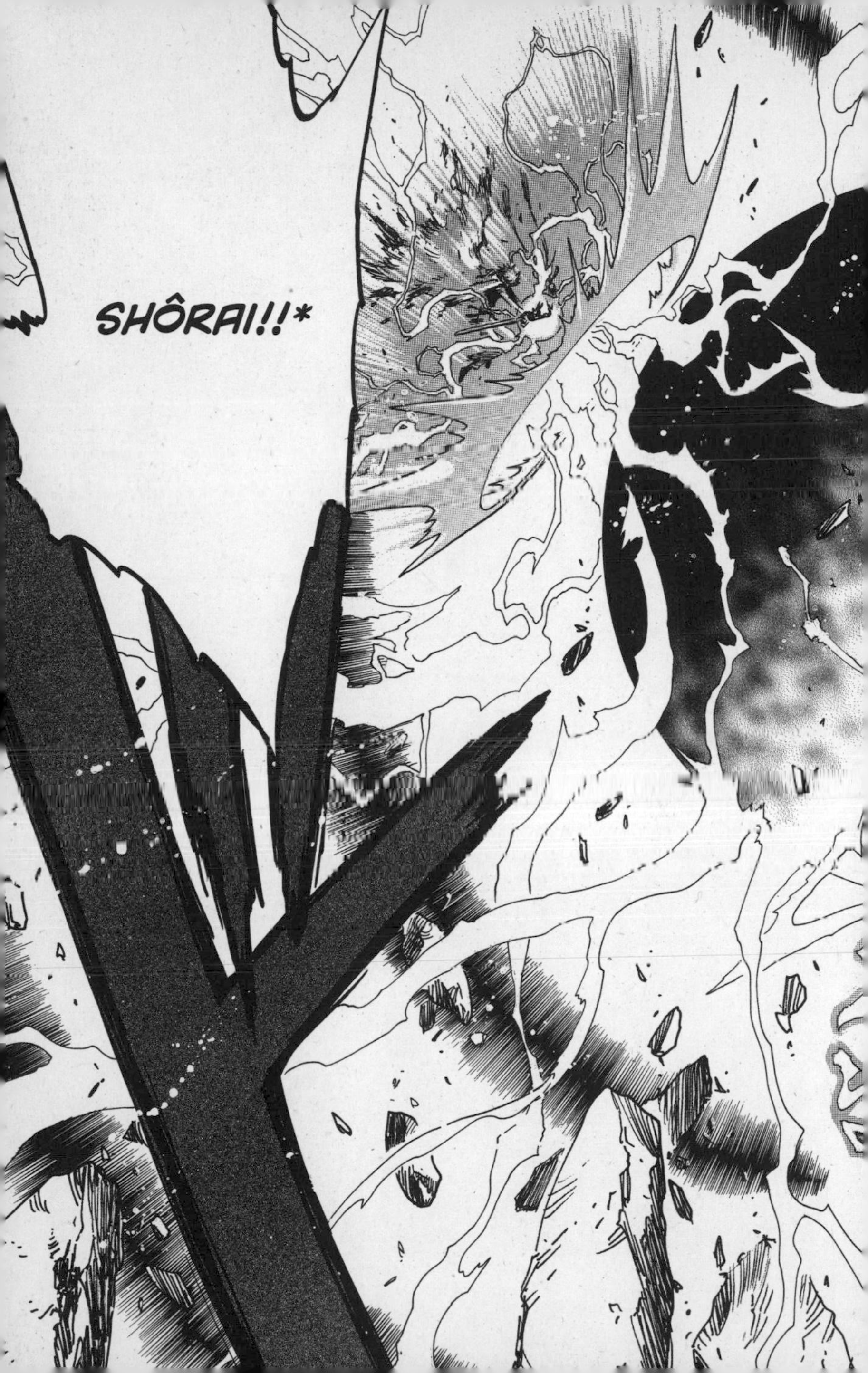
SHÔRAI!!*

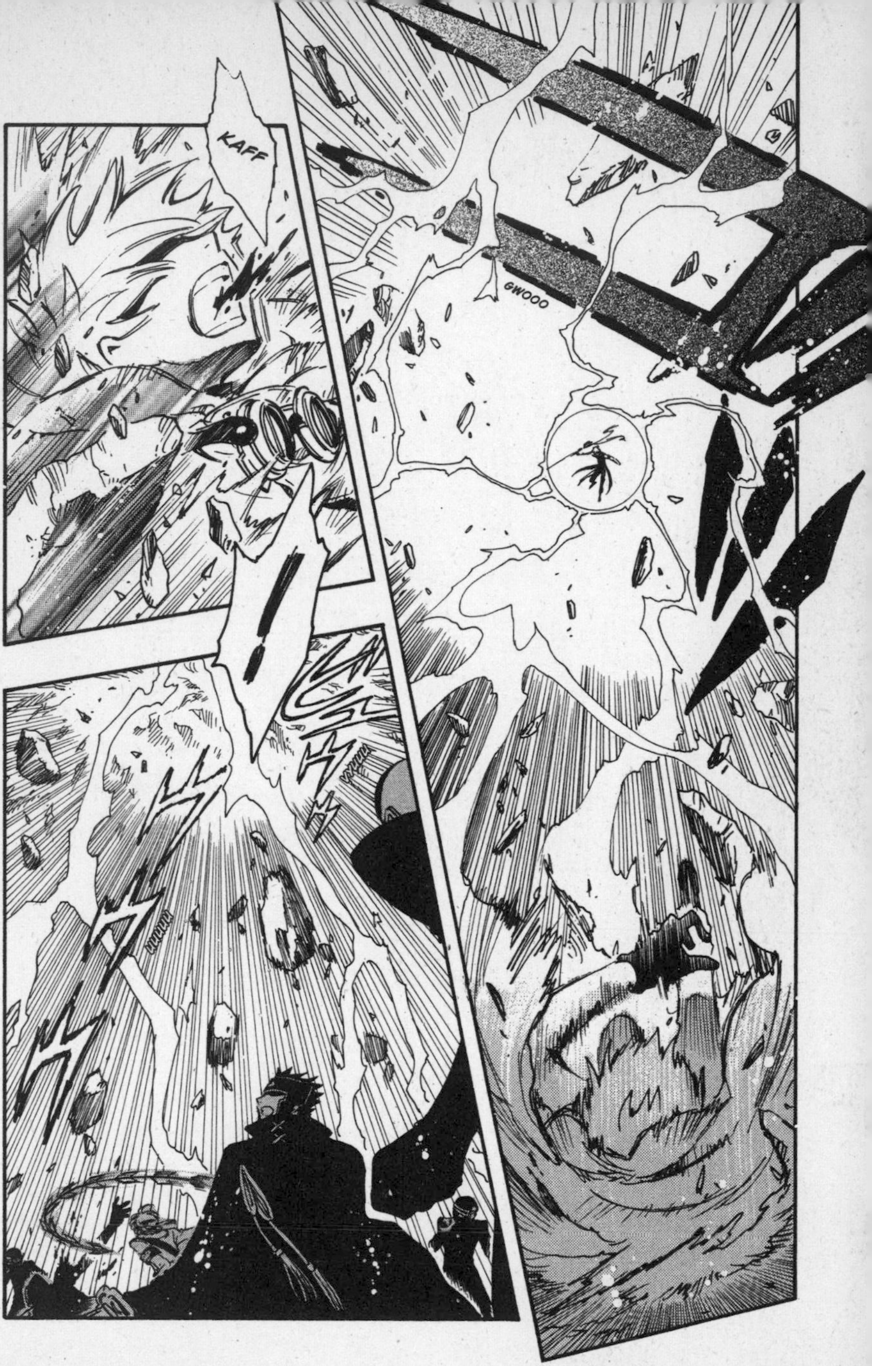
GWOOO
KAFF

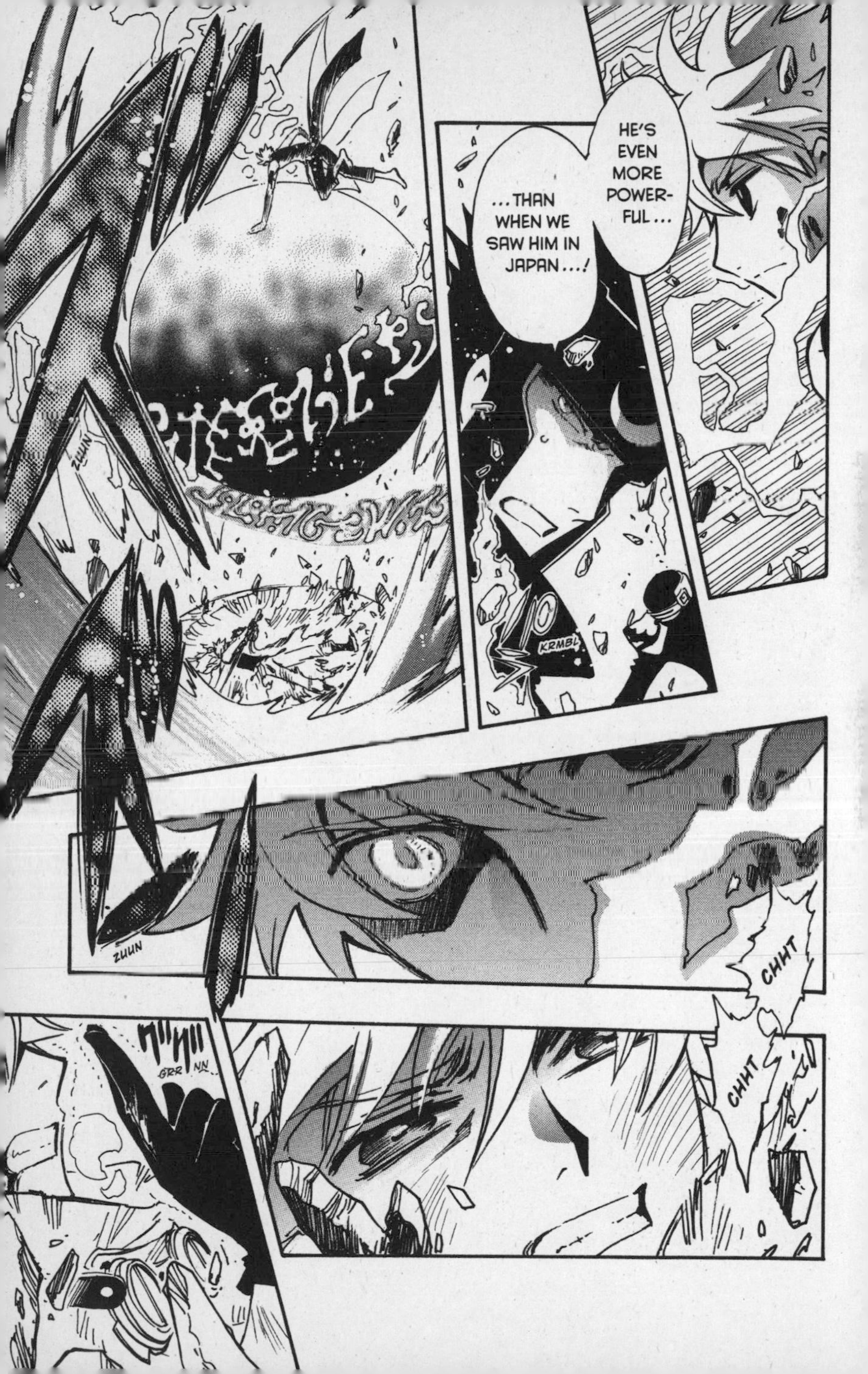
HE'S EVEN MORE POWER-FUL...
...THAN WHEN WE SAW HIM IN JAPAN...!
KRMBL
ZUUN
ZUUN
CHHT
CHHT
GRR NN

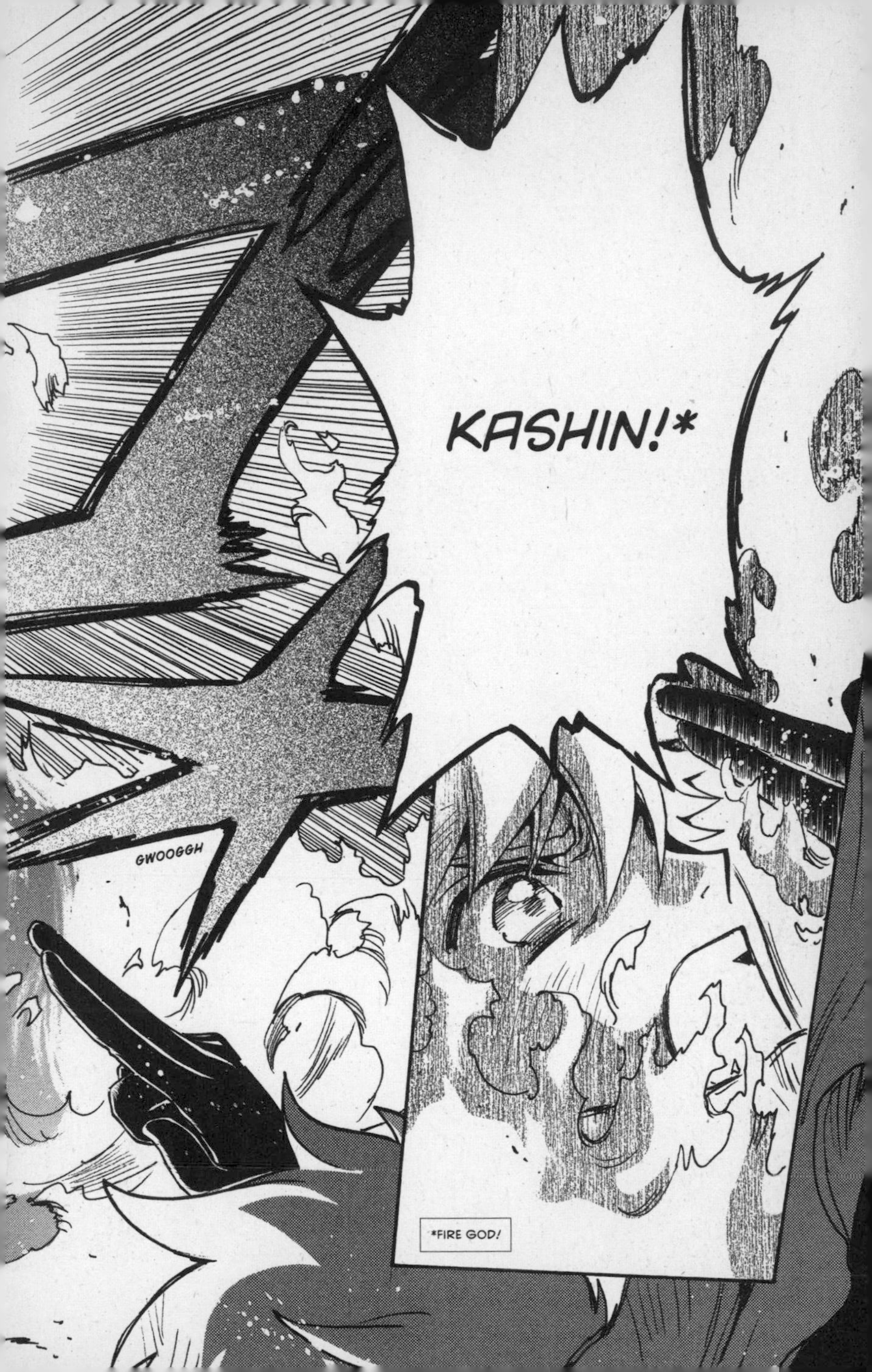
KASHIN!*
GWOOGGH
*FIRE GOD!

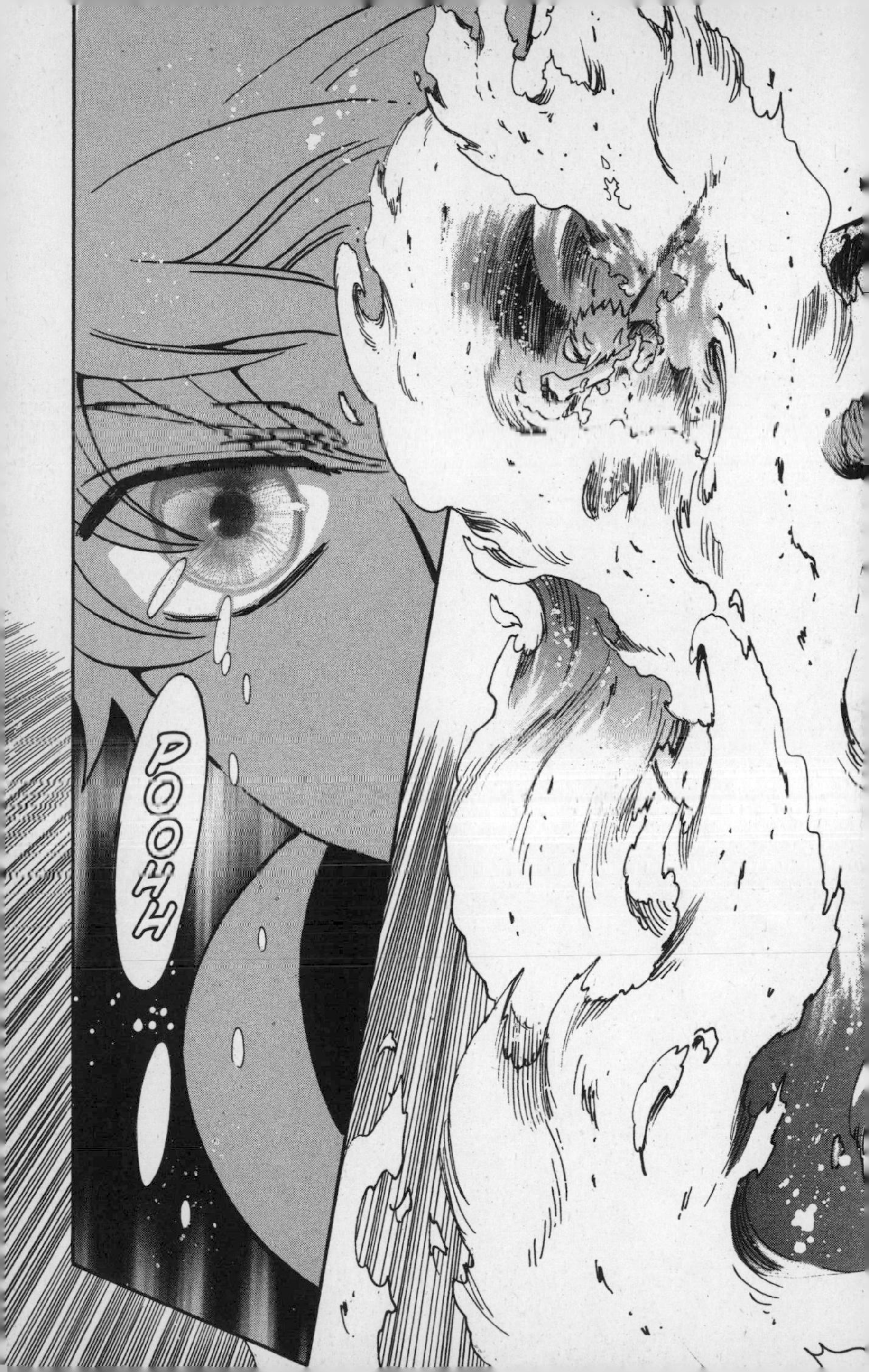
POOHH

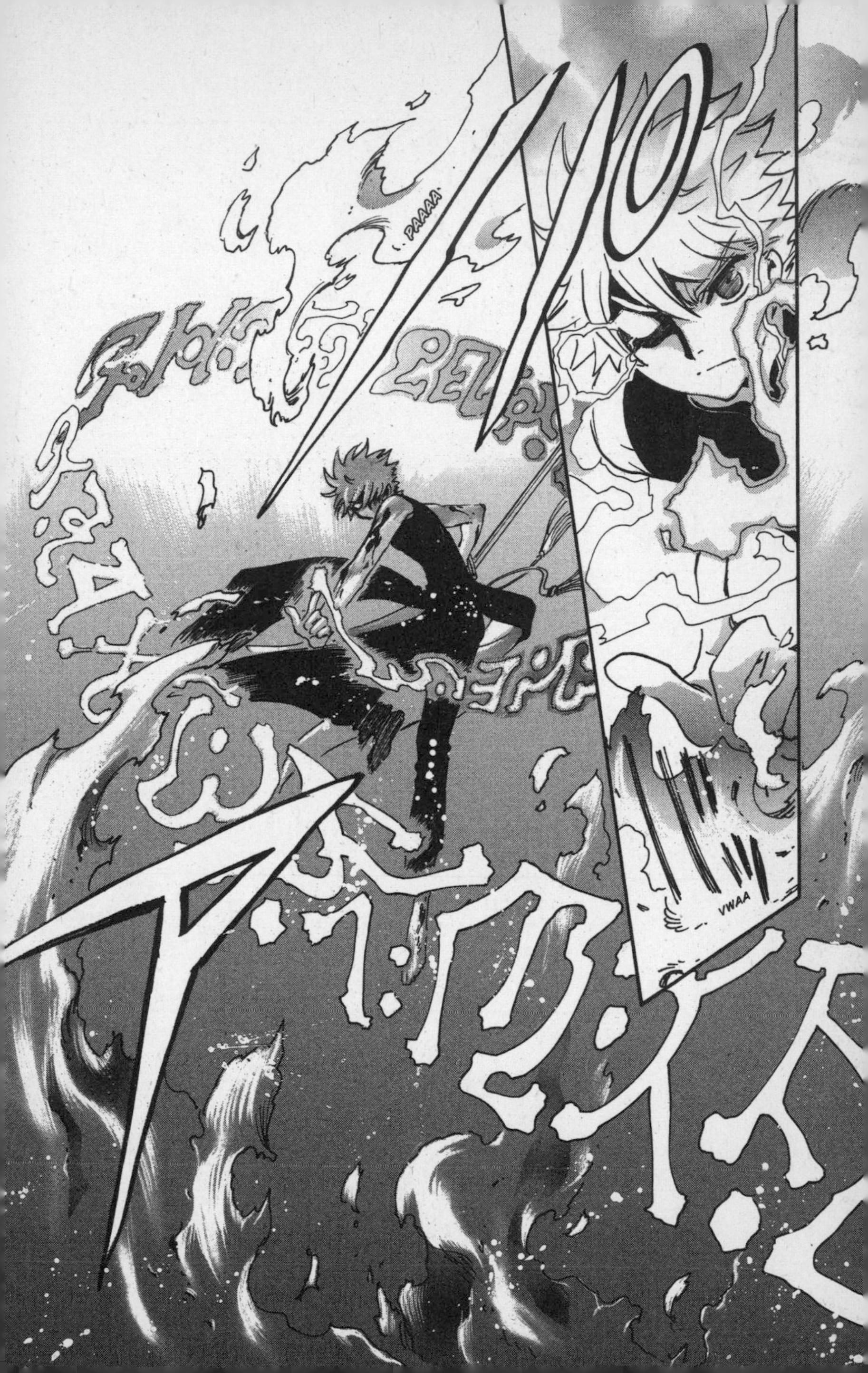
VWAA
PAAAA

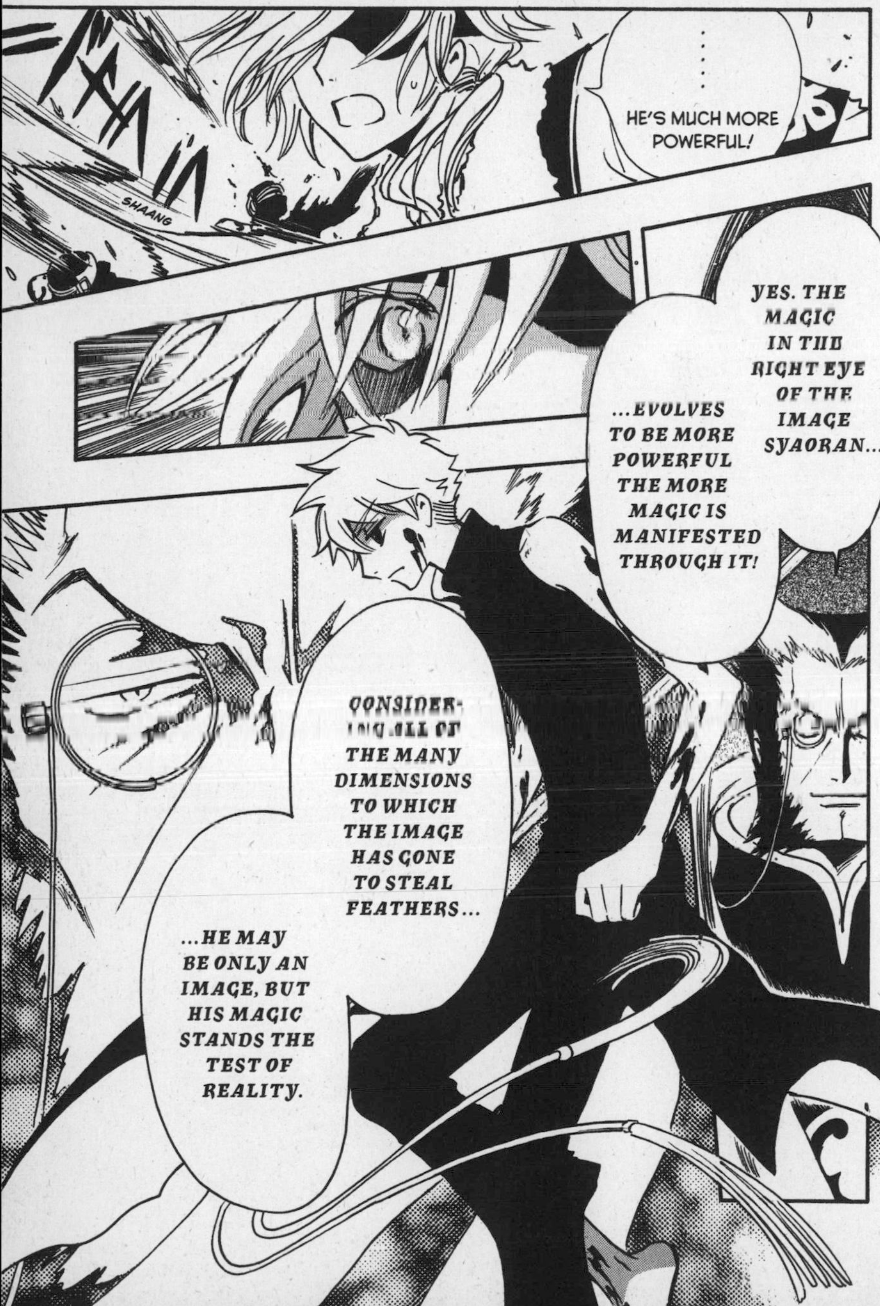
...
HE'S MUCH MORE POWERFUL!
SHAANG
YES. THE MAGIC IN THE RIGHT EYE OF THE IMAGE SYAORAN...
...EVOLVES TO BE MORE POWERFUL THE MORE MAGIC IS MANIFESTED THROUGH IT!
CONSIDER-ING ALL OF THE MANY DIMENSIONS TO WHICH THE IMAGE HAS GONE TO STEAL FEATHERS...
...HE MAY BE ONLY AN IMAGE, BUT HIS MAGIC STANDS THE TEST OF REALITY.

ツバサ

RESERVoir CHRoNiCLE

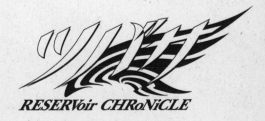

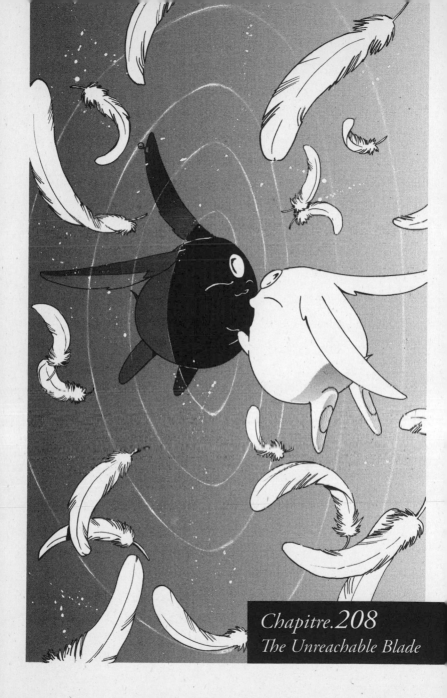

Chapitre.208
The Unreachable Blade

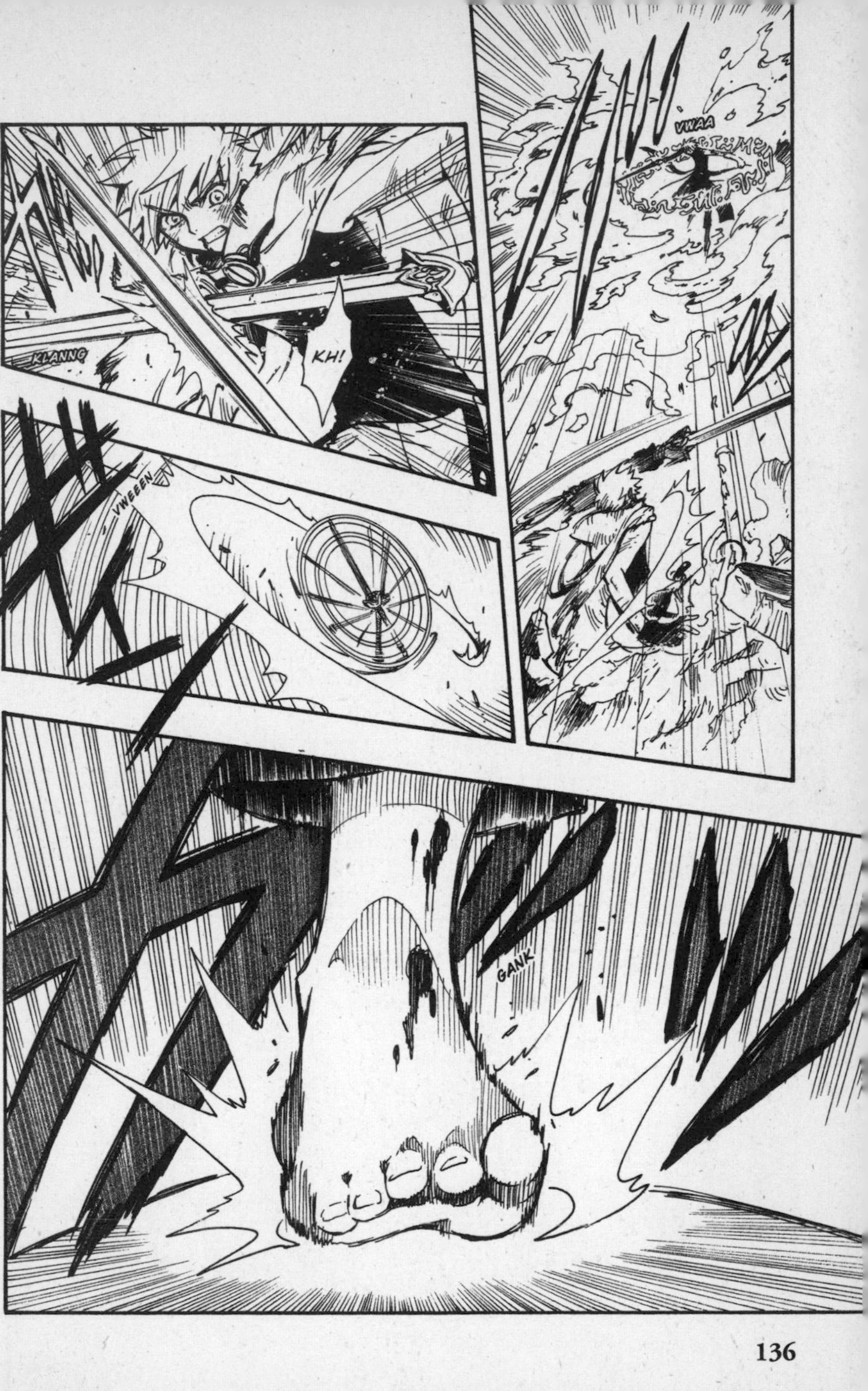
VWAA
KH!
KLANNG
VWEEEN
GANK

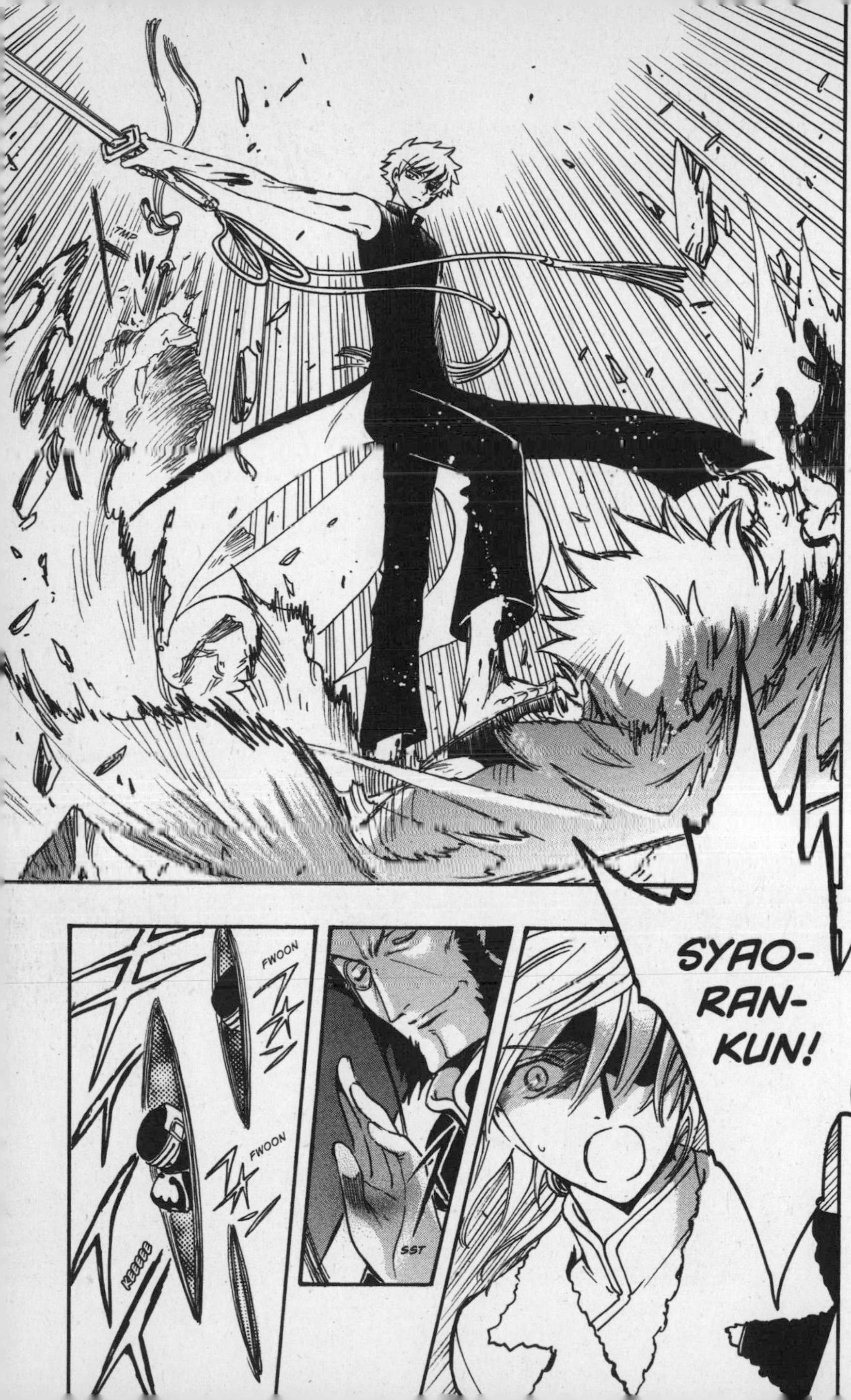
TMP
SYAO-RAN-KUN!
SST
FWOON
FWOON
KEEEEE

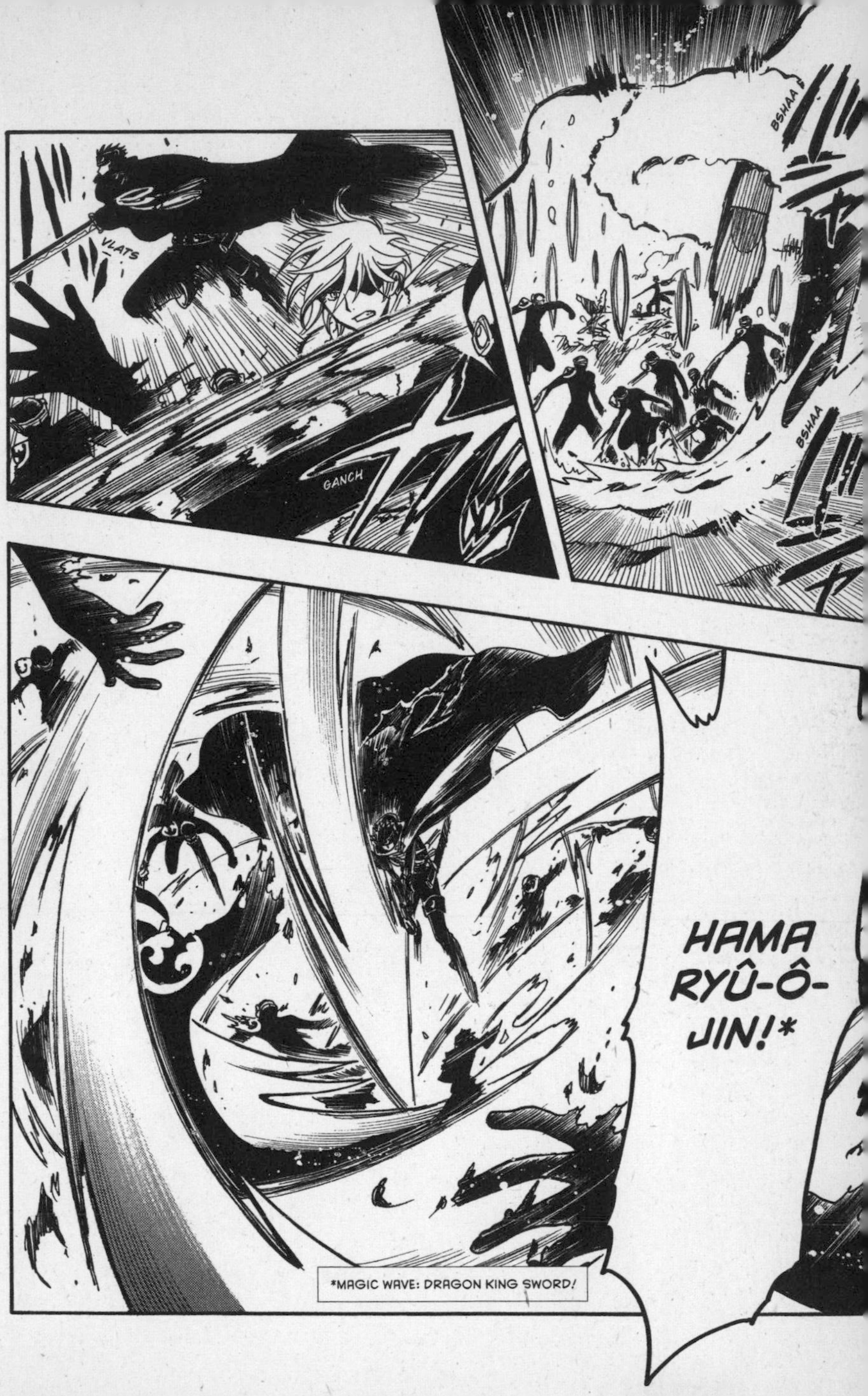
BSHAA
BSHAA
VLATS
GANCH
HAMA RYÛ-Ô-JIN!*
*MAGIC WAVE: DRAGON KING SWORD!

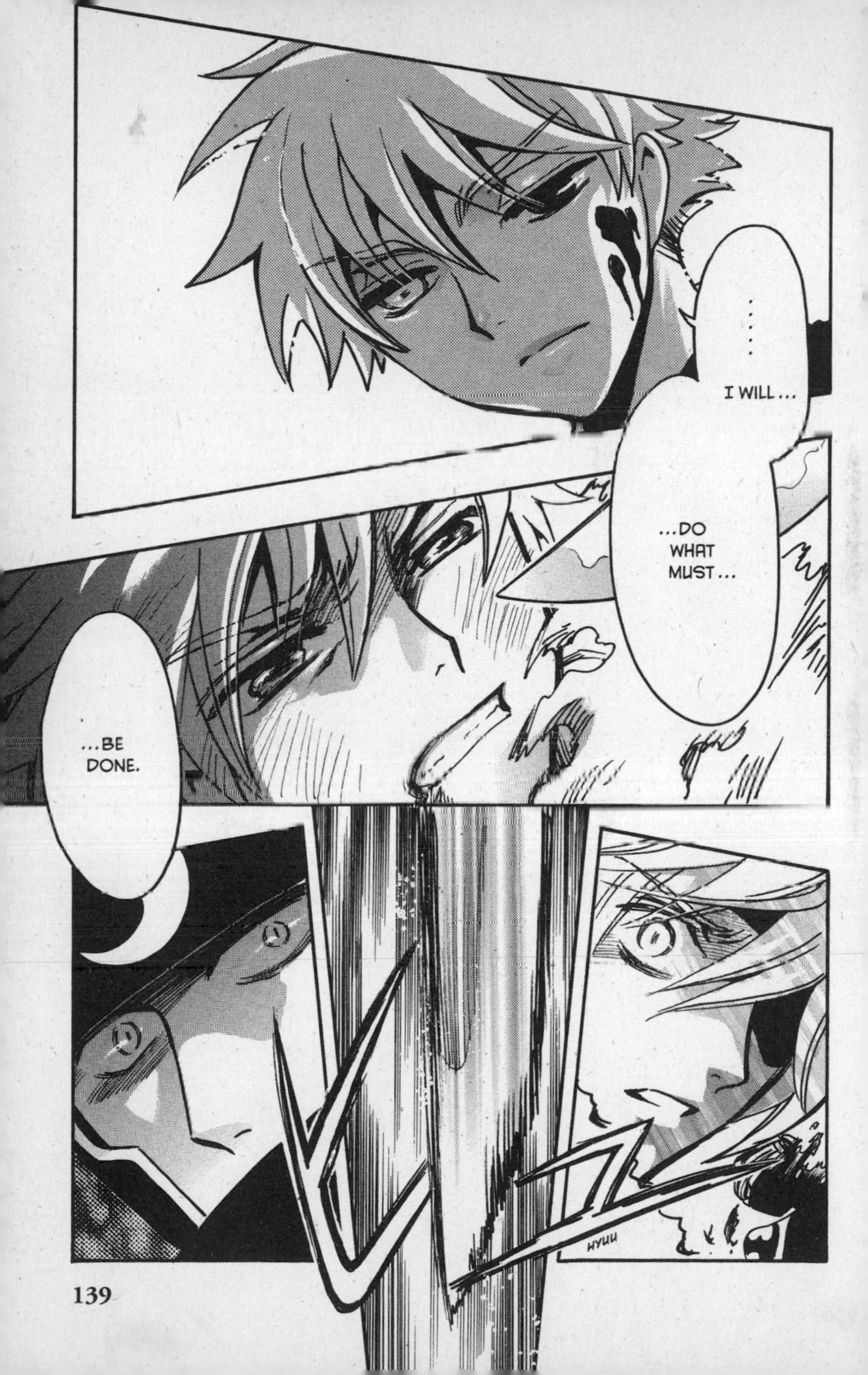
......
I WILL...
...DO WHAT MUST...
...BE DONE.
HYUU

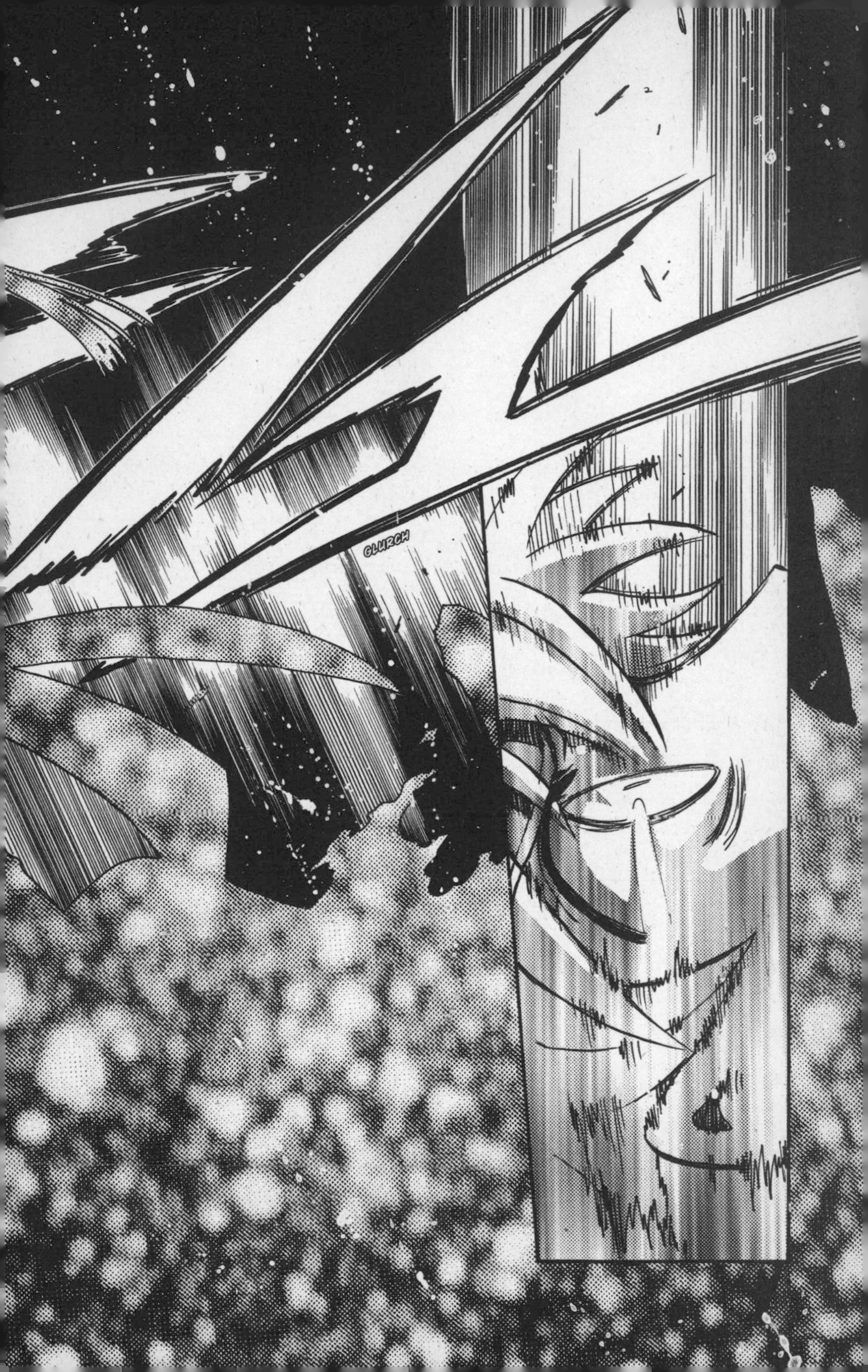
GLURCH

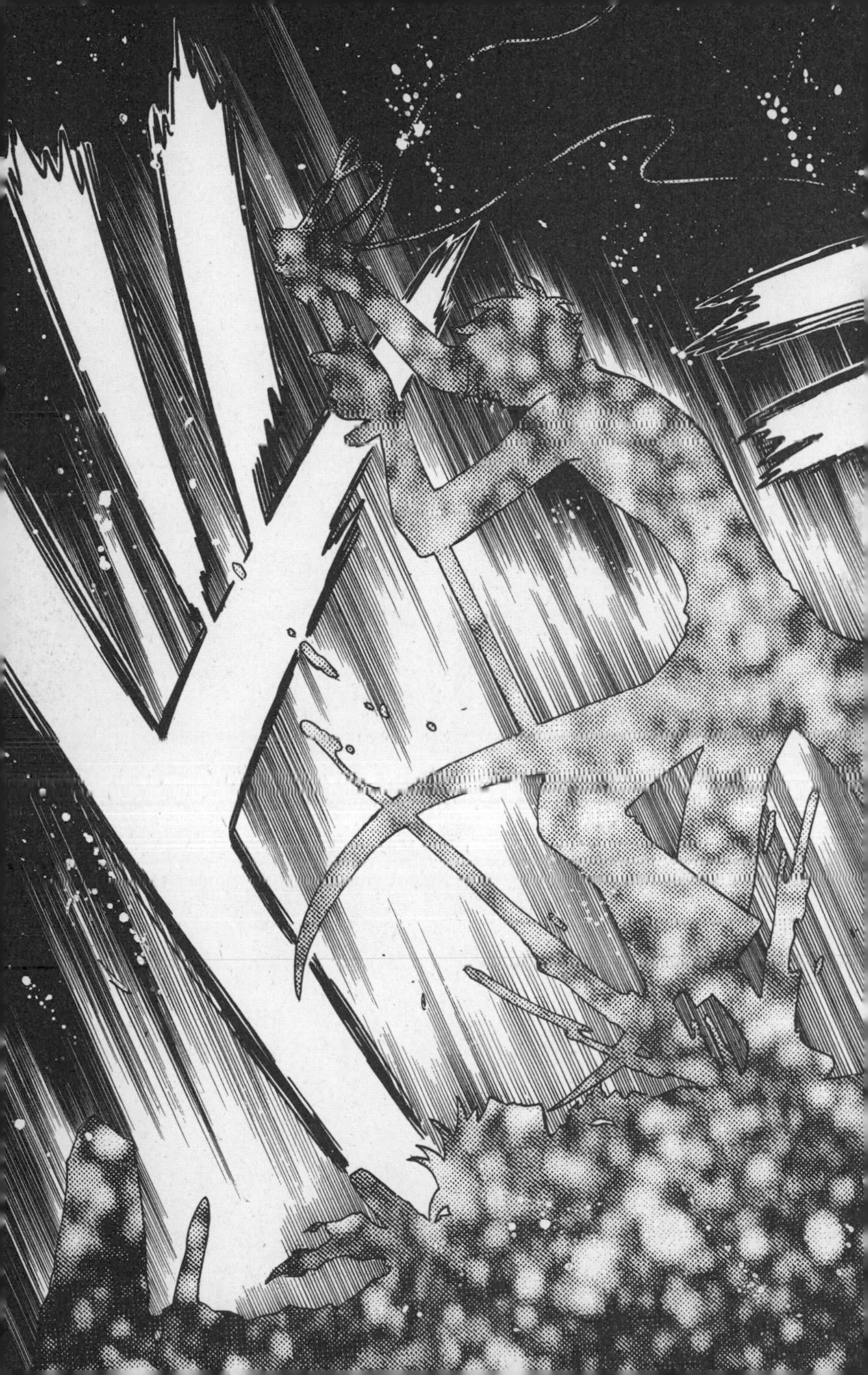

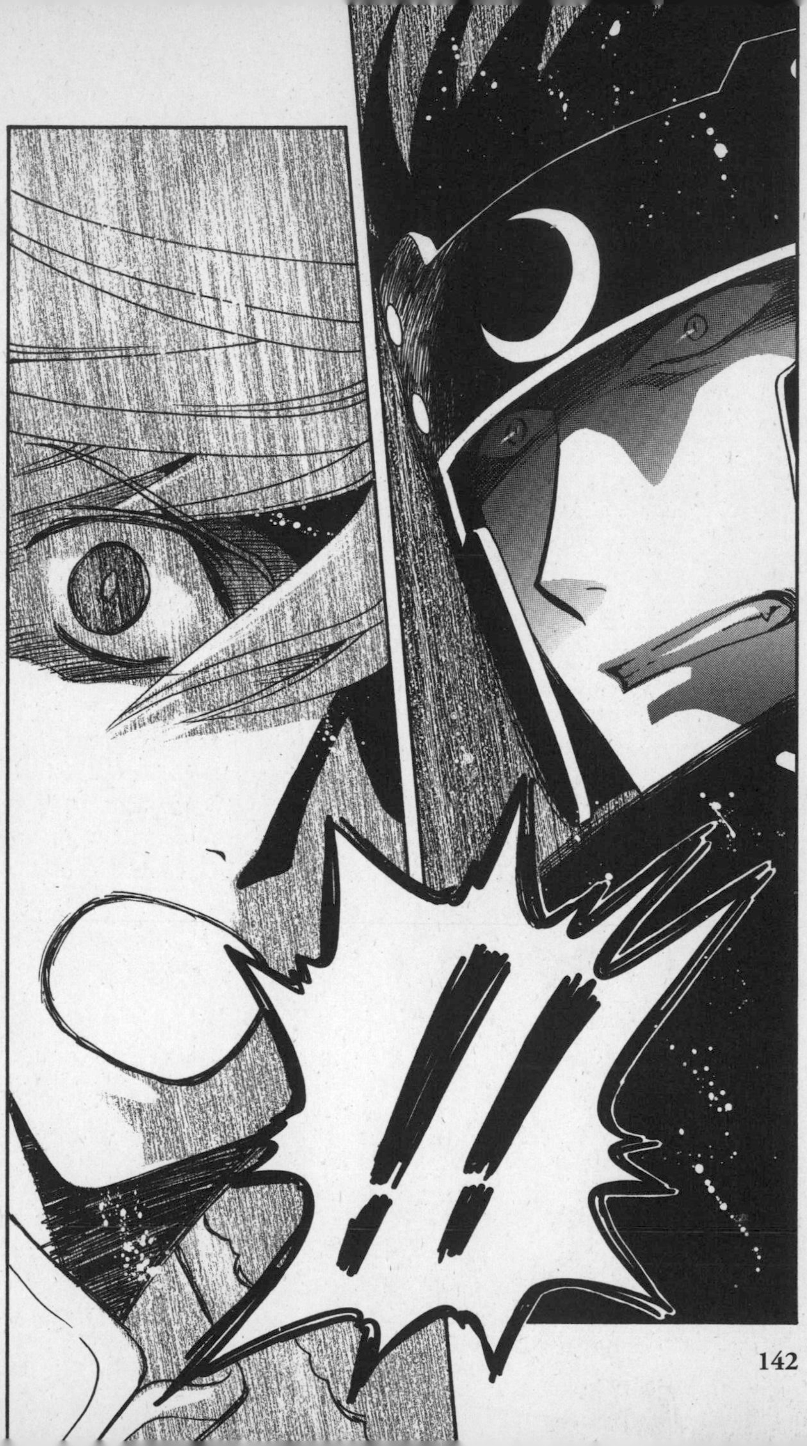
!!

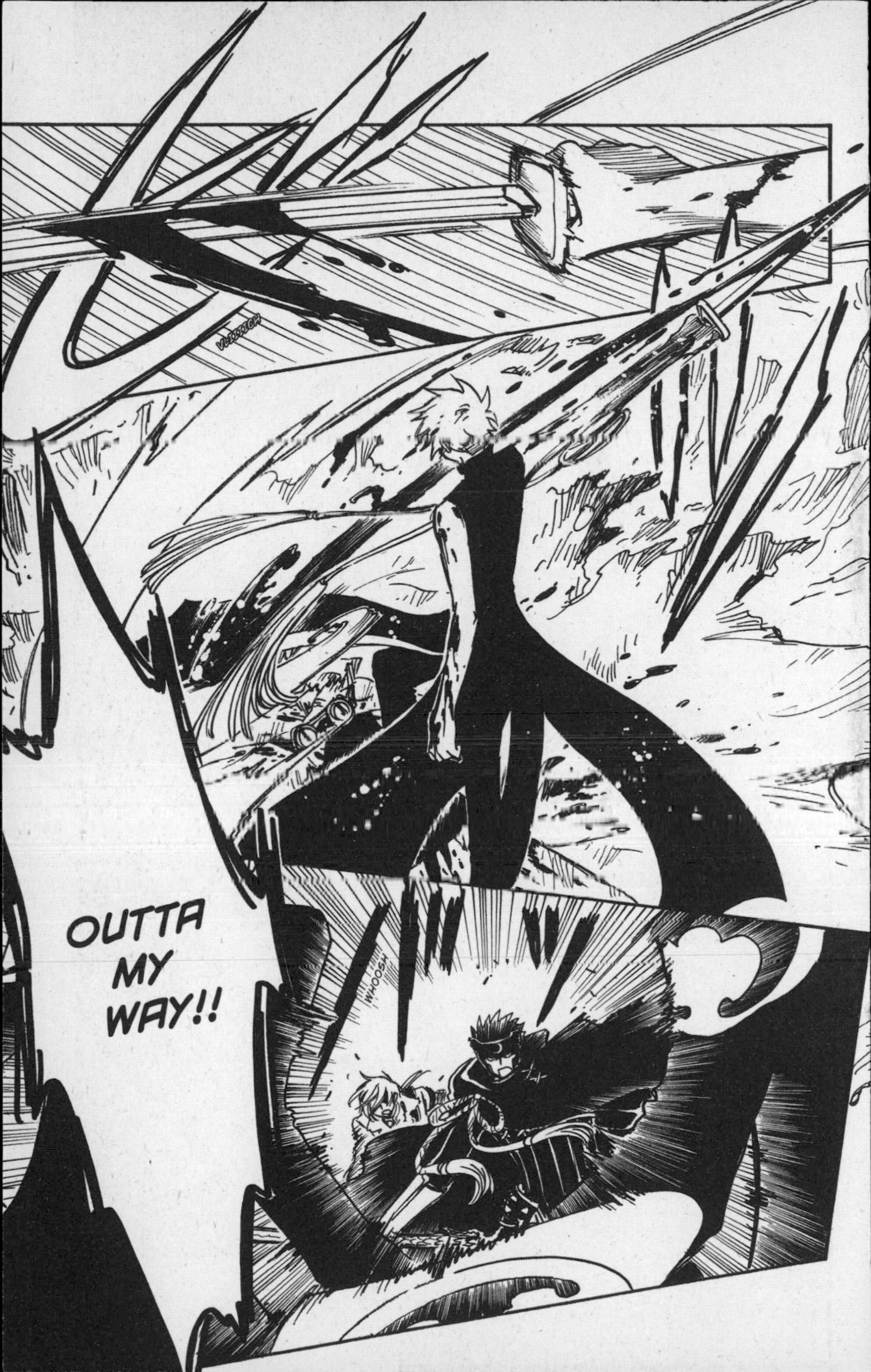
WHOOSH
OUTTA MY WAY!!

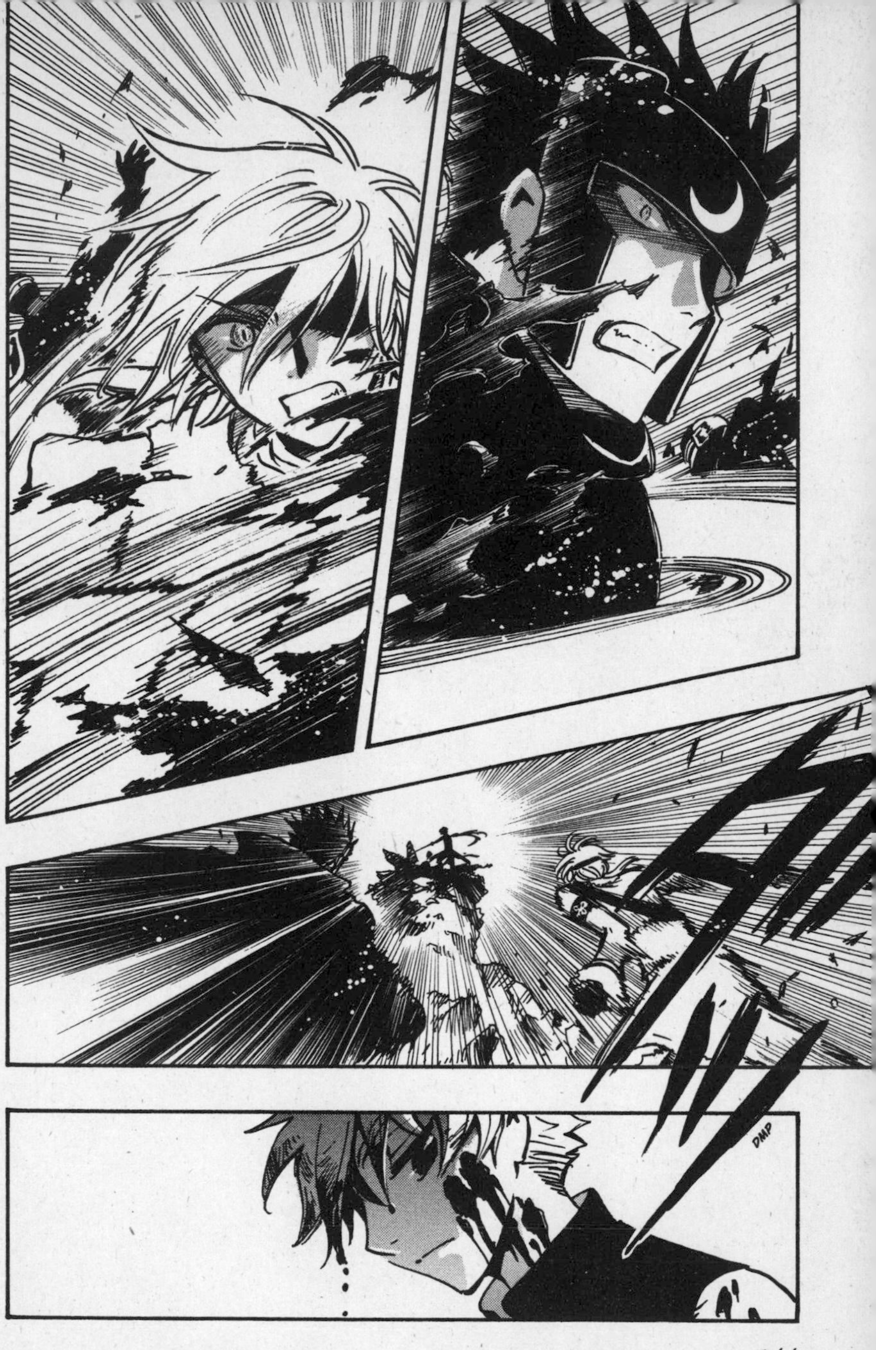
DMP

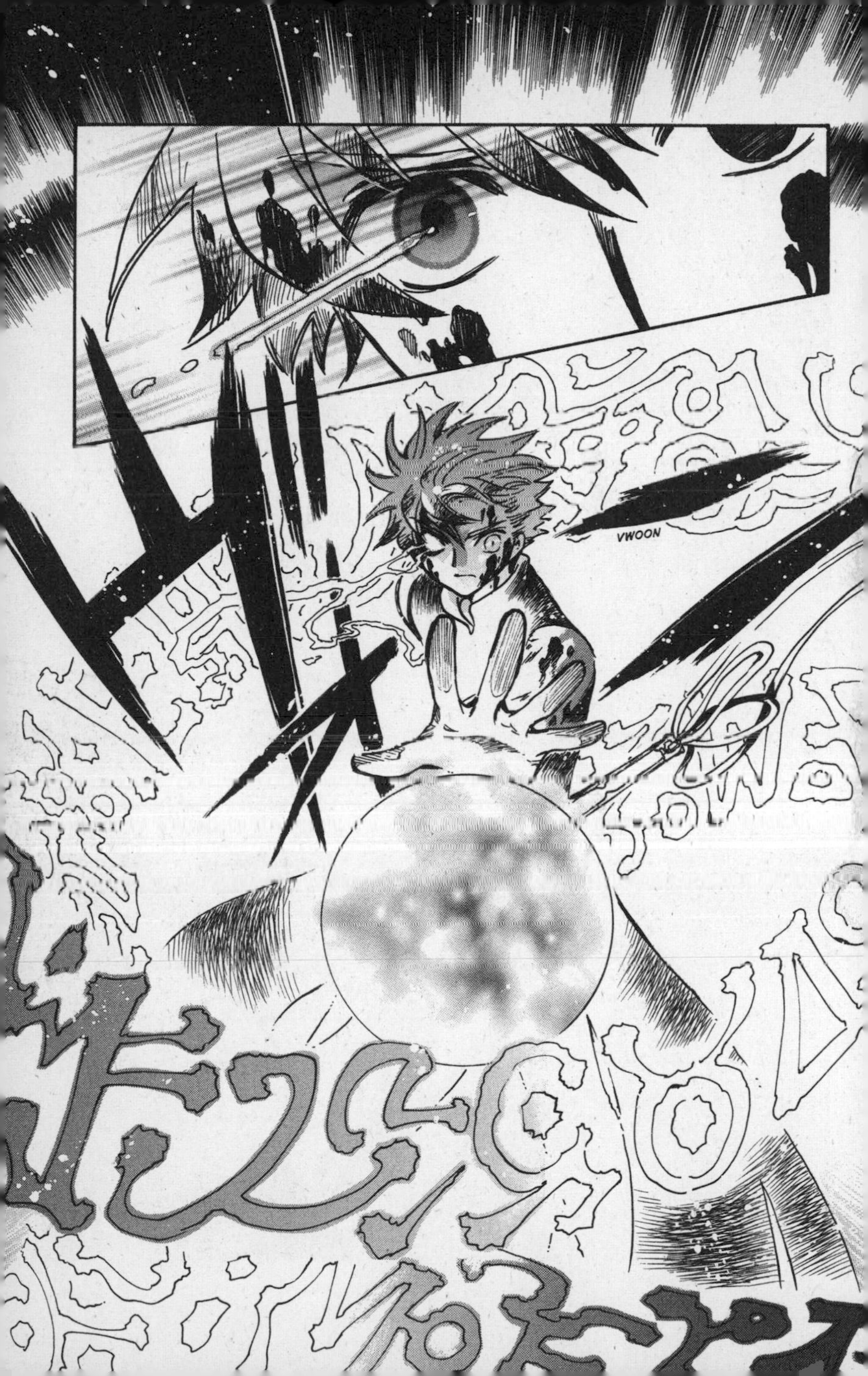
VWOON

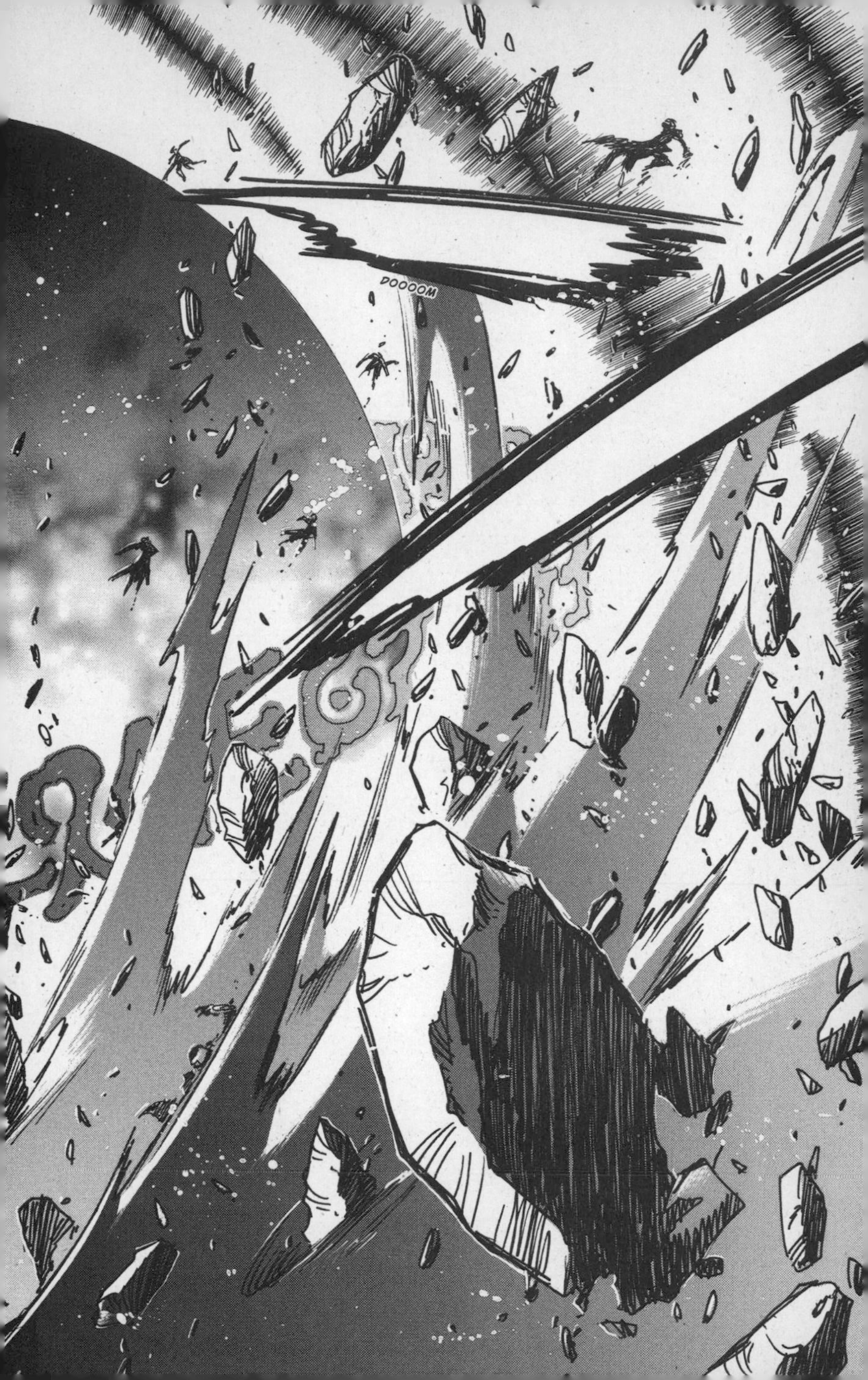
DOOOOM

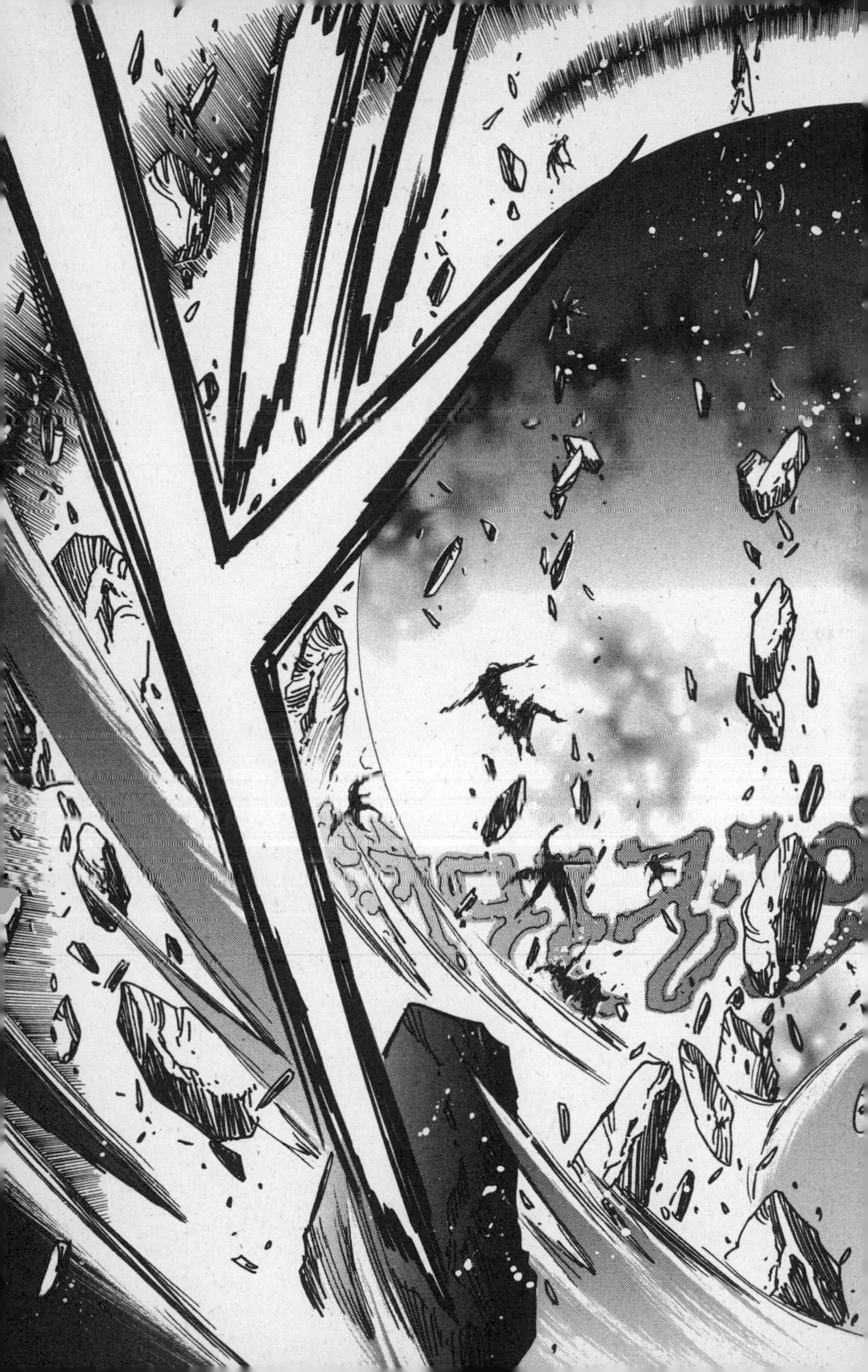

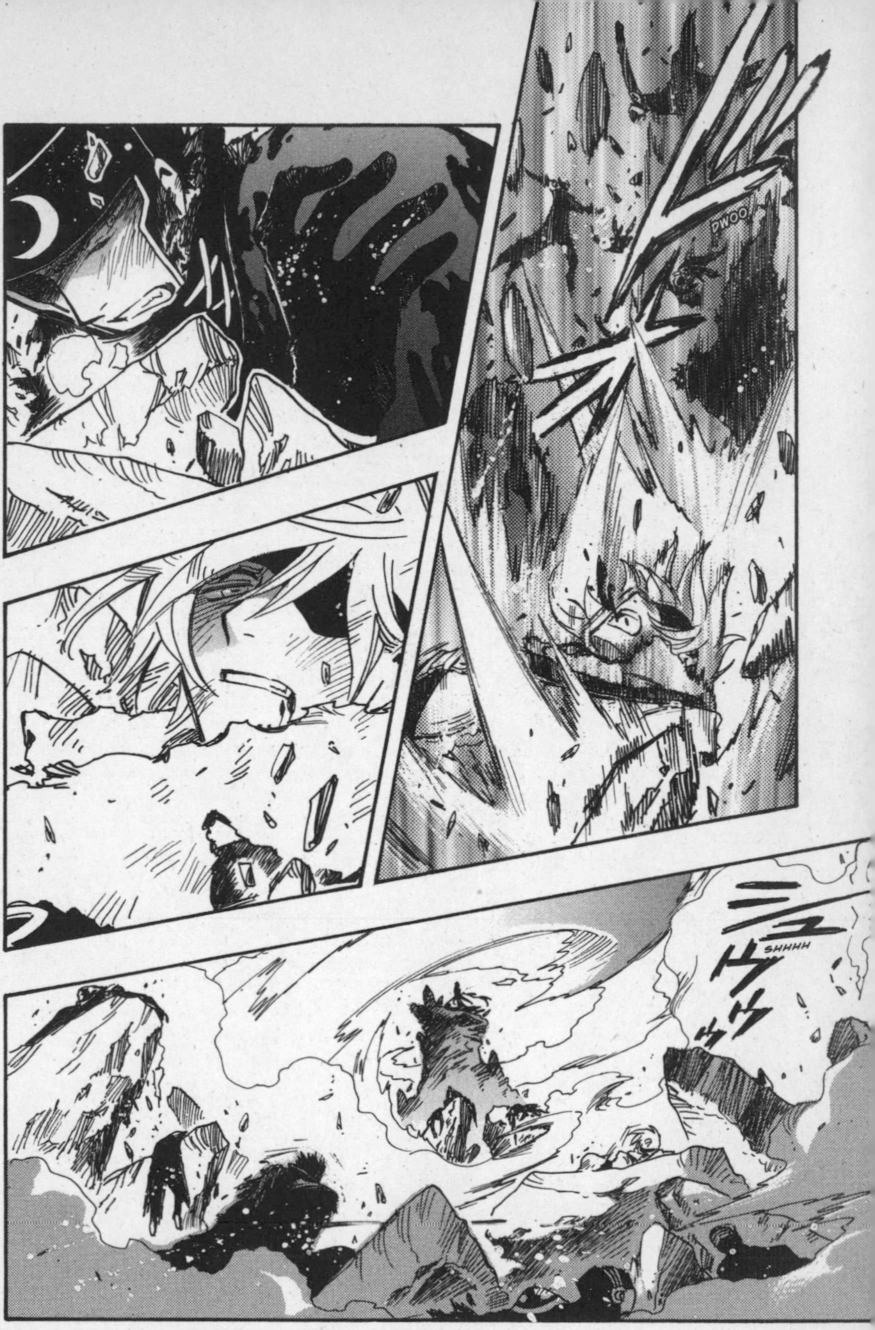
DWOO
SHHHH

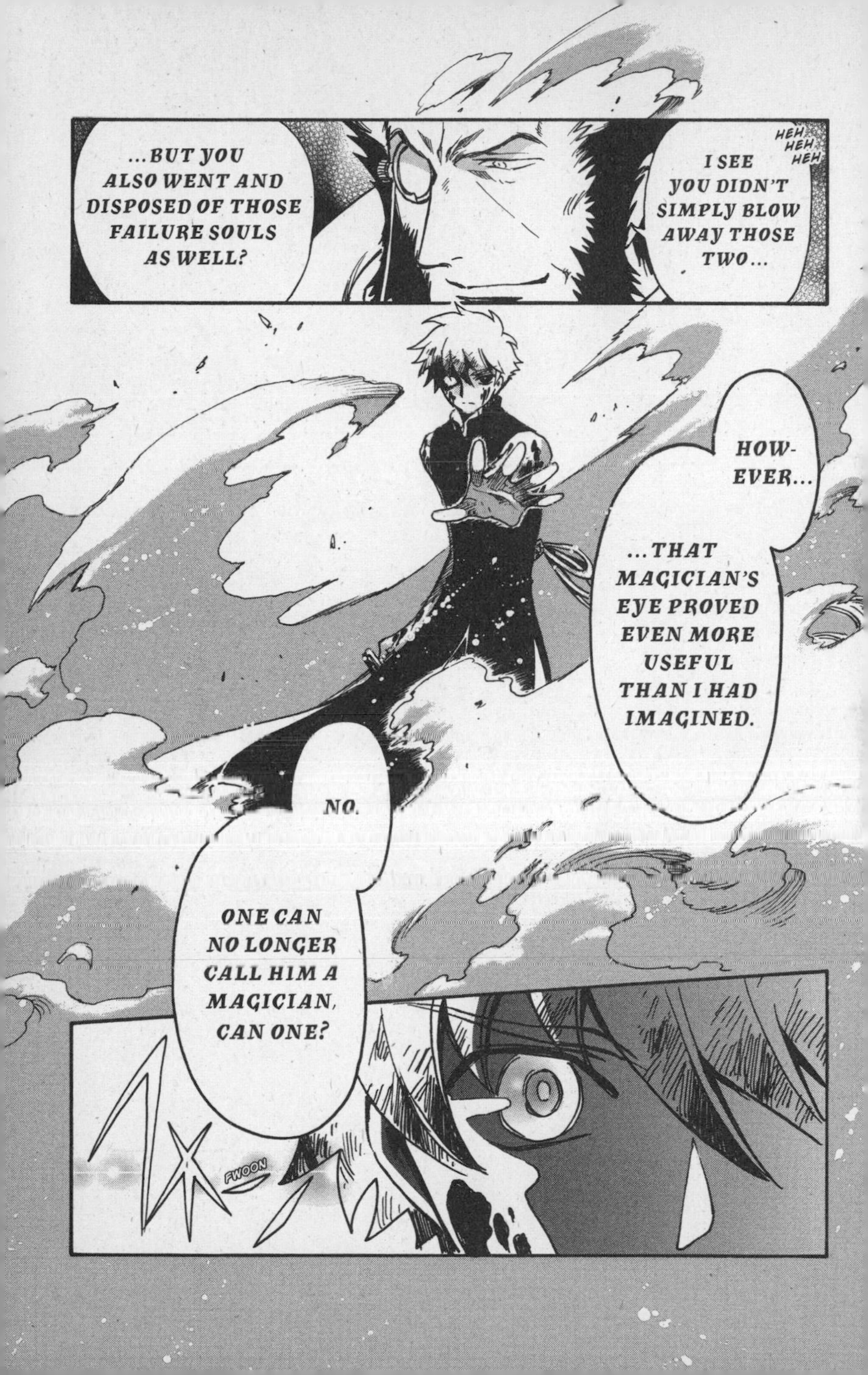
HEH HEH HEH
I SEE YOU DIDN'T SIMPLY BLOW AWAY THOSE TWO...
...BUT YOU ALSO WENT AND DISPOSED OF THOSE FAILURE SOULS AS WELL?
HOW-EVER...
...THAT MAGICIAN'S EYE PROVED EVEN MORE USEFUL THAN I HAD IMAGINED.
NO.
ONE CAN NO LONGER CALL HIM A MAGICIAN, CAN ONE?
FWOON

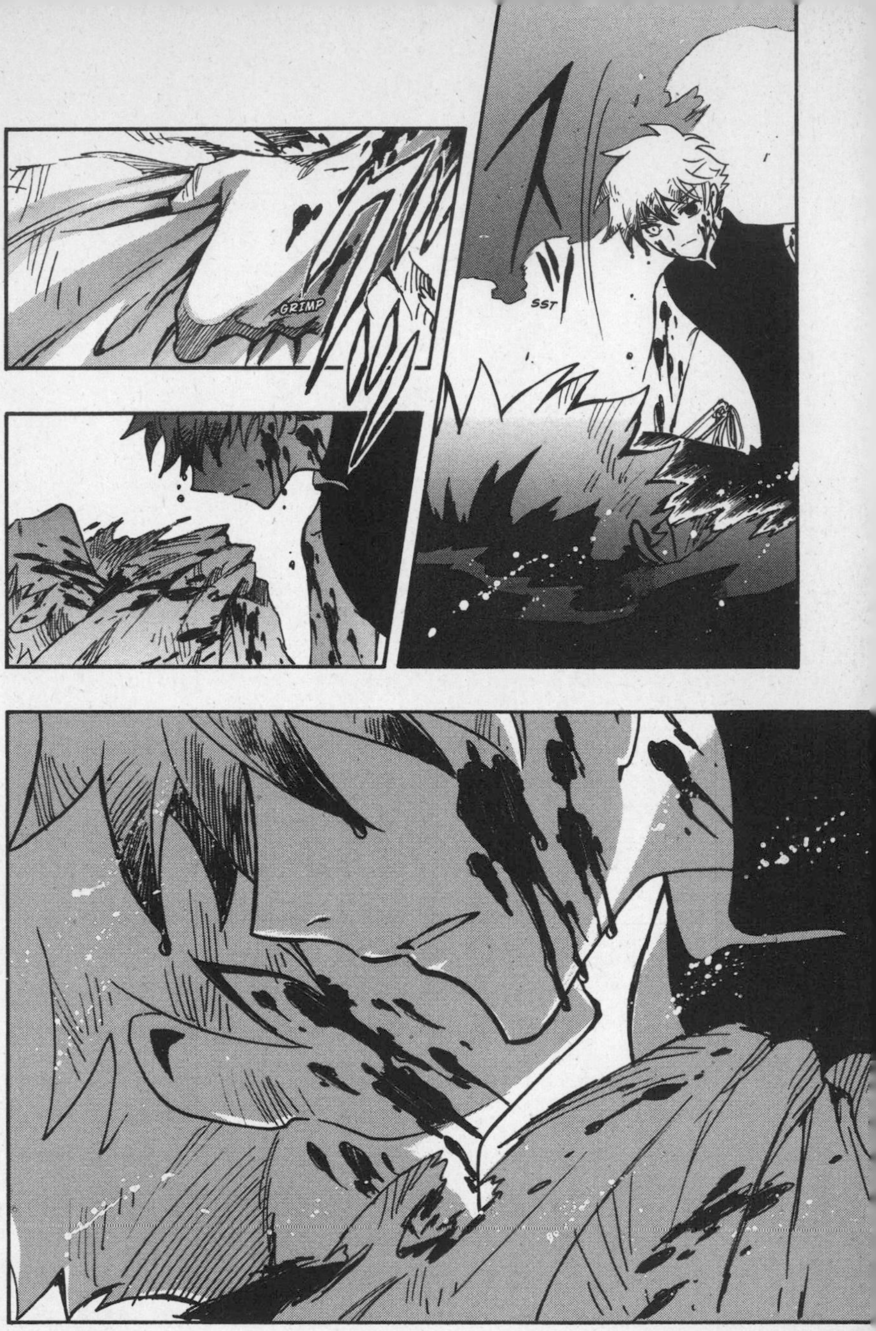
SST
GRIMP

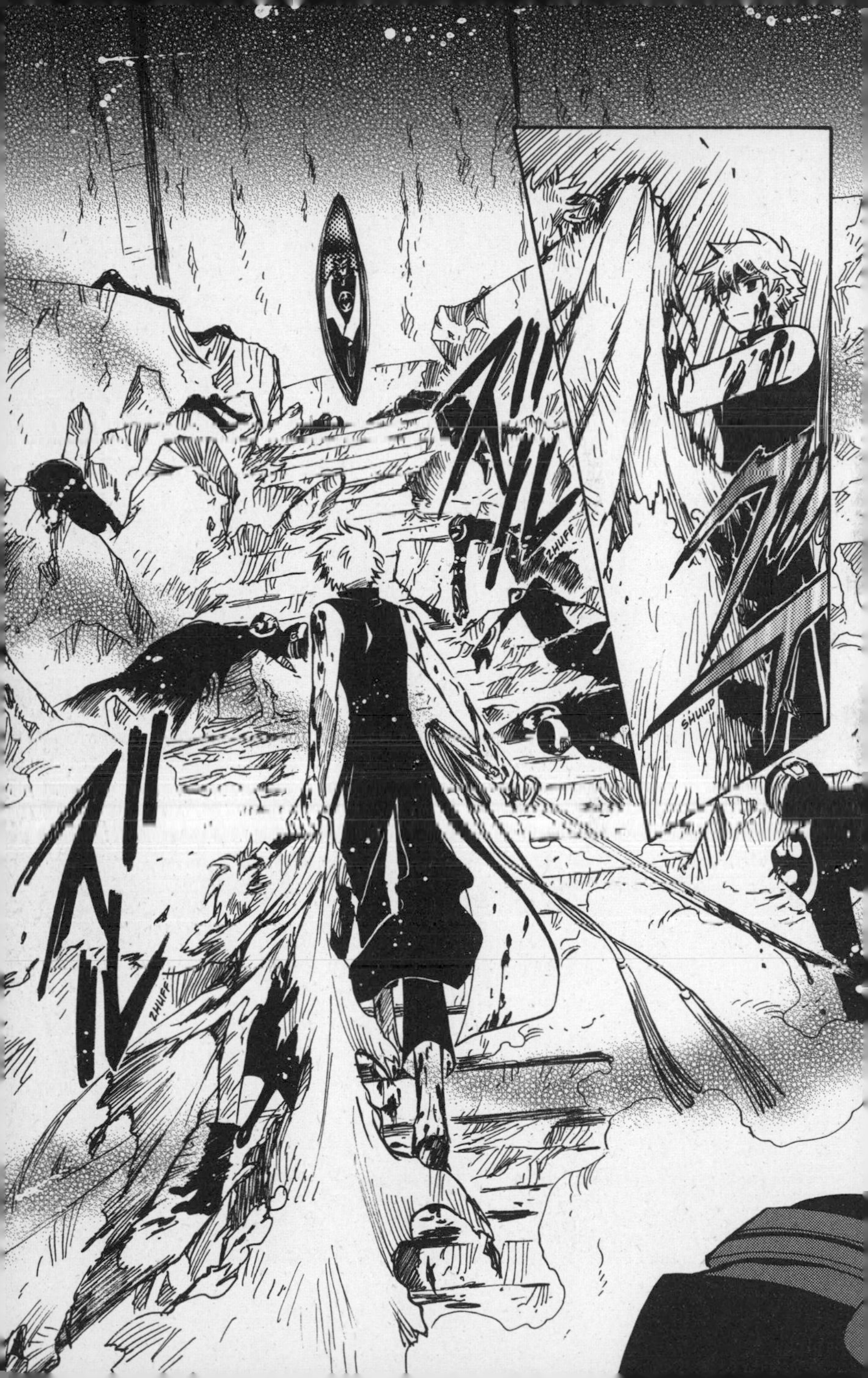
SHUUP
ZHUFF
ZHUFF

RESERVoir CHRoNiCLE

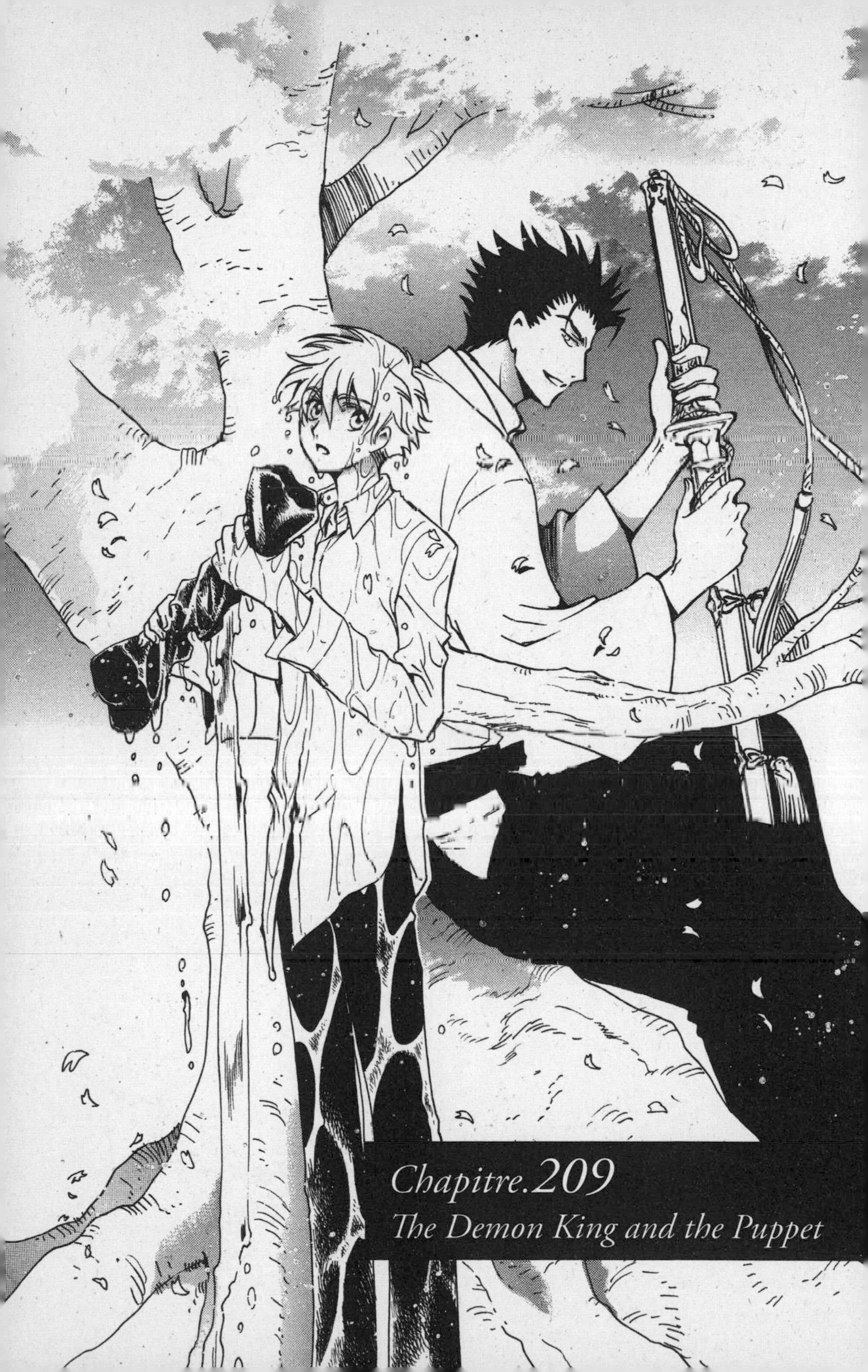
Chapitre.209
The Demon King and the Puppet

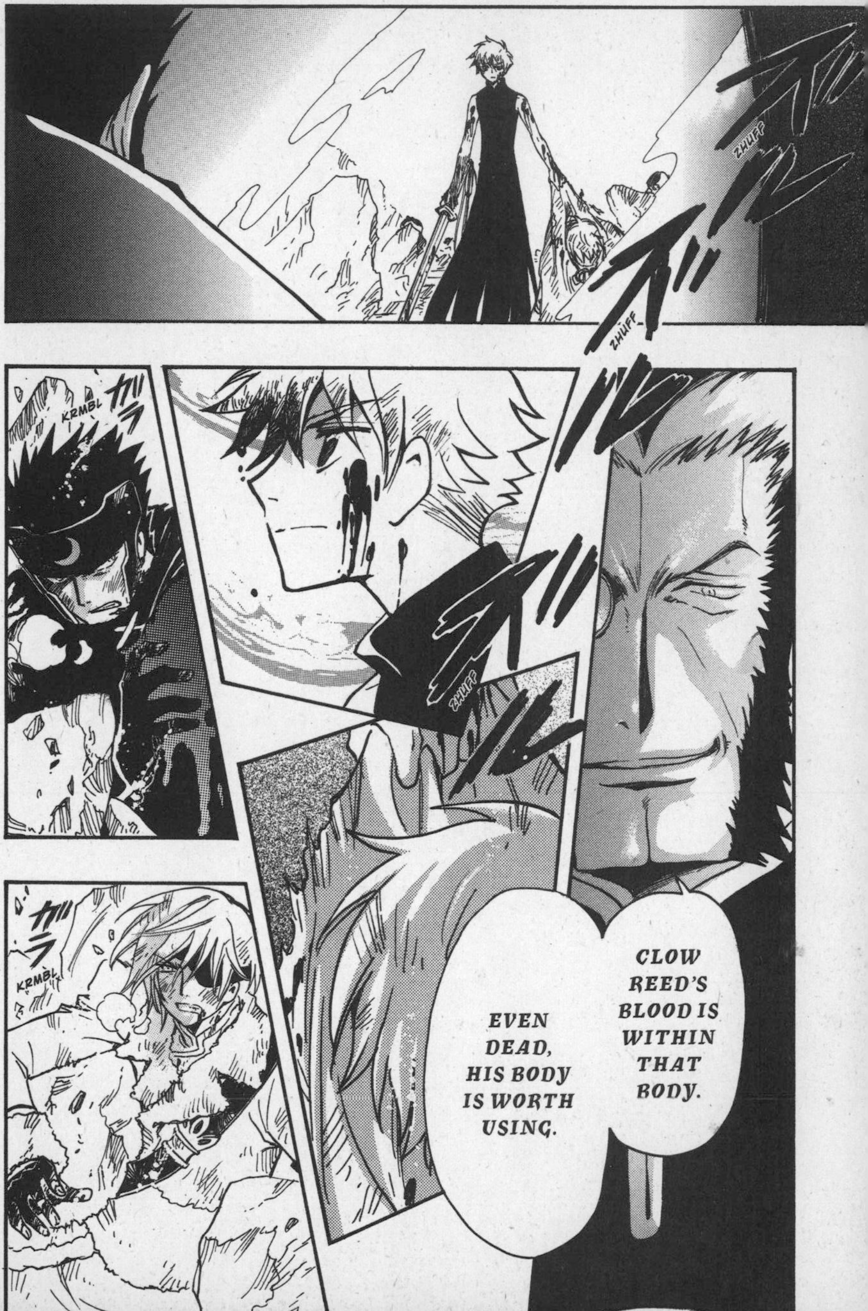
ZHUFF
ZHUFF
ZHUFF
CLOW REED'S BLOOD IS WITHIN THAT BODY.
EVEN DEAD, HIS BODY IS WORTH USING.
KRMBL
KRMBL

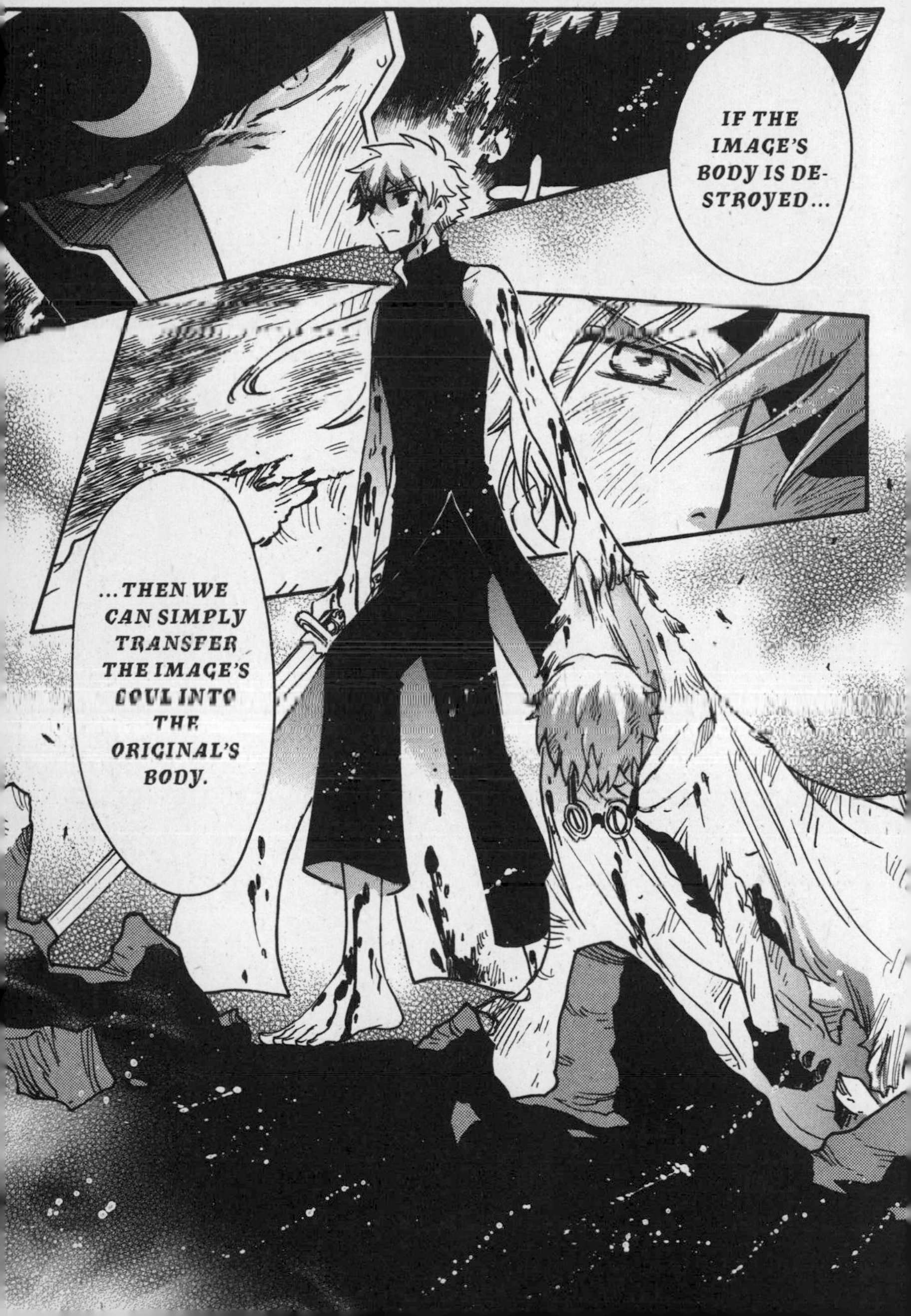
IF THE IMAGE'S BODY IS DE-STROYED...
...THEN WE CAN SIMPLY TRANSFER THE IMAGE'S SOUL INTO THE ORIGINAL'S BODY.

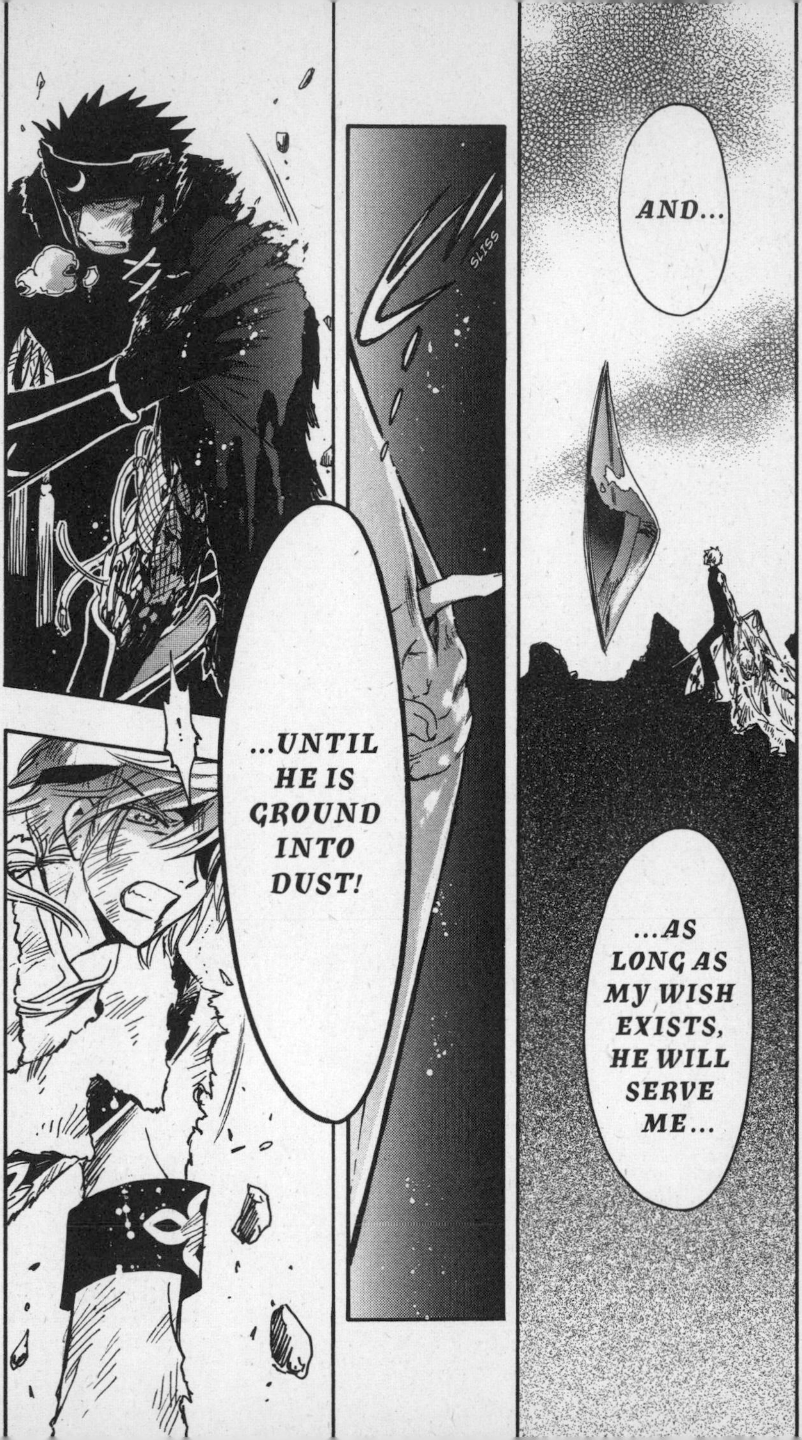
AND...
...AS LONG AS MY WISH EXISTS, HE WILL SERVE ME...
SLISS
...UNTIL HE IS GROUND INTO DUST!

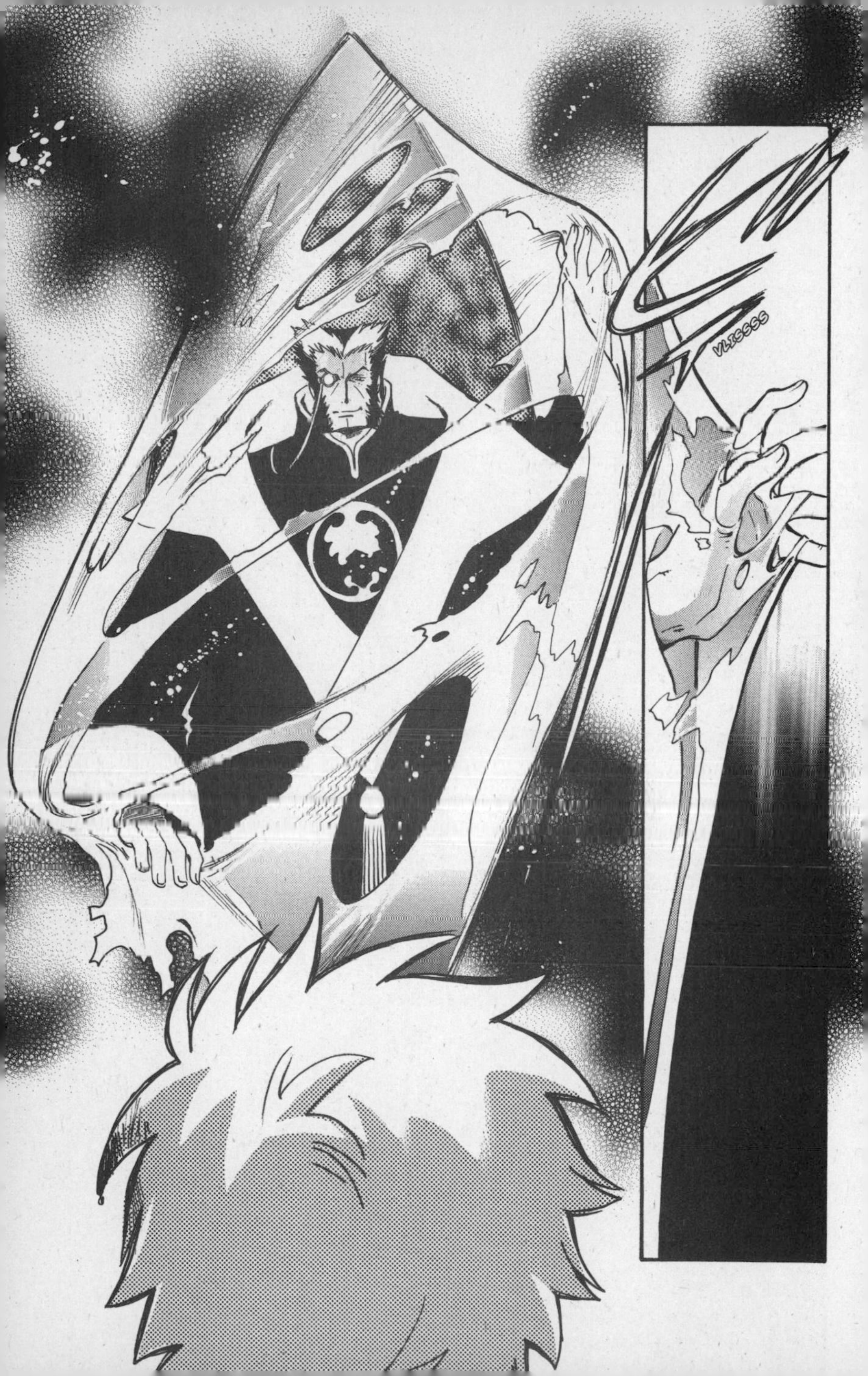
VLISSSS

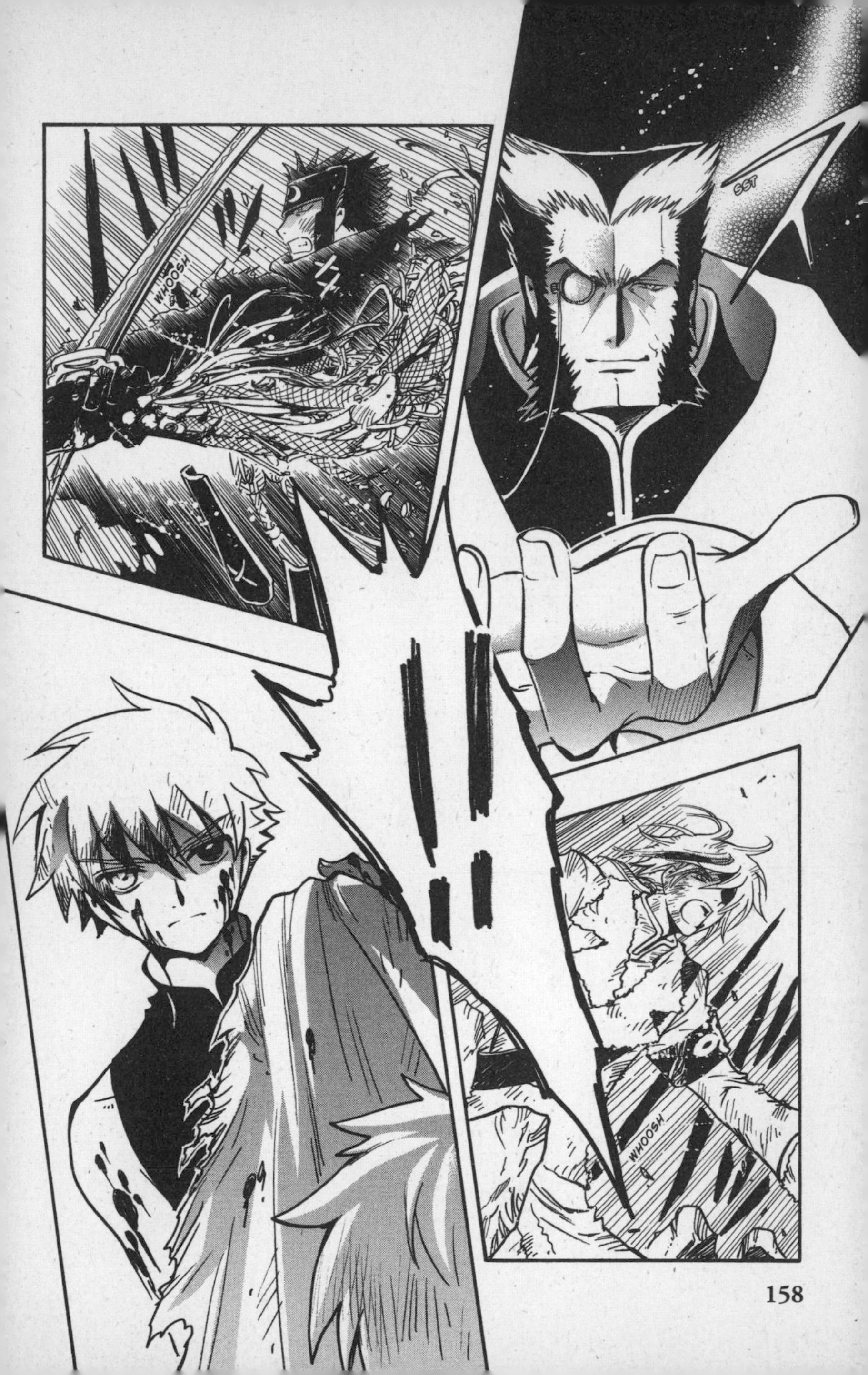
SST
WHOOSH
WHOOSH

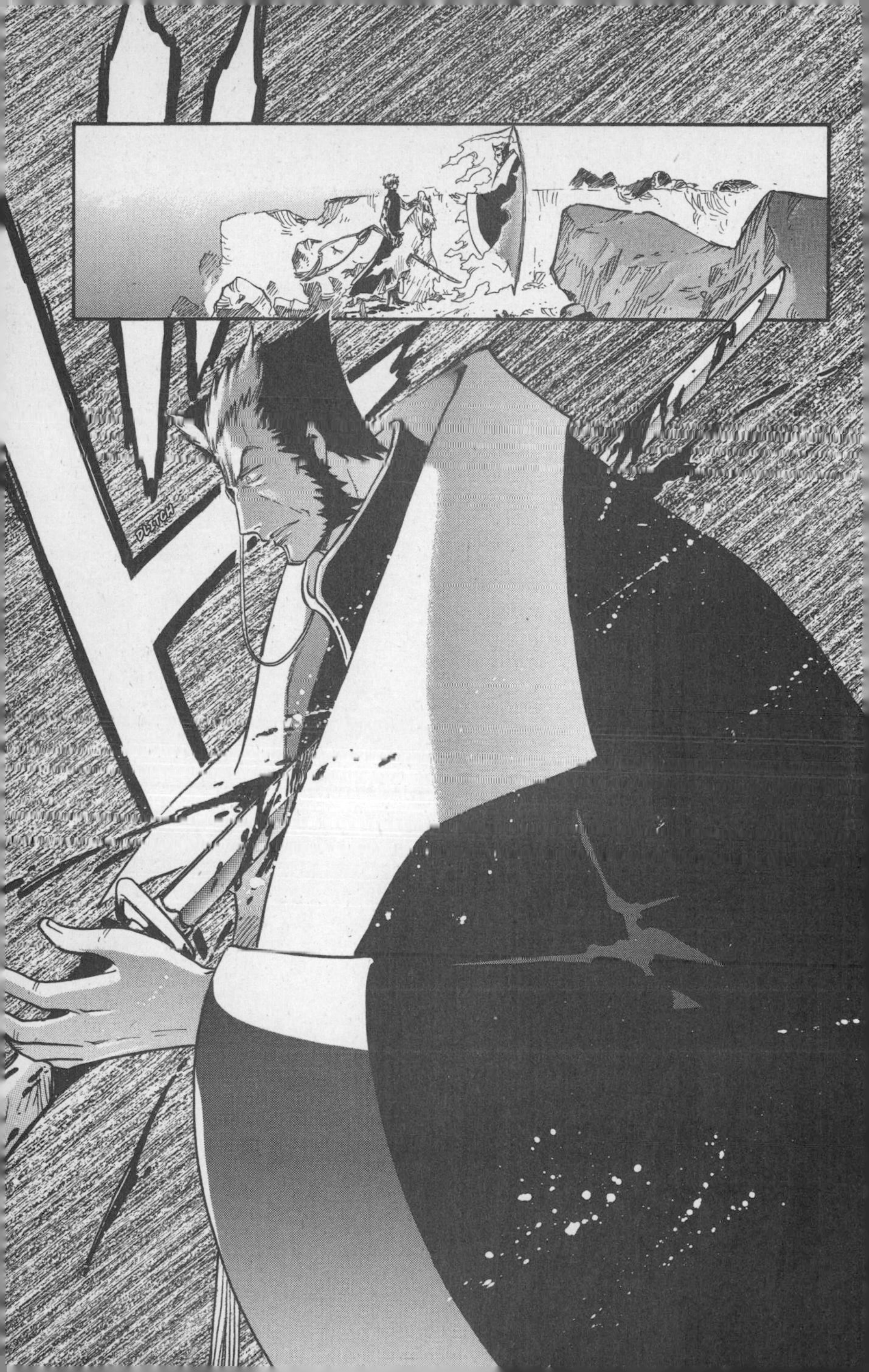
DLITCH

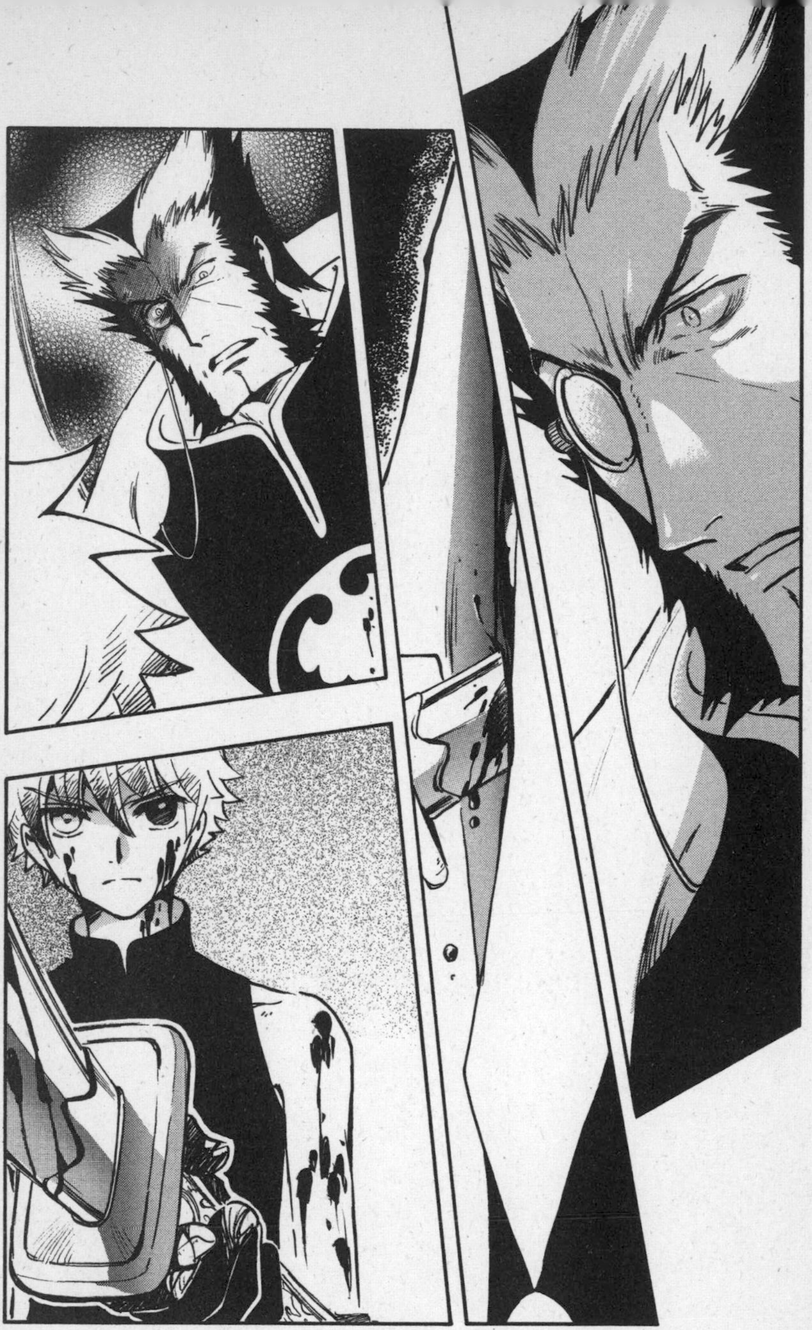

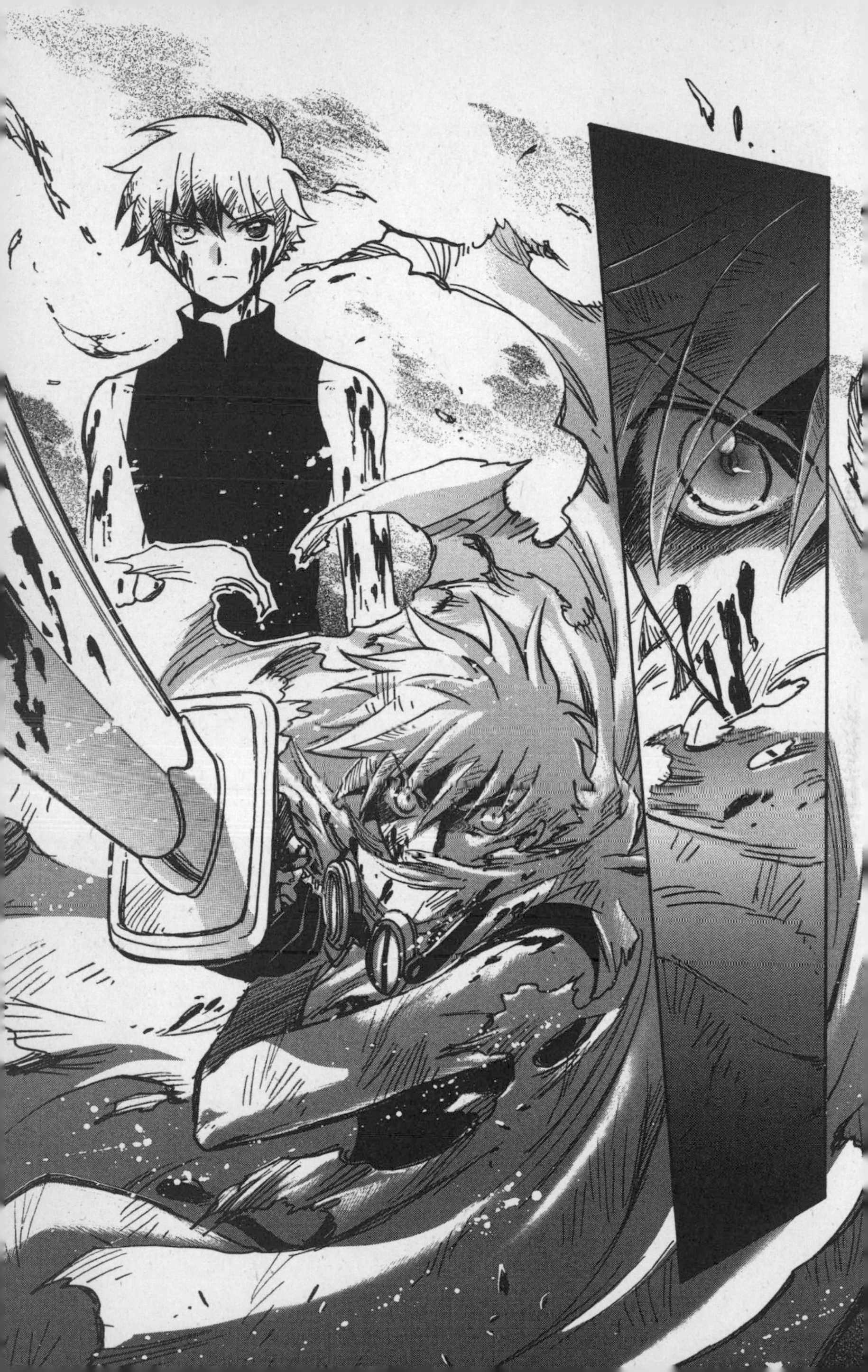

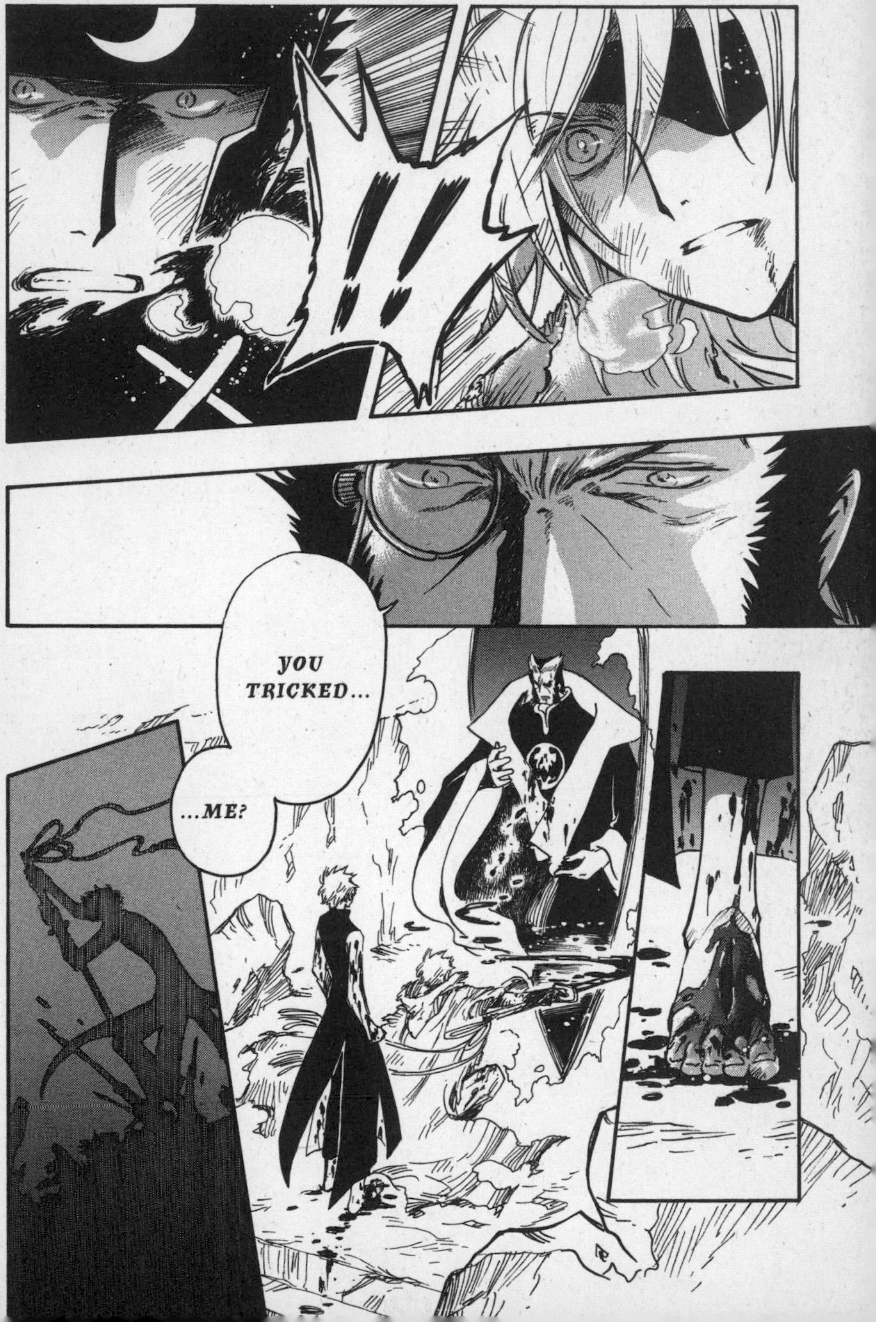
!!
YOU TRICKED...
...ME?

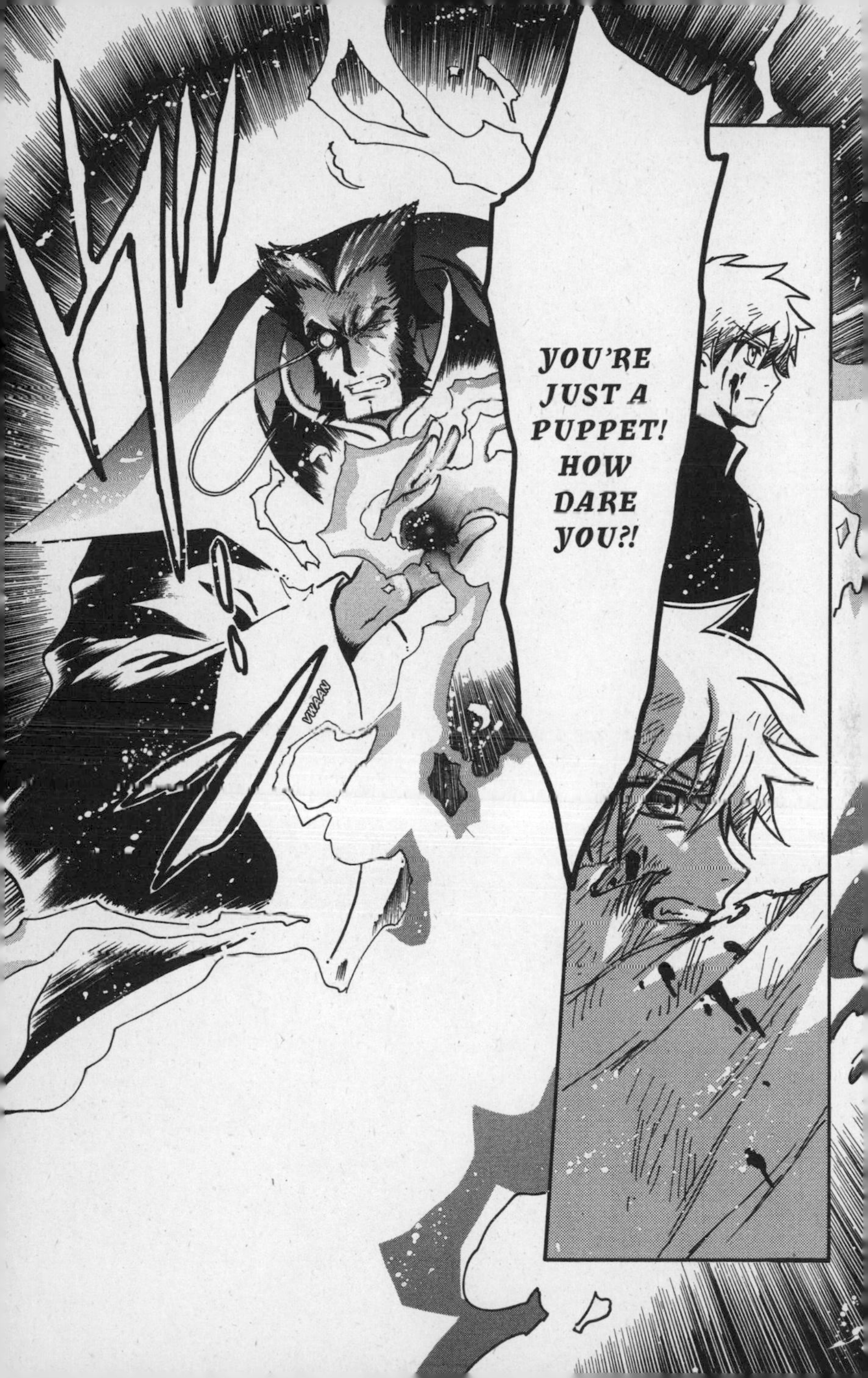
YOU'RE JUST A PUPPET! HOW DARE YOU?!
VWAAN

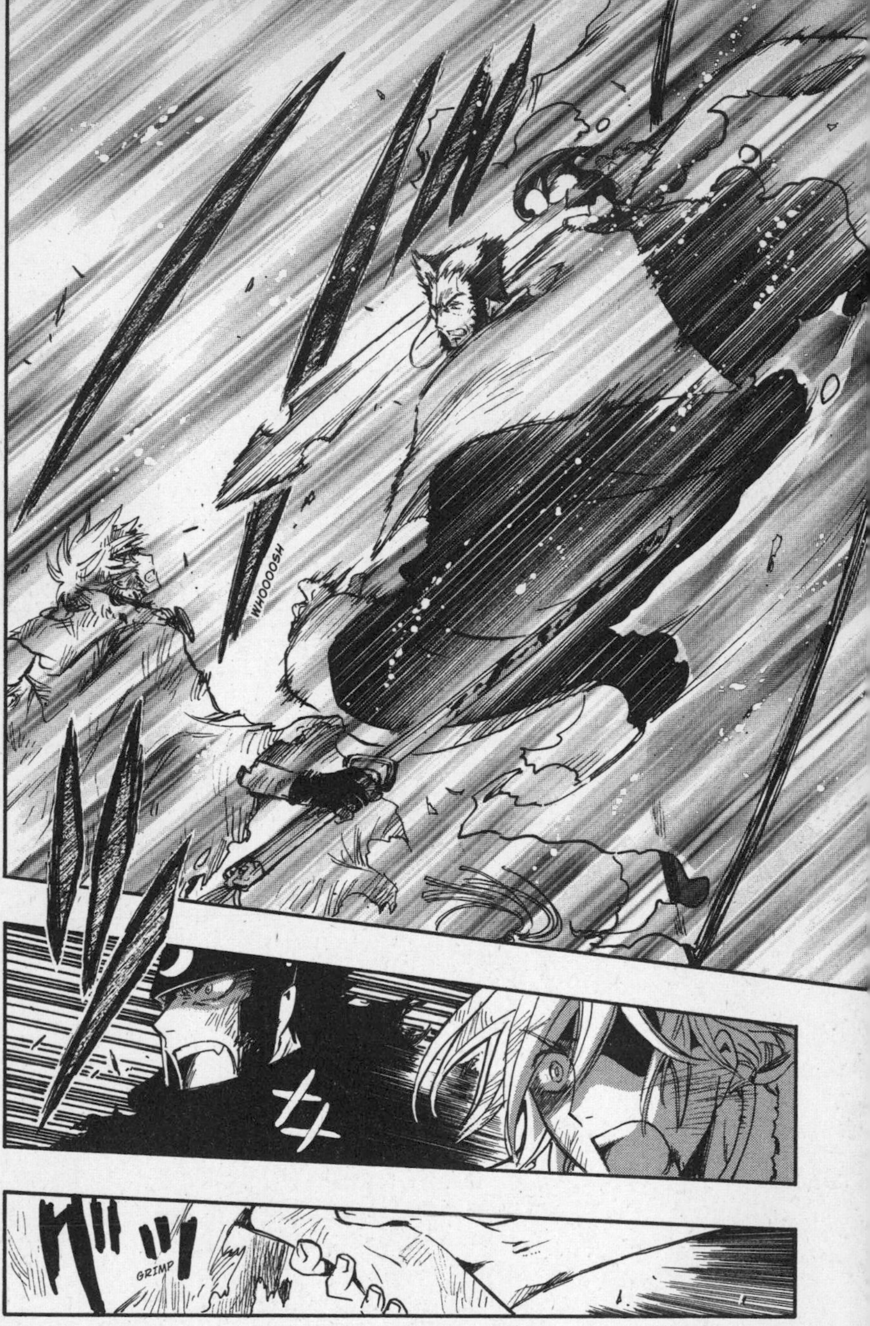
WHOOOOSH
GRIMP

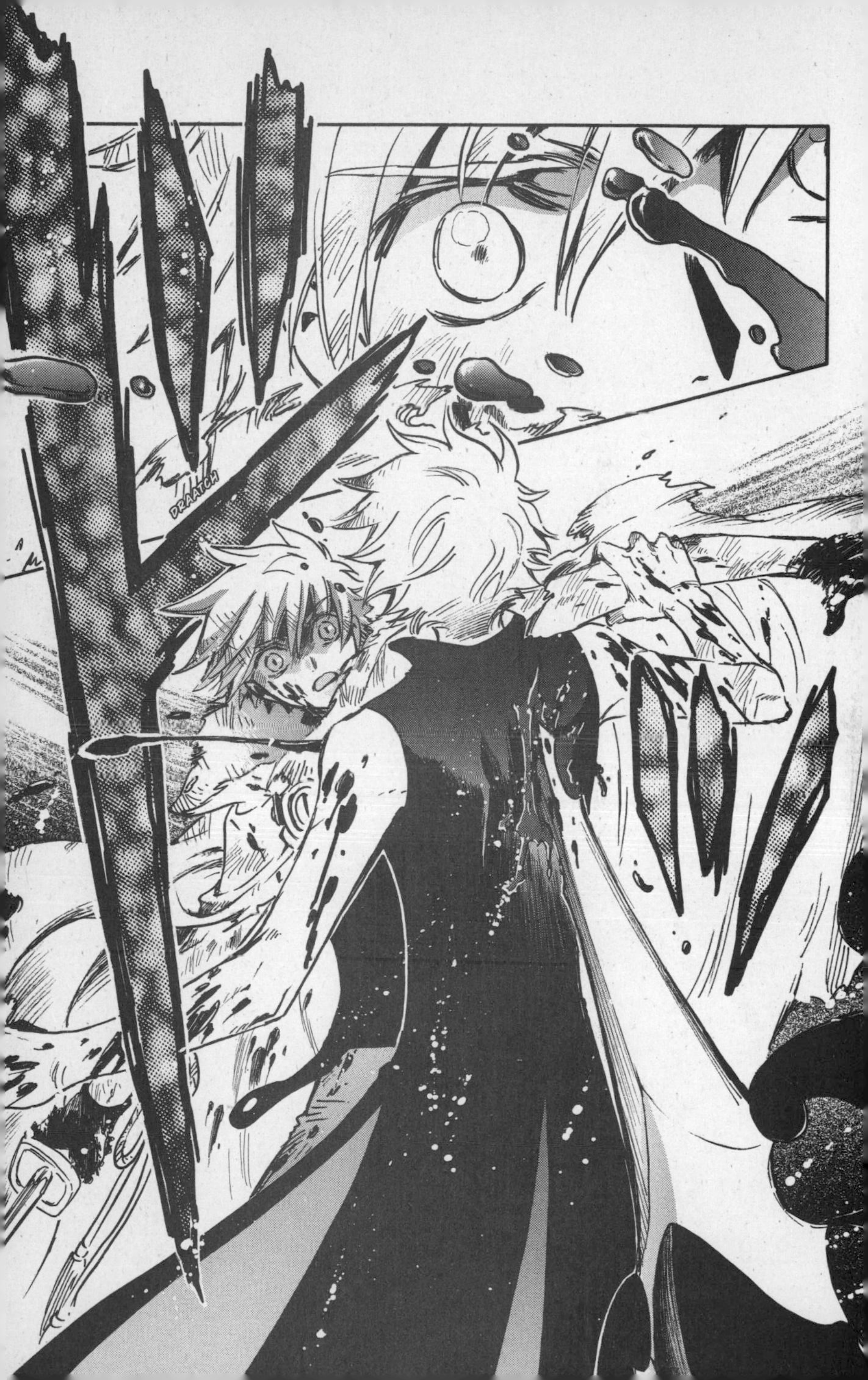
DRAATCH

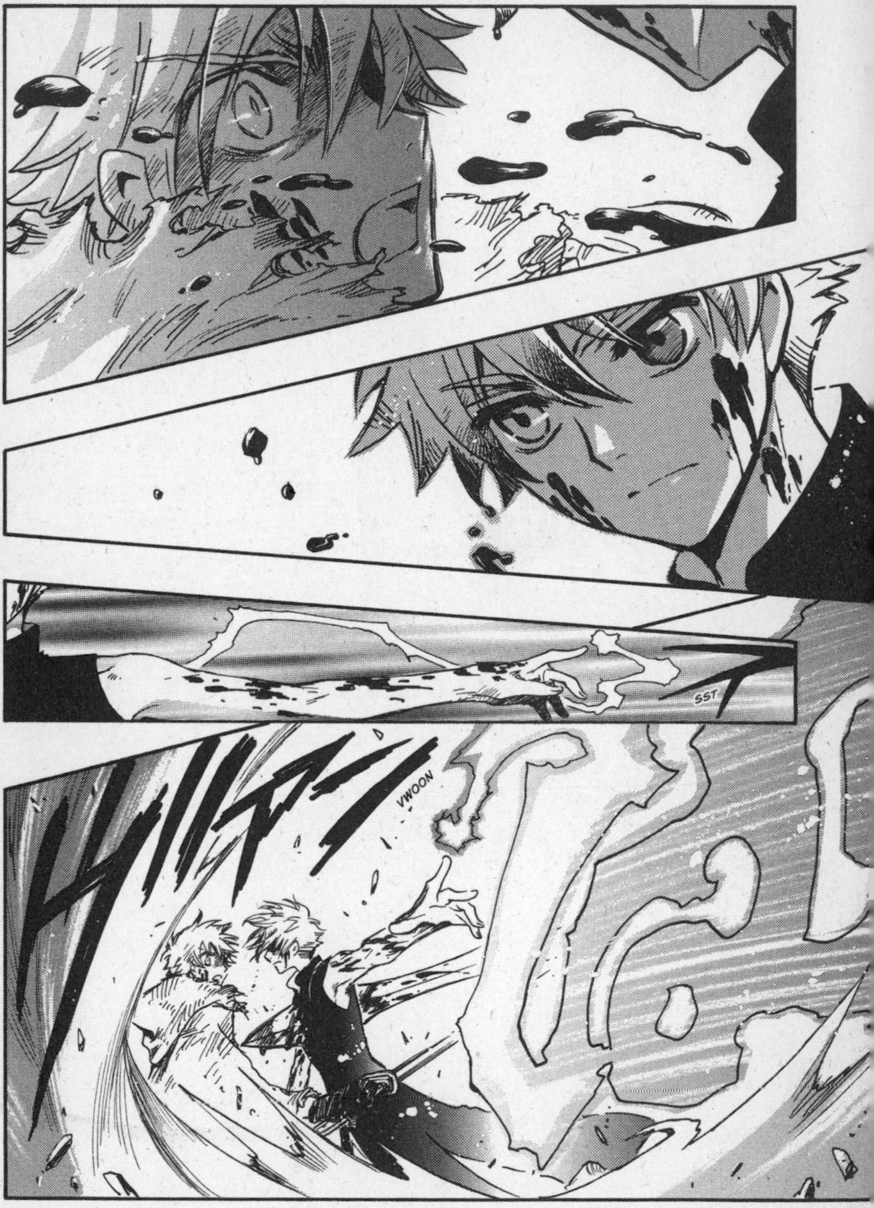
SST
VWOON

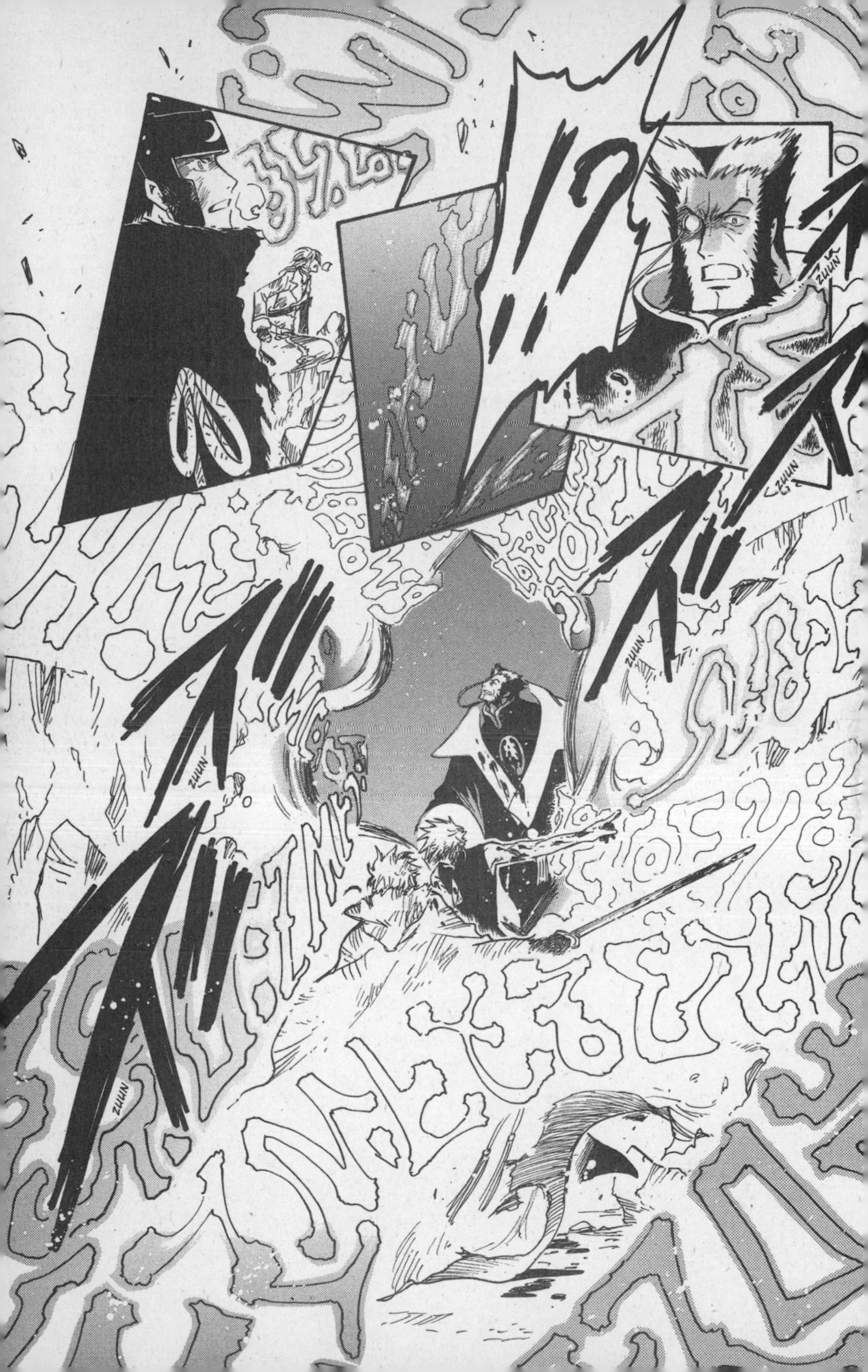
ZUUN
ZUUN
ZUUN
ZUUN
ZUUN

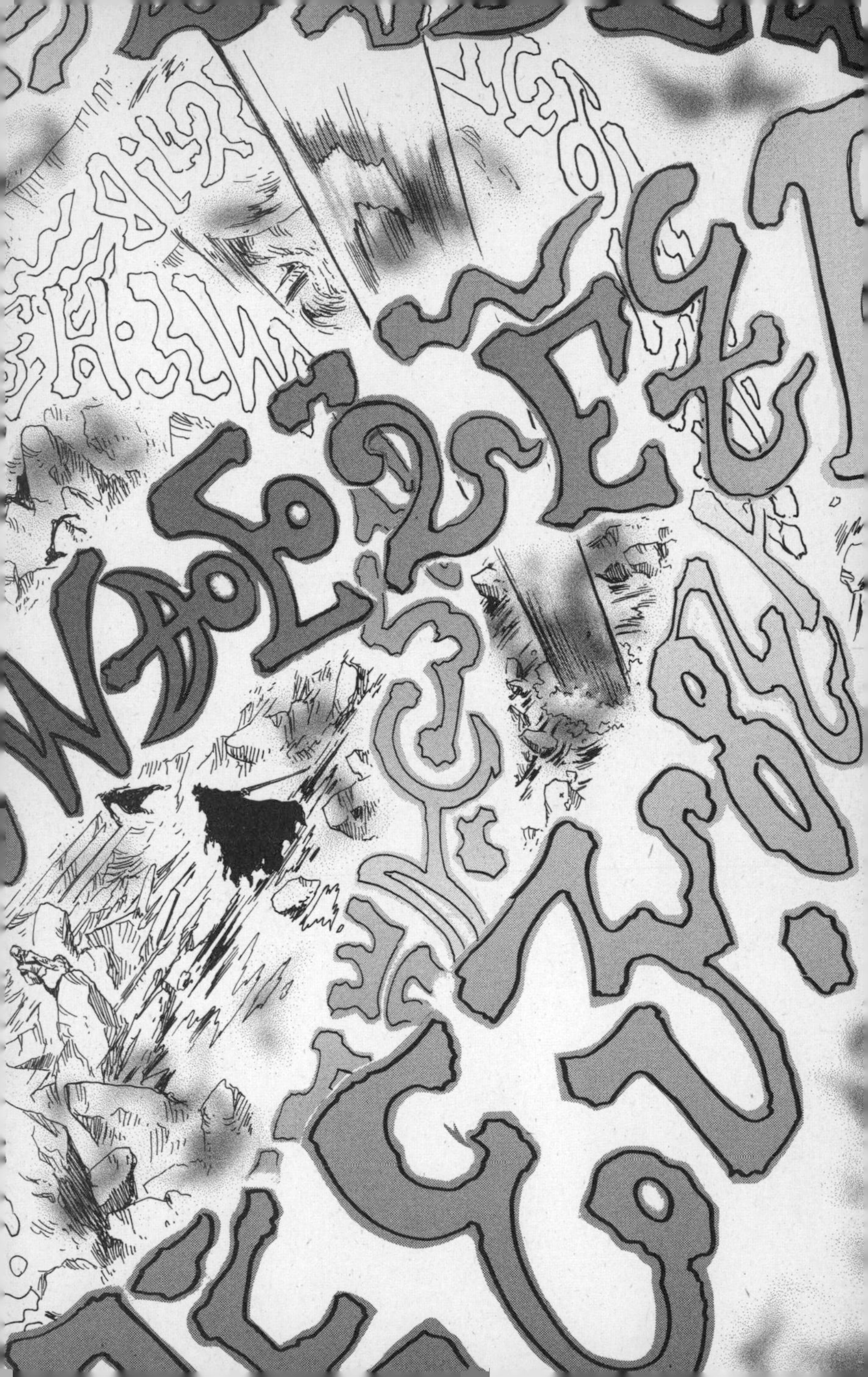

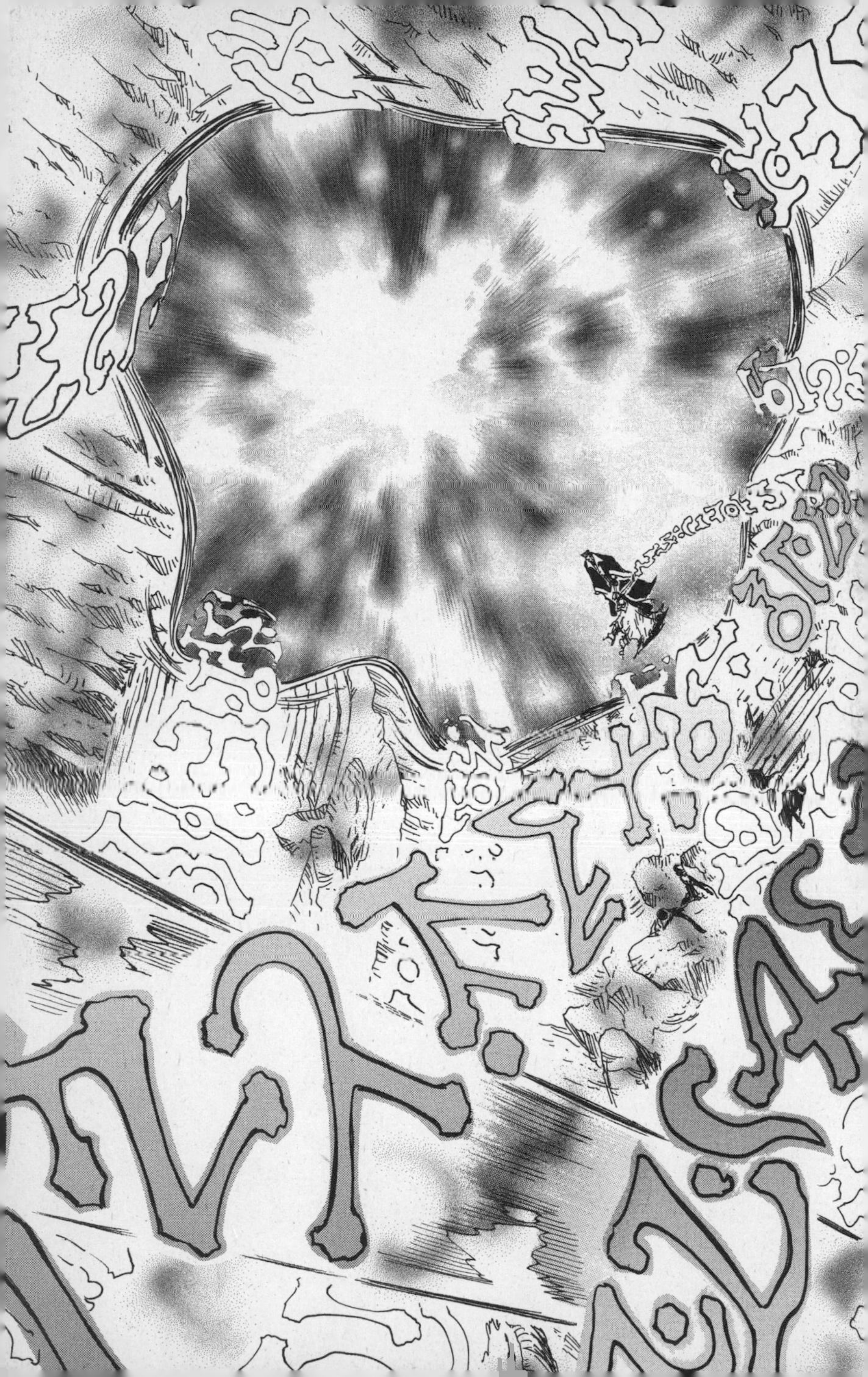

ツバサ

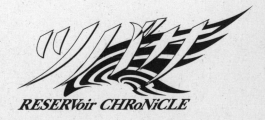

RESERVoir CHRoNiCLE

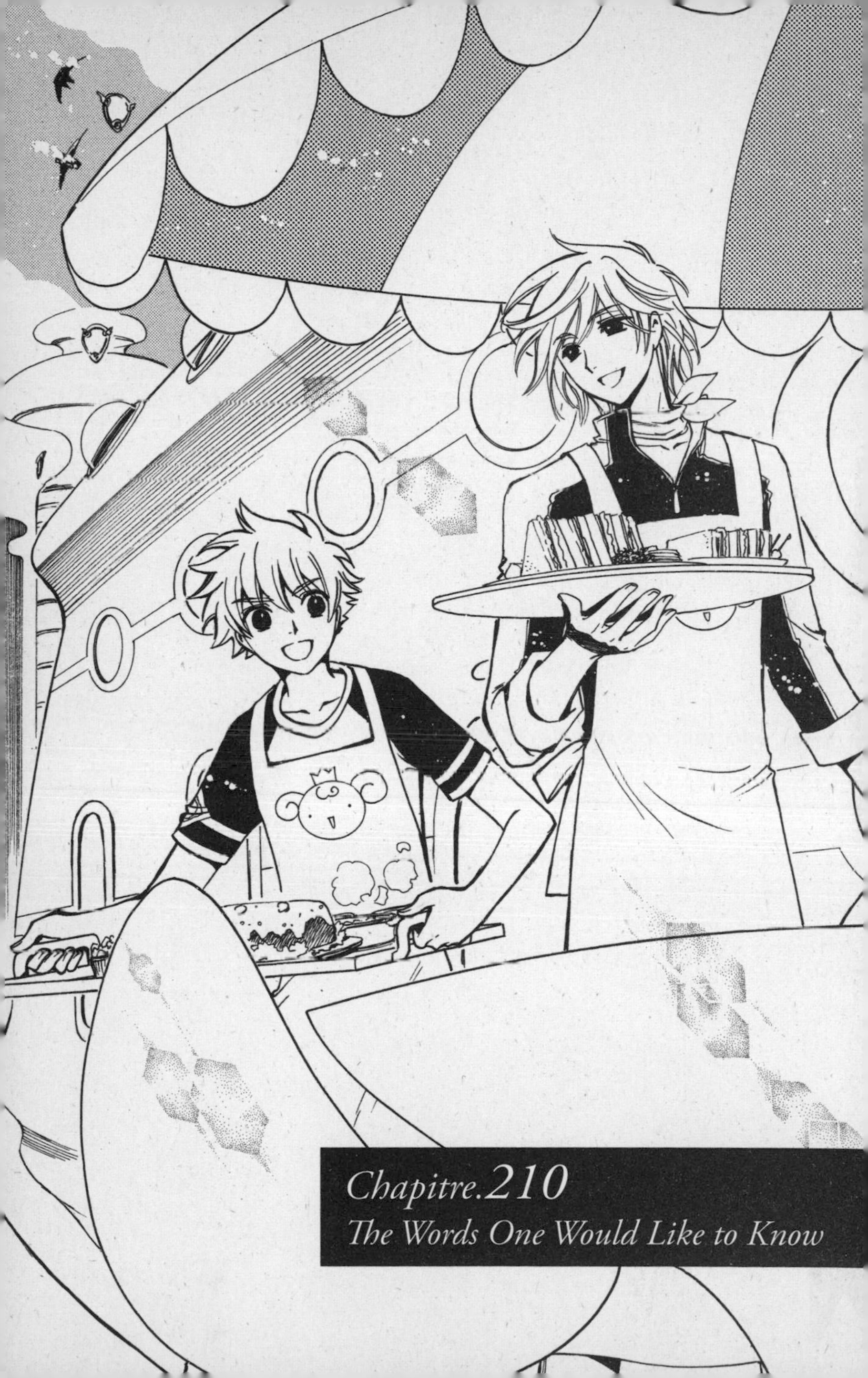
Chapitre.210
The Words One Would Like to Know

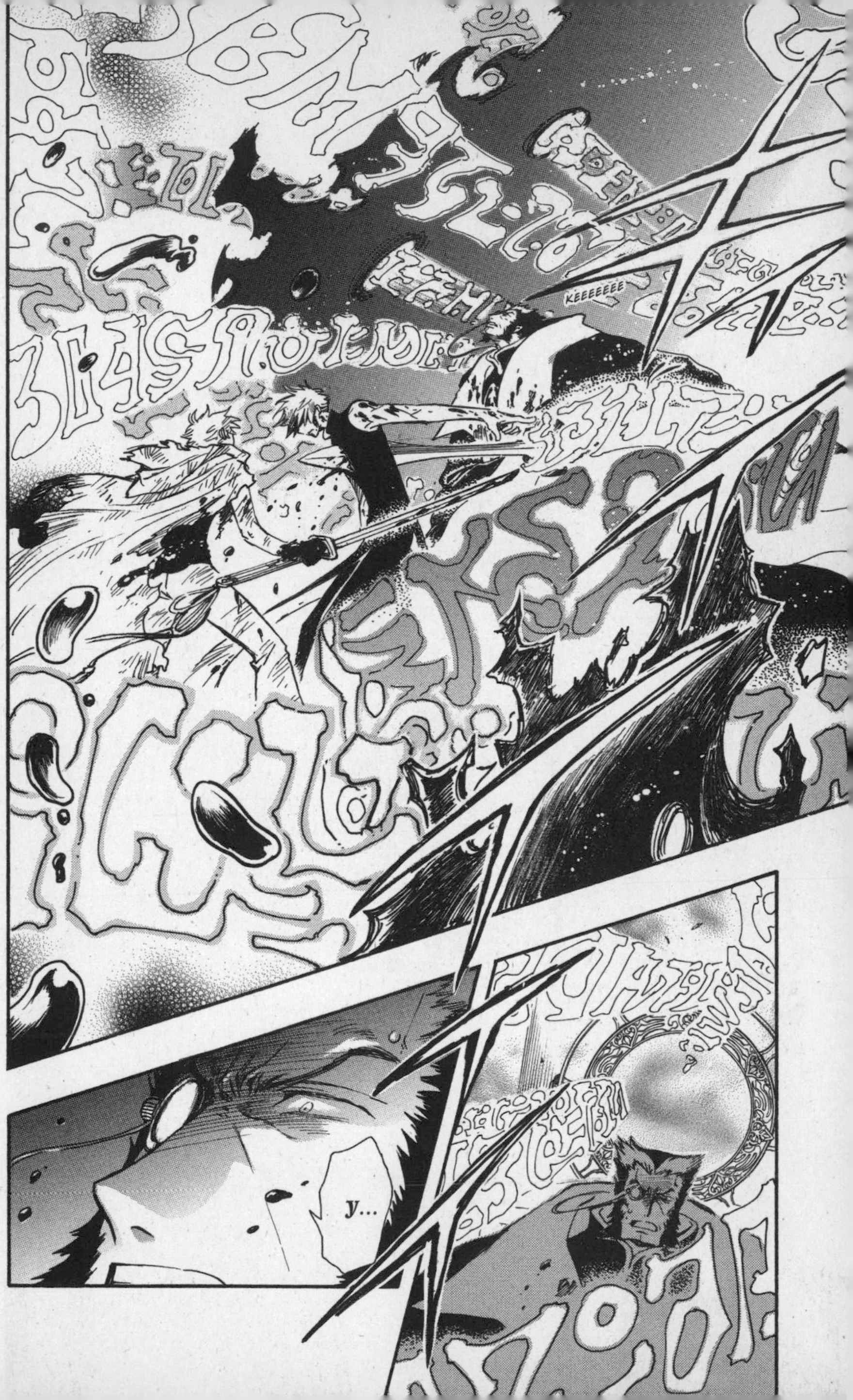
KEEEEEEE
y...

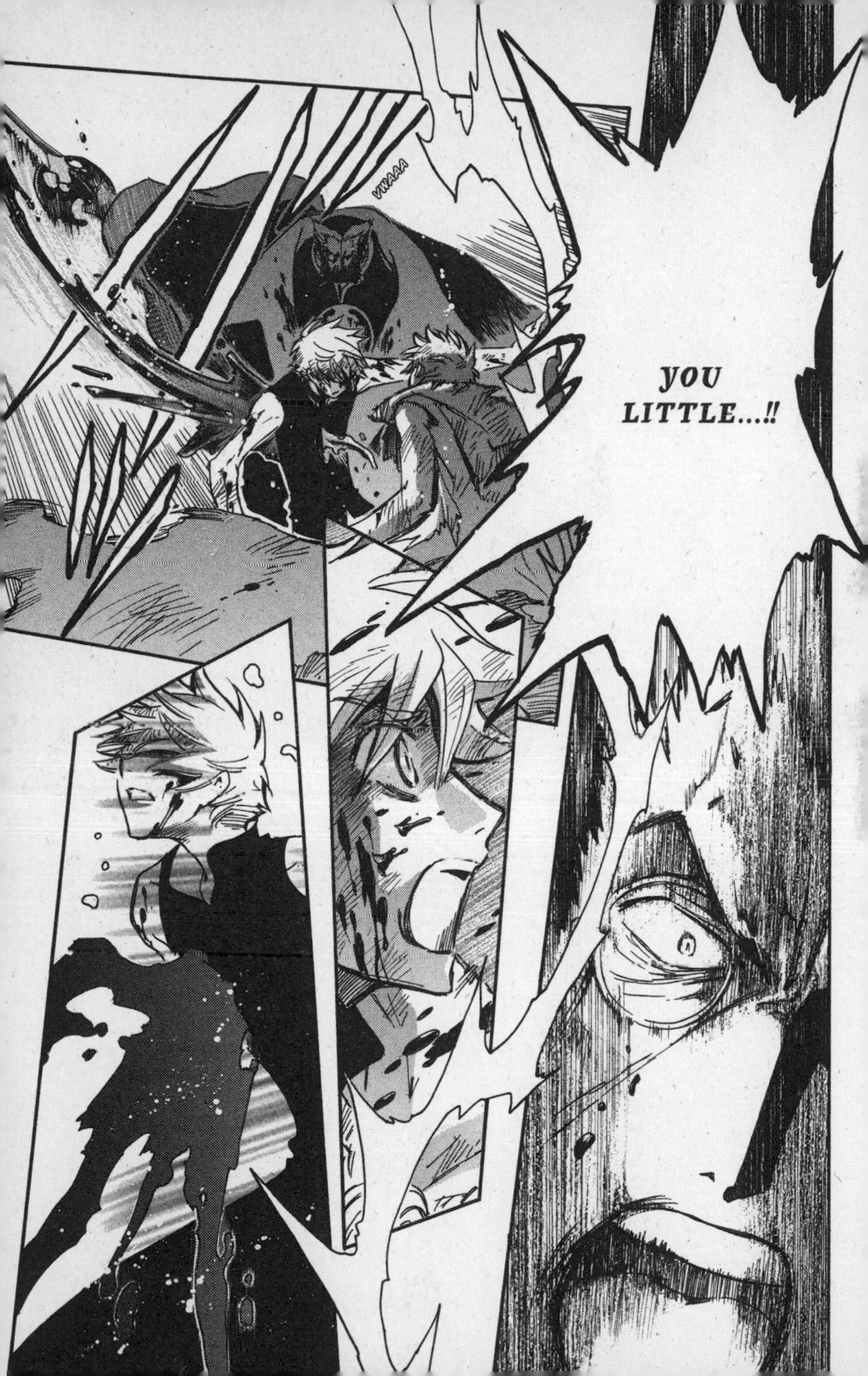
YOU LITTLE...!!
VWAAA

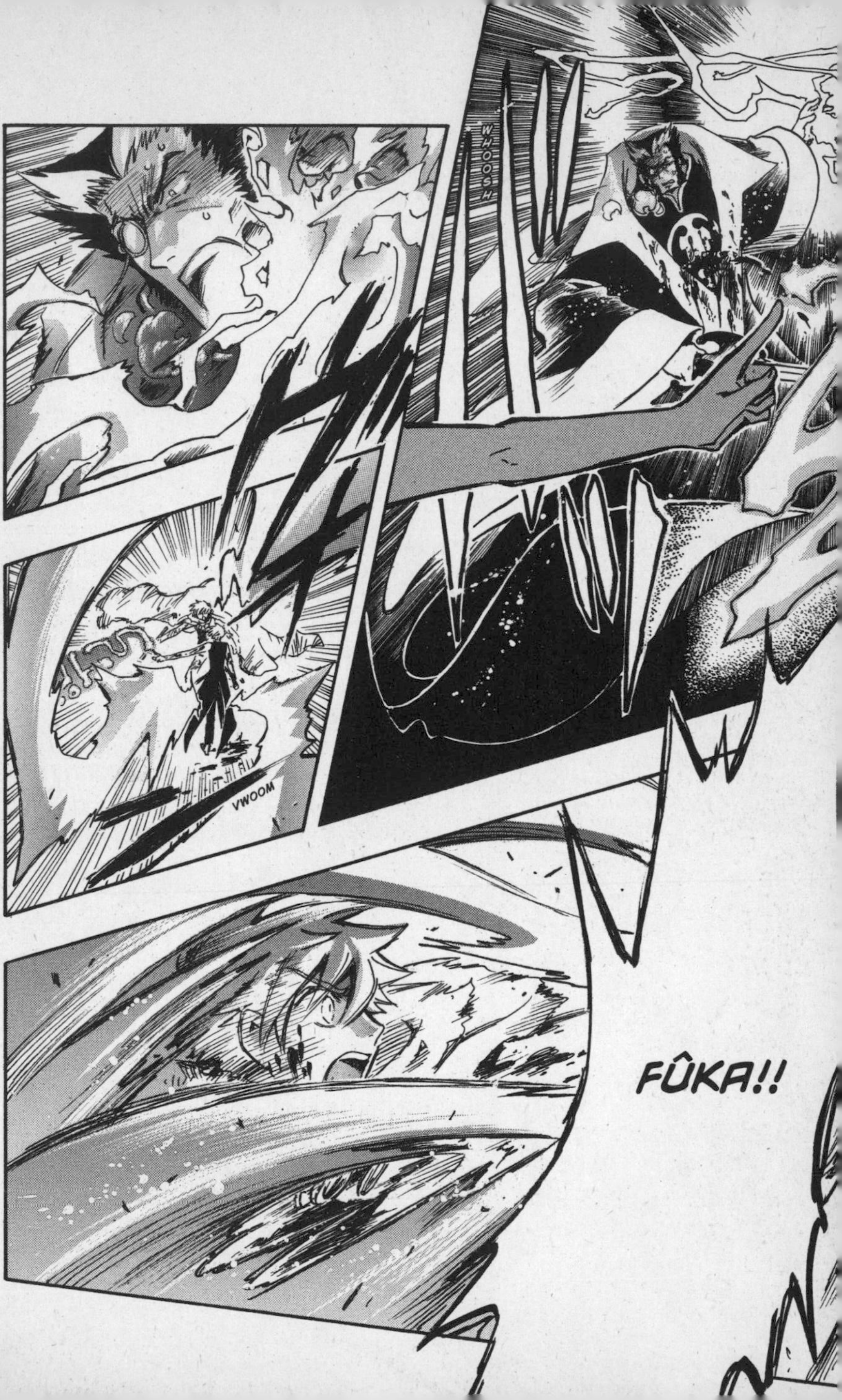
WHOOSH
VWOOM
FÛKA!!

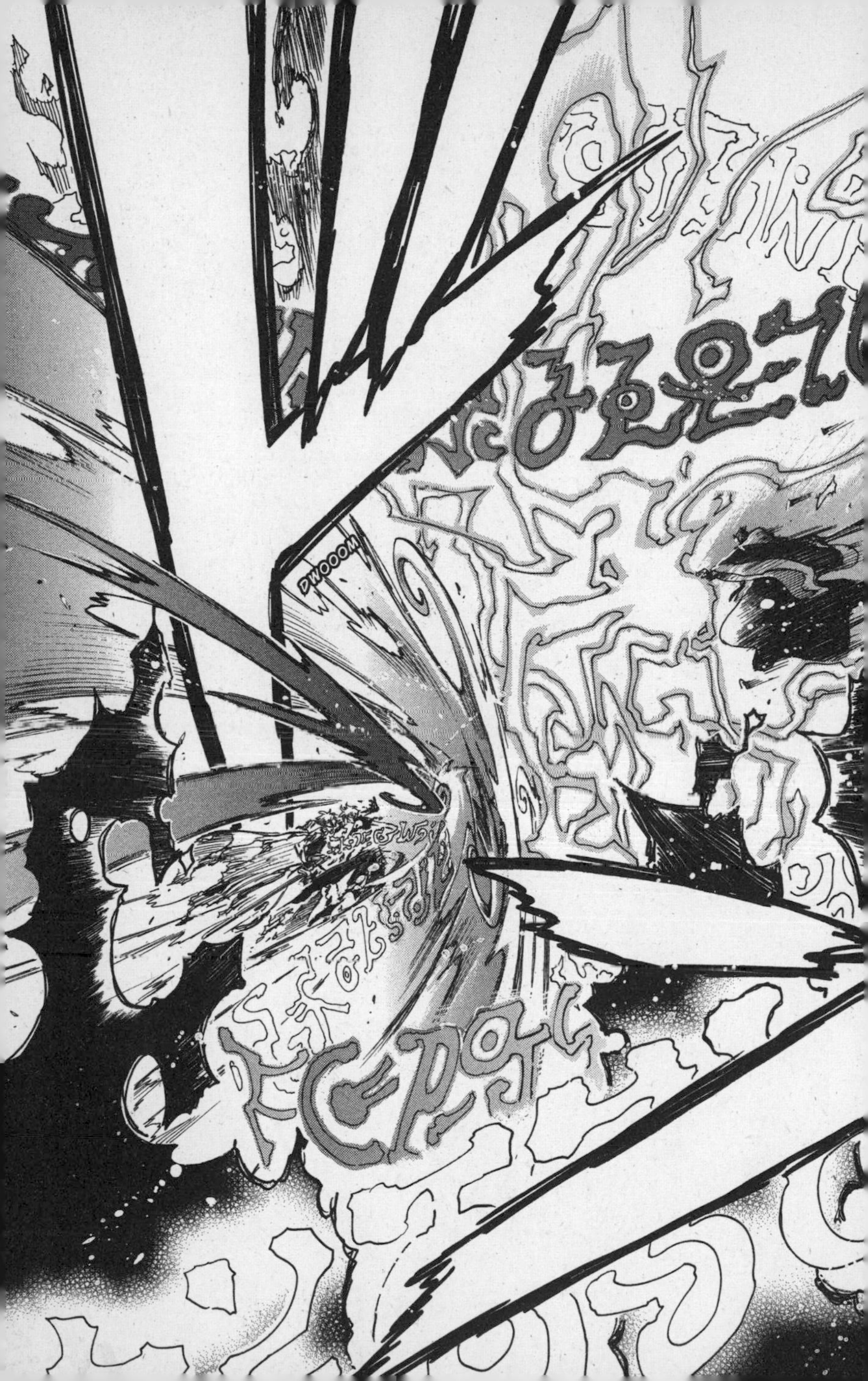
DWOOOM

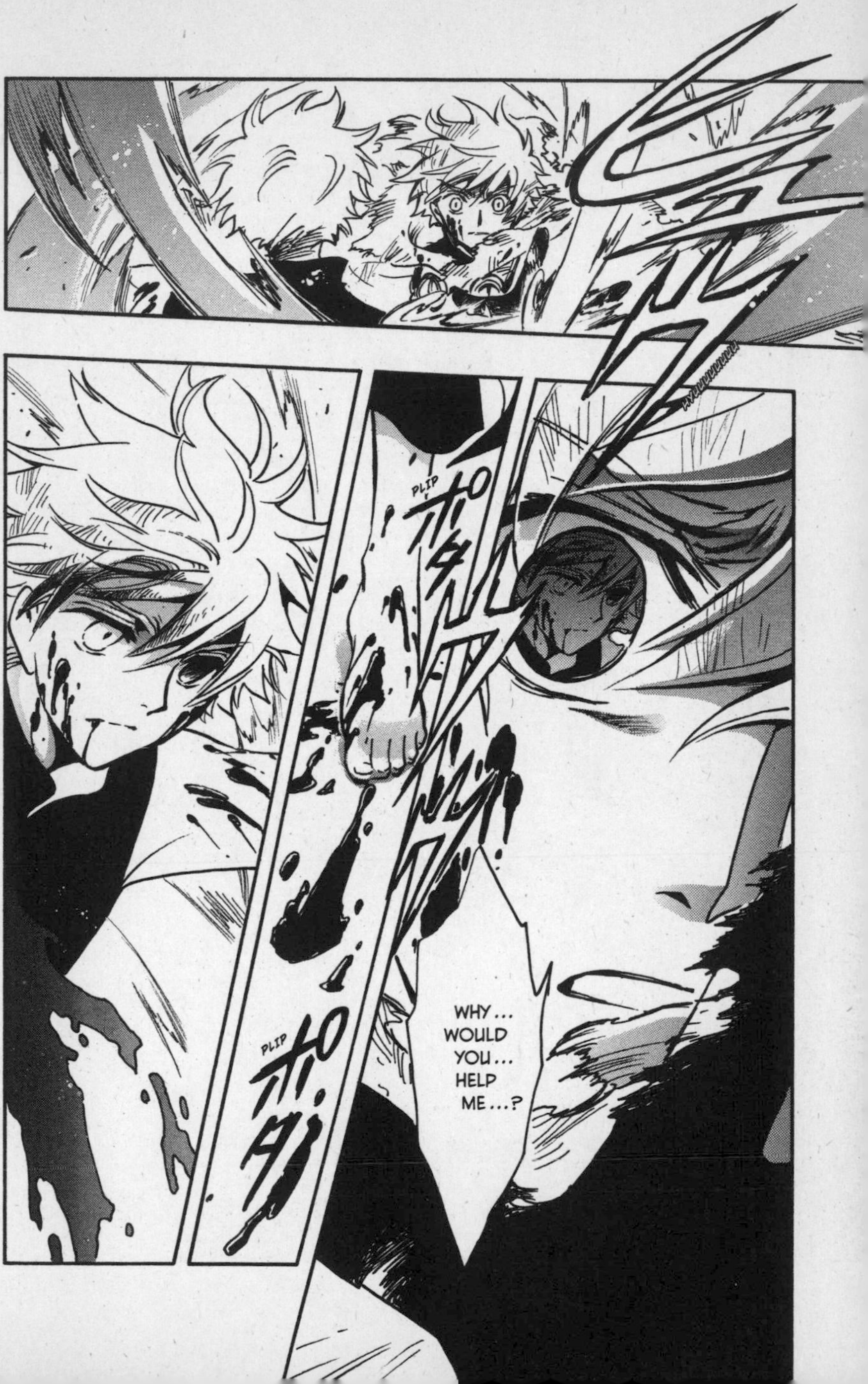
WHY... WOULD YOU... HELP ME...?
PLIP
PLIP

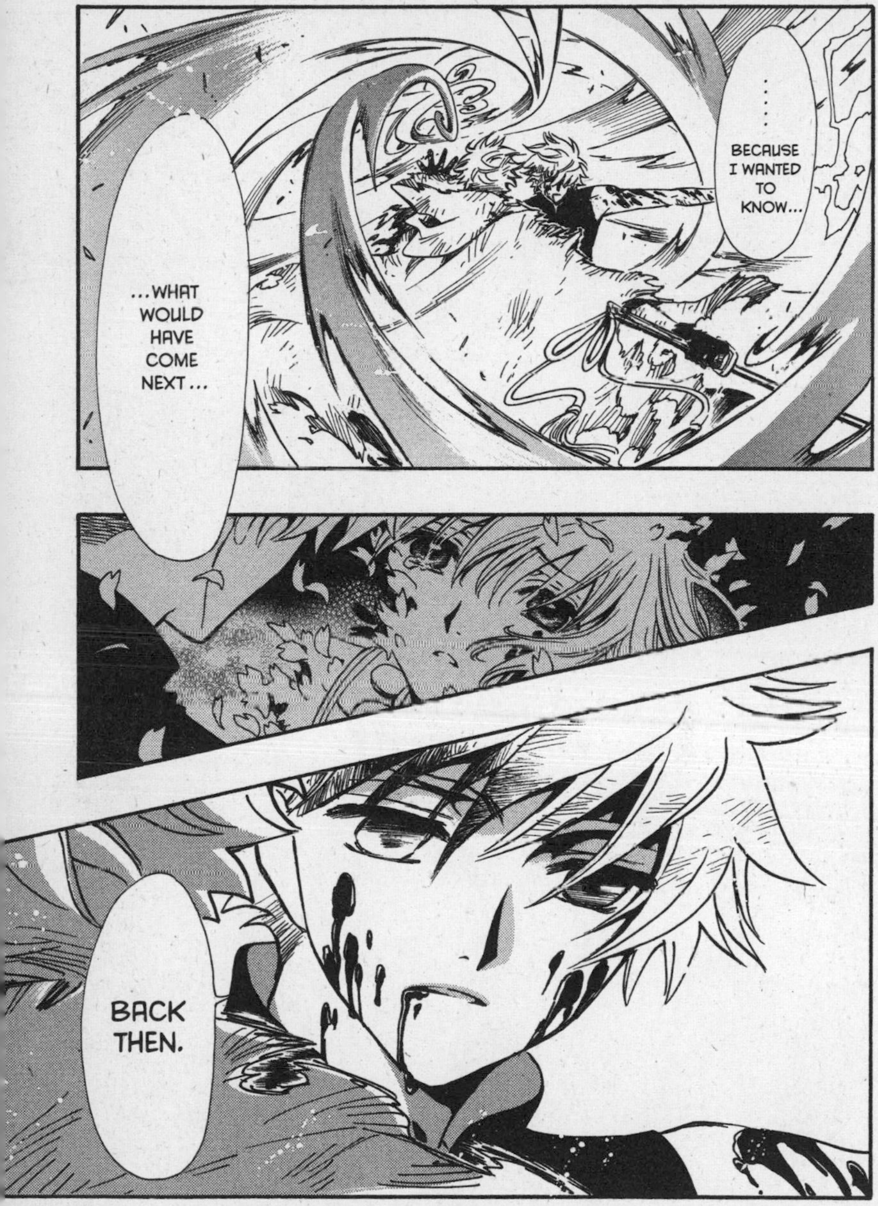
...
BECAUSE I WANTED TO KNOW...
...WHAT WOULD HAVE COME NEXT...
BACK THEN.

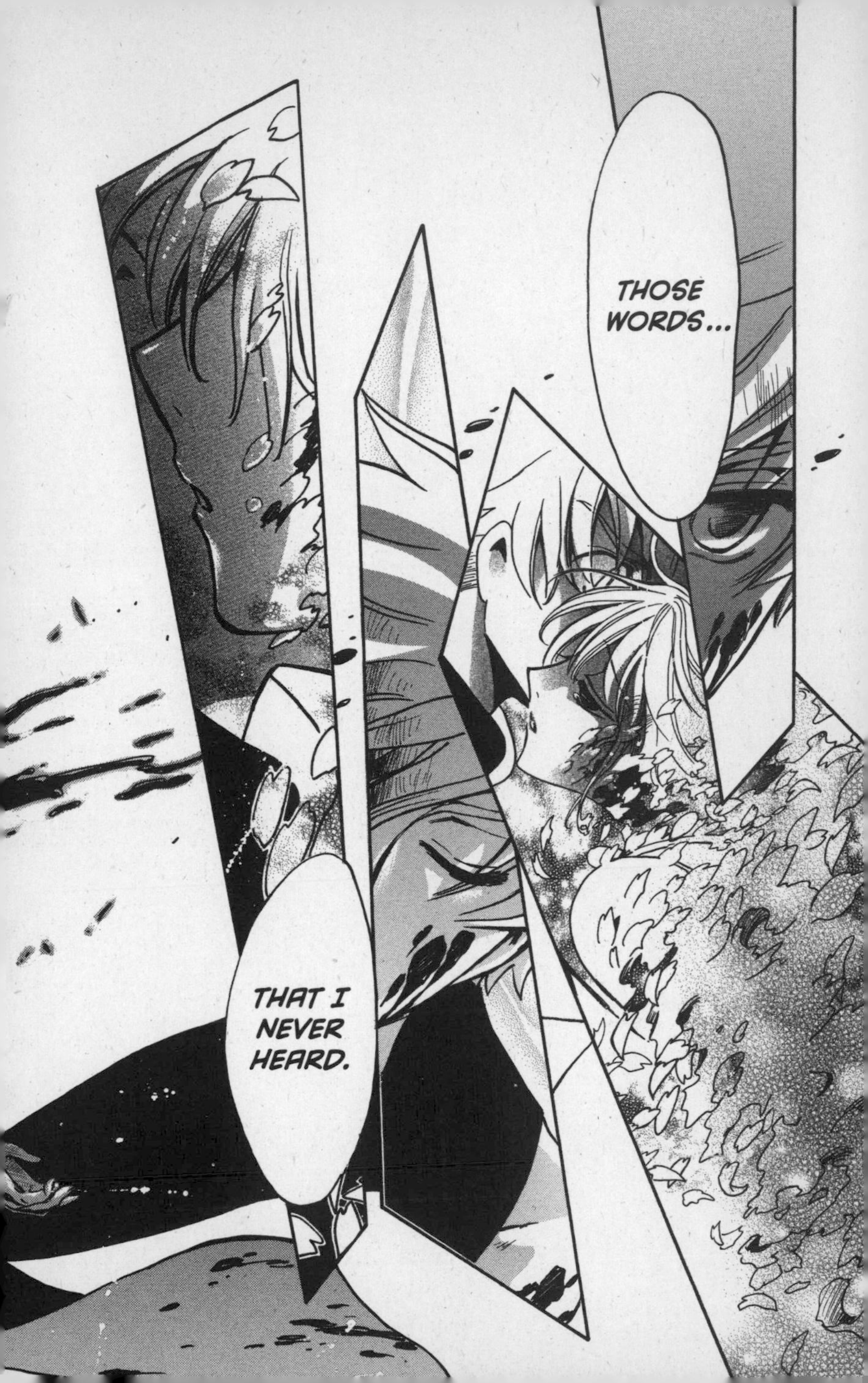
THOSE WORDS...
THAT I NEVER HEARD.

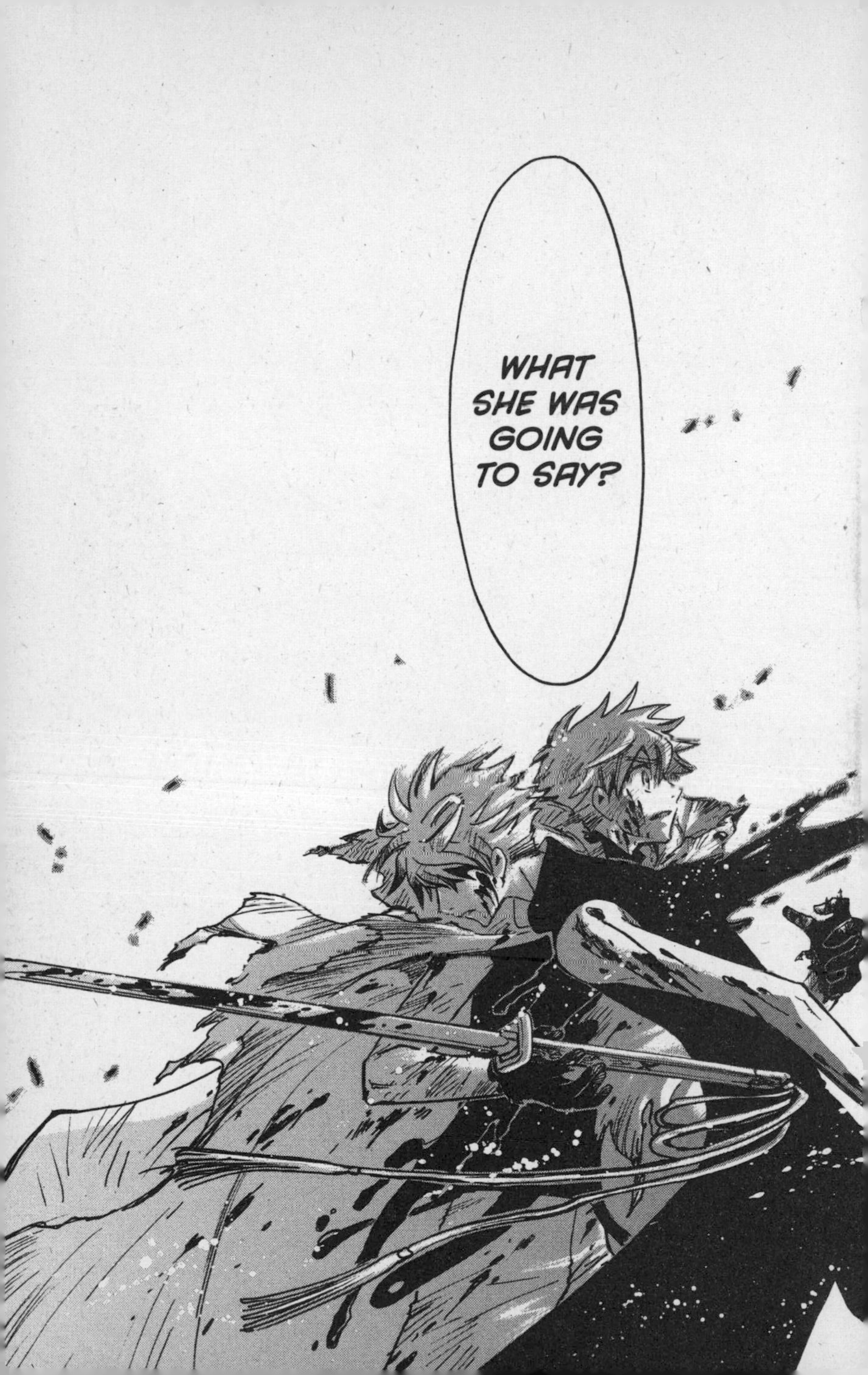
WHAT SHE WAS GOING TO SAY?

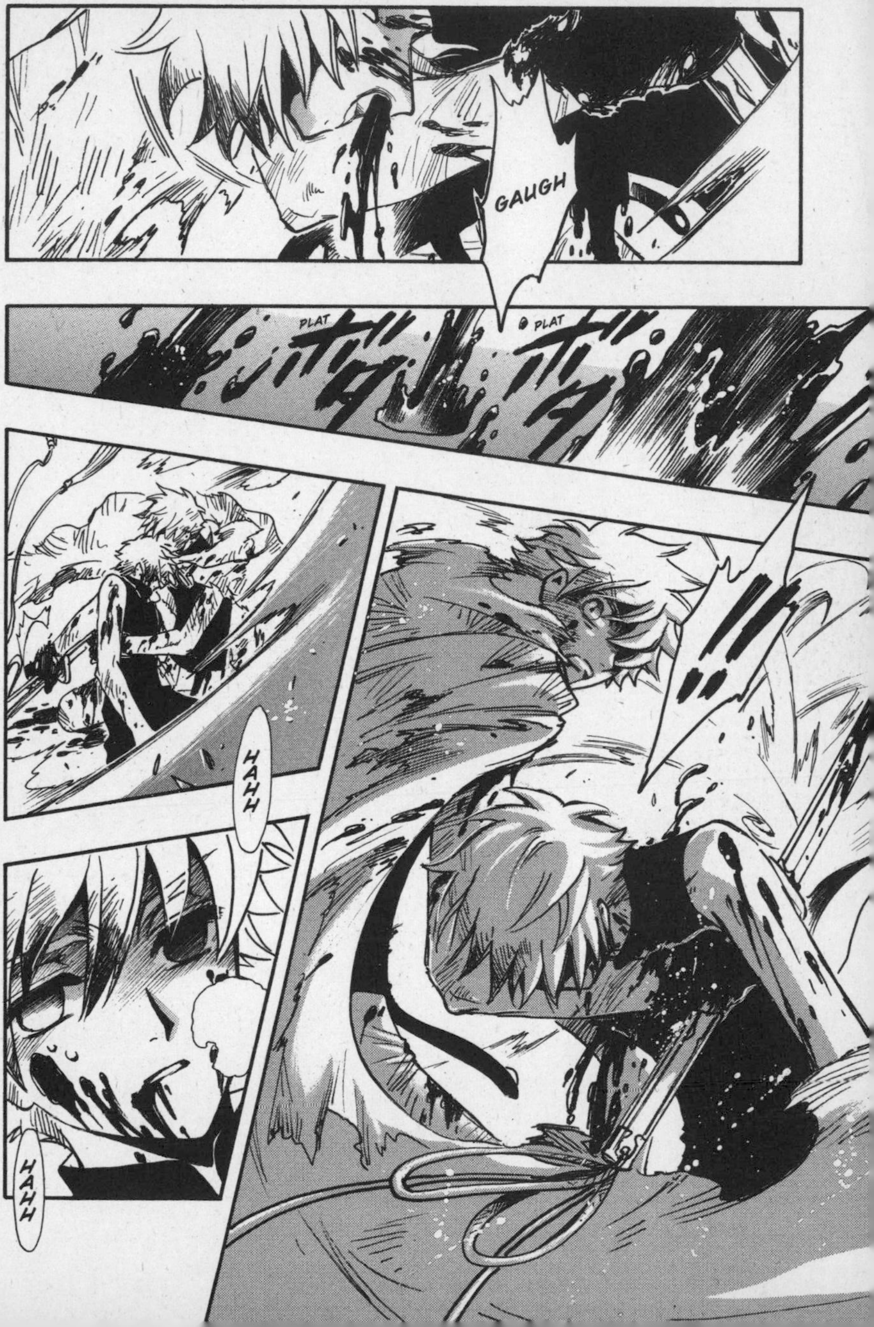
GAUGH
PLAT
PLAT
!!
HAHH
HAHH

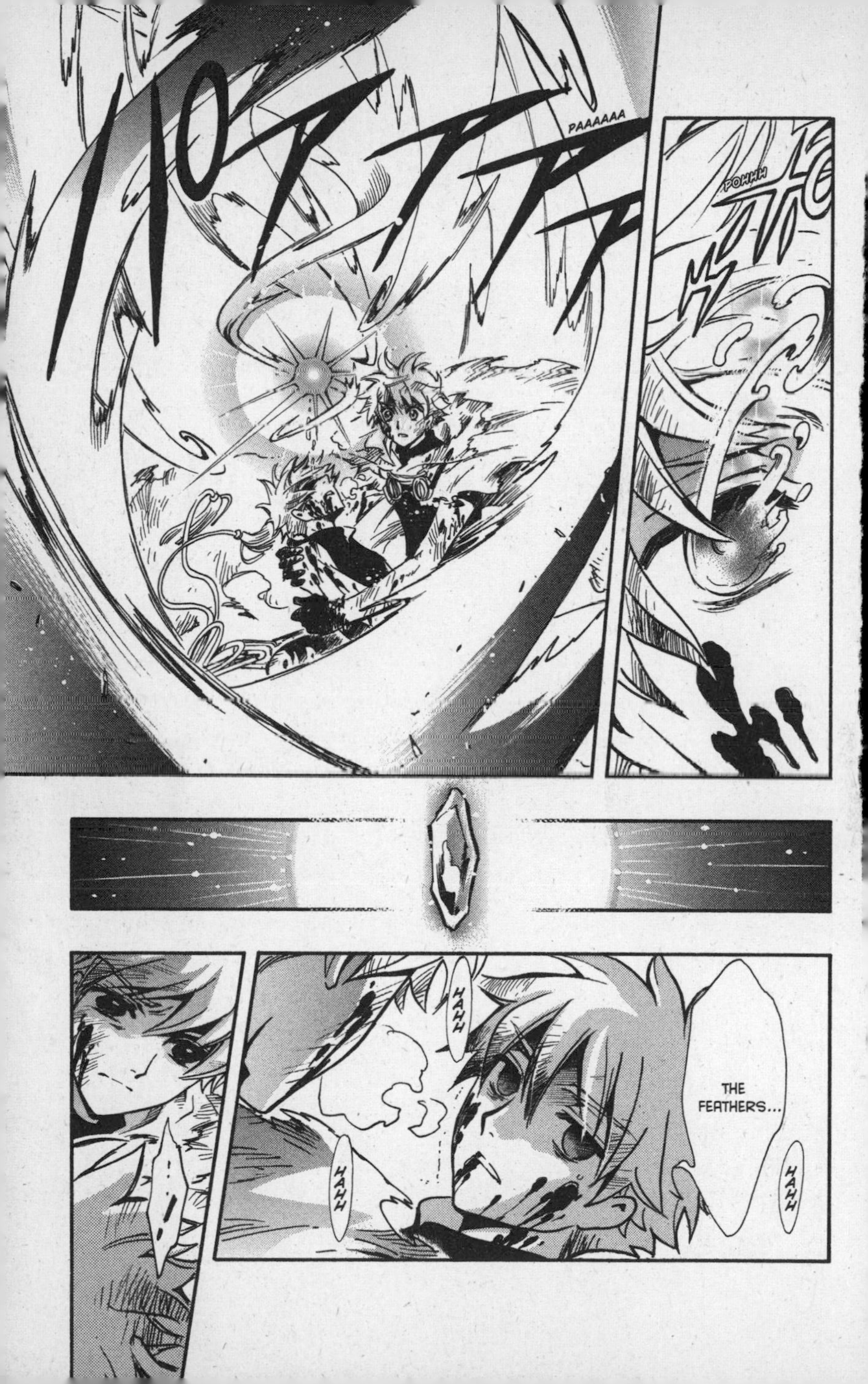
POHHH
PAAAAAA
THE FEATHERS...
HAHH
HAHH
HAHH
!!

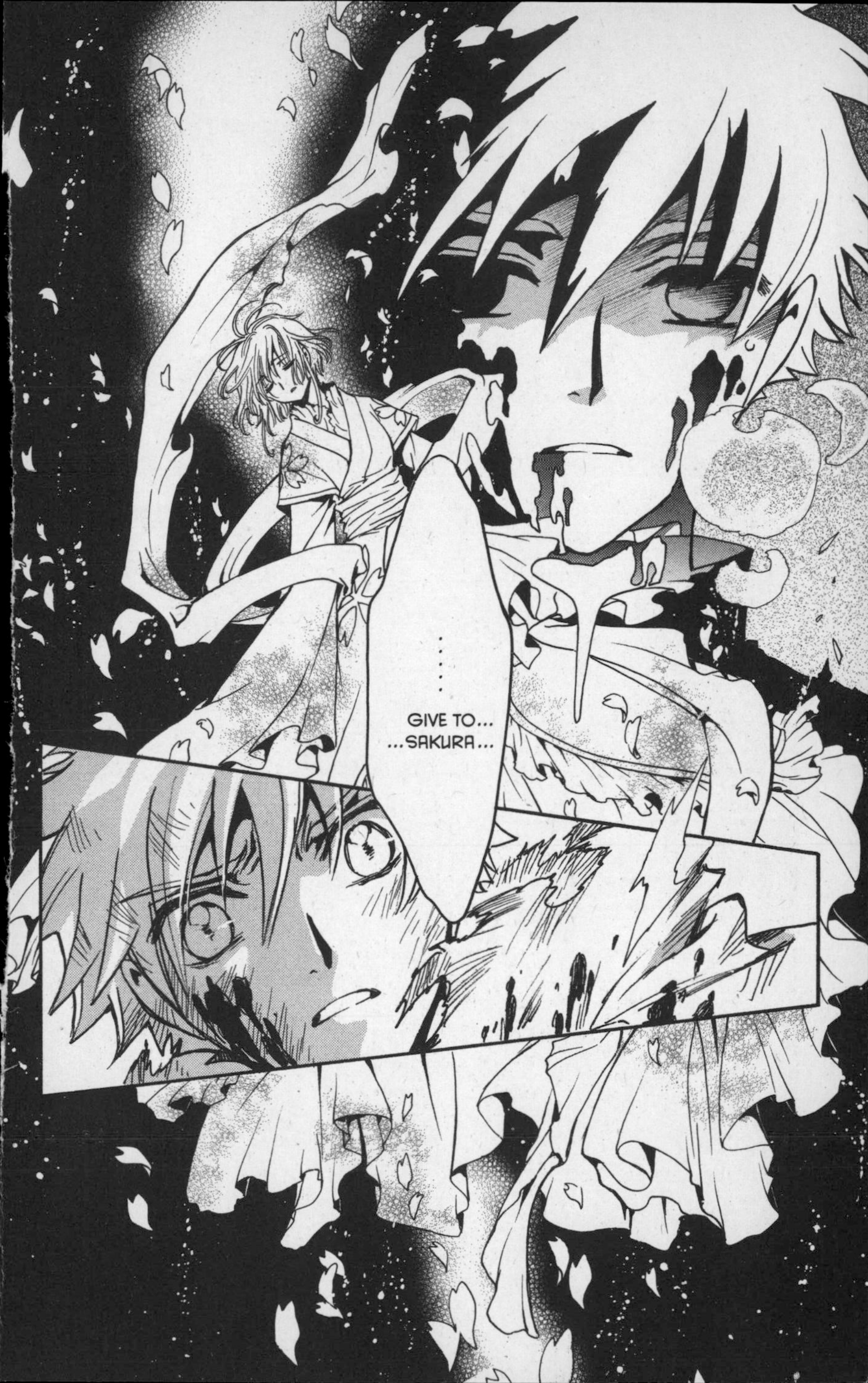
......
GIVE TO...
...SAKURA...

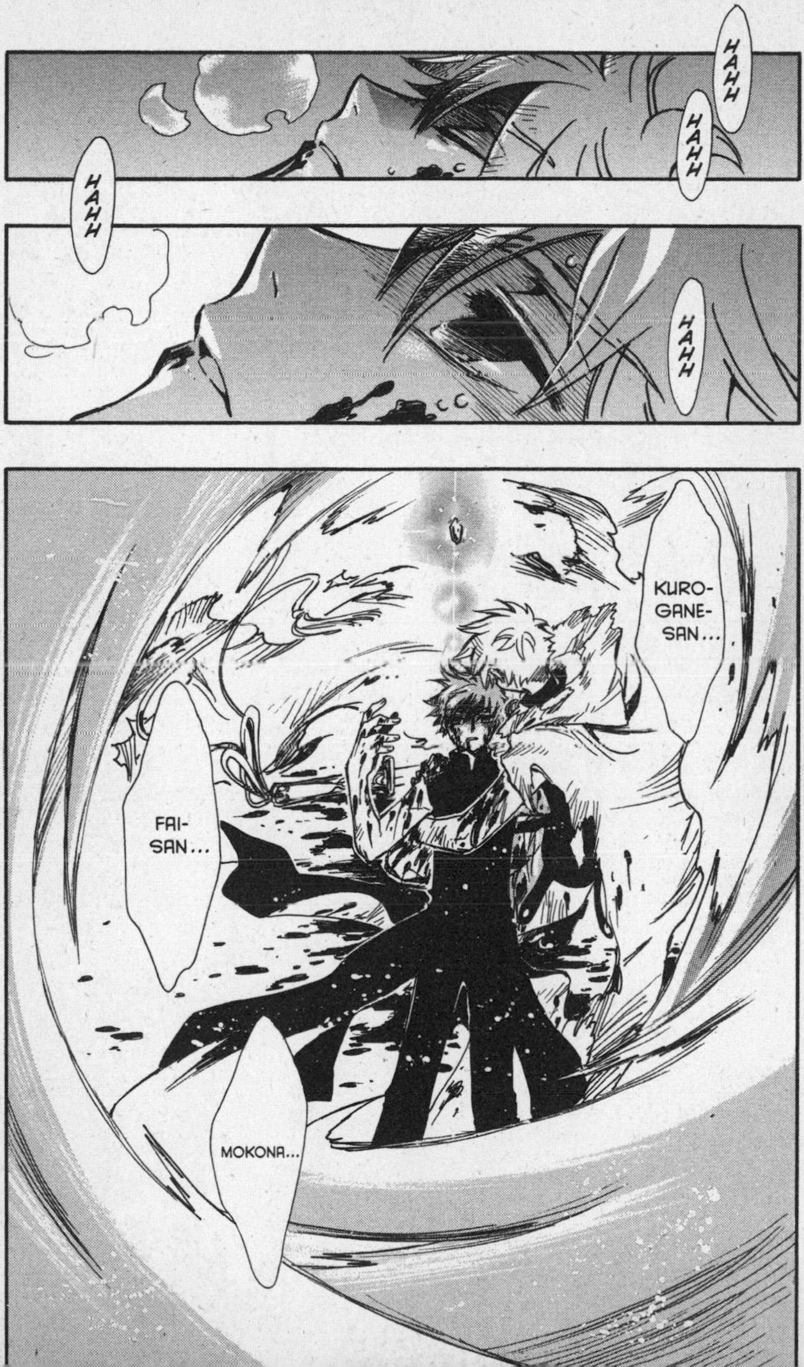
HAHH
HAHH
HAHH
HAHH
KURO-GANE-SAN...
FAI-SAN...
MOKONA...

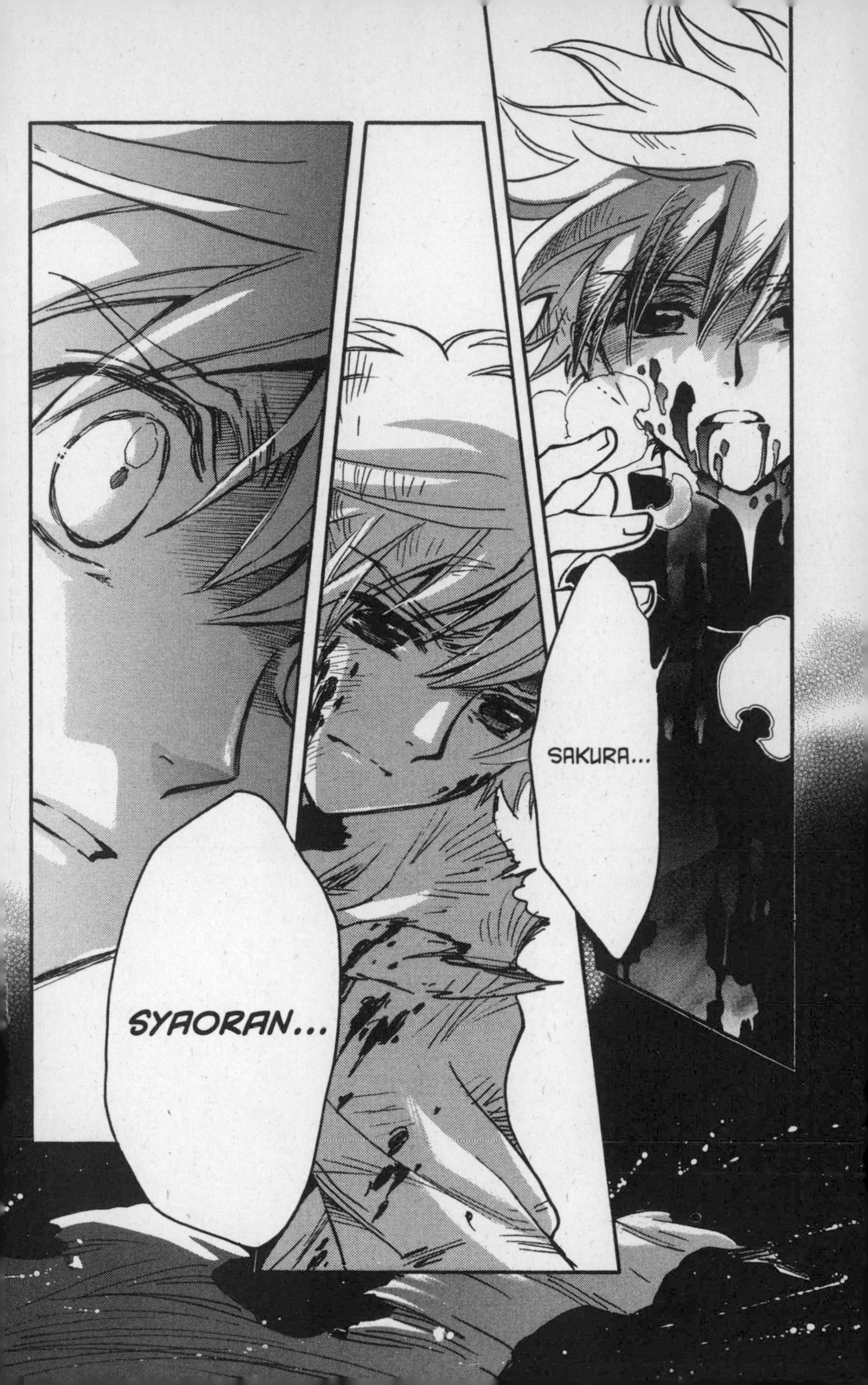
SAKURA...
SYAORAN...

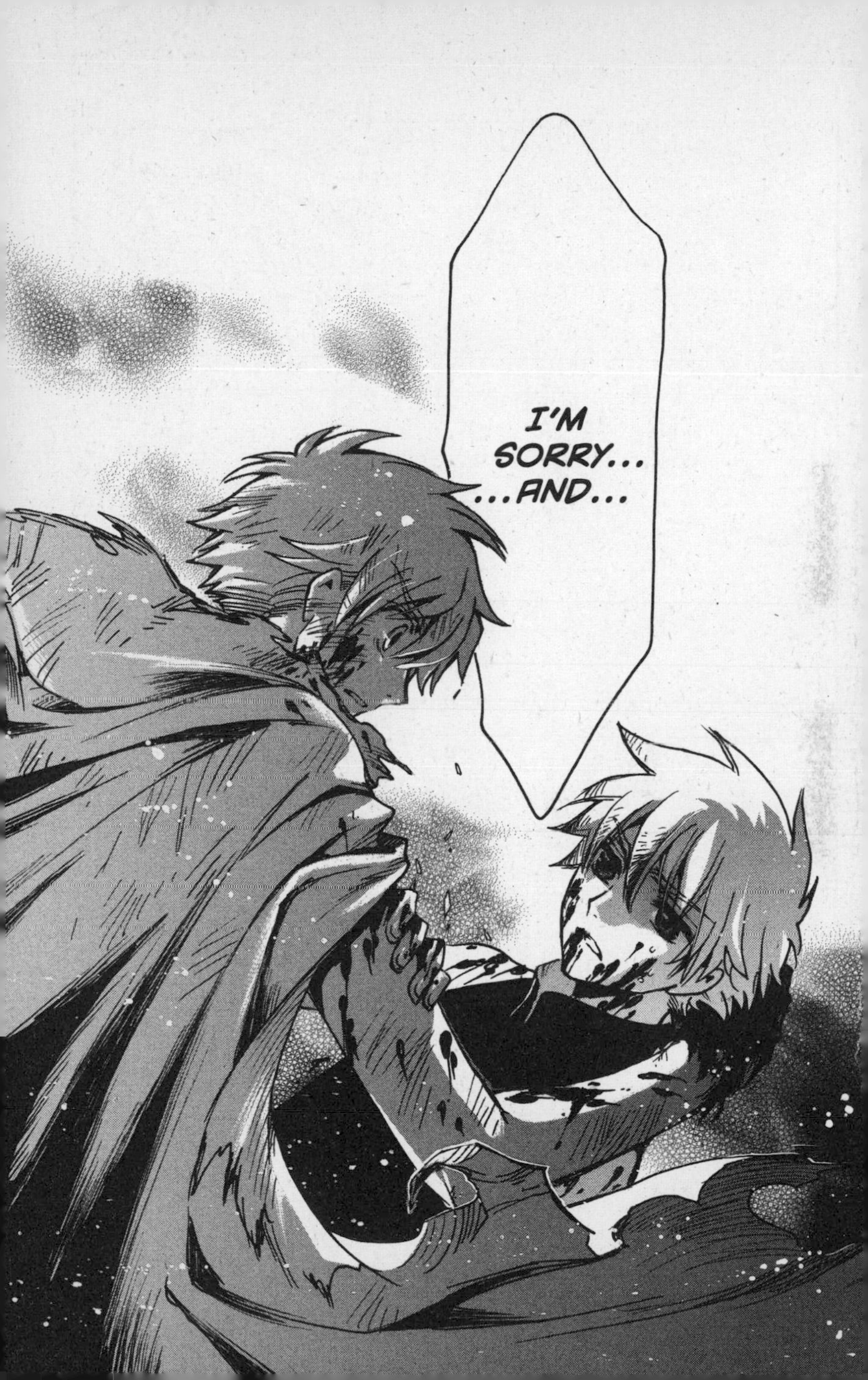
I'M SORRY... ...AND...

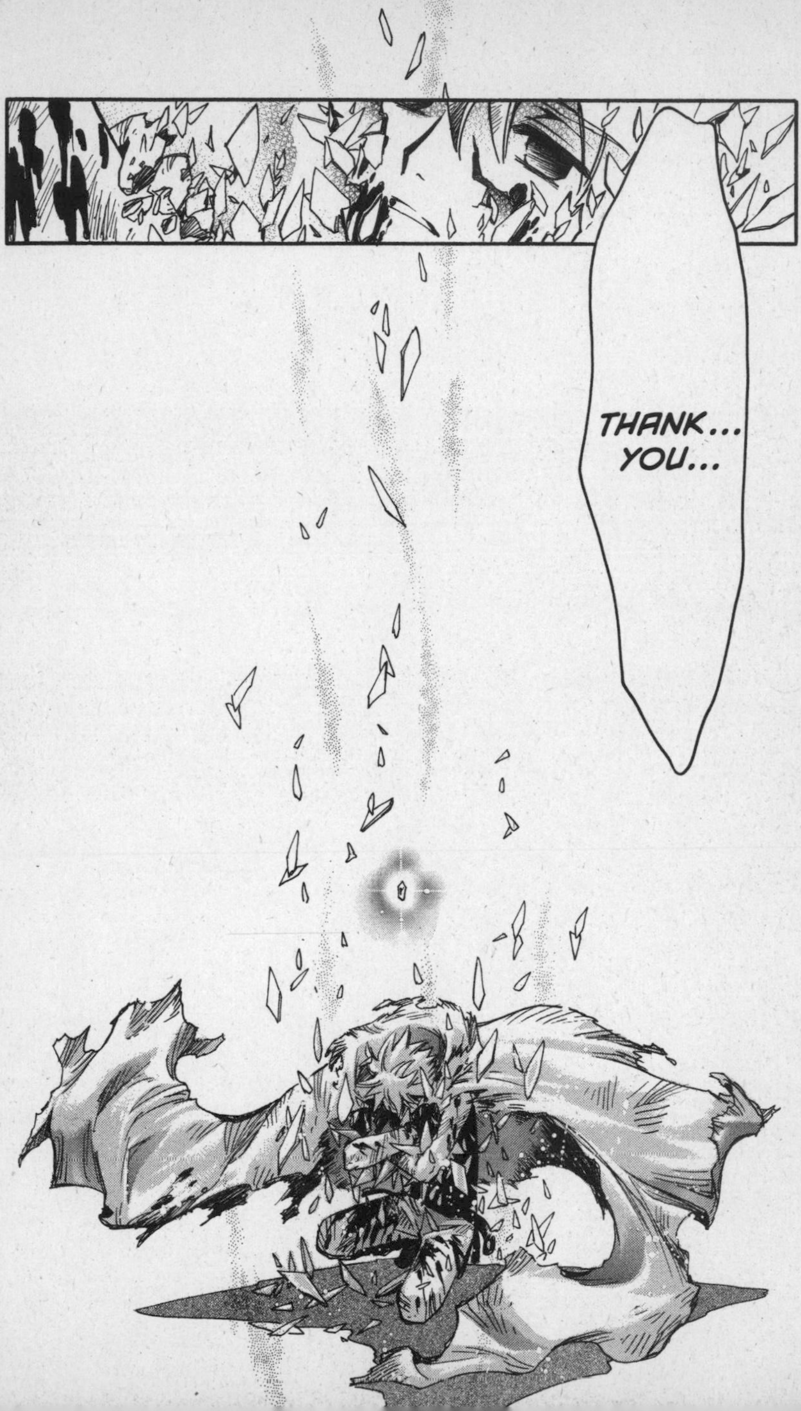
THANK... YOU...

To Be Continued

About the Creators

CLAMP is a group of four women who have become the most popular manga artists in America—Nanase Ohkawa, Mokona, Satsuki Igarashi, and Tsubaki Nekoi. They started out as *doujinshi* (fan comics) creators, but their skill and craft brought them to the attention of publishers very quickly. Their first work from a major publisher was *RG Veda*, but their first mass success was with *Magic Knight Rayearth*. From there, they went on to write many series, including Cardcaptor Sakura and Chobits, two of the most popular manga in the United States. Like many Japanese manga artists, they prefer to avoid the spotlight, and little is known about them personally.

CLAMP is currently publishing three series in Japan: Tsubasa and xxxHOLiC with Kodansha and Gohou Drug with Kadokawa.

Translation Notes

Japanese is a tricky language for most Westerners, and translation is often more art than science. For your edification and reading pleasure, here are notes on some of the places where we could have gone in a different direction in our translation of the work, or where a Japanese cultural reference is used.

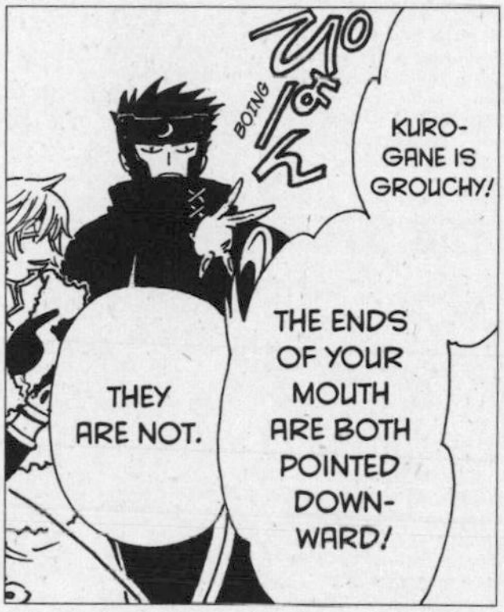
BOING
KURO-GANE IS GROUCHY!
THE ENDS OF YOUR MOUTH ARE BOTH POINTED DOWN-WARD!
THEY ARE NOT.

Ends of mouth pointed downward, page 60

The Japanese used a far more economical description of the shape of Kurogane's mouth. They used the Japanese expression, *he no ji* which means his mouth is shaped like the *kana* symbol for the syllable *he*, which looks something like a lopsided upward pointer. However, to use the expression one would have to assume that the readers are familiar with Japanese *kana* (most aren't). So I had to use a lot more words to describe Kurogane's expression than the original script in Japanese did.

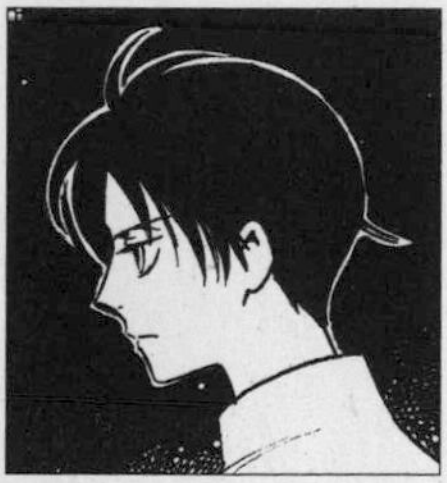

Kimihiro Watanuki, page 65

Readers who do not follow along with Tsubasa's sister book, CLAMP's manga xxxHOLiC, might still recognize Kimihiro Watanuki from his several cameo appearances here in Tsubasa. He has been working as an indentured servant to the shop of the space-time witch, Yûko Ichihara. There he cooks, cleans, and on occasion, helps Yûko fulfill her customer's wishes (for a price). Just as Syaoran is finally revealing his own past, Kimihiro is finally beginning to learn about who he is as well.

Kanji on Kurogane's sword, page 86

Many swords from Japan's feudal period (the era on which Kurogane's world of Japan was based) had names, and those names would have been engraved on the blade or hilt of the sword. In this case, as Kurogane loosens his sword from its scabbard, we catch a glimpse of the engraving on it. The kanji written there is *ryû*, which means "dragon," and is a part of *Ginryû*, the name of his sword.

The Evolved Manifestation, page 119

Although this doesn't quite fall into the "pun" territory, this title is still something of a play on words in Japanese. The Japanese word for "evolution" is *shinka*, with the kanji for *shin* meaning "moving forward" and *ka* meaning "transform" or "appear." The Japanese word for "manifestation" is *keshin*, where *ke* is the same kanji as used for *ka* in *shinka*, but this time the *shin* is a different kanji that means "body." So you have a single kanji with two pronunciations combined with two different kanji that have the same pronunciation. Like I said, it isn't a pun, and wasn't meant to be funny. But, like alliteration in English, such a play on words makes the title memorable. Unfortunately it would have been impossible (as far as I can tell) to translate it as a similar play on words in the English edition.

We're pleased to present you a preview from Tsubasa, volume 27. Please check our website (www.delreymanga.com) to see when this volume will be available.

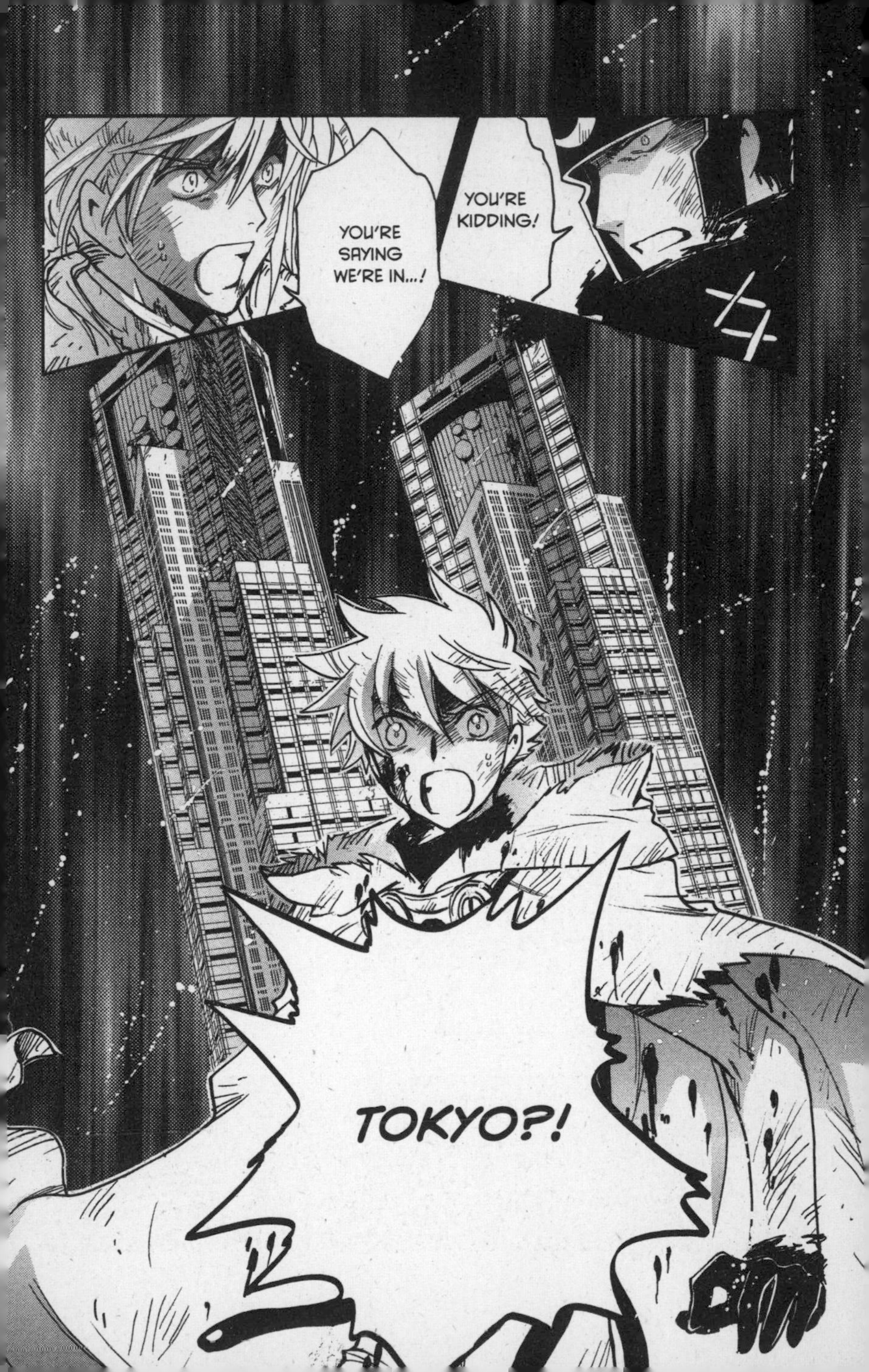
YOU'RE KIDDING!
YOU'RE SAYING WE'RE IN...!
TOKYO?!

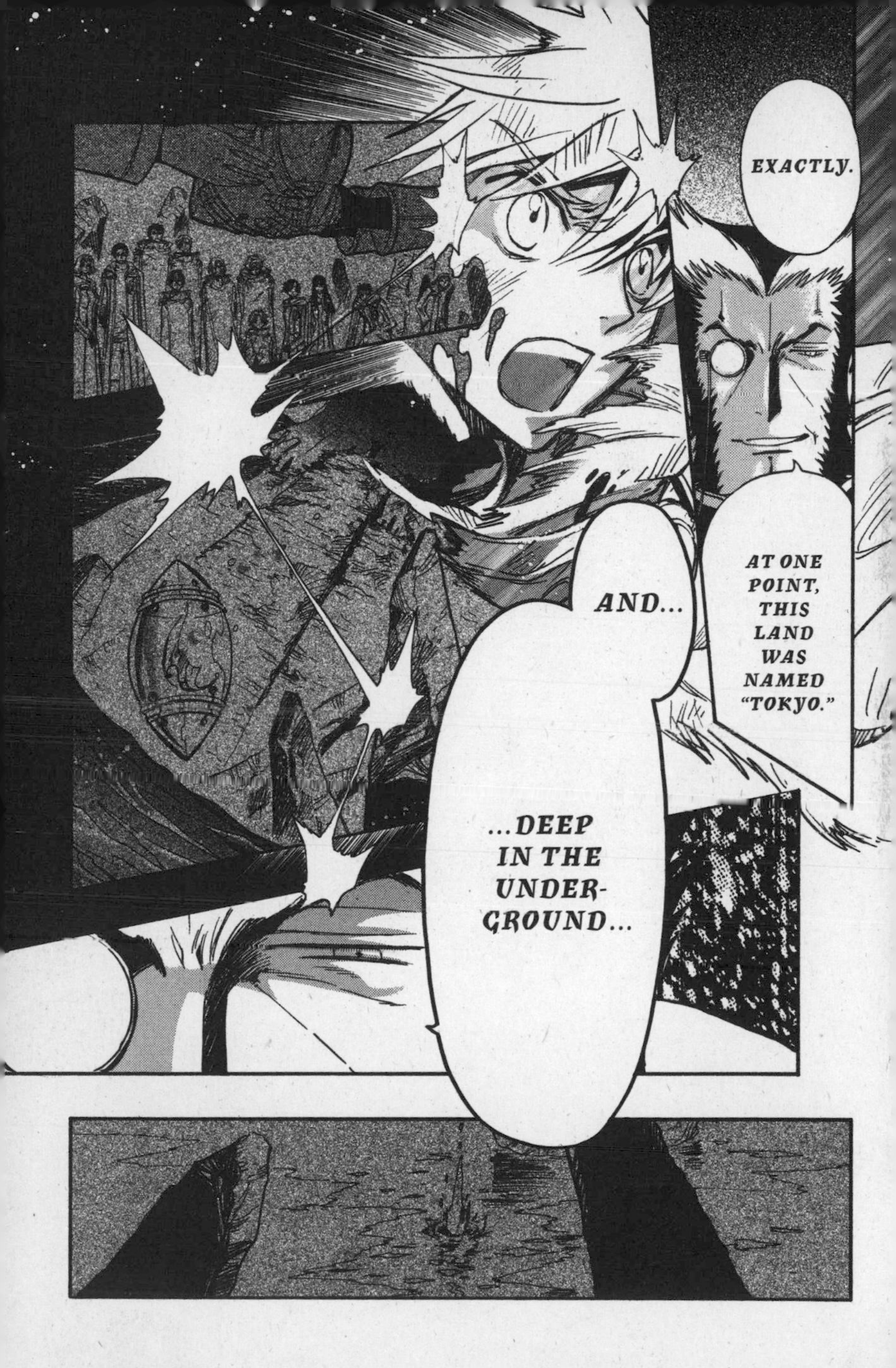
EXACTLY.
AT ONE POINT, THIS LAND WAS NAMED "TOKYO."
AND...
...DEEP IN THE UNDER-GROUND...

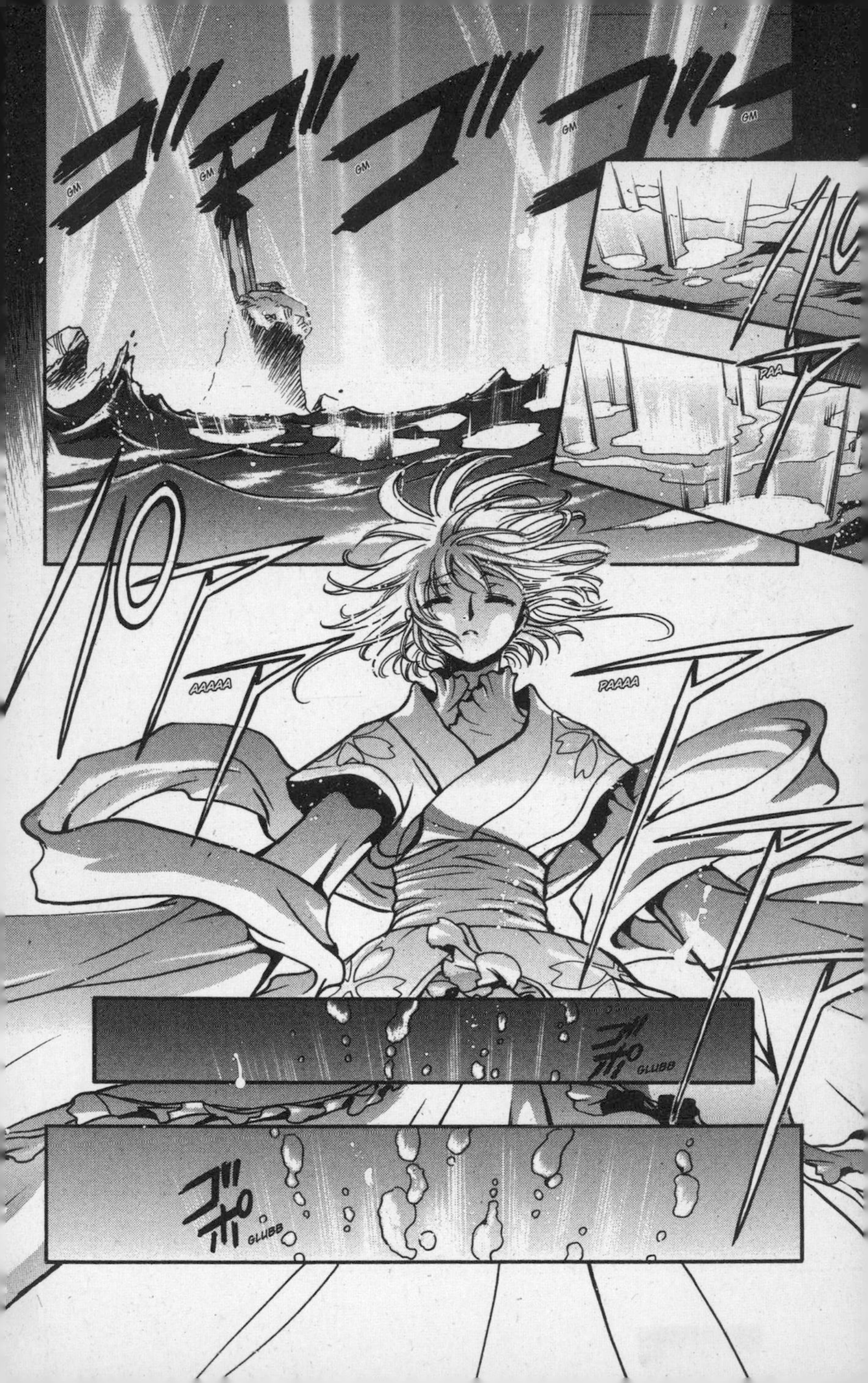
GM
GM
GM
GM
GM
PAA
PAAAA
AAAAA
GLUBB
GLUBB

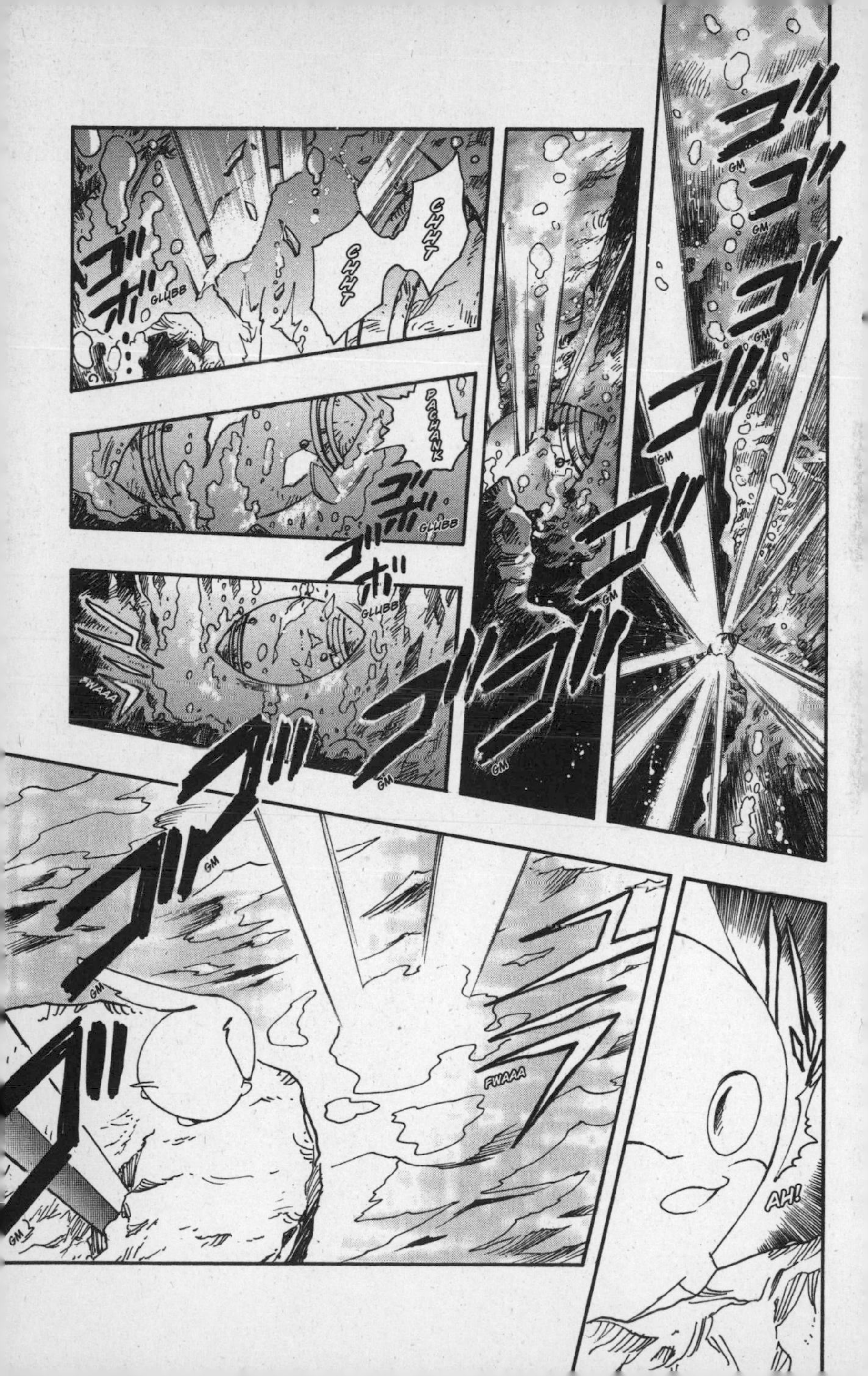
GM
GM
GM
GM
GM
GM
CHHHT
CHHHT
GLUBB
PACHANK
GLUBB
GLUBB
FWAAA
GM
AH!
GM
GM
FWAAA
GM

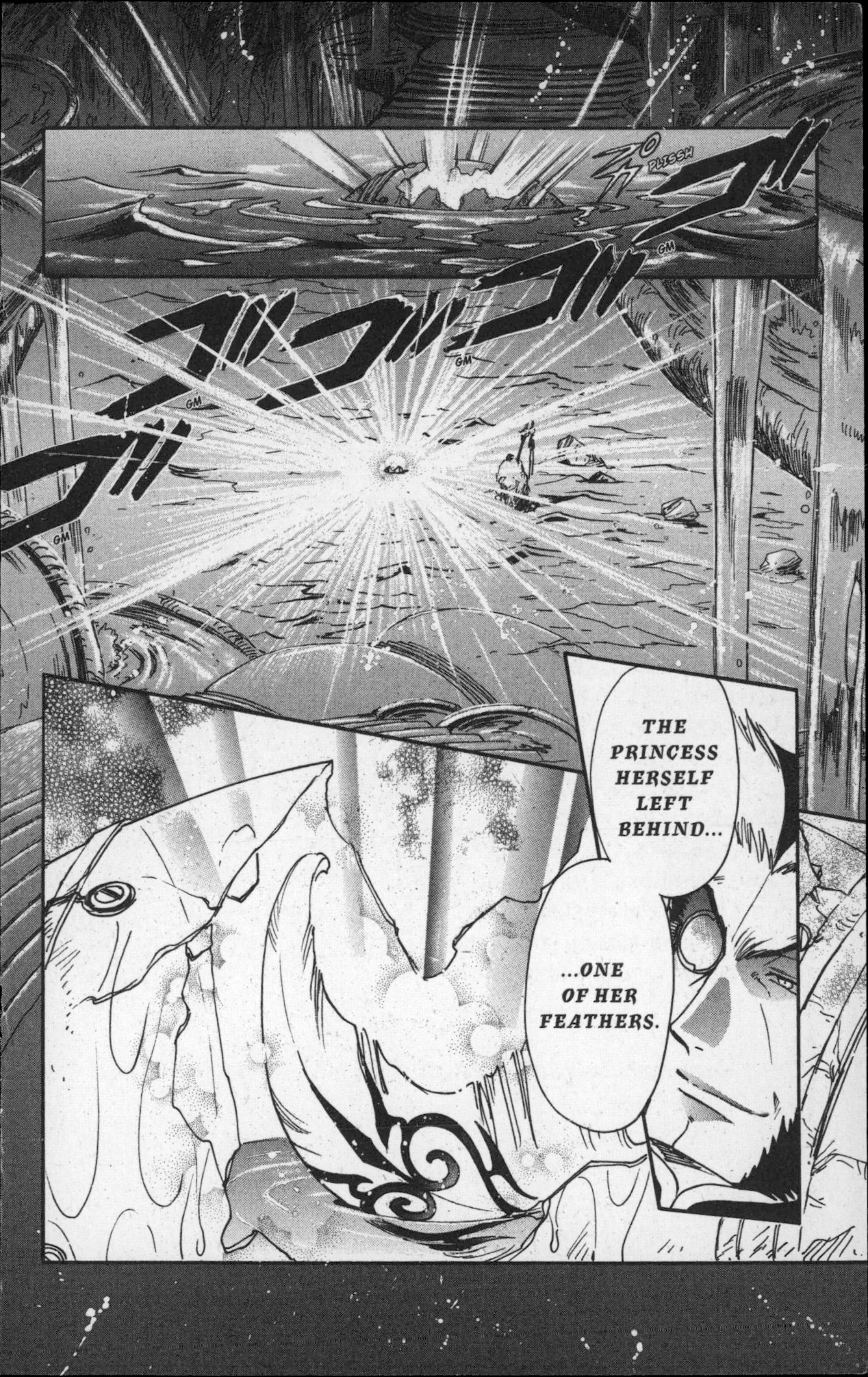
PLISSH
GM
GM
GM
GM
THE PRINCESS HERSELF LEFT BEHIND...
...ONE OF HER FEATHERS.

xxxHOLiC™

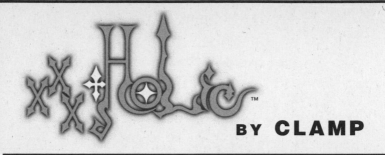

BY CLAMP

Watanuki Kimihiro is haunted by visions. When he finds himself irresistibly drawn into a shop owned by Yûko, a mysterious witch, he is offered the chance to rid himself of the spirits that plague him. He accepts, but soon realizes that he's just been tricked into working for the shop to pay off the cost of Yûko's services! But this isn't any ordinary kind of shop . . . In this shop, Yûko grants wishes to those in need. But they must have the strength of will not only to truly understand their need, but to give up something incredibly precious in return.

CLAMP
CREATORS OF CHOBITS!
1
xxxHOLiC

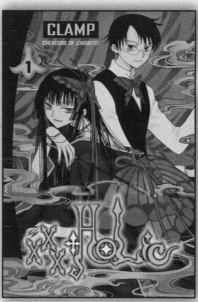

Ages: 13+

Special extras in each volume! Read them all!

DEL REY

VISIT WWW.DELREYMANGA.COM TO:

- View release date calendars for upcoming volumes
- Sign up for Del Rey's free manga e-newsletter
- Find out the latest about new Del Rey Manga series

PEACH-PIT

Creators of *Dears* and *Rozen Maiden*

Everybody at Seiyo Elementary thinks that stylish and super-cool Amu has it all. But nobody knows the *real* Amu, a shy girl who wishes she had the courage to truly be herself. Changing Amu's life is going to take more than wishes and dreams—it's going to take a little magic! One morning, Amu finds a surprise in her bed: three strange little eggs. Each egg contains a Guardian Character, an angel-like being who can give her the power to be someone new. With the help of her Guardian Characters, Amu is about to discover that her true self is even more amazing than she ever dreamed.

Special extras in each volume! Read them all!

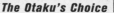

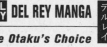

NEGIMA!? NEO
MAGISTER NEGI MAGI

STORY BY KEN AKAMATSU
ART BY TAKUYA FUJIMA

BASED ON THE POPULAR ANIME!

Negi Springfield is only ten years old, but he's already a powerful wizard. After graduating from his magic school in England, the prodigy is given an unusual assignment: teach English at an all-girl school in Japan. Now Negi has to find a way to deal with his thirty-one totally gorgeous (and completely overaffectionate) students—without using magic! Based on the *Negima!* anime, this is a fresh take on the beloved *Negima!* story.

Available anywhere books or comics are sold!

TOMARE!

[STOP!]

You're going the wrong way!

Manga is a completely different type of reading experience.

To start at the *beginning,* go to the *end!*

That's right! Authentic manga is read the traditional Japanese way—from right to left. Exactly the *opposite* of how American books are read. It's easy to follow: Just go to the other end of the book, and read each page—and each panel—from right side to left side, starting at the top right. Now you're experiencing manga as it was meant to be!